*Advances*

# in COMPUTERS
# VOLUME 66

# *Advances in*

# COMPUTERS

## Quality Software Development

*EDITED BY*

# MARVIN V. ZELKOWITZ

Department of Computer Science
and Institute for Advanced Computer Studies
University of Maryland
College Park, Maryland

VOLUME 66

AMSTERDAM • BOSTON • HEIDELBERG • LONDON • NEW YORK • OXFORD
PARIS • SAN DIEGO • SAN FRANCISCO • SINGAPORE • SYDNEY • TOKYO
Academic Press is an imprint of Elsevier

ELSEVIER

ACADEMIC
PRESS

Academic Press is an imprint of Elsevier
525 B Street, Suite 1900, San Diego, California 92101-4495, USA
84 Theobald's Road, London WC1X 8RR, UK
Radarweg 29, PO Box 211, 1000 AE, Amsterdam, The Netherlands
30 Corporate Drive, Suite 400, Burlington, MA 01803, USA

This book is printed on acid-free paper ⊗

**Library of Congress Cataloging in Publication Data**


**British Library Cataloguing in Publication Data**


ISBN-13: 978-0-12-012166-3
ISBN-10: 0-12-012166-2
ISSN (Series): 0065-2458

For information on all Academic Press publications
visit our web site at http://books.elsevier.com

# Contents

## Requirements Management for Dependable Software Systems

### William G. Bail

## Mechanics of Managing Software Risk

### William G. Bail

## The PERFECT Approach to Experience-Based Process Evolution

### Brian A. Nejmeh and William E. Riddle

## The Opportunities, Challenges, and Risks of High Performance Computing in Computational Science and Engineering

### Douglass E. Post, Richard P. Kendall, and Robert F. Lucas

# Contributors

**Dr. William Bail** has worked for The MITRE Corporation in McLean, VA since 1990 as a Computer Scientist in the Software Engineering Center. Dr. Bail's technical areas include dependable software design and assessment, error handling policies, techniques for software specification development, design methodologies, metric definition and application, and verification and validation. At MITRE, Dr. Bail is currently supporting the U.S. Navy, focusing on the practice of software engineering within Integrated Warfare Systems, particularly as applied to large real-time systems. Prior to 1990, Dr. Bail worked at Intermetrics Inc. in Bethesda MD. Since 1989 he has served as an part-time Adjunct Professor at the University of Maryland University College where he develops instructional materials and teaches courses in software engineering, in topics such as Software Requirements, Verification and Validation, Software Design, Software Engineering, Fault Tolerant Software, and others. Previously, Dr. Bail taught part-time at The University of Maryland from 1983–1986 in the Computer Science Department for undergraduate courses in discrete mathematics, computer architecture, and programming language theory. Dr. Bail received a BS in Mathematics from Carnegie Institute of Technology, and an MS and Ph.D. in Computer Science from the University of Maryland.

**Dr. Richard P. Kendall** has been a developer/user/manager of large-scale scientific and engineering simulations for more than 35 years. He recently retired as Chief Information Officer of Los Alamos National Laboratory and is currently a member of the multi-institutional DARPA High Productivity Computing Systems Existing Code Analysis team. Richard received a Ph.D. in Mathematics from Rice University in 1973. He began his professional career at Humble Production Research Co. (now ExxonMobile) in numerical oil reservoir simulation. In 1982 Richard joined a start-up petro-technical software company, J.S. Nolen & Associates, as Vice-President. J.S. Nolen & Assoc. was acquired by Western Atlas International, Inc. in 1983. At Western Atlas, Richard rose to the rank of Chief Operating Officer of the Western Atlas Software Division. In 1995 he joined Los Alamos National laboratory and was appointed Chief Information Officer in 2000. Richard has published over 60 refereed papers. He is a member of the Society of Industrial and Applied Mathematics and the Society of Petroleum Engineers.

**Professor Taghi M. Khoshgoftaar** is a professor of the Department of Computer Science and Engineering, Florida Atlantic University and the Director of the Empirical Software Engineering Laboratory. His research interests are in software engineering, software metrics, software reliability and quality engineering, computational intelligence, computer performance evaluation, data mining, and statistical modeling. He has published more than 250 refereed papers in these areas. He has been a principal investigator and project leader in a number of projects with industry, government, and other research-sponsoring agencies. He is a member of the IEEE, IEEE Computer Society, and IEEE Reliability Society. He served as the general chair of the 1999 International Symposium on Software Reliability Engineering (ISSRE'99), and the general chair of the 2001 International Conference on Engineering of Computer Based Systems. Also, he has served on technical program committees of various international conferences, symposia, and workshops. He has served as North American editor of the *Software Quality Journal*, and is on the editorial boards of the journals *Empirical Software Engineering, Software Quality, and Fuzzy Systems*.

**Dr. Robert F. Lucas** is the Director of the Computational Sciences Division of the University of Southern California's Information Sciences Institute (ISI) where he manages research in computer architecture, VLSI, compilers and other software tools. Prior to joining ISI, he was the Head of the High Performance Computing Research Department in the National Energy Research Scientific Computing Center (NERSC) at Lawrence Berkeley National Laboratory. There he oversaw work in scientific data management, visualization, numerical algorithms, and scientific applications. Prior to joining NERSC, Dr. Lucas was the Deputy Director of DARPA's Information Technology Office. He also served as DARPA's Program Manager for Scalable Computing Systems and Data-Intensive Computing. From 1988 to 1998 he was a member of the research staff of the Institute for Defense Analyses' Center for Computing Sciences. From 1979 to 1984 he was a member of the Technical Staff of the Hughes Aircraft Company. Dr. Lucas received his BS, MS, and PhD degrees in Electrical Engineering from Stanford University in 1980, 1983, and 1988 respectively.

**Brian A. Nejmeh** is the President of INSTEP, a product and market strategy firm specializing in product positioning, product management and process engineering. He is also an Associate Professor of Information Systems and Entrepreneurship at Messiah College. He holds an M.S. degree in Computer Science from Purdue University and a B.S. degree in Computer Science from Allegheny College. He can be reached at nejmeh@instep.com.

**Dr. Douglass E. Post** has been developing and applying large-scale multi-physics simulations for almost 35 years. He is the Chief Scientist of the DoD High Performance Computing Modernization Program and a member of the senior technical staff of the Carnegie Mellon University Software Engineering Institute. He also leads the multi-institutional DARPA High Productivity Computing Systems Existing Code Analysis team. Doug received a Ph.D. in Physics from Stanford University in 1975. He led the tokamak modeling group at Princeton University Plasma Physics Laboratory from 1975 to 1993 and served as head of International Thermonuclear Experimental Reactor (ITER) Joint Central Team Physics Project Unit, and head of ITER Joint Central Team In-vessel Physics Group. More recently, he was the A-X Associate Division Leader for Simulation at Lawrence Livermore National Laboratory and the Deputy X Division Leader for Simulation at the Los Alamos National Laboratory. He has published over 230 refereed papers, conference papers and books in computational, experimental and theoretical physics with over 4700 citations. He is a Fellow of the American Physical Society and the American Nuclear Society and is presently an Associate Editor-in-Chief of the joint AIP/IEEE publication "Computing in Science and Engineering."

**David F. Rico** is a software process improvement consultant specializing in cost, benefit, and return-on-investment analysis. He holds a B.S. in Computer Science and an M.S.A. in Software Engineering. He is pursuing a Doctoral Degree in Information Technology and has been in the field of computer programming since 1983. He has been an international keynote speaker and has published numerous articles in major computer science journals on three continents. Some of his noteworthy accomplishments include designing software for NASA's $20 billion space station, spearheading SW-CMM® and ISO 9001 initiatives for Fujitsu in Tokyo, modernizing a family of U.S. Air Force static radar ranges, reengineering 36 military logistics depots in Cairo, designing a $30 billion constellation of U.S. Air Force satellites, conducting a $42 million U.S. Navy source selection, designing a $70 million cost model for U.S. Navy aircraft, and participating in over 15 SW-CMM® initiatives. David can be contacted at: dave@davidfrico.com.

**Dr. William E. Riddle** is a Senior Solution Architect at Solution Deployment Affiliates. His work focuses on the process modeling and analysis and technology improvement planning. Bill is an IEEE Fellow and recipient of the Most Influential ICSE-8 Paper Award and the 1999 ACM SigSoft Distinguished Service Award.

He holds Engineering Physics and Computer Science degrees from Cornell and Stanford. He can be reached at riddle@WmERiddle.com.

**Pierre Rebours** is a software engineer at Software FX Inc., a leading software component vendor. He received his M.S. degree in Computer Science from Florida Atlantic University, Boca Raton, FL, in 2004. He has a B.S. from l'École des Mines d'Alès, France. His research interests include computational intelligence, data mining and machine learning, software measurement, software reliability and quality engineering, design-patterns, and vector graphics. Pierre may be contacted at prebours@fau.edu.

**Dr. Rini van Solingen** is a principal consultant at LogicaCMG and a professor at Drenthe University, in the Netherlands. Within LogicaCMG, he specializes in industrial software product and process improvement. At Drenthe University-for-professional-education he heads a chair in quality management and quality engineering. Rini holds an MSc in technical informatics from Delft University of Technology and a PhD in management science from Eindhoven University of Technology. Rini has been a senior quality engineer at Schlumberger/Tokheim Retail Petroleum Systems and has been head of the Quality and Process Engineering department at the Fraunhofer Institute for Experimental Software Engineering in Kaiserslautern, Germany. Rini can be contacted at: rini.van.solingen@logicacmg.com.

# Preface

This volume of **Advances in Computers** is number 66 in the series that began back in 1960. This series presents the ever changing landscape in the continuing evolution of the development of the computer and the field of information processing. Each year three volumes are produced presenting approximately 20 chapters that describe the latest technology in the use of computers today. Volume 66, subtitled "Quality Software Development," is concerned about the current need to create quality software. It describes the current emphasis in techniques for creating such software and in methods to demonstrate that the software indeed meets the expectations of the designers and purchasers of that software.

Companies today are engaged in expensive programs to improve their software development technology. However, are they receiving a return on their investment? Do all of the activities, under the general term of "software process improvement," have a positive effect on the organization? In Chapter 1, Rini van Solingen and David Rico discuss "Calculating software process improvement's return on investment." They discuss several measures for calculating this return on investment and provide data that describes the effectiveness that has been achieved for several software process improvement models.

In Chapter 2, Pierre Rebours and Taghi Khoshgoftaar discuss a related issue to the topic of the first chapter. Although we want to compute various measures on software development activities, how do we know if the data we are collecting is accurate? Software development data is notoriously noisy and often inaccurate. Data, which often depends upon programmers and other project members submitting forms, is often missing or incorrect. How can we analyze such data and achieve reliable results? In "Quality Problem in Software Measurement Data," the authors discuss various ways to filter our bad data and "train" the dataset to provide more accurate evaluations.

Chapter 3, "Requirements Management for Dependable Software Systems" by William G. Bail, discusses the role of requirements in the software development process. Many studies over the past 40 years have demonstrated that poor requirements—often missing, misstated or ambiguous—are a major cause of problems during the development process. Fixing these problems is a major contributor toward high software costs. In this chapter Dr. Bail discusses the role of requirements and presents several methods in the proper handling of these requirements to minimize later problems.

In Chapter 4, "Mechanics of Managing Software Risk" also by William G. Bail, the topic is the role of risk in the software development process. Intuitively, in the software development domain a risk is an event that is unexpected and has a cost— generally an increase in needed staff or a delay in completion of the product. The major role of management is to make sure that staff understand their roles, that as many risks as possible are identified early in the development process, and that a plan for mitigating these risks, i.e., for handling these unexpected events, is identified before they occur. Dr. Bail provides a summary of the causes of software risks and various strategies for handling them.

In Chapter 5, "The PERFECT Approach to Experience-Based Process Evolution" by Brian Nejmeh and William Riddle, the authors describe one method of handling process evolution. The previous 4 chapters all describe methods for improving the software development process. Over time as an organization tries to improve its activities, the set of all these development activities, or processes, will change and evolve. How does one understand and manage this change for continued improvement? Based upon their PEDAL framework for describing process evolution steps, they describe a methodology for understanding their process activities and for managing the changes that will occur to those processes.

In Chapter 6, Douglass Post, Richard Kendell, and Robert Lucas discuss "The Opportunities, Challenges, and Risks of High Performance Computing in Computational Science and Engineering." This chapter discusses software development in an application domain that is becoming more important—the high end computing domain. In this domain, machines consisting of thousands of processors work together to solve a single problem that is too complex to solve on a single processor. As the authors state: "The advent of massive parallelization to increase computer performance must be done in a way that does not massively increase the difficulty of developing programs." Four requirements must be met to achieve this: "First, computing power must continue to increase. Second, it must be possible to efficiently develop programs for these highly complex computers. Third, the programs must be accurate, i.e., free of important defects and include all of the necessary effects. Fourth, society must organize itself to develop the application programs." This chapter discusses these requirements in greater detail.

I hope that you find these articles of interest. If you have any suggestions of topics for future chapters, or if you wish to contribute such a chapter, I can be reached at mvz@cs.umd.edu.

Marvin Zelkowitz
College Park, Maryland

# Calculating Software Process Improvement's Return on Investment

## RINI VAN SOLINGEN

*LogicaCMG and Drenthe University
Netherlands*

## DAVID F. RICO

**Abstract**

Many organizations and firms invest in software process improvement (SPI). They do this in order to satisfy business goals for customer satisfaction, time-to-market, cost, quality, and reliability. Return on investment (ROI) is a traditional approach for measuring the business or monetary value of an investment. As such, it can be used for measuring the economic benefit of investing in SPI. Measuring the ROI of SPI is still in its early infancy, in spite of the fact that ROI has been around for many decades and the discipline of SPI itself has also been popular for at least 20 years.

It is important to note that ROI is a metric that can be used before and after an investment in SPI. ROI can be used to evaluate (a priori) investment opportunities and make a proper selection and ROI can be used to evaluate (a posteriori) the extent to which an investment was legitimate. Although the value of using ROI for SPI calculations seems self evident, using ROI in practice often proves difficult. In this chapter we provide an overview of how to apply ROI calculations to enhance decision making processes involving SPI. We approach these calculations from two dimensions: modelling and measuring. For each of these dimensions we provide pragmatic approaches for real-life decision making, all illustrated with actual case studies. The chapter contains guidelines, approaches, and experiences on how to do this in practice. It supports making simple but sound financial evaluations when using SPI to improve organizational performance.

The main message of this chapter is that ROI can and must be calculated for most SPI investment decisions as a means of ultimately satisfying business goals and objectives. ROI can and should be an explicit part of software management and engineering decision making processes when it comes to SPI, which can minimize effort, costs, and financial investments. Software managers

and engineers should include financial considerations such as ROI in their decisions, as well as technical ones, in order to satisfy business goals and objectives
for SPI.

# 1.  Introduction

Software Process Improvement (SPI) is the discipline of characterizing, defining,
measuring, and improving software management and engineering processes. The
goal of SPI is often to achieve better business performance in terms of cost, time-
to-market, innovation, and quality. More importantly, SPI involves change. That is,
there is the fundamental notion that poor organizational performance is associated

with poorly defined processes. While there are numerous types of software processes, software project management and software quality management practices are often the targets of scrutiny, improvement, and institutionalization. Changes to software processes are often based on the notions of adopting or adapting best practices (e.g., experiences of other, not necessarily similar organizations). These changes often include the introduction of new product technologies or tools, but also include designing, deploying, and institutionalizing new organizational policies and procedures for software management and engineering.

SPI now involves the use of many out-of-the-box methodologies, approaches, and techniques. That is, rather than home grow one's organizational improvement from scratch, organizations now have many of pre-packaged approaches from which to choose, examples are:

- Software Capability Maturity Model® (SW-CMM®) [47,59].
- Capability Maturity Model Integration® (CMMI®) [20,19].
- ISO 9000-3 (dedicated to software) [51].
- ISO 15504 (SPICE) [50].
- BOOTSTRAP [10].
- Quality Improvement Paradigm [4].
- Goal/Question/Metric method [4,78].
- Balanced ScoreCard [54].
- Personal Software Process$^{sm}$ (PSP$^{sm}$) [48,34].
- Team Software Process$^{sm}$ (TSP$^{sm}$) [45].
- Software Inspections [33,35].
- Extreme Programming [8].
- Agile Methods [44].

SPI has had the attention of both academics and practitioners since the creation of the Software Capability Maturity Model (SW-CMM®) almost 15 years ago [59]. The general aim of SPI approaches is to make the performance of software development and maintenance more effective and efficient by structuring and optimizing their processes. SPI focuses on software processes. SPI is based on the assumption that well managed organizations with rigorously defined software processes are more likely to provide products and services that satisfy customer requirements. And, these products and services are expected to be rendered within schedule and budget. Poorly managed organizations, on the other hand, are assumed to not achieve such consistent levels of product and service quality without such software processes. As such, SPI is based on the basic assumption that there is a causal relation between process and product, and that the product can be determined through its creation process.

There are a few notable detractors of this so-called over emphasis on the virtues of SPI and software processes [2,3,12,18,21], [43],[1] [49,77]. The main criticism is an over-emphasis on processes with the implicit risk to neglect the product. While even the greatest detractors of SPI admit that sound software processes are prerequisites for software development success, not all software processes or SPI methodologies for that matter are sound. With the amount of international attention, publications, and investments in SPI, more researchers and practitioners are analyzing the extent to which the benefits of these investments are worth their cost [31,65–68].

## 2.  Return-on-Investment for Analysing Cost and Benefits

Return on investment (ROI) is a widely used approach for measuring the value of an investment. In this chapter we consider SPI as a structured investment in which software processes are changed with the intent to achieve benefits in business performance, for example: productivity, customer satisfaction, revenue, profit, cost, quality, time-to-market, culture, and flexibility. The costs of this undertaking are the sum of all direct and indirect cost such as: training, consulting, motivation, implementation, learning, opportunity cost, and material. The benefits are the sum of all direct and indirect benefits, including achievement of goals, increased staff motivation, better quality, productivity, etc. ROI is the numeric calculation in which a financial representation of the benefits is divided by a financial representation of the costs.[2] So, both direct and indirect cost and benefits are converted to a financial number and included in the calculation. An ROI of 3 generally means that for every monetary unit invested, three monetary units are earned. (Detailed examples and explanations will be provided a little later.)

However, ROI still remains a mystery to some practitioners, along with appropriate techniques for determining the ROI of SPI. Surprisingly we find also only a limited number of research reports that contain cost and benefit numbers, and ones that measure ROI. Such ROI numbers are however useful as they can be used to:

- Convince strategic stakeholders to invest money and effort into SPI, and to convince them that organizational performance issues can be solved through SPI.

---

[1] This study shows that 44% of respondents claim limited, little or no success in improvement after having had a CMM assessment (also [36]).

[2] This is a simplified definition of ROI, as: "...yet there is no common understanding of what constitutes an investment and return" [14]. Putnam and Myers even say that these returns should not only payback the investment, but also in addition the capital that would have been generated if these funds would have been invested elsewhere [61].

- Estimate the amount of effort necessary to solve a certain problem, or estimating whether a certain intended benefit is worth its cost.

- Decide how to prioritize software process improvements and which software processes to improve first, as many organizations have severe timing and resource constraints.

- Decide whether to continue SPI initiatives and programs. SPI budgets are assigned and discussed yearly, so if benefits are not made explicit and a sufficient ROI is not shown, continuation is at risk.

- Simply survive, as any investment in an organization should be valued against its return. Or else, it is very likely that money will be wasted and that there is risk of bankruptcy in the long run.

In this chapter we propose some pragmatic solutions on how to calculate cost and benefits, and how to calculate the ROI. One main message is to avoid too detailed calculations. It is in most cases sufficient to know the relative value of the ROI: is it positive, break-even, or negative? In most industrial organizations it is not so important to know whether the ROI is 7.345 or 7.955. Knowing whether the ROI is positive and knowing its range (e.g., between 5 and 10), is for most decision making more than sufficient. The main purpose of ROI calculations is to decide within a specific industrial context (and industry) where to invest the money, or to evaluate whether an investment was worth its money. As SPI is just one possible investment, its ROI should also be calculated. ROI is the magnitude of benefits to costs. If costs are small, ROI is large if benefits are large. If costs are high, ROI is generally lower. Managers often spend too much money to achieve a negligible ROI. Managers need to realize that the goal is to achieve an optimal ROI, not achieve compliance with expensive international standards for SPI. Because the most popular methods for SPI are often the most expensive approaches, managers tend to believe they must spend a lot of money to achieve some level of ROI. This is often a self defeating concept. Managers need to apply methods for SPI with high benefits and low costs. The research community is also responsible for creating methods for SPI with high benefits and low costs.

Research has proven that humans make trade-off analyses continuously; if not based on objective measurements then based on intuition [7]. Making explicit ROI calculations is therefore crucial for SPI, as SPI is an investment with significant cost and not always clearly visible benefits. ROI should therefore be made visible as well, as to avoid wrong intuitive evaluations. Without numbers on costs, benefits, and ROI of SPI, it is be impossible to take proper decisions whether SPI is worth its cost. Even if the overall costs of a SPI undertaking are at a break even point (e.g., costs equal benefits), local benefits may already be worthwhile. For example, if it saves a development team some time: it shortens time-to-market, development can be done faster, and pressure on developers can be decreased. For showing the ROI of SPI it is important to focus on productivity and time-to-market impacts. *"The true cost-benefits occur when projects finish earlier, allowing us to apply more engineering resources to the acquisition and development of new business."* [26].

The ROI of SPI differs, by the way, over different situations. For example, a company with severe quality problems at customer sites can obtain a much higher ROI from SPI than a company with productivity problems, because the business benefits are probably higher in the first case. Building the business case for SPI is therefore always a specific task for a specific environment. Generic numbers on the ROI of SPI can help, e.g., for building ROI models, but the business case should be built along the lines of the specific context, its goals and its problems. A generic benchmark for SPI cannot be given. However, when building the case for SPI in the comparison to other investments, quantifying benefits and ROI will certainly help. It is important to note that a growing body of authoritative literature on the ROI of SPI is now starting to emerge [30,62,63,66,67,73,76].

## 2.1 ROI Metrics

ROI metrics are designed to measure the economic value of a new and improved software process. Each ROI metric is a relevant indicator of how much a new and improved software process is worth. We recommend only six basic metrics related to ROI, as shown in Table I. They are costs, benefits, benefit/cost ratio or B/CR, return on investment or ROI, net present value or NPV, and break even point or BEP [66–68]. Each ROI metric builds upon its predecessor and refines the accuracy of the economic value of a new software process. ROI metrics are not necessarily

TABLE I
ROI METRICS SHOWING SIMPLICITY OF RETURN ON INVESTMENT FORMULAS AND THEIR
ORDER OF APPLICATION

| Metric | Definition | Formula |
|--------|-----------|---------|
| Costs | Total amount of money spent on a new and improved software process | $\sum_{i=1}^{n} Cost_i$ |
| Benefits | Total amount of money gained from a new and improved software process | $\sum_{i=1}^{n} Benefit_i$ |
| B/CR | Ratio of benefits to costs | $\frac{Benefits}{Costs}$ |
| ROI | Ratio of adjusted benefits to costs | $\frac{Benefits - Costs}{Costs} \times 100\%$ |
| NPV | Discounted cash flows | $\sum_{i=1}^{Years} \frac{Benefits_i}{(1 + Discount\ Rate)^{Years}} - Costs_0$ |
| BEP | Point when benefits meet or exceed cost | $\frac{Costs}{Old\ Costs/New\ Costs - 1}$ |

independent or mutually exclusive. Each ROI metric must sometimes be considered individually. For example, costs may be astronomical or benefits may be negligible, marginalizing the relevance of the other metrics.

Costs consist of the amount of money an organization has to pay in order to implement a SPI method. Benefits generally consist of the amount of money saved by implementing a SPI method. B/CR is a simple ratio of the amount of money saved implementing a new SPI method to the amount of money consumed. ROI is also a ratio of money saved to money consumed by a new SPI method expressed as a percentage. However, the ROI metric demands that the costs of implementing the SPI method must first be subtracted from the benefits. NPV is a method of adjusting or reducing the estimated benefits of a SPI method based on projected or future inflation over time. Break even point is a measure of the amount of money that must be spent on a new SPI method before it begins yielding its benefits.

One should note that the basic ROI metric is, in fact, not a very strong metric when calculating investments that exceed the time-span of one year; in such cases net present value (NPV) is stronger. And, there is a growing interest in *real options* as a superior approach towards measuring the value of SPI, versus ROI and NPV [32]. However, for the purpose of this chapter we will continue with ROI, especially because we approach ROI from a pragmatic industrial perspective, and try to keep things simple so exclude interest rates and inflation. Long-term benefits are nice, but industrial investment in general need to show short-term results within the same year.

## 2.2　A Survey of Literature on the ROI Metric for SPI

The ROI of SPI is calculated by dividing a financial representation of the benefits by a financial representation of the cost. So, an ROI of 5 implies that every invested dollar brings 5 dollars in profit. A limited number of publications are available that contain concrete data for calculating the ROI of SPI. Table II presents an overview of the ROI numbers taken from experience reports in literature. Please note that not all reports use the formula: $(benefits - cost)/cost$, for calculating ROI. Some use: $benefits/cost$ (B/CR: benefit cost ratio) or do not present the calculation used. In case of high ROI values, the benefits generally outweigh the costs. However, things get more critical if the ROI approaches 1, which means the monetary costs tend to outweigh the monetary benefits.

The experience reports in Table II show exhibit a range for the ROI of SPI of 1.5 to 19 for every invested dollar or monetary unit.[3] The average ROI is 7 and the median of the data is 6.6. Although, the ROI of any SPI undertaking depends

---

[3] Jones states that he generally observes a ROI between 3 and 30 to every invested dollar.

TABLE II
RETURN-ON-INVESTMENT NUMBERS IN LITERATURE [81]

| Context | Publication | Return on investment |
|---|---|---|
| Unknown[i] | [14] | 1.5 |
| General Dyn. Dec. Systems | [25] | 2.2 |
| BDN International | [74] | 3[ii] |
| Unknown (U[iii]) | [42] | 4 |
| U.S. Navy | [29] | 4.1 |
| Unknown (W[iii]) | [42] | 4.2 |
| Hughes Aircraft | [46] | 5 |
| IBM Global Services India | [37] | 5.5 |
| Tinker Air Force Base | [14] | 6 |
| Unknown (X[iii]) | [42] | 6.4 |
| Motorola | [26] | 6.77 |
| OC-ALC (Tinker) | [17] | 7.5 |
| Philips | [69] | 7.5 |
| Raytheon | [27,28] | 7.7[iv] |
| Boeing | [84] | 7.75 |
| Unknown (Y[iii]) | [42] | 8.8 |
| Unknown | [14] | 10 |
| Hewlett-Packard | [39] | 10.4 |
| Northrop Grumman ES | [64] | 12.5[v] |
| Ogden ALC | [58] | 19 |
| | Average | 7 |
| | Median | 6.6 |

[i] Broadman and Johnson present ROI numbers from several cases (1.5, 2.0, 4, 6, 7.7, 10, 1.26, 5): underlined are likely to be: Tinker, Raytheon, and Hughes Aircraft.
[ii] Slaughter et al. present four ROI numbers: 3.83, 3.65, 2.96, and 2.74.
[iii] Character used to refer to the respective organization in Herbsleb et al.
[iv] This number is calculated based on 6 projects. If the same calculation is followed for the reported 15 projects, this seems to result in an ROI of 4.
[v] Reifer et al. report an ROI by productivity gains of 1,251% on a 5 year planning horizon.

on many influencing factors, it appears that a proper estimation for a SPI-ROI lies between 4 and 10, from this data set. The ROI of SPI is not necessarily constrained by these dimensions, according to some authors [66–68].

The evidence in literature that the above reported ROI will occur when a certain SPI method is used, is however limited. The best that can be attained with studies that focus only on process factors is strong evidence that SPI is associated with some benefits, or that organizations could benefit from SPI activities [31]. This may mean that the benefits of SPI will strongly depend on the reasons (e.g., intended benefits) to use SPI in the first place. Literature findings are diverse and distributed among the several business goals in the software engineering domain. Furthermore, do different SPI approaches have different effects [57,63,68]?

### 2.2.1 A Critical View on Industrial Reported ROI Measurements

Although many publications on the cost and benefits of SPI have been written by respected researchers, and have been through rigorous peer review processes, there are some limitations to the reported data that need to be considered. Especially the validity of these findings (e.g., how good are these findings and are they generically true?) is an essential issue to consider [31,72]. For example, only success stories are reported and failures are not, and it is unknown how many failed attempts have occurred.

Some researchers and practitioners believe that the direct correlation between SPI and the observed business performance improvements has never been proven, because organizations take multiple actions. They never 'bet on one horse.' This means they rarely take only one action to get a certain result. Instead, they take several actions in parallel, with similar expected effects, as they are primarily interested in the effect and not in what actually causes that effect. In addition, the survey-based research results are questionable with respect to the way in which data analysis is performed (e.g., more than one respondent in one organization). Questionnaires are only returned in small quantities, or they are not randomly distributed [13,42], which undermines the reliability and validity of these studies. For more information on the difficulties and limitations in published SPI reports we refer to [31]. This does not mean that such studies are useless, but one should use and adopt these findings carefully [31,41]. They do indicate a positive trend in the ROI of SPI, and also indicate a wide range in ROI values and results. One should consider that these numbers are, however, no guarantee for success.

### 2.2.2 Lack of ROI Expectations

A final observation concerning SPI literature is the total absence of expectations for costs, benefits, and ROI. None of the companies reported that they established explicit expectations for ROI of SPI in advance. Some organizations did mention that they wanted to increase productivity, decrease defects, decrease time-to-market, etc., but no publication indicated what price they were willing to pay for an anticipated range of benefits. It could be that these expectations were defined explicitly, but not reported. However, we strongly suspect that those expectations were not made explicit. This might indicate that starting a SPI effort is often driven by a personal faith that the overall effects of SPI will be positive, and that the investments will have a significant return. This finding also confirms the general tendency that software engineering organizations are not strong in measuring their activities [56,70].

An organization should identify its business goals and after that, select the respective SPI practices that are most likely to have an impact on these goals, to ensure that SPI results address the most important issues for an organization [31].[4] Each organization should describe by itself: the benefits it wants to achieve and the size of these benefits. Just stating that the target is to "reduce time-to-market" is not sufficient. A proper goal is for example: the reduction of average project duration will be reduced with 10% per year so that projects last between 3 and 6 months, with a schedule accuracy of 90% with maximum one calendar month delay for the remaining 10%. Furthermore, the risk of SPI initiatives is so high that establishing only moderate goals for the ROI of SPI may be inherently self defeating, necessitating the establishment of more aggressive targets to counteract negative effects.

The base of scholarly literature on the application of ROI principles is sparse, hard to find, and not ubiquitous. Scientists should take responsibility for creating an industry standard set of metrics and models for ROI of SPI. There are just too many metrics, models, and methods from which to choose. Managers are far too challenged to keep pace with rapidly changing information technologies. They simply cannot keep up with advances in management science. Scholars can help managers by steering them towards cost, benefit, benefit/cost ratio, return on investment, net present value, and break even point analysis using simple mainstream methods.

## 2.3  Cost of SPI

The costs of SPI are almost always expressed in effort, person hours, or engineering hours. This may indicate that effort is considered as the main cost driver of SPI. On the other hand this may also indicate that indirect costs are likely to be overlooked, and that measuring cost and benefits of SPI is not so much a financial investment, but more an effort investment. Managers apparently decide on where to spend their engineering effort to get a return. This is remarkable as most SPI activities involve monetary expenditures training, coaching, and consulting as well. Also, when the costs of SPI are expressed in terms of person effort instead of monetary terms, the financial figures may be more meaningful across a diverse range of organizations, as well as their host nations.

As this chapter intends to give financial numbers to its main questions, Table III provides for each context report, the cost of SPI spent per person per year. These cost are provided in dollars, calculated based on a yearly cost per person of $100,000.

[4] For example: for a study on CMM customisation see [55].

TABLE III
COST OF SPI (MEASURED IN DOLLARS PER PERSON PER YEAR)

| Context | Publication | Cost ($ per person per year) |
|---|---|---|
| Unknown (B[i]) | [42] | 490 |
| Hughes Aircraft | [46] | 800[ii] |
| Unknown (C[i]) | [42] | 858 |
| Unknown (E[i]) | [42] | 1,375 |
| Schlumberger | [83] | 1,500[iii] |
| Motorola | [26] | 1,500[iii] |
| Unknown (D[i]) | [42] | 1,619 |
| HP | [39] | 1,859[iii] |
| AlliedSignal Aerospace | [15] | 2,000[iii] |
| Tokheim | [11] | 2,000[iii] |
| Unknown (A[i]) | [42] | 2,004 |
| Raytheon | [28] | 2,500[iii] |
| Jones | [52] | 6,750[iii] |
| Nasa/SEL | [6] | 11,000[iii] |
| | Average | 2,590 |
| | Median | 1,739 |

[i] Character used to refer to the respective organization in Herbsleb et al.
[ii] Calculated based on 400k$ investment for 500 engineers.
[iii] Calculated based on yearly person cost of $100,000.

Table III shows that SPI cost range between $490 and $11,000 per person per year based on the experience reports from several organisations. The average of the provided numbers is $2,590 and the median of the numbers $1,739. Although, SPI cost depend on the goals of an improvement programme, it seems that a yearly budget of $1,500–$2,500 per person seems reasonable for an SPI programme. This reflects a time expenditure for each person of about 2%.

Today's methods for SPI are often expensive, and range in the millions of dollars. In fact, the most popular method for SPI ranges from five to fifteen million dollars to apply. SPI is very difficult, and can require many attempts over periods as long as a decade before achieving a single instance of success. So, their costs often manifest themselves in multiple applications of the methods. These methods are cost prohibitive for small to medium size enterprises, and may very well place large enterprises at risk of financial instability. Managers could be aware that blindly adopting a method for SPI, in spite of its cost, may place their enterprises at risk, instead of strengthening them. Managers should apply inexpensive versus expensive methods for SPI. There are classes of methods, which are inexpensive, yet highly effective.

## 2.4   Benefits of SPI

One argument often heard in practice is that benefits of SPI cannot be measured, or are at least very difficult to measure. Organizations find it relatively easy to measure cost, but have a hard time in measuring benefits. Investigation of literature supports this partly, as SPI benefits are rarely expressed in a financial value. Benefits are also expressed in dimensions other than cost.

The amount of benefits from SPI claimed in practice is diverse. These benefits are so different that a general number as provided for cost and ROI cannot be given for benefits. Benefits of SPI differ over SPI methodologies and organizations. This is even true for publications that present the benefits of one specific SPI approach (e.g., SW-CMM®), which often obtain different results depending on the different targets set by the respective organization. So, organizations that start SPI efforts to reduce their time-to-market will realise a reduction in project duration, while other organizations starting SPI to increase product reliability will experience a reduction in post-release defects. Organizations should realise that customer perceptions only improve as a by-product of improved performance: being better, faster, and/or cheaper than their competitors [1].

SPI benefits, though different by organization, can be classified among a more generic scheme of benefits. Table IV shows a classification of SPI benefits, based on [14,23,26,36,40,43,52,74,75].

What becomes clear from the benefits mentioned in the SPI publications is that many benefits can be realized. Examples from literature reporting benefits within this classification are shown in Table V.

## 2.5   A Priori and A Posteriori ROI Analysis

ROI is oftentimes applied when it's too late to optimize costs and benefits. In other words, managers often spend millions of dollars on SPI, and then they want to justify their expenditures after-the-fact by looking for ROI. Again, ROI is the magnitude of benefits to costs. If a manager spends too much money, ROI may oftentimes be negligible. Besides, ROI is not always about minimizing costs, but about maximizing benefits! Since managers don't apply ROI, they oftentimes end up with little or no benefits. So, if managers garner few benefits and spend a lot of money, then ROI is sure to be negligible.

ROI calculations should be done before and after the investment:

- Before the investment is made the decision making process should include an explicit step to quantify the cost, benefits and ROI of a SPI investment. This ensures that the most beneficial improvement is made, and that expectations are made explicit.

TABLE IV
CLASSIFICATION OF SPI BENEFITS

| Class | Type of benefit |
|---|---|
| Productivity | Increase in productivity |
| Quality | Increase in quality attributes (e.g., reliability, usability, etc.) |
| | Reduction in defects |
| | Reduction in defect density |
| Cost | Reduction project cost |
| | Reduction product cost |
| | Reduction rework cost |
| | Reduction cost of quality |
| Schedule | Increase in schedule accuracy |
| | Increase of on-time delivery |
| | Reduction of throughput time (time-to-market) |
| Effort | Reduction of work effort |
| | Reduction of rework (cycles) |
| Customer | Increase of customer satisfaction |
| | Increase in sales revenues |
| | Increase in profitability |
| Staff | Increase in staff morale |
| | Decrease in over-time |
| | Decrease of staff turnover |

TABLE V
REPORTED BENEFITS WITHIN SPI CLASSIFICATION FRAMEWORK

| Class | Actual benefit |
|---|---|
| Productivity | 10 time productivity increase (1000%) [17] |
| | 70% productivity increase [58] |
| Quality | 50 times reduction of defects [22] |
| | 80% reduction of defects [38] |
| Cost | 50% to 300% cost reduction [14] |
| | 58% cost reduction [5] |
| | 10% work saving due to inspections [69] |
| | $2M cost saving [82] |
| Schedule | 70% reduction of time-to-market [52] |
| | 15–23% time-to-market reduction [42] |
| | 94% schedule accuracy [83] |
| | >2000% schedule improvement in ten years is feasible [16] |
| Effort | 60% reduction in testing effort [15] |
| | 100% good/excellent customer satisfaction [36] |
| | improved customer satisfaction [84] |
| Staff | Improved staff morale with lesser over-time [28] |
| | 4 times faster assimilation of new engineers [71] |

- After the investment is done, i.e., when the change has been deployed, to evaluate whether the expected improvement actually took place. After all, a change in a process is only an improvement if it actually results in better business performance.

The remainder of this chapter will focus on ROI from these two perspectives. First, modelling will be addressed as this mainly supports decision making on SPI investments. Second, measurement is addressed as this supports in SPI investment evaluations afterwards.

## 3.  Using Quantitative Models for SPI Decision Making

This section includes practical examples for estimating the ROI of Inspections, PSP$^{sm}$, TSP$^{sm}$, SW-CMM®, ISO 9001, and CMMI® through the use of quantitative models. More importantly, this section helps sort through the literature by identifying a small set of practical metrics, models, and examples for the ROI of some SPI approaches. A detailed discussion of the models is beyond the scope of this chapter, however, for clarification, the major inputs, terms, and drivers are explained in Appendix A of this chapter.

Before entering the presentation of the quantitative models, it seems wise to point out that quantitative models have certain limitations. They provide a means to estimate the relevant cost and benefits for ones own situation, calculated from estimates and experiences from others. As such they support in getting a feeling on what to expect based on data from others. However, these models should be treated carefully. Quantitative models tend to provide a level of accuracy which is incorrect, at the same time they provide sufficiently more insight in the size and effects of certain activities than just the qualitative descriptions. One must use discretion and caution with the notion that a single cost model works for every environment (e.g., that for every 4 person team implementing 10,000 LOC using CMMI, process deployment costs $941,700 [Table VIII]). The numbers included in quantitative models support in calculating an estimate for a certain situation. The more numbers from ones own context can be included, the better it is. Also for quantitative models the general rule is valid that all models are wrong, but some models are useful.

### 3.1  Cost Models for SPI

Cost models are simple equations, formulas, or functions that are used to measure, quantify, and estimate the effort, time, and economic consequences of implementing a SPI method. A single cost model may be all that is necessary to estimate the cost

TABLE VI
COST MODELS OF SPI METHODS WITH EXAMPLES FOR A 4 PERSON TEAM IMPLEMENTING
10,000 LOC

| Method | Cost models and worked examples | Hours | Costs |
|---|---|---|---|
| Inspections (effort) | $LOC/(Review\_Rate \times 2) \times (Team\_Size \times 4 + 1)$<br>$10,000/(120 \times 2) \times (4 \times 4 + 1)$ | 708 | [a]$70,833 |
| Inspections (training) | $Team\_Size \times (Fee/Rate + Hours)$<br>$4 \times (410/100 + 24)$ | 112.4 | [b]$11,240 |
| PSP$^{sm}$ (training) | $Team\_Size \times ((Fee + Expenses)/Rate + Hours)$<br>$4 \times ((5,000 + 5,400)/100 + 160)$ | 1,056 | [c]$105,600 |
| TSP$^{sm}$ (training) | $Team\_Size \times ((Fee + Expenses)/Rate + Hours) + PSP$<br>$4 \times ((4,000 + 2,700)/100 + 40) + 1,056$ | 1,484 | [d]$148,400 |
| SW-CMM® (process) | $561 + 1,176 \times Number\_of\_Projects$<br>$561 + 1,176 \times 1$ | 1,737 | [e]$173,700 |
| ISO 9001 (process) | $546 + 560 \times Number\_of\_Projects$<br>$546 + 560 \times 1$ | 1,106 | [f]$110,600 |
| CMMI® (process) | $(10,826 + 8,008 \times Number\_of\_Projects)/2$<br>$(10,826 + 8,008 \times 1)/2$ | 9,417 | [g]$941,700 |

of implementing a SPI method such as PSP$^{sm}$ and TSP$^{sm}$. It may be necessary to combine the results of multiple cost models together in order estimate the costs of implementing SPI methods such as Inspections [67]. The results of multiple cost models must be combined with other empirical data to estimate the complete costs of implementing complex SPI methods such as SW-CMM® and CMMI®. There are eight basic cost models for estimating key cost elements of the six major SPI methods as shown in Table VI. There are cost models for Inspections effort and training, PSP$^{sm}$ and TSP$^{sm}$ training, and SW-CMM®, ISO 9001, and CMMI® processes and products.

## 3.2 Benefit Models for SPI

Benefit models are simple equations, formulas, or functions that are used to measure, quantify, and estimate the economic value, profit, savings, or reward of implementing a new SPI method. SPI methods are designed and implemented in order to yield economic or monetary benefits such as increased customer satisfaction, productivity, quality, cost savings, and cycle time reduction. A long used, classical, and authoritative approach to quantifying the benefits of SPI methods is to measure total life cycle costs before and after the introduction of a new SPI method. There are seven benefit models or total life cycle cost models which are very useful for estimating the economic value of the six major SPI methods as shown in Table VII. There

TABLE VII
BENEFIT MODELS OF SPI METHODS WITH EXAMPLES FOR A 4 PERSON TEAM IMPLEMENTING
10,000 LOC

| Method | Benefit models and worked examples | Hours | Costs |
|--------|-----------------------------------|-------|-------|
| Old Costs | $LOC \times 10.51 - Test\_Hours \times 9$ <br> $10,000 \times 10.51 - 6,666.67 \times 9$ | 45,100 | [h]$4,509,997 |
| Inspections | $LOC \times 10.51 - Inspection\_Hours \times 99 - Test\_Hours \times 9$ <br> $10,000 \times 10.51 - 708.33 \times 99 - 1,950 \times 9$ | 17,425 | [i]$1,742,533 |
| PSP[sm] | $LOC / 25$ <br> $10,000/25$ | 400 | [j]$40,000 |
| TSP[sm] | $LOC / 5.9347$ <br> $10,000/5.9347$ | 1,685 | [k]$168,501 |
| SW-CMM® | $LOC \times 10.2544 - Inspection\_Hours \times 99 - Test\_Hours \times 9$ <br> $10,000 \times 10.2544 - 708.33 \times 99 - 1,950 \times 9$ | 14,869 | [l]$1,486,933 |
| ISO 9001 | $LOC \times 10.442656 - Test\_Hours \times 9 - Rework\_Savings$ <br> $10,000 \times 10.442656 - 6,670 \times 9 - 4,995$ | 39,402 | [m]$3,940,156 |
| CMMI® | $LOC \times 10.2544 - Inspection\_Hours \times 99 - Test\_Hours \times 9$ <br> $10,000 \times 10.2544 - 708.33 \times 99 - 1,950 \times 9$ | 14,869 | [n]$1,486,933 |

are benefit models for old costs, Inspections, PSP[sm], TSP[sm], SW-CMM®, ISO 9001, and CMMI® [67].

Total life cycle cost is an estimate of complete software development and maintenance costs. The basic form of the total life cycle cost model is $LOC \times (Defect\_Rate \times 100 + Software\_Effort/10,000) - Inspection\_Hours \times 99 - Test\_Hours \times 9$. *LOC* refers to lines of code, *Defect_Rate* refers to the defect injection rate, and *Software_Effort* refers to analysis, design, and coding hours. *Inspection_Hours* and *Test_Hours* are self explanatory. With a *Defect_Rate* of 10% or 0.1 and a *Software_Effort* of 5,100, the basic total life cycle cost model simplifies to $LOC \times 10.51 - Inspection\_Hours \times 99 - Test\_Hours \times 9$. This total life cycle cost model signifies complete software development and maintenance costs, less the benefits of inspections and testing. If no inspections or testing are performed, then the total life cycle cost is $LOC \times 10.51$ or 105,100 hours for a 10,000 line of code application. If we perform 708.33 hours of inspections and 1,950 hours of testing, then the total life cycle cost is $LOC \times 10.51 - 708.33 \times 99 - 1,950 \times 9$ or 17,425 hours, a savings of 87,675 hours. (*This is an extensible model which can be calibrated for varying defect rates, software effort, and Inspections and testing efficiencies. Furthermore, it can be augmented to model the economics of automatic static source code analysis and analyzers.*)

The Old Cost benefit model represents a reliance on 6,667 testing hours to remove 667 defects, or 45,100 total life cycle hours for 10,000 lines of code. The

Inspections benefit model represents a balance of 708.33 Inspections hours and 1,950 testing hours, or 17,425 total life cycle hours for 10,000 lines of code. The PSP$^{sm}$ and TSP$^{sm}$ benefit models signify a productivity of 25 and 5.9347 lines of code per hour, or 400 and 1,685 total life cycle hours for 10,000 lines of code. (The PSP$^{sm}$ and TSP$^{sm}$ benefit models don't use the total life cycle cost model because they result in zero defects, and therefore exhibit little or no post-delivery economic activity.) The SW-CMM® benefit model results in 2,544 development hours at Level 3, 708.33 Inspections hours, and 1,950 testing hours, or 14,869 total life cycle hours for 10,000 lines of code. The ISO 9001 benefit model results in 4,426.56 development hours, 6,670 testing hours, and *Rework_Savings* of 4,995 hours, or 39,402 total life cycle hours for 10,000 lines of code. The CMMI® benefit model results in 2,544 development hours at Level 3, 708.33 Inspections hours, and 1,950 testing hours, or 14,869 total life cycle hours for 10,000 lines of code.

## 3.3   Modelling Cost and Benefits of SPI

The cost and benefit summary helps organize the results of the cost and benefit models. The eight major cost and benefit factors are placed against the six major SPI methods as shown in Table VIII. The eight major cost and benefit factors are inspections, training, process (includes products), preparation (for appraisals), appraisal, audit, old costs, and new costs. The values for the first six cost factors are derived from Table VI, with the exception of preparation, appraisal, and audit costs. Preparation costs consist of indoctrination courses, response conditioning exercises,

TABLE VIII

COST AND BENEFIT SUMMARY OF SPI METHODS FOR A 4 PERSON TEAM IMPLEMENTING 10,000 LOC

| Factor | Inspections | PSP$^{sm}$ | TSP$^{sm}$ | SW-CMM® | ISO 9001 | CMMI® |
|---|---|---|---|---|---|---|
| 1. Inspections | [a]$70,833 | n/a | n/a | [a]$70,833 | n/a | [a]$70,833 |
| 2. Training | [b]$11,240 | [c]$105,600 | [d]$148,400 | n/a | n/a | n/a |
| 3. Process | n/a | n/a | n/a | [e]$173,700 | [f]$110,600 | [g]$941,700 |
| 4. Preparation | n/a | n/a | n/a | *$36,800 | *$26,400 | *$48,000 |
| 5. Appraisal | n/a | n/a | n/a | *$30,100 | n/a | *$47,700 |
| 6. Audit | n/a | n/a | n/a | n/a | *$36,000 | n/a |
| Costs | $82,073 | $105,600 | $148,400 | $311,433 | $173,000 | $1,108,233 |
| 7. Old Costs | [h]$4,509,997 | [h]$4,509,997 | [h]$4,509,997 | [h]$4,509,997 | [h]$4,509,997 | [h]$4,509,997 |
| 8. (New Costs) | [i]($1,742,533) | [j]($40,000) | [k]($168,501) | [l]($1,486,933) | [m]($3,940,156) | [n]($1,486,933) |
| Benefits | $2,767,464 | $4,469,997 | $4,341,496 | $3,023,064 | $569,841 | $3,023,064 |

\* Preparation, appraisal, and audit costs determined without the aid of a cost model.

and mock appraisals. Appraisal costs consist of the costs for the planning, preparation, and appraisal stages, as well as the appraisal fees. The preparation, appraisal, and audit costs were based on bottom up estimates, and no cost models were created to aid in their estimation. The total costs are a simple summation of the values from cost factors one through six. (The letters a through g correspond to the cost model values from Table VI.) The values for old costs and new costs are derived from Table VII. The total benefits are the difference of old costs and new costs. (The letters h through n correspond to the benefit model values from Table VII.)

## 3.4   ROI Models for SPI

The ROI summary illustrates total costs and benefits and the calculation of benefit/cost ratio, return on investment, net present value, and break even point for each of the six SPI methods. Table IX shows the values of B/CR, ROI, NPV, and BEP using the metrics from Table I. B/CR is used to determine the magnitude of benefits to costs using the formula $Benefits/Costs$. ROI is used to determine the magnitude of benefits to costs based on adjusted benefits using the formula $(Benefits - Costs)/Costs \times 100\%$. NPV is used to discount the cash flows using the formula, equation, or discounting method from Table I (e.g., SUM $(Benefits_i/(1 + Discount\ Rate)^{Years}) - Costs_0)$. BEP is used to determine when the SPI method begins yielding its benefits using the formula $Costs/(Old\ Costs/New\ Costs - 1)$.

The BEP values represent *total costs* spent on a new SPI method *before* the benefits are realized. The BEP values should be divided by 400 to account for *Team Size* and *Rate*. The BEP for Inspections is 129 hours or three weeks, PSP$^{sm}$ is two hours, and TSP$^{sm}$ is 14 hours or two days. The BEP for SW-CMM® is 383 hours or 2.2 months, ISO 9001 is 2,991 hours or 1.4 years, and CMMI® is 1,363 hours or eight months. Figure 1 is a graphical representation of the costs, benefits, and ROI values from Table IX. Notice that the costs dramatically increase from left to right as illustrated by the red bar in Fig. 1. Also notice that the benefits and ROI sharply decrease from left to right as illustrated by the green and blue bars in Fig. 1.

TABLE IX

ROI METRIC EXAMPLES OF SPI METHODS FOR A 4 PERSON TEAM IMPLEMENTING 10,000 LOC

| Method | Costs | Benefits | B/CR | ROI | NPV | BEP |
|--------|-------|----------|------|-----|-----|-----|
| Inspections | $82,073 | $2,767,464 | 34:1 | 3,272% | $2,314,261 | $51,677 |
| PSP$^{sm}$ | $105,600 | $4,469,997 | 42:1 | 4,133% | $3,764,950 | $945 |
| TSP$^{sm}$ | $148,400 | $4,341,496 | 29:1 | 2,826% | $3,610,882 | $5,760 |
| SW-CMM® | $311,433 | $3,023,064 | 10:1 | 871% | $2,306,224 | $153,182 |
| ISO 9001 | $173,000 | $569,841 | 3:1 | 229% | $320,423 | $1,196,206 |
| CMMI® | $1,108,233 | $3,023,064 | 3:1 | 173% | $1,509,424 | $545,099 |

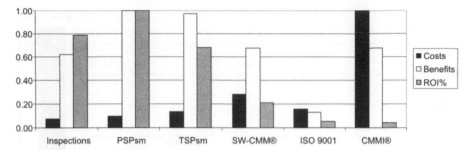

FIG. 1. ROI examples (normalized) showing increasing costs, decreasing benefits, and decreasing return on investment from left to right.

## 3.5  Limitations of the Quantitative Models

Six simple ROI metrics were introduced for costs, benefits, benefit/cost ratio, return on investment, net present value, and break even point. And, fourteen cost and benefit models were introduced for Inspections, PSP$^{sm}$, TSP$^{sm}$, SW-CMM®, ISO 9001, and CMMI®. More importantly, each of the ROI metrics and models were thoroughly exercised to demonstrate how ROI is estimated for SPI. (*As an aside, important concepts in total life cycle costs were introduced to estimate the benefits of SPI. The estimation of benefits is perhaps the most elusive concept in the fields of ROI and SPI.*)

As mentioned numerous times, ROI metrics are not mutually exclusive. The result or value of one ROI metric should not overshadow the value of another. For instance, Fig. 1 illustrates impressive ROI values of 3,272%, 4,133%, 2,826%, 871%, 229%, and 173% for Inspections, PSP$^{sm}$, TSP$^{sm}$, SW-CMM®, ISO 9001, and CMMI®. Before running out and immediately implementing one of these methods, one should consider the costs. The cost per person for these SPI methods is $20,518, $26,400, $37,100, $77,858, $43,250, and $277,058 as shown in Fig. 2. These figures may not seem daunting for monolithic well endowed non-profit organizations. However, one can rest assured knowing that the average commercial firm could not afford the least expensive of these SPI methods. The probability of sustained commitment and execution of expensive and manually-intensive software processes is nearly zero.

The ROI metrics and models exhibited in this chapter are simple and not perfect at all. We do not claim perfection or ultimate accuracy. However, the models are highly useful on getting a grip on the abstract character of SPI and on getting some insight on where to expect benefits for which cost. As such the models are useful for making ROI analysis a priori of the investment, and as such support in the basic character of investment decision making. Use the ROI models in this chapter, however, with great care and customize them to other organizations as much as necessary.

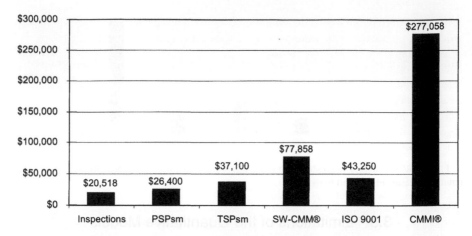

FIG. 2. Cost per person showing increasing costs for various SPI methods from left to right.

## 4. Using Quantitative Measurements for SPI Investment Evaluations

This section includes practical examples on the measurement of the ROI of SPI. Measuring the ROI of SPI is a prerequisite for evaluating a posteriori whether the benefits of an investment were worth their costs. Measuring costs and benefits is often considered as a difficult task. In this section we present pragmatic solutions and examples for putting a quantitative measurement on SPI cost and benefits.

### 4.1 Measuring Benefits Is Just as Easy as Measuring Cost

One argument often heard in practice is that benefits of SPI cannot be measured, or are at least difficult to measure. Organizations find it relatively easy to measure cost by measuring effort, but have a hard time in measuring benefits. This is however, based on a serious misunderstanding of cost measurement: costs are much broader than effort alone. For example, cost also involves other resources such as office-space, travel, and computer infrastructure. When calculating cost, a fixed hour-rate is used that is assumed to approach the real value of cost acceptably. Measuring cost in such way is commonly accepted and agreed upon; however, such a cost calculation is in fact: an estimate. This in itself is of course not wrong. It is a pragmatic agreement on how to approach the actual cost with an acceptable level of accuracy. However, if we accept that cost measurement is just a matter of estimating and agreeing on the procedure, why don't we do the same for benefits? If we (just as with costs) agree that approaching the actual value is sufficient and we agree on the estimation procedure, then we can measure benefits to the same extent as we measure cost.

Measuring benefits is in fact just as easy as measuring cost, or better: just as difficult. We only need to agree on the required level of accuracy. As ROI calculations for SPI generally do not need to be very accurate, benefits can be easily measured based on stakeholder involvement and estimation. As such, explicit ROI calculations can be incorporated into SPI investments and evaluations can be made on whether the SPI activities were worth the effort.

ROI requires the application of metrics and models. Software measurement is not in wide spread use by the general body of managers. Metrics and models are usually relegated to a few well placed scholars, management consultants, and high maturity organizations. Worse yet, statistical analysis is not considered a necessary component of the most popular approaches to SPI. So, managers don't generally apply ROI, and see it as part of the field of scientific study; ignoring it because mainstream methods don't require its application. Managers should apply quantitative methods for SPI, especially metrics and models for SPI. They should overcome the myths that metrics and models are only for special circumstances, such as large, expensive, mission critical systems. Shortly: managers should apply metrics in all circumstances, in all projects, and in all maturity levels.

## 4.2   Involve Stakeholders for Benefit Estimations

The basic starting point for measuring SPI benefits is that: *"Although intangible benefits may be more difficult to quantify, there is no reason to value them at zero. Zero is, after all, no less arbitrary than any other number."* [53]. So, estimating a benefit based on stakeholder involvement is fairly better than just estimating the benefit as zero. Stakeholder involvement for benefit quantification seems logical. Stakeholders have an overview on impacts and values of benefits from specific viewpoints. Most people will agree that it is in practice impossible to find one single person with a full overview on SPI benefits, who is also capable of expressing those in terms of money. Multiple stakeholders should therefore be involved. For example, knowing that SPI caused a time-to-market reduction of two weeks, it is possible to ask the marketing department what this will bring in financial values: a number or an estimated range will be provided. Calculations can be made with such estimates. Also it should not be forgotten to ask the project manager whether there would have been a delay in his opinion if there had not been the SPI activities: a so-called 'what-if-not-analysis' [53]. If so, the marketing department can be asked what the cost of this delay would have been: another benefit. It is important to include all of these SPI benefits and to transfer them to a financial value. 'Money' is after all, a measurement scale that most stakeholders understand.

Pure calculation of cash-flow benefits for SPI is often considered difficult [9,75]. An alternative to quantifying benefits is by asking the people involved (e.g., management) what a certain improvement is 'worth'. So, don't simply measure the effort of the improvement activities, but to look at what the value of that improvement is, and take this value as the benefit. *"Rather than attempting to put a dollar tag on benefits that by their nature are difficult to quantify, managers should reverse the process and estimate first how large these benefits must be in order to justify the proposed investment."* [53]. For example, if a manager states that his team has clearly a better motivation due to the SPI initiatives, ask the manager for what price he would be willing to 'buy' that increased motivation. Ask the manager for example, how many days of education he would be willing to spend on his staff to acquire this increased motivation. If it is for example 5 days of training, a quantitative estimation of this benefit is: number of staff × number of days training × (daily rate of staff + daily fee of one-person training). This illustrates clearly: not difficult to quantify as long as there is agreement on how this benefit is quantified.

## 4.3  Case 1: GQM-Based Measurement Program

A first case was made for a GQM measurement program as published in [80] and [81]. It was undertaken in a systems development department (hardware and software) in an industrial company that produces and services systems for fuel stations. This particular team developed an embedded software product that controls a fuel pump and manages all fuel-transaction communications. This case involves a goal-oriented measurement program in which developer distortions (so-called 'interrupts') were addressed. The measurement program had the objective to find out the reasons for developer-interruptions and as a result reduce the number of developer-interruptions. During a period of three months, a development team of six people measured and improved their processes.

When making an analysis of the cost we find that the effort of the software team was 80 hours, and the effort of the GQM measurement team was 240 hours. So, the total cost of this improvement program was: $(320/1,600) \times \$100,000^5 = \$20,000$.

When considering the benefits, we measured a saving in engineering effort of the software team of 260 hours due to the improvements (e.g., reduced number of interrupts) and a saving of 60 hours for the GQM measurement team (e.g., from reusable material). These benefits were directly related to the objectives of the improvement program. Therefore, the financial benefits for the software team were $16,000 and of the GQM team $4,000. The ROI for the software team is therefore 2, and for the

---

[5] We calculated with 1,600 productive engineering hours per year and a yearly cost of $100,000 per engineer (the case took place in The Netherlands).

TABLE X
DETAILED MEASUREMENTS FOR THE ROI CALCULATION OF CASE 1 [81]

| Cost/Benefits | Value | Explanation |
|---|---|---|
| Cost | | |
| Effort engineering team | $5,000 | 80 hours effort expenditure in measurement program related tasks, measured from hour registration system |
| Effort GQM team | $15,000 | 240 hours effort expenditure for measurement program, measured from hour registration system |
| Total cost | $20,000 | |
| Benefits | | |
| Effort saving due to less interrupts | $16,000 | 260 hours effort saving during the measurement program due to a measured reduction of interrupts |
| Effort saving reuse (GQM team) | $4,000 | 60 hours effort saving due to reusable material on interrupt reduction |
| Total direct benefits | $20,000 | |
| Early delivery due to effort saving | $100,000 | One week early delivery of the product, measured from value indicated by marketing manager |
| Effort saving due to spin-off | $50,000 | Effort saving during remainder of the year due to the reduction of interrupts |
| Increased quality awareness | $100,000 | Increased focus on quality and time expenditure, both in the project as in other groups, measured from value for group manager (combination of buy-in and personal value) |
| Update of engineering documentation | $16,000 | Some documentation was updated due to a measurable number of interrupts on these documents, measured from value for engineers |
| Total indirect benefits | $266,000 | |
| Total benefits | $286,000 | |
| Return-on-Investment | 1:13 | |

whole program it was break even. The ROI is calculated by dividing the profit of the investment by the investment, e.g., *(benefit − cost)/cost*.

However, when also considering the indirect benefits, it became clear in the feedback sessions of the measurement program, and based on conclusions by the project manager, that the benefits were higher. Some of the benefits were that:

- The project finished at least one week earlier thanks to the measurements (according to marketing a saving of at least: $100,000).

- Documentation was updated based on the measurement analysis, preventing at least 250 hours on interrupts (which makes $16,000).

- Increased quality awareness and interruption awareness of the software team (which was valued by the project manager as at least: $100,000).

- Saved interruptions in other projects in the same department due to increased awareness outside the department (which was valued by the project manager to be worth at least more than $50,000).

Total benefits can be calculated to be at least: $286,000, giving an ROI of 55 for the software team ($286,000 − $4,000 − $5,000/$5,000), and an ROI of 13 for the whole organization ($286,000 − $20,000/$20,000). Making the distinction between direct and indirect benefits supports the business case for SPI. Especially the indirect benefits (those that are difficult to correlate directly to the SPI efforts, because they are initiated from multiple initiatives) tend to have large financial benefits. Although quantification of those benefits requires some effort, it serves to explain to managers, why SPI initiatives support to attain business goals.

## 4.4 Case 2: CMM-Based Improvement Program

The second case presents the results of an ROI evaluation of an industrial SPI program. This program applied the SW-CMM® as a starting point for improvement and applied it pragmatically as a checklist for potential improvement actions. This particular organization had defined its improvement goals in terms of development throughput-time, schedule accuracy and customer satisfaction. The respective organization develops and services a software simulation package that is capable of executing virtual tests using finite element modeling. Such simulations provide production companies safety feedback on products that are still on the 'drawing table'. The market success of this package is in fact mainly due to its high return-on-investment. Imagine what the savings are for a manufacturer when receiving safety flaws in design-phase compared to receiving these flaws in delivery-phase.

ROI was evaluated after one year in the SPI program, as contractually agreed upon with the SPI consulting company. The approach undertaken was similar as described in this article. Available measurements were used expanded with five stakeholder interviews (marketing and product manager, development manager, software engineer, test engineer, release coordinator). These interviews indicated that the main benefits of the SPI program were: process documentation (description of standard processes, definition of templates and best-practices, and a group wide process-web-infrastructure), progress monitoring (periodic reporting by progress metrics and 'traffic-light'-indicators), software engineering role and responsibility definitions, and improved product documentation.

For each of these benefits, estimations were made based on stakeholder involvement by: asking for effort saving, value range (between min and max), or a purchase value (what if you had to buy this change?). In every case the lowest value of the stakeholder numbers were used; implying that the calculated ROI number was a minimum agreement. One specific addition was made by adding so-called "contribution percentages." As many improvements can not be attributed solely to the SPI program because they result from multiple initiatives, the contribution to the improvement was indicated in such a percentage. Take for example, the benefit "best-practices." Best-practices would probably also be documented if there would not have been a SPI program. However, the R&D manager estimated that the SPI program would have a partial contribution of about 25%, due to the focus on best-practice capturing. In this example, only 25% of the value was measured as benefit.

The cost of the SPI program in the first year was $50,000. For the benefits a distinction was made between the direct benefits (directly accounted to activities in the improvement program) and the indirect benefits (results more indirectly accounted to the improvement program) of the SPI program. The direct benefits were valued to be $147,000. The indirect benefits were valued to be $300,000. This was calculated from the separate values for project management and control ($65,000), on-time releasing of the product ($45,000) and role and responsibility definitions ($190,000).

Based on these collected numbers it was relatively easy to calculate ROI numbers. The direct ROI was 2 to every invested dollar and the total ROI (including both direct and indirect benefits) was 8. This ROI is calculated by dividing the profit of the investment by the investment $(benefit - cost)/cost$. The respective interviewed stakeholders agreed with the numbers used for these calculations. When presenting these calculations to the complete software engineering team, the engineers indicated that they did not recognize all of the values. It appeared that not everyone was aware of the overall improvements and impacts. We concluded that more intermediate communication on SPI activities and results should have been done, instead of this one yearly ROI analysis only. This could have improved common understanding of the benefits of the improvement program for the department.

## 4.5   Limitations of Quantitative Measurements

We have explained and illustrated an approach to quantitatively measure the costs, benefits, and ROI of SPI in practice. Although the cases show that this approach provides useful results, there are also some limitations. First of all, the accuracy of the numbers is limited. The main cause of this is that both cost and benefit measurements are derived from estimates. Estimates are by definition not very accurate, although often better than measuring them as zero. In addition, these benefits are quantified by applying stakeholder input and experiences, which make them strongly influenced by personal perceptions, characteristics, and attitudes. Secondly, the presented measurements are limited in their external validity, i.e., they are only meaningful within the respective context. Using these measurements outside that specific project or organization should not be allowed. There is no evidence that the presented ROI effects will occur in other environments that apply the same approach. In other words: the

TABLE XI
DETAILED MEASUREMENTS FOR THE ROI CALCULATION OF CASE 2 [81]

| Cost/Benefits | Value | Explanation | Allocation | Value |
|---|---|---|---|---|
| **Cost** | | | | |
| Company effort | $35,000 | 305 person hours with an average hourly fee of $115, measured from project accounting system. | 100% | $35,000 |
| External coaching | $15,000 | External coaching hours from consulting company, measured from bills. | 100% | $15,000 |
| Total cost | | | | $50,000 |
| **Benefits** | | | | |
| Process awareness | $20,000 | Measured from value for R&D manager, through buy-in comparison: 5 days by external trainer | 100% | $20,000 |
| Documented processes available | $160,000 | V-model reflected in set-of procedures and standard WBS for projects: Effort saving at least $4,000 per project, 40 projects per year, measured from value for R&D manager | 50% | $80,000 |
| Documentation templates | $120,000 | Buy-in value of good template: $1,000, 3 templates set-up, 40 projects per year, measured from value for R&D manager and engineers | 25% | $30,000 |
| Best practices documented | $32,000 | Effort saving of at least $800 per project, 40 projects, measured from value for engineers | 25% | $8,000 |
| Requirements training followed | $16,000 | Cost of requirements training in effort and external trainer, measured from project accounting system | 25% | $4,000 |
| Project documentation updated | $5,000 | Updated documentation based on findings, measured from value for R&D manager | 100% | $5,000 |
| Total direct benefits | | | | $147,000 |
| Project management support | $650,000 | Calculated from value for R&D manager and product manager of the overall set of PM actions (e.g., traffic light progress monitoring, customer planning alignment, less late deliveries) | 10% | $65,000 |
| Release on time | $180,000 | Effort/cost saving from releasing on time: $30,000, 6 releases, calculated from value for R&D manager and product manager | 25% | $45,000 |
| Role separation | $255,000 | Effort saving of 1.5 person-year, due to role and responsibility separation, measured from value for R&D manager | 75% | $190,000 |
| Total indirect benefits | | | | $300,000 |
| Total benefits | | | | $447,000 |
| Return-on-investment | 1:8 | | | |

predictive value of the measurements is low. Finally, SPI is by definition an activity that changes things. When implementing change, cost and benefit factors such as resistance and learning effects are present. Such factors can have a strong influence on costs and benefits, and directly influence the final ROI measurement. As a consequence, it is unclear to which extend the presented measurements represent the cost and benefits of the software process improvement itself, from the change process, or from both.

# 5.  Conclusions

There is one basic concern about ROI measurement in the context of SPI: How to measure benefits? This leads to several questions, such as: Can benefits be measured, at all? Can a monetary value be placed on benefits? And, if all such ROI benefit analysis shows an ROI for 6:1 up to 10:1, why are companies so reluctant to do this, and if management stops pushing, the process usually dies? If companies really believed the 6-fold payoff, why are they reluctant to continue to pay $100K per year (for example) with a demonstrated saving of $600K per year? These are legitimate questions, which cannot be answered completely based on the currently available research material. However, one thing is clear: the fact that benefits are often difficult to measure or even more difficult to quantify financially, is not an excuse not to do so. As Gilb's law says: "Anything you need to quantify can be measured in some way that is superior to not measuring it at all" [24]. In this chapter we have provided some insights and support on how to (financially) quantify the unquantifiable.

Research has shown that the lack of explicit expectations (e.g., hypothesis) has a drastic negative effect in the learning effects of SPI programs [77,79]. Without making such expectations explicit, it will be difficult to evaluate whether a certain benefit was worth its cost, or whether an ROI of 3 is sufficient. When planned numbers are compared with actual numbers, it can be evaluated whether the SPI action was successful and whether anything was learned at all from the effects of the SPI program or initiative. The fact that all too often no quantitative or financial evaluation is made of SPI investment is probably one of the reasons that SPI initiatives are ended too soon. If managers are given the promise of an ROI between 6 and 10, but no effort is spend on actually proving this ROI, the chances rise that support and commitment start to deteriorate.

Pragmatic ROI calculations are feasible and not difficult at all. If detailed measurements are not available: estimates and models can help. Such estimations may not be very accurate, but they are at least better than no number at all. Furthermore, we intended to show that pragmatic ROI calculations open a discussion on the cost, benefits, and ROI of SPI. Pragmatism is crucial: apply an approach for measuring cost and benefits that is simple and fast by involving stakeholders. Accept that such estimations of costs and benefits might not be perfectly accurate, but accuracy is not the main purpose. The purpose is to indicate value: to indicate whether costs and benefits are balanced, and to obtain a ROI number for communication purposes.

ROI belongs to the discipline of applying metrics and models for software management and engineering. Software managers believe that software measurement requires the application of advanced tools in statistics. And, of course, software managers believe software measurement requires years of data collection, data points, and impeccable statistical justification. Scholarly methods for determining ROI also require large investments in capital improvements to apply. Therefore, managers believe large amounts of money need to be invested in order to apply methods for ROI. Managers should understand that ROI can be applied to SPI early, easily, and inexpensively. They should overcome the myths that ROI is only for the scientific community, and realize it doesn't require large capital investments. ROI calculations can be performed early based on top down estimates without years of data collection.

Expressing costs, benefits, and ROI in financial or monetary terms is crucial. If there is one generic term for which people share perception, then it is: money.

### ACKNOWLEDGEMENTS

The authors would like to thank professor Egon Berghout from University Groningen for his contribution and feedback on earlier versions of this work. And, of course, we owe a debt of gratitude to professor Marvin Zelkowitz from the University of Maryland for soliciting, supporting, and championing the completion of this much needed work.

## Appendix A: Background of the Quantitative Models

This appendix provides simple, but powerful, authoritative, and relatively accurate examples of how to apply basic techniques for estimating the ROI of six major approaches to SPI. Benefit to cost ratio (B/CR) and return on investment percentage (ROI%) formulas will be applied to benefit data from Rico [65] as well as other sources of SPI data. Phillips [60] served as the basis for selecting these arithmetical techniques for estimating the ROI of SPI. The six approaches to SPI that are examined here are:

- Inspection: The software inspection process is a highly-structured and facilitated group meeting to objectively identify the maximum number of software defects with the purpose of improving software quality.

- PSP$^{sm}$: The PSP$^{sm}$ is a training curriculum to teach simple, but powerful techniques in software project management and quality management.
- TSP$^{sm}$: The TSP$^{sm}$ is an extension of PSP$^{sm}$, which introduces group software project management techniques versus the individual focus taught by PSP$^{sm}$.
- SW-CMM®: The SW-CMM® is a supplier selection model created by the U.S. DoD to evaluate and select software contractors that practice minimum software project management techniques.
- ISO 9001: ISO 9001, like the SW-CMM®, is a supplier selection model created by the European Union to evaluate, identify, and select suppliers that practice minimum quality management techniques.
- CMMI®: The CMMI®, which is the newest version of SW-CMM®, is also a supplier selection model created by the U.S. DoD to evaluate and select systems engineering contractors that practice minimum systems engineering management techniques.

## A.1 Inspection: Detailed ROI Estimation Procedures

Let's examine the dynamics of estimating the costs, benefits, and ROI of the software inspection process using the formulas for B/CR and ROI%.

- Training costs for inspections: Let's begin by modeling the training costs for implementing Inspections on a four-person project. The average market price for Inspection training is about $410 per person. The average length of time for Inspection training is three days or 24 business hours. At a minimum cost of $100 per hour, training time comes to $2,400. Add $410 to $2,400 for a total of $2,810 per person for Inspection training. Multiply $2,810 by four people and that comes to $11,240 to train four people to perform Inspections.
- Implementation costs for inspections: Now let's examine the cost of implementing Inspections by our four trained inspectors. Let's assume the project will develop 10,000 software source lines of code (SLOC), which is not unlikely for a web project in modern times. (Inspections of requirements, designs, and tests drive the Inspection costs even higher, but are omitted for simplicity's sake.) At an Inspection rate of 240 SLOC per meeting, that comes to approximately 41.67 meetings. Since each Inspection run requires about 17 hours for planning, overviews, preparation, meetings, rework, and follow-up, we then multiply 41.67 by 17 for a total of 708.33 hours. Once again, at $100 per hour, that comes to $70,833 for our four trained inspectors to perform Inspections on 10,000 SLOC.

- Costs for inspections: So, we add the training cost of $11,240 to the implementation cost of $70,833, and we arrive at a total cost of $82,073 for four trained inspectors to Inspect 10,000 SLOC.

- Benefits for inspections: The estimated total life cycle costs for 10,000 SLOC after our four trained inspectors perform their Inspections are $1,742,533 (as illustrated from the benefit model in Table VII). The estimated total life cycle costs for 10,000 SLOC without Inspections are $4,509,997 (as also shown in Table VII). So, our four trained inspectors have saved $2,767,464 on their very first implementation of Inspections.

- B/CR for inspections (the formula for B/CR is *benefits* divided by *costs*): Therefore, divide the $2,767,464 in Inspection benefits by the $82,073 in Inspection costs and the B/CR for Inspections is 34:1.

- ROI% for inspections (the formula for ROI% is *benefits* less *costs* divided by *costs* times 100): Therefore, first subtract the $82,073 in Inspection costs from the $2,767,464 in Inspection benefits and divide the results by the $82,073 in Inspection costs and multiply by 100 for an impressive ROI% of 3,272%.

## A.2 PSP$^{sm}$: Detailed ROI Estimation Procedures

Now, let's examine the dynamics of estimating the costs, benefits, and ROI of PSP$^{sm}$ using the formulas for B/CR and ROI%.

- Costs for PSP$^{sm}$: Let's begin by modeling the training costs for implementing PSP$^{sm}$ on a four-person project. The Software Engineering Institute's (SEI's) price for PSP training is $5,000 per person. The costs of the airline, hotels, meals, and parking are about $5,400 for two weeks. The length of time for PSP$^{sm}$ training is 10 days or 80 business hours. Each hour of classroom time requires approximately one hour of non-classroom time for a total of 80 more hours. At a minimum cost of $100 per hour, training time comes to $16,000. Add $5,000, $5,400, and $16,000 for a total of $26,400 per person for PSP$^{sm}$ training. Multiply $26,400 by four people and that comes to $105,600 to train four people to perform PSP$^{sm}$.

- Benefits for PSP$^{sm}$: The estimated total life cycle costs for 10,000 SLOC after our four trained PSP$^{sm}$ engineers apply PSP$^{sm}$ are $40,000 (as illustrated from the benefit model in Table VII). The estimated total life cycle costs for 10,000 SLOC without PSP$^{sm}$ are $4,509,997 (as also shown in Table VII). So, our four trained PSP$^{sm}$ engineers have saved $4,469,997 on their very first implementation of PSP$^{sm}$.

- B/CR for PSP$^{sm}$ (the formula for B/CR is *benefits* divided by *costs*): Therefore, divide the $4,469,997 in PSP$^{sm}$ benefits by the $105,600 in PSP$^{sm}$ costs and the B/CR for PSP$^{sm}$ is 42:1.

- ROI% for PSP$^{sm}$ (the formula for ROI% is *benefits* less *costs* divided by *costs* times 100): Therefore, first subtract the $105,600 in PSP$^{sm}$ costs from the $4,469,997 in PSP$^{sm}$ benefits, divide the results by the PSP$^{sm}$ $105,600 in costs, and multiply by 100 for an impressive ROI% of 4,133%.

## A.3 TSP$^{sm}$: Detailed ROI Estimation Procedures

Now, let's examine the dynamics of estimating the costs, benefits, and ROI of TSP$^{sm}$ using the formulas for B/CR and ROI%.

- Costs for TSP$^{sm}$: Let's begin by modeling the training costs for implementing TSP$^{sm}$ on a four-person project. The SEI's price for TSP$^{sm}$ training is $4,000 per person. The costs of the airline, hotels, meals, and parking are about $2,700 for one week. The length of time for TSP$^{sm}$ training is 5 days or 40 business hours. At a minimum cost of $100 per hour, training time comes to $4,000. Add $4,000, $2,700, and $4,000 for a total of $10,700 per person for TSP$^{sm}$-specific training. Add the $26,400 for PSP$^{sm}$ training to the $10,700 for TSP$^{sm}$ training and the total overall TSP$^{sm}$ costs come to a breathtaking $37,100 per person. Multiply $37,100 by four people and that comes to a budget-busting $148,400 to train four people to use TSP$^{sm}$.

- Benefits for TSP$^{sm}$: The estimated total life cycle costs for 10,000 SLOC after our four trained TSP$^{sm}$ engineers apply TSP$^{sm}$ are $168,501 (as illustrated from the benefit model in Table VII). The estimated total life cycle costs for 10,000 SLOC without TSP$^{sm}$ are $4,509,997 (as also shown in Table VII). So, our four trained TSP$^{sm}$ engineers have saved $4,341,496 on their very first implementation of TSP$^{sm}$.

- B/CR for TSP$^{sm}$ (the formula for B/CR is *benefits* divided by *costs*): Therefore, divide the $4,341,496 in TSP$^{sm}$ benefits by the $148,400 in TSP$^{sm}$ costs and the B/CR for TSP$^{sm}$ is 29:1.

- ROI% for TSP$^{sm}$ (the formula for ROI% is *benefits* less *costs* divided by *costs* times 100): Therefore, first subtract the $148,400 in TSP$^{sm}$ costs from the $4,341,496 in TSP$^{sm}$ benefits and divide the results by the $148,400 in TSP$^{sm}$ costs and multiply by 100 for an impressive ROI% of 2,826%.

## A.4 SW-CMM®: Detailed ROI Estimation Procedures

Now, let's examine the dynamics of estimating the costs, benefits, and ROI of SW-CMM® using the formulas for B/CR and ROI%.

- Inspection costs for SW-CMM®: SW-CMM® may involve the use of Inspections for SW-CMM® Level 3 compliance. So, let's examine the cost of implementing Inspections for SW-CMM® Level 3 compliance by our four trained inspectors. Let's assume the project will develop 10,000 software source lines of code (SLOC), which is not unlikely for a web project in modern times. (Inspections of requirements, designs, and tests drive the Inspection costs even higher, but are omitted for simplicity's sake.) At an Inspection rate of 240 SLOC per meeting, that comes to approximately 41.67 meetings. Since each Inspection run requires about 17 hours for planning, overviews, preparation, meetings, rework, and follow-up, we then multiply 41.67 by 17 for a total of 708.33 hours. Once again, at $100 per hour, that comes to $70,833 for our four trained inspectors to perform Inspections on 10,000 SLOC.

- Process costs for SW-CMM®: Let's begin by modeling the costs for developing the policies and procedures for SW-CMM® Levels 2 and 3. SW-CMM® Levels 2 and 3 require 13 policies and 38 procedures at 11 hours each. That comes to 561 hours for 51 SW-CMM® Level 2 and 3 policies and procedures. Multiply 561 by $100, and the cost of developing Level 2 and 3 policies and procedures is $56,100. Now let's examine the cost of putting SW-CMM® Level 2 and 3 into practice for a single software project. Levels 2 and 3 require 28 documents, 30 work authorizations, 66 records, 55 reports, and 30 meeting minutes at 5.63 hours each. That comes to 1,176 hours for 209 Level 2 and 3 documents, work authorizations, records, reports, and meeting minutes. Multiply 1,176 by $100, and the cost of Level 2 and 3 documents, work authorizations, records, reports, and meeting minutes is $117,600. Add 561 hours for developing SW-CMM® policies and procedures to 1,176 hours for developing SW-CMM® Level 3-compliant documentation and this totals 1,737 hours or $173,700 (at $100 per hour).

- Assessment preparation costs for SW-CMM®: Let's estimate one software project of four people in 13 indoctrination courses at 2 hours each which totals 104 hours. Let's similarly estimate one software project of four people in 13 response-conditioning courses at 2 hours. This totals another 104 hours. Finally, let's estimate one software project of four people in one 40 hour mock assessment or two 20 hour mock assessments. This totals 160 hours. Now, let's add 104 indoctrination hours, 104 response conditioning hours, and 160 mock assessment hours. And, this totals of 368 assessment preparation hours. Finally, let's multiply 368 by $100 for a total of $36,800 in assessment preparation costs.

- Assessment costs for SW-CMM®: And, let's not forget the assessment itself. An assessment requires up to 642 hours of internal labor (not including the assessor's effort). However, for our one project of four people let's estimate 13 hours for planning and 47 hours for preparation. Additionally, let's estimate 129 hours for the appraisal itself and 12 hours of follow-up which totals 201 hours for the assessment. Now multiply 201 by $100 for a total labor cost of $20,100 plus $10,000 in assessment fees for a total cost of $30,100.

- Costs for SW-CMM®: Finally, add $70,833 for Inspections, $173,700 for processes, $36,800 for appraisal preparation, and $30,100 for the appraisal itself. This comes to a grand total of $311,433 to achieve SW-CMM® Level 3 compliance and implement Inspections for 10,000 SLOC.

- Benefits for SW-CMM®: The estimated total life cycle costs for 10,000 SLOC after our software engineers apply SW-CMM® Level 3-compliant policies and procedures are $1,486,933 (as illustrated from the benefit model in Table VII). The estimated total life cycle costs for 10,000 SLOC without SW-CMM® are $4,509,997 (as also shown in Table VII). So, our software engineers have saved $3,023,064 on their very first implementation of a SW-CMM®-compliant software project.

- B/CR for SW-CMM® (the formula for B/CR is *benefits* divided by *costs*): Therefore, divide the $3,023,064 in SW-CMM® benefits by the $311,433 in SW-CMM® costs and the B/CR for SW-CMM® is 10:1.

- ROI% for SW-CMM® (the formula for ROI% is *benefits* less *costs* divided by *costs* times 100): Therefore, first subtract the $311,433 in SW-CMM® costs from the $3,023,064 in SW-CMM® benefits and divide the results by the $311,433 in SW-CMM® costs and multiply by 100 for an impressive ROI% of 871%.

## A.5 ISO 9001: Detailed ROI Estimation Procedures

Now, let's examine the dynamics of estimating the costs, benefits, and ROI of ISO 9001 using the formulas for B/CR and ROI%.

- Process costs for ISO 9001: Let's begin by modeling the costs for developing the policies and procedures for ISO 9001. ISO 9001 requires 144 policy statements, 144 quality manual paragraphs, and 51 procedures at 1.61 hours each. That comes to 546 hours for 339 ISO 9001 policy statements, quality manual paragraphs, and procedures. Multiply 546 by $100, and the cost of developing ISO 9001 policies and procedures is $54,600. Now let's examine the cost of putting ISO 9001 into practice for a single software project. ISO 9001 requires

51 plans and 144 records at about 2.87 hours each. That comes to 560 hours for 195 ISO 9001 plans and records for a single software project. Multiply 560 by $100, and the cost of ISO 9001 plans and records is $56,000 for a single software project. Therefore, the total process cost for ISO 9001 is 1,106 hours or $110,600.

- Audit preparation for ISO 9001: Let's estimate one software project of four people in 23 indoctrination courses at one hour each which totals 92 hours. Let's similarly estimate one project of four people in 23 response conditioning courses at one hour each which also totals 92 hours. Finally, let's estimate one software project of four people in one 20 hour mock quality system audit, for a total of 80 hours. Now, let's add 92 indoctrination hours, 92 response conditioning hours, and 80 mock quality system audit hours. This totals 264 quality system audit preparation hours. Finally, let's multiply 264 by $100 for a total of $26,400 in quality system audit preparation costs.

- Audit for ISO 9001: And, let's not forget the quality system audit itself. An ISO 9001 quality system audit may cost around $48,000. However, let's isolate this cost to $12,000 per software project. Typically, internal labor associated with quality system audits is about twice that of the cost of the audit itself. Therefore, let's assume $24,000 in internal costs to support the actual quality system audit. So, add $12,000 in external costs and $24,000 in internal costs, and we arrive at $36,000 per quality system audit per project.

- Costs for ISO 9001: Finally, add $110,600 for processes, $26,400 for audit preparation, and $36,000 for the audit itself. This comes to a grand total of $173,000 to acquire ISO 9001 registration for 10,000 SLOC.

- Benefits for ISO 9001: The estimated total life cycle costs for 10,000 SLOC after our software engineers apply ISO 9001-compliant policies and procedures are $3,940,156 (as illustrated from the benefit model in Table VII). The estimated total life cycle costs for 10,000 SLOC without ISO 9001 are $4,509,997 (as also shown in Table VII). So, our software engineers have saved $569,841 on their very first implementation of an ISO 9001-compliant software project.

- B/CR for ISO 9001 (the formula for B/CR is *benefits* divided by *costs*): Therefore, divide the $569,841 in ISO 9001 benefits by the $173,000 in ISO 9001 costs and the B/CR for ISO 9001 is an admirable 3:1.

- ROI% for ISO 9001 (the formula for ROI% is *benefits* less *costs* divided by *costs* times 100): Therefore, first subtract the $173,000 in ISO 9001 costs from the $569,841 in ISO 9001 benefits and divide the results by the $173,000 in ISO 9001 costs and multiply by 100 for an impressive ROI% of 229%.

## A.6 CMMI®: Detailed ROI Estimation Procedures

Now, let's examine the dynamics of estimating the costs, benefits, and ROI of CMMI® using the formulas for B/CR and ROI%.

- Inspection costs for CMMI®: CMMI® may involve the use of inspections for CMMI® Level 3 compliance. So, let's examine the cost of implementing inspections for CMMI® Level 3 compliance by our four trained inspectors. Let's assume the project will develop 10,000 software source lines of code (SLOC), which is not unlikely for a web project in modern times. (Inspections of requirements, designs, and tests drive the Inspection costs even higher, but are omitted for simplicity's sake.) At an Inspection rate of 240 SLOC per meeting, that comes to approximately 41.67 meetings. Since each Inspection run requires about 17 hours for planning, overviews, preparation, meetings, rework, and follow-up, we then multiply 41.67 by 17 for a total of 708.33 hours. Once again, at $100 per hour, that comes to $70,833 for our four trained inspectors to perform Inspections on 10,000 SLOC.

- Process costs for CMMI®: Let's begin by modeling the costs for developing the policies and procedures for CMMI® Levels 2 and 3. CMMI® Levels 2 and 3 require 416 policies and procedures at approximately 26.02 hours each. That comes to 10,826 hours for 416 CMMI® Level 2 and 3 policies and procedures. Multiply 10,826 by $100. The cost of developing CMMI® Level 2 and 3 policies and procedures is $1,082,600. However, let's assume only half of this cost is for software engineering. Let's adjust it accordingly to $541,300. Now let's examine the cost of putting CMMI® Level 2 and 3 into practice for a single project. CMMI® Levels 2 and 3 require 429 work products at about 18.67 hours each. That comes to 8,008 hours for 429 CMMI® Level 2 and 3 work products for a single project. Multiply 8,008 by $100, and the cost of CMMI® Level 2 and 3 work products is $800,800 for a single project. However, let's assume only half of this cost is for software engineering, and adjust it accordingly to $400,400. Add 5,413 hours for developing CMMI® policies and procedures to 4,004 hours for developing CMMI® Level 3-compliant documentation and this totals 9,417 hours or $941,700 (at $100 per hour).

- Assessment preparation costs for CMMI®: Let's estimate one project of eight people in 20 indoctrination courses at 2 hours each which totals 320 hours. Let's similarly estimate one project of eight people in 20 response conditioning courses at 2 hours, each which also totals 320 hours. Finally, let's estimate one project of eight people in one 40 hour mock assessment or two 20 hour mock assessments. This totals 320 hours. Now, let's add 320 indoctrination hours,

320 response conditioning hours, and 320 mock assessment hours. This totals 960 hours. Finally, let's multiply 960 by $100 for a total of $96,000 in assessment preparation costs. Half of this is software engineering, which amounts to $48,000.

- Assessment costs for CMMI®: And, let's not forget the assessment itself. For our one software project of four people, let's estimate 127 hours for the plan and prepare for appraisal stage. Let's estimate 204 hours for the conduct appraisal stage. And, let's estimate 21 hours for the report results stage. This totals to 352 hours. Multiply 352 by $100 for an internal labor estimate of $35,200. Add an assessment fee of $12,500 for a total assessment cost of $47,700.

- Costs for CMMI®: Finally, add $70,833 for Inspections, $941,700 for processes, $48,000 for appraisal preparation, and $47,700 for the appraisal itself. This comes to a grand total of $1,108,233 to achieve CMMI® Level 3 compliance and implement Inspections for 10,000 SLOC.

- Benefits for CMMI®: The estimated total life cycle costs for 10,000 SLOC after our software engineers apply CMMI® Level 3-compliant policies and procedures are $1,486,933 (as illustrated from the benefit model in Table VII). The estimated total life cycle costs for 10,000 SLOC without CMMI® are $4,509,997 (as also shown in Table VII). So, our software engineers have saved $3,023,064 on their very first implementation of a CMMI®-compliant software project.

- B/CR for CMMI® (the formula for B/CR is *benefits* divided by *costs*): Therefore, divide the $3,023,064 in CMMI® benefits by the $1,108,233 in CMMI® costs and the B/CR for CMMI® is 3:1.

- ROI% for CMMI® (the formula for ROI% is *benefits* less *costs* divided by *costs* times 100): First subtract the $1,108,233 in CMMI® costs from the $3,023,064 in CMMI® benefits and divide the results by the $1,108,233 in SW-CMM® costs and multiply by 100 for an impressive ROI% of 173%.

## REFERENCES

[1] Arthur L.J., "Quantum improvements in software system quality", *Commun. ACM* (1997) 46–52.
[2] Bach J., "The immaturity of the CMM", *Amer. Programmer* (September 1994) 13–18.
[3] Bach J., "Enough about process: What we need are heroes", *IEEE Software* (March 1995) 96–98.

[4] Basili V.R., Caldiera G., Rombach H.D., van Solingen R., "Goal Question Metric Approach (GQM)", in: Marciniak J.J. (Ed.), *Encyclopaedia of Software Engineering*, vol. 1, second ed., John Wiley & Sons, New York, 2002.

[5] Basili V.R., Caldiera G., McGarry F., Pajerski R., Page G., Waligora S., "The software engineering laboratory—an operational software experience factory", in: *Proceedings of the 14th International Conference on Software Engineering*, 1992.

[6] Basili V.R., Zelkowitz M., McGarry F., Page J., Waligora S., Pajerski R., "SEL's software process improvement program", *IEEE Software* (November 1995) 83–87.

[7] Beach L.R., *Image Theory: Decision Making in Personal and Organizational Contexts*, John Wiley & Sons, New York, 1990.

[8] Beck K., "Embracing change with extreme programming", *IEEE Computer* **32** (10) (1999) 70–77.

[9] Berghout E.W., "Evaluation of information system proposals: design of a decision support method", PhD thesis, Delft University of Technology, The Netherlands, 1997.

[10] Bicego A., Kuvaja P., "BOOTSTRAP: Europe's assessment method", *IEEE Software* (May 1993).

[11] Birk A., van Solingen R., Jarvinen J., "Business impact, benefit and cost of applying GQM in industry", in: *Proceedings of the 5th International Symposium on Software Metrics (Metrics'98), Bethesda, Maryland*, November 19–21, 1998.

[12] Bollinger T., McGowan C., "A critical look at software capability evaluations", *IEEE Software* (July 1991) 25–41 (plus pp. 42–46 comments on this article by Humhrey W.S., Curtis B.).

[13] Brodman J., Johnson D., "What small businesses and small organizations say about the CMM", in: *Proceedings of the 16th International Conference on Software Engineering*, 1994, pp. 331–340.

[14] Brodman J., Johnson D., "Return on investment from software process improvement as measured by U.S. industry", *Crosstalk* **9** (4) (April 1996) 23–29.

[15] Buchman C., "Software process improvement at allied signal aerospace", in: *Proceedings of the 29th Annual Hawaii International Conference on Systems Science, vol. 1: Software Technology and Architecture*, 1996, pp. 673–680.

[16] Burke S., "Radical improvements require radical actions: simulating a high-maturity organization", CMU/SEI-96-TR-024, 1996.

[17] Butler K., "The economic benefits of software process improvement", *Crosstalk* **8** (7) (July 1995) 14–17.

[18] Card D., "Understanding process improvement", *IEEE Software* (July 1991) 102–103.

[19] Chrissis M.B., Konrad M., Shrum S., *CMMI: Guidelines for Process Integration and Product Improvement*, Addison–Wesley, Reading, MA, 2003.

[20] CMMI Product Development Team, "CMM-i for systems engineering/software engineering/integrated product and process development, version 1.02, CMMISM-SE/SW/IPPD, v1.02", Staged representation, CMU/SEI-2000-TR-030, ESC-TR-2000-095, 2000.

[21] Curtis B., "A mature view of the CMM", *Amer. Programmer* (September 1994) 19–28.

[22] Daskalantonakis M.K., "A practical view of software measurement and implementation experiences within Motorola", *IEEE Trans. Software Engrg.* (November 1992) 998–1010.

[23] Deephouse C., Goldenson D., Kellner M., Mukhopadhyay T., "The effects of software processes on meeting targets and quality", in: *Proceedings of the Hawaiian International Conference on Systems Sciences*, vol. 4, 1995, pp. 710–719.

[24] DeMarco T., Lister T., *Peopleware: Productive Projects and Teams*, Dorset House Publishing, 1987.

[25] Diaz M., King J., "How CMM impacts quality, productivity, rework, and the bottom line", *CrossTalk* (March 2002) 9–14.

[26] Diaz M., Sligo J., "How software process improvement helped Motorola", *IEEE Software* (September/October 1997) 75–81.

[27] Dion R., "Elements of a process improvement program", *IEEE Software* (July 1992) 83–85.

[28] Dion R., "Process improvement and the corporate balance sheet", *IEEE Software* (July 1993) 28–35.

[29] Dunaway D.K., Berggren R., des Rochettes G., Iredale P., Lavi I., Taylor G., "Why do organizations have assessments? Do they pay off?", CMU/SEI-99-TR-012, 1999.

[30] El Emam K., *The ROI from Software Quality*, Auerbach, New York, 2005.

[31] El Emam K., Briand L., "Cost and benefits of software process improvement", International Software Engineering Research Network (ISERN) technical report, ISERN-97-12, http://www.iese.fhg.de/network/ISERN/pub/technical_reports/isern-97-12.ps.gz, 1997.

[32] Erdogmus H., Favaro J., "Keep your options open: Extreme programming and the economics of flexibility", in: Marchesi M., Succi G., Wells J.D., Williams L. (Eds.), *Extreme Programming Perspectives*, Addison–Wesley, New York, 2003, pp. 503–552.

[33] Fagan M.E., "Advances in software inspections", *IEEE Trans. Software Engrg.* (July 1986) 741–755.

[34] Ferguson P., Humphrey W.S., Khajenoori S., Macke S., Matyva A., "Results of applying the personal software process", *IEEE Computer* (May 1997) 24–31.

[35] Gilb T., Graham D., *Software Inspection*, Addison–Wesley, Reading, MA, 1993.

[36] Goldenson D.R., Herbsleb J.D., "After the appraisal: A systematic survey of process improvement, its benefits, and factors that influence success", Technical Report, CMU/SEI-95-TR-009, Software Engineering Institute, 1995.

[37] Goyal A., Kanungo S., Muthu V., Jayadevan S., "ROI for SPI: Lessons from initiatives at IBM global services India". Best Paper at the India SEPG Conference 2001 (24 page report).

[38] Grady R.B., Caswell D., *Software Metrics: Establishing a Company-Wide Program*, Prentice Hall, New York, 1987.

[39] Grady R.B., van Slack T., "Key lessons in achieving widespread inspection usage", *IEEE Software* (July 1994) 46–57.

[40] Haley T.J., "Software process improvement at Raytheon", *IEEE Software* (November 1996) 33–41.

[41] Henry J., Rossman A., Snyder J., "Quantitative evaluation of software process improvement", *J. Systems Software* **28** (1995) 169–177.

[42] Herbsleb J., Carleton A., Rozum J., Siegel J., Zubrow D., "Benefits of CMM-based software process improvement: Executive summary of initial results", Technical Report, CMU-SEI-94-SR-13, Software Engineering Institute, 1994.

[43] Herbsleb J., Zubrow D., Goldenson D., Hayes W., Paulk M., "Software quality and the capability maturity model", *Commun. ACM* (June 1997) 30–40.

[44] Highsmith J., *Agile Software Development Ecosystems*, Addison–Wesley, Boston, MA, 2002.

[45] Humphrey W.S., *Introduction to the Team Software Process*, Addison–Wesley, Reading, MA, 1999.

[46] Humphrey W., Snyder T., Willis R., "Software process improvement at Hughes aircraft", *IEEE Software* (July 1991) 11–23.

[47] Humphrey W.S., *Managing the Software Process*, SEI Series in SoftwareEngineering, Addison–Wesley, Reading, MA, 1989.

[48] Humphrey W.S., *A Discipline for Software Engineering*, Addison–Wesley, Reading, MA, 1995.

[49] Humphrey W.S., Curtis B., "Comments on 'a critical look' ", *IEEE Software* **8** (4) (July 1991) 42–46.

[50] "ISO 15504, Information technology—software process assessment—Part 2: A reference model for process and product capability", Technical Report Type 2, International Organization for Standardisation, 1998.

[51] "ISO 9000-3, Quality management and quality assurance standards—Part 3: Guidelines for the application of ISO 9001 to develop, supply install and maintain software", 1994.

[52] Jones C., "The economics of software process improvement", *IEEE Computer* (January 1996) 95–97.

[53] Kaplan R.S., "Must CIM be justified by faith alone?", *Harvard Business Rev.* (March–April 1986) 87–95.

[54] Kaplan R.S., Norton D.P., *The Balanced Scorecard: Translating Strategy into Action*, Harvard Business School Press, Boston, 1996.

[55] Kitson D., Masters S., "An analysis of SEI software process assessment results: 1987–1991", in: *Proceedings of the International Conference on Software Engineering*, 1993, pp. 68–77.

[56] Kulik P., "Software metrics "State of the art"—2000", http://www.klci.com/, December 2000.

[57] McGibbon T., "A business case for software process improvement revised: Measuring return on investment from software engineering and management", A DACS state-of-the-art report, SP0700-98-4000, 1999.

[58] Oldham L.G., Putnam D.B., Peterson M., Rudd B., Tjoland K., "Benefits realized from climbing the CMM ladder", *CrossTalk* **12** (5) (1999) 7–10.

[59] Paulk M.C., Curtis B., Chrissis M.B., Weber C.V., "Capability maturity model for software, version 1.1", SEI-CMU-93-TR-24, Software Engineering Institute, 1993.

[60] Phillips J.J., *Return on Investment in Training and Performance Improvement Programs*, Gulf Publishing Company, Houston, TX, 1997.

[61] Putnam L.H., Myers W.M., *Measures for Excellence: Reliable Software on Time, within Budget*, Prentice Hall, New York, 1992.

[62] Reifer D.J., *Making the Software Business Case: Improvement by the Numbers*, Addison–Wesley, Reading, MA, 2001.

[63] Reifer D.J., "Let the numbers do the talking", *CrossTalk* **15** (3) (2002) 4–8.

[64] Reifer D., Chatmon A., Walters D., "The definitive paper: quantifying the benefits of software process improvement", *Software Tech. News* (November 2002), http://www.dacs.dtic.mil/awareness/newsletters/stn5-4/toc.html.

[65] Rico D.F., "Using cost benefit analyses to develop software process improvement (SPI) strategies" (Contract Number SP0700-98-D-4000), Air Force Research Laboratory—Information Directorate (AFRL/IF), Data and Analysis Center for Software (DACS), Rome, NY, 2000.

[66] Rico D.F., "How to estimate ROI for Inspections, PSP, TSP, SW-CMM, ISO 9001, and CMMI", *DoD Software Tech. News* **5** (4) (2002) 23–31.

[67] Rico D.F., *ROI of Software Process Improvement: Metrics for Project Managers and Software Engineers*, J. Ross Publishing, Boca Raton, FL, 2004.

[68] Rico D.F., "Practical metrics and models for return on investment", *TickIT International* **7** (2) (2005) 10–16.

[69] Rooijmans J., Aerts H., van Genuchten M., "Software quality in consumer electronics products", *IEEE Software* (January 1996) 55–64.

[70] Rubin H., "Software process maturity: Measuring its impact on productivity and quality", in: *Proceedings of the International Conference on Software Engineering*, 1993, pp. 468–476.

[71] Rubin H.A., Johnson M., Yourdon E., "With the SEI as my copilot: using software process flight simulation to predict the impact of improvements in process maturity", *Amer. Programmer* (September 1994) 50–57.

[72] Sheard S., Miller C.L., "The Shangri-La of ROI", Software Productivity Consortium, http://www.software.org/pub/externalpapers/Shangrila_of_ROI.doc, 2000.

[73] Sikka V., *Maximizing ROI on Software Development*, Auerbach, New York, NY, 2004.

[74] Slaughter S.A., Harter D.E., Krishnan M.S., "Evaluating the cost of software quality", *Commun. ACM* (August 1998) 67–73.

[75] Sorqvist L., "Difficulties in measuring the cost of poor quality", *European Quality* **4** (2) (1997) 40–42.

[76] Tockey S., *Return on Software: Maximizing the Return on Your Software Investment*, Addison–Wesley, Reading, MA, 2004.

[77] van Solingen R., "Product focused software process improvement: SPI in the embedded software domain", BETA Research Series, Nr. 32, http://www.gqm.nl/, 2000, Eindhoven University of Technology.

[78] van Solingen R., Berghout E., *The Goal/Question/Metric Method: A Practical Guide for Quality Improvement of Software Development*, McGraw–Hill, 1999, http://www.gqm.nl/.

[79] van Solingen R., Berghout E., "Integrating goal-oriented measurement in industrial software engineering: industrial experiences with and additions to the Goal/Question/Metric method (GQM)", in: *Proceedings of the 7th International Software Metrics Symposium*, London, April 4–6, 2001, IEEE Comput. Soc., Los Alamitos, CA, 2001, pp. 246–258.

[80] van Solingen R., Berghout E., van Latum F., "Interrupts: Just a minute never is", *IEEE Software* (September/October 1998) 97–103.

[81] van Solingen R., "Measuring the ROI of software process improvement", *IEEE Software* (May/June 2004) 32–38.

[82] Willis R.R., Rova R.M., Scott M.D., Johnson M.I., Ryskowski J.F., Moon J.A., Shumate K.C., Winfield T.O., "Hughes aircraft's widespread deployment of a continuously improving software process", CMU/SEI-98-TR-006, 1998.

[83] Wohlwend H., Rosenbaum S., "Schlumberger's software improvement program", *IEEE Trans. Software Engrg.* (November 1994) 833–839.

[84] Yamamura G., Wiggle G.B., "SEI CMM level 5: For the right reasons", *CrossTalk* (August 1997).

# Quality Problem in Software Measurement Data

PIERRE REBOURS AND TAGHI M. KHOSHGOFTAAR

*Empirical Software Engineering Laboratory*
*Department of Computer Science and Engineering*
*Florida Atlantic University*
*Boca Raton, FL 33431*
*USA*
*prebours@fau.edu*
*taghi@cse.fau.edu*

## Abstract

An approach to enhance the quality of software measurement data is introduced in this chapter. Using poor-quality data during the training of software quality models can have costly consequences in software quality engineering. By removing such noisy entries, i.e., by filtering the training dataset, the accuracy of software quality classification models can be significantly improved.

The Ensemble-Partitioning Filter functions by splitting the training dataset into subsets and inducing multiple learners on each subset. The predictions are then combined to identify an instance as noisy if it is misclassified by a given number of learners. The conservativeness of the Ensemble-Partitioning Filter depends on the filtering level and the number of iterations. The filter generalizes some commonly used filtering techniques in the literature, namely the Classification, the Ensemble, the Multiple-Partitioning, and the Iterative-Partitioning Filters. This chapter also formulates an innovative and practical technique to compare filters using real-world data. We use an empirical case study of a high assurance software project to analyze the performance of the different filters obtained from the specialization of the Ensemble-Partitioning Filter. These results allow us to provide a practical guide for selecting the appropriate filter for a given software quality classification problem. The use of several base classifiers as well as performing several iterations with a conservative filtering scheme can improve the efficiency of the filtering scheme.

**43**

# 1. Introduction

Software failures or incorrect software requirements can have severe consequences including customer dissatisfaction, the loss of financial assets and even the loss of human lives [1,2]. *Software Quality Models* (SQMs) can be used toward providing a reliable and high-quality software product. By detecting likely faulty modules, SQMs allow improvement efforts to be focused on software modules with higher risks [3–5]. Resources can then be allocated for software testing, inspection, and quality enhancement of the most likely faulty modules prior to system release. In the context of two-group classification, SQMs can *classify* modules (i.e., instances) as either *fault-prone* (*fp*) or *not fault-prone* (*nfp*).

SQMs are often based on inductive learning algorithms which generalize the concepts learned from a set of training instances (i.e., fit dataset) and apply these concepts to the unseen or new instances (i.e., test dataset) [6]. Different data mining algorithms have been investigated for software quality modeling, such as Case-Based Reasoning [7], Logistic Regression [5], Genetic Programming [8] and decision trees [9]. In an ideal inductive learning problem, the predictions generated by the induced hypotheses should agree with the actual class of the instances. In practice, however, the training set could be cluttered with poor-quality instances, often referred to as *noise*. Using poor-quality data during training lowers the predictive accuracy of the learning techniques [10–12]. As illustrated by Redman [13], "decisions are not better than the data on which they are based."

Noise can occur for various reasons such as poor interface design, data entry errors, lack of necessary information, or measurement subjectivity of the entity being measured [14,15]. Unless effective measures are taken to prevent errors in data, the error rate related to data entry and data acquisition is generally more than 5% [13,16]. It is generally considered that noise can be classified into two types: *attribute noise* and *class noise* [10,17]. Attribute noise represents errors introduced in the attribute values of the instances (i.e., independent variables or features). Class noise are mislabeling errors introduced in the class labels (i.e., dependent variables). Inconsistent instances (i.e., instances with similar attributes but with different class labels) and instances labeled with a wrong class (i.e., mislabeled) [18] are the two very likely causes for class noise.

Table I illustrates some obvious quality problems that can be found in software measurement data. Each instance $I_k$ is described by four metrics: (1) number of branches, (2) total number of lines, (3) number of lines of comments, and (4) number of operands. The dependent variable $c_k$ is either *nfp* or *fp*. Instances 1 and 2 are contradictory examples because they have identical attributes but different class labels. Therefore, one instance is either noisy (class noise) or the selected software measurements do not represent the underlying characteristics of the quality of this software system. It can also be argued that one of the instances is an exception (see Section 2.2. In instance 3, the 'total number of lines' is less than the 'number of lines of comments.' Because the 'total number of lines' includes comments as well as executable code [1], it is likely that $I_3$ contains noisy attributes originating from inaccurate measurements. Finally, $I_4$ has only a total of five lines but is labeled as *fp*.

TABLE I
NOISY INSTANCES IN A SOFTWARE QUALITY DATASET

| $I_k$ | Branches | Total lines | Lines of comments | Operands | $c_k$ |
|---|---|---|---|---|---|
| 1 | 41 | 194 | 44 | 140 | *nfp* |
| 2 | 41 | 194 | 44 | 140 | *fp* |
| 3 | 61 | 149 | 168 | 305 | *nfp* |
| 4 | 1 | 5 | 0 | 3 | *fp* |

It is rather surprising to have a *fp* instance with such a simple implementation. This makes us suspect that the instance has been mislabeled. Only a manual check by a software engineering and domain expert could address this issue. But detecting noise manually becomes very complex and time-consuming because real-world software repositories have thousands of instances (i.e., program modules) and incorporate a large number of independent variables. Therefore, detecting noise requires automatic noise-handling algorithms.

This work focuses on *class-noise filters* to automatically detect and remove training instances suspected of being mislabeled. Quinlan [19] showed that when the level of noise increases, removing attribute noise decreases the performance of the classifier if the test dataset presents the same attribute noise. In contrast, filtering class noise in the training dataset will result in a classifier with significantly higher predictive accuracy for the test dataset [20,21].

When identifying noisy instances, two types of misclassifications can occur. The first type (false positive) occurs when an instance is incorrectly detected as *noisy* and is subsequently discarded. The second type of error (false negative) occurs when a noisy instance is detected as *clean* [17,20]. Filtering needs to balance the amount of noise removed from the dataset with the amount of data retained for training [21]. Consequently, an *efficient* filter is defined as being capable of removing noisy instances while retaining clean instances. Filtering may not be feasible with only a meager amount of data available [10,21].

In this chapter we present the Ensemble-Partitioning Filter. The training dataset is first split into subsets, and base learners are induced on each of these splits. The predictions are then combined in such a way that an instance is identified as noisy if it is misclassified by a certain number of base learners. The amount of noise removed (i.e., the conservativeness of the filter) is tuned by either the voting scheme or the number of iterations. This filter unifies commonly used filters in the literature, namely the Classification Filter [10], the Ensemble Filter [20,21], the Multiple-Partitioning Filter and the Iterative-Partitioning Filter [22]. The advantages of the proposed filter are threefold:

(1) the practitioner can decide on a trade-off between the efficiency and the complexity of the filter;
(2) the filter is an out-of-the-box solution which allows the practitioner to plug in any familiar classifiers; and
(3) the algorithm is scalable because it allows filtering small, large, or distributed data repositories.

This study strives to produce empirical results that offer sound knowledge for the practitioner to tune up the filtering process. Many empirical works [11,17,20] evaluated noise handling mechanisms on datasets in which noise is artificially injected. This seems to be far from the real-world scenario, in which the practitioner generally does not have any knowledge of the existing noise rate nor the noise distribution in the dataset. Because there is no direct way to know which instances are noisy (as opposed to injecting artificial noise), we developed a technique called the *efficiency paired comparison* that evaluates the relative efficiency of filters on real-world datasets. Based on our comparative results, we recommend using several base classifiers as well as performing several iterations with a conservative voting scheme in order to improve the efficiency of the Ensemble-Partitioning Filter.

The rest of the chapter is organized as follows. In Section 2, we present a literature review on existing noise-handling techniques. Section 3 details the implementation of the Ensemble-Partitioning Filter. In Section 4, we describe the modeling methodology involved in our empirical investigation. Section 5 outlines the empirical study and analyzes the results. Finally, in Section 6, we draw some practical recommendations for applying the Ensemble-Partitioning Filter on other real-world problems.

## 2. Noise-Handling Techniques

We describe four class-noise filtering techniques introduced in the literature, namely the Classification Filter, the Ensemble Filter, the Multiple-Partitioning Filter, and the Iterative-Partitioning Filter. These filters provide the theoretical foundations for the Ensemble-Partitioning Filter which will be formulated and presented in Section 3. We then present the difference between noise and exceptions in a given dataset. Finally, we review related works on noise detection.

### 2.1   Class-Noise Filters

The *Classification Filter* was first introduced in [10] and is often used as a baseline to compare more advanced noise detection schemes [10,17,20]. For a given dataset, predictions of a classification algorithm, called the *base learner* of the filter [20], are obtained by $k$-fold cross-validation. In $k$-fold cross-validation, the data is divided into $k$ subsets of (approximately) equal size. The learner is trained $k$ times, each time leaving out one of the subsets during training [6]. The instances in the remaining subset that are misclassified are filtered; it is assumed that machine learning algorithms usually treat misclassified instances as noisy (i.e., mislabeled) [10]. In a recent study [21], we argue that using only one base classifier may be risky because this classifier may not have the appropriate bias to learn the concepts for a given domain.

The *Ensemble Filter* [20] overcomes the limitations of the Classification Filter by combining $m$ base learners to filter the data. An instance is labeled as noisy if it is misclassified by a majority of the base learners (i.e., majority voting scheme) or all the $m$ learners (i.e., consensus voting scheme). Similar to the Classification Filter, the predictions are based on cross-validations. The results reported in [20] with three base learners have empirically substantiated that filtering can improve classification accuracy for the datasets with poor-quality data. However, since some learning algorithms are better suited for certain types of data than others, it is possible that the most appropriate classifier may be outweighed [6,21]. Our previous work [21, 23] concluded that the number of base classifiers is a key factor when the Ensemble Filter approach is used to detect and eliminate noise. Because classifiers do not perform consistently well across different domains, experimenting with a large number of classifiers can ensure that the probability of eliminating good data decreases. Twenty-five distinct base classifiers were selected in [21]. They come from different categories such as instance-based, rule-based, decision-tree based, and pattern-based. Because of the large number of base learners, the number of instances removed (i.e., *level of conservativeness*) can be tuned more precisely than the original Ensemble Filter developed in [20]. The *filtering level*, noted as λ [21,22], is defined as the number of classifiers which should misclassify a given instance to identify it as noisy.

Zhu et al. [17] argued that the Classification Filter and the Ensemble Filter are sometimes inadequate for large and/or distributed datasets because the induction of the base classifiers is too time-consuming, or the datasets cannot be handled at once by these base learners. In a recent study [22], we proposed a modification of the partitioning approach developed in [17]. The training dataset is first split into $n$ subsets, and $m$ different base learners are induced on each of these data splits. Two filters are implemented: the Multiple-Partitioning Filter and the Iterative-Partitioning Filter. The Multiple-Partitioning Filter combines several classifiers induced on each split. The Iterative-Partitioning Filter uses only one base learner on each split, but performs multiple filtering iterations. Similar to the Ensemble Filter [21], this approach allows us to modify the amount of filtered instances by varying the filtering level and/or the number of iterations [22].

All the above filters use supervised learning algorithms, i.e., algorithms which need to be trained on datasets where the dependent variable (*fp* or *nfp*) is available. Therefore, noisy data can only be removed from the training dataset. It is worth noticing that the filters are all based on the same assumption: the more often an instance is misclassified by the base learners, the more likely it is noisy. After removing instances detected as noisy from the training set, *final classifiers* [20] are built on the noise-free training dataset. Hence, the separation of noise detection and hypothesis induction has the advantage that the noisy instances do not influence the hypotheses constructed [10].

It is also worth pointing out that combining multiple learners is a well-known data mining technique also used to improve the predictive accuracy [24,25]. It was found that the multiple-learners approach does increasingly better than the single-learner as the number of irrelevant attributes is increased [26]. Much of the work in learning from multiple models is motivated by the Bayesian learning theory which suggests that in order to maximize the predictive accuracy, all hypotheses in the hypothesis space should be used [26,27].

## 2.2   Data Noise and Exceptions

The previously mentioned filters automatically remove instances that cannot be correctly classified by a certain number of base learners. Some of these instances might be exceptions to the general rules, hence causing a false positive filtering error. Filtering with different base learners may overcome this problem because the bias of at least one of the learning algorithms will enable it to learn the exceptions [20,23]. Therefore, even if one classifier (or more) has difficulty capturing a particular exception, it cannot cause the exception to be erroneously eliminated from the training data.

It is recommended to take a consensus vote rather than a majority vote because consensus approach is more conservative and will result in fewer instances being erroneously eliminated from the training data [20]. Khoshgoftaar et al. [21] argued that the use of twenty-five classifiers combined with a conservative filtering level ($\lambda = 23$, for example) decreases the rate of misclassification of exceptions as noisy, to a certain degree. Of course, a conservative approach increases the risk of retaining bad data (false negative filtering errors).

Exceptions may have the same effects as noisy instances from an induction point of view [10]. In order to avoid overfitting the fit dataset, some final classifiers do not induce the hypotheses covering these exceptions [19]. Therefore, it is not practical to keep unfiltered exceptions from a data mining point of view.

## 2.3   Other Methods to Handle Data Noise

Robust learning algorithms are often employed to avoid overfitting possible noisy training instances. Typically, these algorithms try to reduce the complexity of the induced hypotheses [28]. For example, post-pruning is a popular technique to simplify decision trees and has shown to perform well in noisy environments [19,29,30]. Other post-processing techniques such as boosting [31] and bagging [32] can also make the learners less sensitive to noise.

In [33], instances that are misclassified by the $k$-NN classifier are eliminated from the training set that will be later used to build the final 1-NN classifier. Tomek [34] extended the method by experimenting with several increasing values of nearest neighbors in order to eliminate noisy data. Aha et al. [35] showed that if the instances are selected on the basis of their contribution towards the classification accuracy of an instance-based classifier, the accuracy of the resulting classifier can be improved. Applicability of the instance selection techniques is not only limited to instance-based classifiers. Winston [36] demonstrated the utility of selecting *near misses* when learning structural descriptions. A new metric for measuring the possibility of an instance being noisy based on the $k$-NN algorithm was presented in [37]. Wilson et al. [33] offered an overview of instance selection techniques for exemplar-based learning algorithms. Lorena et al. [38] evaluated the effectiveness of five data-processing algorithms based on [33,34] in the context of genomic identification.

Teng [39] explored a different approach called polishing. Instead of removing the instances identified as being noisy, corrections are made to either one or more features or the class label of the instances suspected of being noisy. The concept assumes that different components in a dataset may not be totally independent except in the case of irrelevant attributes. However, further noise may be introduced unintentionally in an attempt to correct the noisy data. Yang et al. [18] illustrated an algorithm that produces better results for the independent variables that cannot be predicted by using the class and other independent variables. Polishing was compared against other filtering techniques in [11].

In [10], a target theory was built using a rule induction algorithm to correctly classify all instances in the dataset. Instances that maximize the Minimum Description Length cost of encoding the target theory are removed until the cost cannot be reduced further. The same authors in [40] also outlined a theoretical approach of the noise detection problem based on the Occam's Razor principle. Zhao et al. [41] adopted a fuzzy logic approach to represent and calculate inaccuracies in the training data. Their method dynamically determines fuzzy intervals for inaccurate data, and calls for domain knowledge to be able to divide the features into sets whose members are qualitatively dependent. Guyon et al. [42] described a method for data cleaning by discovering meaningless or garbage patterns likely to be noise. Lawrence et al. [43] proposed a probabilistic noise model for constructing a Fisher kernel discriminant from training examples with noisy labels. Muhlenbach et al. [44] based their strategy on the cut weight statistic defined by geometrical neighborhoods and associated with 1-NN predictions. They evaluated their technique with relaxation labeling procedures which originate in computer vision and pattern recognition [45]. Zhu et al. [46] proposed a cost-guided class noise algorithm to identify noise for effective cost-sensitive learning.

Hipp et al. [47] and Marcus et al. [48] demonstrated that association rule mining can be useful in identifying not only interesting patterns but also patterns that uncover errors in the data sets. In their study, ordinal association rules identify potential errors in the dataset with reasonably low computational complexity and high efficiency. Khoshgoftaar et al. [49] analyzed boolean rules to detect mislabeled instances in the training data set. Finally, Hulse et al. [50] presented the pairwise attribute noise detection algorithm which can be used with or without the knowledge of class labels.

# 3. Ensemble-Partitioning Filter

The Ensemble-Partitioning Filter is designed to unify the implementations of the filters presented in Section 2.1. Figure 1 details the unified implementation using pseudo-code. The algorithm can be divided into four logical blocks detailed in the following sections: (1) partitioning the dataset; (2) building the base learners induced on the partitions; (3) combining the output of the base learners; (4) evaluating the stopping criterion.

Given a set $X$, $\|X\|$ denotes the number of instances in set $X$. '!', '&' and '|' are the symbols for the logical NOT, AND and OR operators, respectively. $L_j(I_k, P_i)$ is the predictive class (*nfp* or *fp* in our case) of instance $I_k$ obtained by inducing the learning scheme $L_j$ on the training set $P_i$. The predictive class is either equal to or different from the actual class $c_k$ of instance $I_k$. If $I_k \in P_i$, the predictions are evaluated using cross-validation; the notation hence becomes $L_j^{cv}(I_k, P_i)$. The remaining notations used in Fig. 1 will be defined throughout our discussion of the algorithm.

## 3.1   Partitioning the Dataset

The training dataset $E$ is first partitioned into $n$ disjoint almost equally sized subsets $P_{i=1,\ldots,n}$ (step 2). For each partition $P_i$, two subsets are defined. $A_i$ (step 4) is the set of instances detected as noisy in $P_i$. $G_i$ (step 5) is the set of good examples in $P_i$. Good examples are used for the iterative step and are described later in Section 3.4.

## 3.2   Creation of the Base Learners

Given $m$ base classifiers $L_{j=1,\ldots,m}$, each classifier $L_j$ is induced on each subset $P_i$. Hence, $m \times n$ models are computed. Similar to [17], given an instance $I_k$, two error count variables are defined: $S_k^{le}$, local error count and $S_k^{ge}$, global error count (step 8). The values of these counters are incremented as follows:

(1) If $I_k$ belongs to $P_i$ and $I_k$'s classification from $L_j$ (using cross-validation) induced on $P_i$ is different from its original label $c_k$, the local error count $S_k^{le}$ is incremented (step 11);
(2) If $I_k$ does not belong to $P_i$ and $I_k$'s classification from $L_j$ induced on $P_i$ is different from its original label $c_k$, the global error count $S_k^{ge}$ is incremented (step 12).

| | |
|---|---|
| **Input:** | $E$, training set with $\|E\|$ examples |
| **Parameters:** | $n$, number of subsets |
| | $L_{j=1,...,m}$, base learners |
| | $bCv$, cross-validation constraint flag |
| | $\lambda$, filtering level |
| | $\beta$, rate of good examples to be removed after each iteration |
| | Stopping criterion |
| **Output:** | $A$, detected noisy subset of $E$ |

(1) $A \leftarrow \emptyset$
(2) Form $n$ subsets $P_i$, where $\bigcup_{i=1}^{n} P_i = E$ ⎫
(3) **for** $i = 1, \ldots, n$ **do** ⎪
(4)     $A_i \leftarrow \emptyset$ ⎬ Partition, see Section 3.1
(5)     $G_i \leftarrow \emptyset$ ⎪
(6) **endfor** ⎭
(7) **for** $k = 1, \ldots, \|\bigcup_{i=1}^{n} P_i\|$ **do** ⎫
(8)     $S_k^{le} = S_k^{ge} = 0$ ⎪
(9)     **for** $j = 1, \ldots, m$ **do** ⎪
(10)     **for** $j = 1, \ldots, n$ **do** ⎪
(11)         **if** $I_k \in P_i \& L_j^{cv}(I_k, P_i) \neq c_k$ **then** $S_k^{le} ++$ ⎬ Base learners, see Section 3.2
(12)         **elseif** $I_k \notin P_i \& L_j(I_k, P_i) \neq c_k$ **then** $S_k^{ge} ++$ ⎪
(13)         **endfor** ⎪
(14)     **endfor** ⎭
(15)     **if** $(!bCv \& (S_k^{ge} + S_k^{le}) \geqslant \lambda) \|$ ⎫
(16)     $(bCv \& S_k^{le} = m \& S_k^{le} + S_k^{ge} \geqslant \lambda)$ ⎪
(17)         **then** $A_i \leftarrow A_i \cup \{I_k\}$ ⎬ Voting, see Section 3.3
(18)     **elseif** $S_k^{le} = 0 \& S_k^{ge} = 0$ ⎪
(19)         **then** $G_i \leftarrow C_i \cup \{I_k\}$ ⎪
(20)     **endfor** ⎭
(21) **for** $i = 1, \ldots, n$ **do** ⎫
(22)     $G_i' \leftarrow$ SelectPortionOfGoodExamples$(\beta, G_i)$ ⎪
(23)     $P_i \leftarrow P_i \setminus A_i$ ⎪
(24)     $P_i \leftarrow P_i \setminus G_i'$ ⎬ Iteration, see Section 3.4
(25)     $A \leftarrow A \cup A_i$ ⎪
(26) **endfor** ⎪
(27) **if** the stopping criterion is satisfied **then** exit ⎪
(28) **else goto** step 3 ⎭

FIG. 1. Algorithm of the Ensemble-Partitioning Filter.

It is assumed that noisy instances receive larger values for $S_k^{le}$ and $S_k^{ge}$ than clean instances [17]. By selecting $m$ classifiers from distinct data mining families, the biases of the learners will cancel out one another and make the filter more efficient in detecting exceptions [21]. Moreover, splitting the training dataset makes the filter more adequate to large and/or distributed datasets, partially because the induction of the base classifiers is less time-consuming [17].

## 3.3   Voting Scheme

The filtering level ($\lambda$) and the cross-validation constraint ($bCv$) are used to combine the predictions of the $m \times n$ models. When the cross-validation constraint is enabled, a distinction is made between the local and the global error counts. More specifically, two situations can occur:

(1) $bCv = false$ (step 15). An instance is labeled as noise if at least $\lambda$ models misclassify it.
(2) $bCv = true$ (step 16). An instance is labeled as noise if at least $\lambda$ models misclassify it *and* if it is also mislabeled by all the $m$ classifiers induced on the subset which includes that instance. A classifier often has a higher prediction accuracy with instances of the training dataset [17].

A filter with the cross-validation constraint is more conservative than a filter without it. The filtering level ($\lambda$) could vary from $m \times n$ (i.e., consensus scheme) to $(m \times n)/2 + 1$ (i.e., majority scheme). The higher the filtering level, the less instances are detected as noisy.

A model generated by a machine learner can be regarded as an *expert* [20,6]. In contrast to the Ensemble Filter [20], the Ensemble-Partitioning Filter makes the distinction between two types of experts. A *local expert* classifies instances which are part of the training subset on which the expert is induced. In this case, the predictions are obtained by cross-validation. A *global expert* predicts the class labels of instances which do not belong to the training subset of this expert. When the cross-validation constraint is used, the votes of local experts weigh much more than the votes of global experts. While local experts produce accurate predictions, global experts avoid overfitting the data. The Ensemble-Partitioning Filter uses $m$ local experts and $(m \times n) - m$ global experts. Consequently, if the dataset is not split ($n = 1$), the filter only combines the votes of local experts. It is also worth noticing that in case of consensus voting, the distinction between local experts and global experts is irrelevant [51].

Table II presents an example where three different base learners ($L_{j=1,...,3}$) are combined on a dataset preliminary partitioned threefold ($P_{i=1,...,3}$). The filtering level is set to five ($\lambda = 5$) and the cross-validation constraint is enabled. This table presents three instances $I_{i=1,...,3}$ where $I_1$ and $I_2$ are part of subset $P_1$ and $I_3$ is part of subset $P_2$. Bold fonts indicate the predictions of local experts. For example, because instance 1 is part of the first partition ($I_1 \in P_1$), the three local experts ($m = 3$) of $I_1$ are trained on $P_1$. $I_1$ is classified as noisy since it is misclassified

TABLE II
NOISE DETECTION WITH THE ENSEMBLE-PARTITIONING FILTER

|  | $I_1$ | $I_2$ | $I_3$ |
|---|---|---|---|
| Class $c_k$ | nfp | fp | fp |
| $P_i \, (I_k \in P_i)$ | 1 | 1 | 2 |
| $L_1(I_k, P_1)$ | **fp** | **nfp** | fp |
| $L_1(I_k, P_2)$ | fp | nfp | **nfp** |
| $L_1(I_k, P_3)$ | nfp | nfp | fp |
| $L_2(I_k, P_1)$ | **fp** | **fp** | fp |
| $L_2(I_k, P_2)$ | nfp | fp | **nfp** |
| $L_2(I_k, P_3)$ | nfp | nfp | fp |
| $L_3(I_k, P_1)$ | **fp** | **nfp** | nfp |
| $L_3(I_k, P_2)$ | nfp | nfp | **nfp** |
| $L_3(I_k, P_3)$ | fp | fp | fp |
| $S_k^{le}$ | 3 | 2 | 3 |
| $S_k^{ge}$ | 2 | 4 | 1 |
| Noisy | ✓ |  |  |

$\lambda = 5, n = 3, m = 3, bCv = \text{true}$.

by five experts including all the related local experts ($S_1^{le} = 3$ and $S_1^{ge} = 2$). $I_2$ is not identified as noisy because it is properly classified by one of its local experts ($L_2(I_2, P_1) = c_2$). If the cross-validation constraint was disabled, $I_2$ would be labeled as noisy. Despite that $I_3$ is misclassified by all its local experts, there are still not enough experts misclassifying it. Hence, $I_3$ is labeled as *clean*.

## 3.4  Iterative Approach

Similar to the Iterative-Partitioning Filter [22], noise elimination is accomplished in multiple iterations. The stopping criterion (step 27) is defined as follows: in $T_1$ consecutive iterations, if the number of identified noisy examples in each iteration is less than $T_2$, noise elimination will stop. The study in [17] recommended to set $T_1$ to 3 and $T_2$ to 1% of the size of the original training dataset (i.e., $T_2 = 0.01 \times \|E\|$). The filtering procedure can be also executed for a fixed number of iterations.

Table III illustrates how the stopping criterion works when $T_1$ and $T_2$ are set to their recommended values. $\|A_i\|$ represents the number of instances detected as noisy in $P_i$. In this example, the stopping criterion is met at the 5th iteration, because each of the last three iterations (i.e., iterations 3, 4 and 5) detects less than one percent of the training dataset as being noisy.

In addition, a portion ($\beta$) of good instances (step 22) is removed at each iteration (step 24) [17]. In this study, $\beta = 50\%$. A good instance is one that is not misclassified by any of the models (step 18). $G_{i=1,...,n}$, is the set of good examples detected in $P_i$.

TABLE III
ITERATIVE STOPPING CRITERION

| Round | Noise count $\| A_i \|$ | | | Total $\| A \| = \sum_{i=1}^{3} \| A_i \|$ | |
|---|---|---|---|---|---|
| | $\| A_1 \|$ | $\| A_2 \|$ | $\| A_3 \|$ | Count | Proportion (%) |
| 1 | 132 | 140 | 125 | 397 | 19.85 |
| 2 | 51 | 42 | 61 | 154 | 7.7 |
| 3 | 8 | 6 | 2 | 16 | 0.8 |
| 4 | 9 | 4 | 2 | 15 | 0.75 |
| 5 | 2 | 1 | 4 | 7 | 0.35 |

$\| E \| = 2000$, $n = 3$, $T_1 = 3$, $T_2 = 0.01 \times \| E \| = 20$.

$G'_{i=1,\ldots,n}$ is the set of good examples removed from $P_i$. $G'_i$ is made up of $\beta \times \| G_i \|$ instances randomly selected from $G_i$ while respecting the original proportion of *fp* and *nfp* instances [22]. There are two benefits when some good examples are removed. Firstly, the dataset size is reduced, making the induction learning schemes run faster in the next iteration. Secondly, the exceptions in the subsets of the previous iteration may form new rules in the next iteration [17].

## 3.5 Specialized Filters

By varying the parameters associated to the Ensemble-Partitioning Filter (i.e., $m$, $n$, $bCv$, $\lambda$, $\beta$, and the stopping criterion), the four filters presented in Section 2.1 can be instantiated. The Classification Filter [10], abbreviated *cf* in this study, only uses one base classifier ($m = 1$) induced on the entire dataset ($n = 1$) without any filtering iterations. The Ensemble Filter implemented in [21,23] uses twenty-five distinct classifiers ($m = 25$) on the whole dataset ($n = 1$) at filtering level 13, 17, 20, and 23. Our recent work [22] implemented the Multiple-Partitioning Filter with and without the cross-validation constraint ($bCv = true$ and $bCv = false$, respectively) by using five different classifiers ($m = 5$) and by splitting the training dataset into five subsets ($n = 5$). The Multiple-Partitioning Filter with and without the cross-validation constraint are referred to as *mpfcv* and *mpf*, respectively. In [22], the Iterative-Partitioning Filter is implemented with the cross-validation constraint. One learner ($m = 1$) is successively induced on the five splits of the training dataset ($n = 5$). As its name indicates, the filtering is carried out in multiple iterations. The majority and consensus schemes are successively used by the Iterative-Partitioning Filter. The filters are referred to as *ipfcons* and *ipfmaj*, respectively.

Table IV summarizes the values of the parameters used to specialize the Ensemble-Partitioning Filter. L and G represent the number of Local and Global experts, respectively. The value of $bCv$ is irrelevant for both the Classification Filter and the Ensemble Filter because only local experts are used ($n = 1$).

TABLE IV
SPECIALIZATION OF THE ENSEMBLE-PARTITIONING FILTER

| Filter | $m$ | $n$ | $bCv$ | $\lambda$ | Iteration | L | G |
|--------|-----|-----|-------|-----------|-----------|---|---|
| cf | 1 | 1 | NA | 1 | no | 1 | 0 |
| ef | 25 | 1 | NA | 13–25 | no | 25 | 0 |
| mpf | 5 | 5 | false | 13–25 | no | 5 | 20 |
| mpfcv | 5 | 5 | true | 13–25 | no | 5 | 20 |
| ipfcons | 1 | 5 | true | 5 | yes | 1 | 4 |
| ipfmaj | 1 | 5 | true | 3 | yes | 1 | 4 |

## 3.6  Configuration of the Parameters

The filtering requirements determine the values of the input parameters of the Ensemble-Partitioning Filter. Four criteria need to be considered:

**Efficiency:** An efficient filter is capable of removing instances which are *noisy* and retaining instances which are *clean*. However, the definition of efficiency is relatively subjective. Depending on the dataset at hand and on the study environment, the characteristics of the selected filter may vary. On one hand, it is preferable to choose a conservative filter for the situations in which there is a paucity of data. On the other hand, when there is an abundance of data, selecting an aggressive filter makes more sense [20]. The level of conservativeness of the Ensemble-Partitioning Filter can be tuned up by the filtering level and/or the stopping criterion.

**Complexity:** The complexity of a filter is determined by the total number of models (i.e., experts) which need to be built. There are ($m \times n \times$ number of iterations) models in the case of the Ensemble-Partitioning Filter. The more complex the filter, the more computation is required.

**Expertise:** The expertise that is required to build the filter is directly related to the total number of distinct learners that are used by the practitioner. While the Classification Filter and the Iterative-Partitioning Filter only require one learner, the Ensemble Filter presented in [21] uses twenty-five distinct learners.

**Scalability:** Partitioning the training set makes the Ensemble-Partitioning Filter scalable to distributed and/or large datasets [17,22]. It is recommended to maintain enough instances in the training partitions to induce relevant hypotheses [6].

## 4.  Modeling Methodology

This section lays out the methodology employed and presents the principles of the efficiency paired comparisons which assess the relative efficiency of filters compared to one another. The efficiency of the Ensemble-Partitioning Filter for different input parameters will later be determined empirically in Section 5.

## 4.1   Model-Selection Strategy

Our empirical study is related to the two-group classification in the context of software quality. Software program modules are typically labeled as either fault-prone (*fp*) or not fault-prone (*nfp*). Hence, two types of misclassification errors can occur: *Type I error* (or false positive) and *Type II error* (or false negative). In software quality classification, the Type I and Type II errors are generally inversely proportional. Hence, software quality engineers often recommend selecting a classification model that has a preferred balance between the two error rates.

Our previous studies, which focused on high assurance systems similar to the one in this chapter, selected a preferred balance of equality between Type I and Type II errors, with Type II being as low as possible. Having both Type I and Type II low ensures detection of significantly large number of *fp* modules, and at the same time, keeps the number of *nfp* modules predicted to be *fp* (i.e., ineffective testing and inspection) low. In this study, we use the same model selection strategy to select the base learners as well as the final learners.

## 4.2   Performance Evaluation

Comparing the performance of different classification methods based on the two misclassification rates (Type I and Type II) can be a difficult task, especially when the performance of the base classifiers is being evaluated across a range of datasets (with different levels of noise, in our case).

In the context of (two-group) software quality classification, where there is likely to be a vast disparity between the prior probabilities of the two classes (*fp* and *nfp*) and the cost of the two types of misclassification, the Expected Cost of Misclassification (ECM) is more appropriate as a practical measure for comparison [21]

$$ECM = C_I Pr(fp|nfp)\pi_{nfp} + C_{II}Pr(nfp|fp)\pi_{fp} \tag{1}$$

where $C_I$ and $C_{II}$ are costs of Type I and Type II misclassification errors respectively, $\pi_{fp}$ and $\pi_{nfp}$ are prior probabilities of *fp* modules and *nfp* modules, $Pr(fp|nfp)$ is the probability that a *nfp* module would be misclassified as *fp*, and $Pr(nfp|fp)$ is the probability that a *fp* module would be misclassified as *nfp*.

In practice, it is difficult to quantify the actual costs of misclassification at the time of modeling. Hence, we define the Normalized Expected Cost of Misclassification

(NECM):

$$\text{NECM} = \frac{\text{ECM}}{C_I} = Pr(fp|nfp)\pi_{nfp} + \frac{C_{II}}{C_I}Pr(nfp|fp)\pi_{fp} \qquad (2)$$

NECM facilitates the use of cost ratio $C_{II}/C_I$, which can be more readily estimated using software engineering heuristics for a given application.

## 4.3  Efficiency Paired Comparison

Many empirical tests have been conducted on datasets in which noise is artificially injected [11,17,20]. For example, the method of artificial universes [52], the model of the classification noise process [53] or a simple pairwise scheme [17,54] can be used to generate artificial noise. It allows the researchers to compare which noise-handling technique performs the best in terms of false positive and false negative filtering errors (see Section 2.2).

We introduce the principle of *Efficiency Paired Comparisons* to determine which filter of a given pair is more efficient. This technique does not require to inject artificial noise and can validate filtering schemes on a real world case. Hence, the software quality engineer gets a realistic view of the performance improvements that are possible when poor quality instances are removed from the dataset.

### 4.3.1  Principles

Suppose that the performance of the final learning algorithms on the dataset filtered by filter $f_1$ is better (i.e., having a lower NECM value) than the performance of the same learners on the dataset processed by filter $f_2$. $f_1$ is likely to identify more noise than $f_2$ because improving performance means that more actual noisy data is removed [21]. But concluding that filter $f_1$ is more effective than filter $f_2$ is too shortsighted. The more aggressive the filter, the more likely it will filter instances which are actually clean. An efficient filter is capable of improving the classification accuracies of the final learners while keeping the number of removed instances low.

This argument leads to conclude that filter $f_1$ is more efficient than filter $f_2$ if one of the two following criteria is fulfilled:

(1) The NECM values of the final learners built on the dataset filtered by $f_1$ are lower than the NECM values of the final learners built on the dataset filtered by $f_2$ *and* if the number of instances removed by $f_1$ is not higher than that removed by $f_2$.

(2) The NECM values of the final learners built on the dataset filtered by $f_1$ are not higher than the NECM values of the final learners built on the dataset

filtered by $f_2$ *and* if the number of instances removed by $f_1$ is lower than that removed by $f_2$.

On the other hand, $f_1$ is as efficient as $f_2$ if the NECM values of the learners built on the dataset filtered by $f_1$ are the same as the NECM values of the learners built on the dataset filtered by $f_2$ *and* if the number of instances removed by $f_1$ is the same as that removed by $f_2$. No conclusion can be reached when $f_1$ ($f_2$)'s NECM is lower than $f_2$ ($f_1$) and that $f_1$ ($f_2$) removes more instances than $f_2$ ($f_1$).

## 4.3.2 Hypothesis Testings

The principle of the efficiency paired comparison can be translated into two successive hypothesis testings: *HA* and *HB*. The null hypothesis $HA_0$ is that the proportion of instances filtered by $f_1$ ($p_1$) is equal to the proportion of instances filtered by $f_2$ ($p_2$). If $HA_0$ is true at a given significance level $\alpha$, filter $f_1$ is as conservative as filter $f_2$. In other words, both $f_1$ and $f_2$ statistically remove the same number of instances:

$$\begin{cases} HA_0: \ p_1 = p_2, \\ HA_1: \ p_1 \neq p_2. \end{cases} \tag{3}$$

The value of the test statistic $z$ for the comparison of proportion is computed as follows [55]:

$$z = \frac{\hat{p}_1 - \hat{p}_2}{\sqrt{2\frac{\bar{p}\bar{q}}{\|E\|}}} \quad \text{where } \bar{p} = \frac{\hat{p}_1 + \hat{p}_2}{2} \text{ and } \bar{q} = 1 - \bar{p} \tag{4}$$

where $\hat{p}_1 = \|A_1\|/\|E\|$ and $\hat{p}_2 = \|A_2\|/\|E\|$ are the two sample proportions where $\|A_1\|$ and $\|A_2\|$ are the number of instances detected as noisy by $f_1$ and $f_2$, respectively, and $\|E\|$ is the number of instances in the original training dataset.

The null hypothesis $HB_0$ is that the NECM of the final learners induced on the dataset filtered by $f_1$ is equal to that filtered by $f_2$:

$$\begin{cases} HB_0: \ \mu_D = 0, \\ HB_1: \ \mu_D \neq 0 \end{cases} \tag{5}$$

where $\mu_D$ is the difference between the population means of the costs of misclassification (NECM) related to $f_1$ and $f_2$. Let $k$ be the number of final learners. The value of the test statistic $t$ for the sample mean is computed as follows [55]:

$$t = \frac{\bar{D}}{\left(\frac{\sigma_D}{\sqrt{k}}\right)} \tag{6}$$

where $D_{j=1,\ldots,k}$ is the sample of difference scores between paired observations, $\sigma_D$ is the standard deviation of $D$ and $\bar{D}$ is the mean value of the sample of differences [55]. For example, suppose that three learners are used ($k = 3$). The costs of misclassification of the three learners on dataset $E$ filtered by $f_1$ are 0.34, 0.36 and 0.35, respectively. Similarly, the costs of misclassification of these same three learners training on $E$ filtered by $f_2$ are 0.39, 0.34 and 0.34, respectively. $\bar{D}$ is then computed as follows:

$$\bar{D} = \frac{1}{3} \times \left( (0.34 - 0.39) + (0.36 - 0.34) + (0.35 - 0.34) \right)$$

$$= \frac{-0.05 + 0.02 + 0.01}{3} = -\frac{0.02}{3}.$$

In this case, $f_1$ performs better than $f_2$ on average ($\bar{D} < 0$).

Table V summarizes how the outcomes of the hypotheses are combined. If $HA_0$ is true, filter $f_1$ is as conservative as filter $f_2$. On the other hand, $f_1$ is more aggressive than $f_2$ if $HA_0$ is false *and* the sample proportion of instances eliminated by $f_1$ is greater than the sample proportion eliminated by $f_2$ (i.e., $\hat{p}_1 > \hat{p}_2$). Conversely, $f_2$ is more aggressive than $f_1$ if $HA_0$ is false *and* the sample proportion of instances eliminated by $f_2$ is greater than the sample proportion eliminated by $f_1$ (i.e., $\hat{p}_2 > \hat{p}_1$).

Along the same lines, $HB$ is divided into three different situations. If $HB_0$ is true (i.e., $\mu_D = 0$), the performance on the dataset filtered by $f_1$ is as good as the performance on the dataset filtered by $f_2$ (i.e., with similar NECM). On the other hand, the performance related to $f_1$ is better than the performance related to $f_2$ if $HB_0$ is false *and* the mean value of the sample of differences is lower than zero (i.e., $\bar{D} < 0$), or the performance related to $f_1$ is worse than the performance related to $f_2$ if $HB_0$ is false and $\bar{D} > 0$.

TABLE V

RELATIVE EFFICIENCY BETWEEN TWO FILTERS

|  | $HA_0$ true (i.e., $p_1 = p_2$) | $HA_1$ true *and* | |
|---|---|---|---|
|  |  | $\hat{p}_1 < \hat{p}_2$ | $\hat{p}_1 > \hat{p}_2$ |
| $HB_0$ true (i.e., $\mu_D = 0$) | $f_1$ as efficient as $f_2$ | $f_1$ more efficient than $f_2$ | $f_2$ more efficient than $f_1$ |
| $HB_1$ $\bar{D} < 0$ true | $f_1$ more efficient than $f_2$ | $f_1$ more efficient than $f_2$ | Cannot conclude |
| *and* $\bar{D} > 0$ | $f_2$ more efficient than $f_1$ | Cannot conclude | $f_2$ more efficient than $f_1$ |

# 5. Empirical Evaluation

## 5.1  System Description

The software metrics and quality data used in our study are from a NASA software project written in C and referred to as JM1. The data is available through the Metrics Data Program (MDP) at NASA, and includes software measurement data and associated error (fault) data collected at the function/subroutine/method level. The dataset consists of 10883 software modules of which 2105 modules have errors (ranging from 1 to 26) while the remaining 8778 modules are error-free, i.e., have no software faults. In this case study, a module is considered not fault-prone (*nfp*) if it has no faults, and fault-prone (*fp*) otherwise [4]. Note that we interchangeably use the terms errors, defects, and faults in this chapter [1].

Each module in the JM1 project is characterized by twenty-one software measurements [1]: three McCabe metrics (Cyclomatic_Complexity, Essential_ Complexity, Design_Complexity); four basic Halstead metrics (Unique_ Operators, Unique_Operands, Total_Operators, Total_Operands); eight derived Halstead metrics (Halstead_Length, Halstead_Volume, Halstead_Level, Halstead_Difficulty, Halstead_Content, Hal- stead_Effort, Halstead_Error_Est, Halstead_Prog_Time); five metrics of Line Count (Loc_Code_And_Comment, Loc_Total, Loc_ Comment, Loc_Blank, Loc_Executable); and one metric for Branch Count. The types and numbers of available software metrics are determined by the NASA Metrics Data Program. Other types of software metrics, including software process measurements are not available for analysis. The quality of the modules is described by their *Error Rate* (number of defects in the module) and *Defect* (whether or not the module has any defects). The latter is used as the class label. For additional details regarding software measurements and software quality metrics, the reader is referred to [1].

Upon removing obvious inconsistent modules (those with identical software measurements but with different class labels) and those with missing values, the dataset is reduced from 10883 to 8850 modules. We denote this reduced dataset as JM1-8850, which now had 1687 modules (19%) with one or more defects and 7163 modules (81%) with no defects. We only used thirteen metrics in our analysis. The eight derived Halstead metrics are not used during modeling since these metrics are derived from the four basic Halstead metrics. Classifiers are built using the thirteen software metrics as independent variables and the module-class as the dependent variable, i.e., *fp* or *nfp*.

It is important to note that the software measurements used for the software system are primarily governed by their availability, the internal workings of the respective projects, and the data collection tools used by the project. The use of specific software metrics in the case study does not advocate their effectiveness—a different software project may collect and consider a different set of software measurements for analysis [1,21,22].

## 5.2    Creation of the Filters

This section presents how the different filters issued from the specialization of the Ensemble-Partitioning Filter (Table IV) are created for the JM1-8850 dataset. In this study, we use a 10-fold cross-validation. Extensive tests on numerous different datasets, with different learning techniques, show that ten is about the right number of folds to get the best estimate of error [6].

### 5.2.1    Classification Filter

J48 [56] is selected to be the base classifier for the Classification Filter (*cf*) since it generally produces fairly good results on a large variety of datasets. Besides, J48 is a robust algorithm, making it tolerant to noisy data [10,19]. The Type I and Type II error rates of classifier J48 on JM1-8850 obtained using 10-fold cross-validation are 32.56% and 32.42%, respectively. The high error rates indicate that JM1 is potentially very noisy [21].

### 5.2.2    Ensemble Filter

In this chapter, we use the Ensemble Filter implemented in our previous studies [21,23]. The filter is based on the performance of twenty-five different base classification techniques (*m* = 25): Case-Based Reasoning [7]; J48 [6,56]; Treedisc [57]; Lines-of-Code [23]; Logistic Regression [58]; Artificial Neural Network [59]; Genetic Programming [60]; Logit Boost [58]; Rule-Based Modeling [61]; Bagging [32]; Rough Sets [62]; Meta Cost combined with J48 [63]; Ada Boost combined with J48 [31]; Decision Table [64]; Alternate Decision Tree [65]; Sequential Minimal Optimization [66]; IB1 [67]; IB*k* [67]; Partial Decision Tree [68]; 1R [69]; Repeated Incremental Pruning to Produce Error Reduction (RIPPER) [70]; Ripple Down Rule (RIDOR) [71]; Naive Bayes [72]; Hyper Pipes [73]; and Locally Weighted Learning [74] with Decision Stump (LWLStump). For most classification techniques, the predictions are obtained using 10-fold cross-validation.[1] By selecting classifiers from different data mining families such as rule-based, tree-based and instance-based classifiers, the bias of the learners will complement one to another [21].

---

[1] Exceptions due to infeasibility or limitation of the tool used for Treedisc, Logistic Regression, Artificial Neural Network, Genetic Programming, Rule-Based Modeling, and Rough Sets.

Similar to [21,23], we only experiment with four different filtering levels. More specifically, an instance is considered to be noisy if it is misclassified by: 23 or more classifiers (the most conservative approach, i.e., misclassification by over 90% classifiers); 20 or more classifiers (misclassification by over 80% classifiers); 17 or more classifiers (misclassification by over 68% classifiers); and 13 or more classifiers (the majority approach—the least conservative one). The Ensemble Filter is denoted by *ef* and its filtering level $\lambda$. For example, the Ensemble Filter at filtering level 17 is referred to as *ef-17*.

### 5.2.3 Multiple-Partitioning Filter

Similar to the Multiple-Partitioning Filter implemented in [22], the dataset is initially split into five equal subsets ($n = 5$), and five base algorithms ($m = 5$) are selected: J48 [56,6]; 1R [69]; LWLStump [74]; RIPPER [70]; and IB$k$ [67]. Two types of filters are then defined: with or without the cross-validation constraint. Similar to the Ensemble Filter defined in the previous section, twenty-five models are built ($m \times n = 25$), and the same filtering levels are selected: 13, 17, 20, and 23. The Multiple-Partitioning Filter with the cross-validation constraint is denoted by *mpfcv* and its filtering level $\lambda$. For example, the notation *mpfcv-17* corresponds to the Multiple-Partitioning Filter with the cross-validation constraint at filtering level 17. Likewise, *mpf* refers to the Multiple-Partitioning Filter without the cross-validation. For example, *mpf-23* symbolizes the Multiple-Partitioning Filter without the cross-validation constraint at filtering level 23.

### 5.2.4 Iterative-Partitioning Filter

The Iterative-Partitioning Filter only uses one base classifier ($m = 1$). As suggested in [17], the dataset is split into five equal parts ($n = 5$). In our case study, J48 [56] is selected for the same reasons as with the Classification Filter. J48 is built on each of the five splits at each iteration. In 3 continuous iterations, if the number of identified noisy examples in each round is less than 1% of the size of the original training dataset, the iterative execution stops (Section 3.4).

Figure 2 indicates the number of instances removed at each iteration for both the consensus and the majority schemes. Seven iterations are required with the majority scheme for this specific dataset in order to reach the stopping criterion. On the other hand, nine iterations are necessary to fulfill the stopping criterion with the consensus filter. This can be explained by the fact that the filter with majority scheme removes much more instances at each given iteration than the filter with consensus scheme does. Therefore, all the potentially noisy (i.e., mislabeled) instances are removed quicker, making the majority filter reach the stopping criterion in fewer rounds.

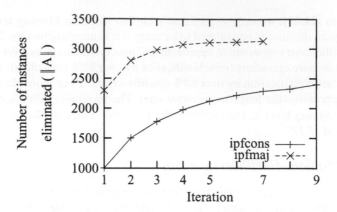

FIG. 2.  Noise elimination at different iterations.

The level of conservativeness of the Iterative-Partitioning Filter depends on the number of iterations and on the filtering scheme. Similar to [22,51,75], the first five iterations as well as the last one are selected for this study. The Iterative-Partitioning Filter is denoted by *ipf*, its voting scheme (*cons* or *maj*, for either consensus or majority scheme), and the number of filtering iterations. For example, *ipfcons-9* symbolizes the Iterative-Partitioning Filter with consensus scheme at its ninth (and last) iteration, and *ipfmaj-2* is related to the Iterative-Partitioning Filter with majority scheme at its second iteration.

## 5.3   Noise Elimination Results

Table VI lists the number of instances eliminated by the filters at different filtering levels or at different iterations. For each filter, the table provides the number as well as the proportion of *nfp* and *fp* modules in the set of instances detected as noisy. We observe that the Classification Filter and the Iterative-Partitioning Filter with majority scheme are the most two aggressive filters. Moreover, the Ensemble Filter with a high filtering level is much more conservative as compared with the Multiple-Partitioning Filter at the same filtering level. It is also worth noting that the proportions of *nfp* and *fp* modules eliminated by the filters remain almost the same as the initial proportions found in dataset JM1-8850 before filtering, because our model selection strategy attempts to keep the Type I error rate to be balanced with the Type II error rate (Section 4.1).

Figure 3 plots the number of instances removed by *ef*, *mpf* and *mpfcv* at different filtering levels. The Ensemble Filter is more conservative than the Multiple-Parti-

TABLE VI
NUMBER AND PROPORTION OF INSTANCES REMOVED BY THE FILTERS

| Filters | *nfp* modules | | *fp* modules | | Total |
|---------|-------|----------------|-------|----------------|-------|
|         | Count | Proportion (%) | Count | Proportion (%) | count |
| cf        | 2332 | 81.00 | 547 | 19.00 | 2879 |
| ef-23     | 877  | 82.81 | 182 | 17.19 | 1059 |
| ef-20     | 1440 | 83.00 | 295 | 17.00 | 1735 |
| ef-17     | 1823 | 82.19 | 395 | 17.81 | 2218 |
| ef-13     | 2302 | 81.14 | 535 | 18.86 | 2837 |
| mpf-23    | 1155 | 81.51 | 262 | 18.49 | 1417 |
| mpf-20    | 1567 | 80.32 | 384 | 19.68 | 1951 |
| mpf-17    | 1865 | 79.33 | 486 | 20.67 | 2351 |
| mpf-13    | 2258 | 78.84 | 606 | 21.16 | 2864 |
| mpfcv-23  | 1055 | 81.78 | 235 | 18.22 | 1290 |
| mpfcv-20  | 1264 | 81.97 | 278 | 18.03 | 1542 |
| mpfcv-17  | 1345 | 82.11 | 293 | 17.89 | 1638 |
| mpfcv-13  | 1402 | 82.18 | 304 | 17.82 | 1706 |
| ipfcons-1 | 780  | 77.69 | 224 | 22.31 | 1004 |
| ipfcons-2 | 1212 | 80.69 | 290 | 19.31 | 1502 |
| ipfcons-3 | 1443 | 81.20 | 334 | 18.80 | 1777 |
| ipfcons-4 | 1590 | 80.47 | 386 | 19.53 | 1976 |
| ipfcons-5 | 1693 | 79.82 | 428 | 20.18 | 2121 |
| ipfcons-9 | 1896 | 79.00 | 504 | 21.00 | 2400 |
| ipfmaj-1  | 1849 | 80.53 | 447 | 19.47 | 2296 |
| ipfmaj-2  | 2246 | 80.30 | 551 | 19.70 | 2797 |
| ipfmaj-3  | 2384 | 80.03 | 595 | 19.97 | 2979 |
| ipfmaj-4  | 2457 | 80.01 | 614 | 19.99 | 3071 |
| ipfmaj-5  | 2483 | 79.92 | 624 | 20.08 | 3107 |
| ipfmaj-7  | 2501 | 79.88 | 630 | 20.12 | 3131 |

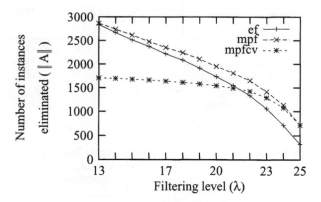

FIG. 3. Noise elimination at different filtering levels.

tioning Filter without the cross-validation constraint at any filtering level. However, the amount of noise eliminated by *ef* and *mpf* gets closer as the level of filtering decreases. The Multiple-Partitioning Filter with the cross-validation constraint (*mpfcv*) is less conservative than the Ensemble Filter when the filtering level is greater than or equal to 22. However, at lower filtering levels ($\lambda < 22$), the number of instances removed by *mpfcv* is much lower than the other two filters. In a previous study [51], we explained that the maximum number of instances which can be detected as potential noise by the Multiple-Partitioning Filter with the cross-validation constraint (*mpfcv*) is less than that of its counterparts, i.e., the Multiple-Partitioning Filter without the cross-validation constraint (*mpf*) and the Ensemble Filter (*ef*).

## 5.4　Performance of the Final Learners

The experimental design is illustrated in Fig. 4. Similar to [21], the following steps are executed for each filtering technique:

(1) Instances detected as *noisy* by the filter (set *A*) are removed from the domain dataset (*E*), i.e., JM1-8850 in our case.
(2) The filtered dataset ($E' = E \setminus A$) is randomly split into two equal parts while keeping an equal proportion of the *nfp* and the *fp* modules in the splits. One split will be used as fit dataset ($E'_{fit}$) and the other as test dataset ($E'_{test}$).
(3) Four final classifiers—J48, 1R, RIPPER and IB*k*—are built on the fit dataset ($E'_{fit}$) by following a balanced strategy (Section 4.1). Inducing more than one

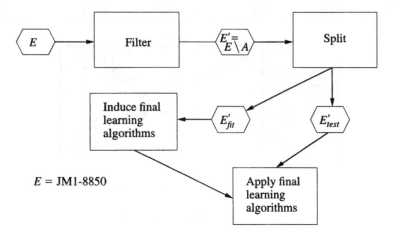

FIG. 4. General procedure for building final learners.

classifier gives a better estimate of the predictive performance since the accuracy often depends on the bias of the learner [17]. These classifiers are also used to create the Multiple-Partitioning Filter (Section 5.2.3). Using only four final learners was considered relevant and accurate enough for the purpose of our experiment work [22].

(4) The selected models are applied to the test dataset ($E'_{test}$). It is worth noting that the level of noise in the fit and test datasets is similar, because the two sets have been randomly split.

The performance of the final learners are evaluated by using NECM with cost ratio ($C_{II}/C_I$) values of 10, 20, 30 and 50. These values are considered to be practical for the JM1 software system [21].

In order to evaluate the efficiency of filters, noise is often artificially injected into the datasets, either in the class label or in the attribute values [17,20]. However, this approach does not take into account the quality of the fit dataset prior to injecting noise. Moreover, without a noise-free test dataset, the predictive performance of the final classifiers may not be the true indicators of how these techniques perform. In contrast, our approach analyzes the effect of the filtering techniques on a real world dataset with inherent noise.

Table VII summarizes the quality-of-fit in terms of NECM (using 10-fold cross-validation) for the final classifiers built on the JM1-8850 filtered by the Classification Filter, the Ensemble Filter, the Multiple-Partitioning Filter and the Iterative-Partitioning Filter, respectively. The confidence ranges [76] of the costs of misclassification, at a significance level of 0.05, are presented as well. Similarly, the quality-of-test is presented in Table VIII. It is evident that as more noise is removed from the dataset (i.e., lower filtering level or higher number of iterations), both the quality-of-fit and the predictive performance improve for all the final classifiers.

It is assumed that noise occurrence is random. If instances are systematically corrupted in both training and test sets, it is expected that training on the erroneous training set would yield good performance on the test set which is also erroneous [6]. Therefore, the improvement of the classification accuracy for both the fit and test datasets indicates that the filter discards instances which are actually *noisy*. In fact, the more aggressive the filter, the better the performance compared to other filters from the *same* filtering scheme family.

## 5.5   Results of the Efficiency Paired Comparisons

Table IX summarizes the possible paired comparisons at different cost ratios ($C_{II}/C_I$) and for both the fit and test datasets. The outcome of the efficiency paired comparison (Section 4.3) is listed at each cost ratio and for both the fit and test

TABLE VII
COSTS OF MISCLASSIFICATION (NECM) ON THE FIT DATASET

| Filters | $C_{II}/C_I = 10$ | $C_{II}/C_I = 20$ | $C_{II}/C_I = 30$ | $C_{II}/C_I = 50$ |
|---|---|---|---|---|
| cf | 0.34 ± 0.11 | 0.58 ± 0.19 | 0.82 ± 0.27 | 1.30 ± 0.42 |
| ef-23 | 0.68 ± 0.02 | 1.17 ± 0.04 | 1.65 ± 0.06 | 2.62 ± 0.10 |
| ef-20 | 0.49 ± 0.05 | 0.84 ± 0.09 | 1.19 ± 0.12 | 1.89 ± 0.20 |
| ef-17 | 0.34 ± 0.03 | 0.57 ± 0.05 | 0.81 ± 0.06 | 1.28 ± 0.10 |
| ef-13 | 0.15 ± 0.02 | 0.26 ± 0.04 | 0.37 ± 0.05 | 0.59 ± 0.08 |
| mpf-23 | 0.56 ± 0.04 | 0.95 ± 0.07 | 1.34 ± 0.10 | 2.12 ± 0.16 |
| mpf-20 | 0.39 ± 0.03 | 0.66 ± 0.05 | 0.93 ± 0.07 | 1.47 ± 0.10 |
| mpf-17 | 0.22 ± 0.03 | 0.38 ± 0.05 | 0.53 ± 0.07 | 0.83 ± 0.11 |
| mpf-13 | 0.06 ± 0.04 | 0.10 ± 0.07 | 0.15 ± 0.11 | 0.23 ± 0.17 |
| mpfcv-23 | 0.59 ± 0.04 | 1.01 ± 0.06 | 1.43 ± 0.09 | 2.26 ± 0.14 |
| mpfcv-20 | 0.52 ± 0.05 | 0.90 ± 0.08 | 1.27 ± 0.12 | 2.02 ± 0.19 |
| mpfcv-17 | 0.52 ± 0.05 | 0.88 ± 0.08 | 1.24 ± 0.12 | 1.97 ± 0.19 |
| mpfcv-13 | 0.48 ± 0.03 | 0.83 ± 0.05 | 1.17 ± 0.07 | 1.85 ± 0.12 |
| ipfcons-1 | 0.67 ± 0.08 | 1.14 ± 0.15 | 1.61 ± 0.23 | 2.55 ± 0.38 |
| ipfcons-2 | 0.53 ± 0.06 | 0.90 ± 0.10 | 1.27 ± 0.14 | 2.01 ± 0.22 |
| ipfcons-3 | 0.47 ± 0.07 | 0.80 ± 0.13 | 1.12 ± 0.18 | 1.78 ± 0.29 |
| ipfcons-4 | 0.39 ± 0.04 | 0.67 ± 0.08 | 0.94 ± 0.11 | 1.49 ± 0.18 |
| ipfcons-5 | 0.35 ± 0.10 | 0.59 ± 0.17 | 0.83 ± 0.24 | 1.31 ± 0.37 |
| ipfcons-9 | 0.22 ± 0.12 | 0.38 ± 0.20 | 0.53 ± 0.28 | 0.84 ± 0.45 |
| ipfmaj-1 | 0.40 ± 0.05 | 0.67 ± 0.08 | 0.95 ± 0.11 | 1.50 ± 0.17 |
| ipfmaj-2 | 0.26 ± 0.09 | 0.43 ± 0.16 | 0.61 ± 0.22 | 0.97 ± 0.35 |
| ipfmaj-3 | 0.17 ± 0.08 | 0.28 ± 0.14 | 0.40 ± 0.19 | 0.63 ± 0.30 |
| ipfmaj-4 | 0.15 ± 0.11 | 0.25 ± 0.18 | 0.35 ± 0.25 | 0.56 ± 0.40 |
| ipfmaj-5 | 0.12 ± 0.09 | 0.21 ± 0.15 | 0.30 ± 0.21 | 0.47 ± 0.34 |
| ipfmaj-7 | 0.12 ± 0.08 | 0.20 ± 0.14 | 0.28 ± 0.20 | 0.45 ± 0.31 |

datasets. The significance level $\alpha$ for the hypothesis testings outlined in Table V is 0.05. The paired comparisons, which are indexed for convenience, are ordered from the least to the most aggressive pairs of filters.

Three situations can occur:

(1) $f_1$ is more efficient than $f_2$ at a given cost ratio and for a given dataset; it is symbolized by '+'.
(2) $f_1$ and $f_2$ are as efficient at a given cost ratio and for a given dataset; it is symbolized by '='.
(3) We cannot conclude at a given cost ratio and for a given dataset; the related cell of the table is left empty.

For example, *mpf-13* is more efficient than *ef-13* except on the test dataset for cost ratios 30 and 50, when the two filters have the same efficiency (# 44). According to Table VI, *ef-13* and *mpf-13* remove 2837 and 2864, respectively. Even though *mpf-13*

TABLE VIII
COSTS OF MISCLASSIFICATION (NECM) ON THE TEST DATASET

| Filters | $C_{II}/C_I = 10$ | $C_{II}/C_I = 20$ | $C_{II}/C_I = 30$ | $C_{II}/C_I = 50$ |
|---|---|---|---|---|
| cf | $0.35 \pm 0.09$ | $0.58 \pm 0.12$ | $0.82 \pm 0.15$ | $1.29 \pm 0.22$ |
| ef-23 | $0.68 \pm 0.08$ | $1.15 \pm 0.16$ | $1.62 \pm 0.25$ | $2.55 \pm 0.41$ |
| ef-20 | $0.52 \pm 0.03$ | $0.90 \pm 0.09$ | $1.28 \pm 0.16$ | $2.03 \pm 0.29$ |
| ef-17 | $0.34 \pm 0.06$ | $0.56 \pm 0.11$ | $0.79 \pm 0.16$ | $1.24 \pm 0.26$ |
| ef-13 | $0.16 \pm 0.04$ | $0.28 \pm 0.07$ | $0.39 \pm 0.10$ | $0.62 \pm 0.17$ |
| mpf-23 | $0.62 \pm 0.09$ | $1.10 \pm 0.25$ | $1.57 \pm 0.41$ | $2.52 \pm 0.72$ |
| mpf-20 | $0.42 \pm 0.03$ | $0.71 \pm 0.04$ | $1.01 \pm 0.05$ | $1.60 \pm 0.08$ |
| mpf-17 | $0.24 \pm 0.05$ | $0.40 \pm 0.12$ | $0.56 \pm 0.19$ | $0.88 \pm 0.35$ |
| mpf-13 | $0.08 \pm 0.03$ | $0.13 \pm 0.07$ | $0.18 \pm 0.11$ | $0.28 \pm 0.21$ |
| mpfcv-23 | $0.70 \pm 0.13$ | $1.26 \pm 0.32$ | $1.82 \pm 0.50$ | $2.94 \pm 0.87$ |
| mpfcv-20 | $0.59 \pm 0.09$ | $1.02 \pm 0.20$ | $1.45 \pm 0.31$ | $2.32 \pm 0.53$ |
| mpfcv-17 | $0.53 \pm 0.08$ | $0.90 \pm 0.23$ | $1.26 \pm 0.39$ | $2.00 \pm 0.70$ |
| mpfcv-13 | $0.53 \pm 0.05$ | $0.90 \pm 0.10$ | $1.27 \pm 0.15$ | $2.01 \pm 0.25$ |
| ipfcons-1 | $0.66 \pm 0.05$ | $1.12 \pm 0.14$ | $1.58 \pm 0.24$ | $2.50 \pm 0.43$ |
| ipfcons-2 | $0.54 \pm 0.08$ | $0.92 \pm 0.13$ | $1.30 \pm 0.18$ | $2.05 \pm 0.29$ |
| ipfcons-3 | $0.47 \pm 0.04$ | $0.79 \pm 0.08$ | $1.11 \pm 0.12$ | $1.75 \pm 0.22$ |
| ipfcons-4 | $0.40 \pm 0.11$ | $0.68 \pm 0.22$ | $0.96 \pm 0.33$ | $1.52 \pm 0.55$ |
| ipfcons-5 | $0.36 \pm 0.08$ | $0.62 \pm 0.19$ | $0.88 \pm 0.31$ | $1.41 \pm 0.54$ |
| ipfcons-9 | $0.24 \pm 0.09$ | $0.42 \pm 0.19$ | $0.60 \pm 0.28$ | $0.95 \pm 0.47$ |
| ipfmaj-1 | $0.38 \pm 0.04$ | $0.63 \pm 0.06$ | $0.87 \pm 0.08$ | $1.36 \pm 0.14$ |
| ipfmaj-2 | $0.24 \pm 0.06$ | $0.41 \pm 0.09$ | $0.57 \pm 0.11$ | $0.90 \pm 0.16$ |
| ipfmaj-3 | $0.18 \pm 0.08$ | $0.30 \pm 0.15$ | $0.43 \pm 0.22$ | $0.68 \pm 0.36$ |
| ipfmaj-4 | $0.14 \pm 0.09$ | $0.23 \pm 0.12$ | $0.32 \pm 0.15$ | $0.49 \pm 0.21$ |
| ipfmaj-5 | $0.14 \pm 0.11$ | $0.23 \pm 0.18$ | $0.32 \pm 0.25$ | $0.50 \pm 0.39$ |
| ipfmaj-7 | $0.13 \pm 0.10$ | $0.20 \pm 0.15$ | $0.28 \pm 0.20$ | $0.42 \pm 0.30$ |

is more aggressive than *ef-13*, the proportion is not significantly different (i.e., $HA_0$ is true, see Eq. (3)). Tables VII and VIII indicate that the final learners induced on the dataset filtered by *mpf-13* perform better than those induced on the dataset filtered by *ef-13*. The differences are statistically significant ($HB_0$ is false, see Eq. (5)), except on the test dataset for cost ratios 30 and 50 because the confidence ranges are too large in these two situations ($HB_0$ is true).

We have not found any pairs of filters for which $f_1$ is more efficient than $f_2$ at a given cost ratio ($C_{II}/C_I$) and for a given dataset (either fit or test datasets) and, for which $f_2$ is also more efficient than $f_1$ for another cost ratio and/or another dataset. In addition, only relevant comparisons where one conclusive outcome was reached at least for both the fit and test dataset are included in Table IX.

*cf* is outperformed by all the other filters (# 17, 20, 22, 25, 26, 30, 35, 36, 45, and 50). These results were previously confirmed by [17,20]. The Iterative-Partitioning Filter with majority voting is the second worst filter (# 19, 21, 24, 27, 29, 31, 32, 33,

TABLE IX
EFFICIENCY PAIRED COMPARISONS ON THE FIT AND TEST DATASETS

| # | $f_1$ | $f_2$ | Fit dataset | | | | Test dataset | | | |
|---|-------|-------|----|----|----|----|----|----|----|----|
|   |       |       | 10 | 20 | 30 | 50 | 10 | 20 | 30 | 50 |
| 1 | ef-23 | ipfcons-1 | = | = | = | = | = | = | = | = |
| 2 | mpf-23 | mpfcv-20 |  | + | + | + | + | + | + | + |
| 3 | ipfcons-2 | mpf-23 | + | + | + | + | = | = | = | = |
| 4 | ipfcons-2 | mpfcv-17 | + | + | + | + | + | + | + | + |
| 5 | mpfcv-20 | ipfcons-2 | = | = | = | = | = | = | = | = |
| 6 | mpfcv-20 | mpfcv-13 |  | + | + | + | + | + | + | + |
| 7 | mpfcv-17 | mpfcv-20 | = | = | = | = | = | = | = | = |
| 8 | mpfcv-17 | ipfcons-3 | + | + | + | + | + | + | + | + |
| 9 | mpfcv-13 | mpfcv-17 | + | + | + | + | = | = | = | = |
| 10 | ef-20 | mpfcv-17 | + | + | + | + | = | = | = | = |
| 11 | ef-20 | mpfcv-13 | = | = | = | = | = | = | = | = |
| 12 | ef-20 | ipfcons-3 | = | = | = | = | = | = | = | = |
| 13 | ipfcons-3 | mpfcv-13 | = | = | = | = | + | + | = | = |
| 14 | ipfcons-3 | mpf-20 | + | + | + | + |  | + | + | + |
| 15 | mpf-20 | ipfcons-4 | = | = | = | = | = | = | = | = |
| 16 | mpf-20 | ipfcons-5 | + | + | + | + |  | + | + | + |
| 17 | mpf-20 | cf | + | + | + | + | + |  |  |  |
| 18 | ipfcons-4 | ipfcons-5 | + | + | + | + | + | + | + | + |
| 19 | ipfcons-4 | ipfmaj-1 | + | + | + | + | + | + | + | + |
| 20 | ipfcons-4 | cf | + | + | + | + |  | + | + | + |
| 21 | ipfcons-5 | ipfmaj-1 | + | + | + | + | + | + | + | + |
| 22 | ipfcons-5 | cf | + | + | + | + | + | + | + | + |
| 23 | ef-17 | ipfcons-5 | = | = | = | = | + | = | = | = |
| 24 | ef-17 | ipfmaj-1 | + | + | + | + | + | = | = | = |
| 25 | ef-17 | cf | + | + | + | + | + | + | + | + |
| 26 | ipfmaj-1 | cf | + | + | + | + | + | + | + | + |
| 27 | mpf-17 | ipfmaj-1 | + | + | + | + | + | + | + | + |
| 28 | mpf-17 | ipfcons-9 | = | = | = | = | = | = | = | = |
| 29 | mpf-17 | ipfmaj-2 | + | + | + | + | + | + | + | + |
| 30 | mpf-17 | cf | + | + | + | + | + | + | + | + |
| 31 | mpf-17 | ipfmaj-4 | + | + | + | + | + | + | + | + |
| 32 | ipfcons-9 | ipfmaj-1 | + | + | + | + | + | + | + | = |
| 33 | ipfcons-9 | ipfmaj-2 | + | + | + | + | + | + | + | + |
| 34 | ipfcons-9 | ef-13 | + | + | + | + |  |  |  | + |
| 35 | ipfcons-9 | cf | + | + | + | + | + | + | + | + |
| 36 | ipfmaj-2 | cf | + | + | + | + | + | + | + | + |
| 37 | ef-13 | ipfmaj-2 | + | + | + | + | + | + | + | + |
| 38 | ef-13 | cf | + | + | + | + | + | + | + | + |
| 39 | ef-13 | ipfmaj-3 | + | + | + | + | + | + | + | + |
| 40 | ef-13 | ipfmaj-4 | + | + | + | + | + | + |  |  |
| 41 | ef-13 | ipfmaj-5 | + | + | + | + | + | + | + | + |

(*continued on the next page*)

TABLE IX — *continued*

| # | $f_1$ | $f_2$ | Fit dataset | | | | Test dataset | | | |
|---|---|---|---|---|---|---|---|---|---|---|
| | | | 10 | 20 | 30 | 50 | 10 | 20 | 30 | 50 |
| 42 | ef-13 | ipfmaj-7 | + | + | + | + | + | + | | |
| 43 | mpf-13 | ipfmaj-2 | + | + | + | + | + | + | + | + |
| 44 | mpf-13 | ef-13 | + | + | + | + | + | + | = | = |
| 45 | mpf-13 | cf | + | + | + | + | + | + | + | + |
| 46 | mpf-13 | ipfmaj-3 | + | + | + | + | + | = | = | = |
| 47 | mpf-13 | ipfmaj-4 | + | + | + | + | + | + | + | + |
| 48 | mpf-13 | ipfmaj-5 | + | + | + | + | + | + | + | + |
| 49 | mpf-13 | ipfmaj-7 | + | + | + | + | + | + | + | + |
| 50 | ipfmaj-3 | cf | + | + | + | + | + | + | + | + |
| 51 | ipfmaj-4 | ipfmaj-3 | = | = | = | = | + | + | + | + |
| 52 | ipfmaj-4 | ipfmaj-5 | = | = | = | = | = | = | = | = |
| 53 | ipfmaj-5 | ipfmaj-7 | = | = | = | = | = | = | = | = |
| 54 | ipfmaj-7 | ipfmaj-4 | + | = | = | = | = | = | = | = |

37, 39, 40 to 43, 46 to 49), but performs better than the Classification Filter (# 26, 36 and 50). It is also worth noting that *cf* and *ipfmaj* are the most aggressive filters (Table VI).

The use of only one base classifier with majority scheme (i.e., *ipfmaj*) is, in most cases, less efficient than the use of five base classifiers with the majority scheme (i.e., *mpf-13*) according to the paired comparisons # 43 and 46 to 49. Similarly, using one base classifier with majority scheme is less efficient at any iterations than using twenty-five base classifiers with an aggressive voting scheme (i.e., $\lambda = \{13, 17\}$, # 24, 37, 39 to 42). Using only one base classifier turns out to be risky, because the classifier may not have the appropriate bias to learn the concepts from a given domain.

*ipfcons-9* is more efficient than *ipfmaj-1* and *ipfmaj-2* (# 32 and 33). *ipfmaj-1* is worse than *ipfcons-4* and *ipfcons-5* (# 19 and 21). It is generally recommended [20, 21] to take a consensus vote instead of a majority vote because the approach is more conservative, and therefore, will result in fewer *clean* instances being wrongly eliminated from the training data.

The Iterative-Partitioning Filter with consensus scheme performs better than or similar to both the Multiple-Partitioning Filter and the Ensemble Filter in most cases (# 1, 3, 4, 5, 12, 13, 14, 15, 28, and 34). However, *mpfcv-17*, *mpf-20*, and *ef-20* beat *ipfcons-3*, *ipfcons-5*, and *ipfcons-5*, respectively (# 8, 16, and 23). Therefore, using a conservative scheme with one base classifier and going through multiple iterations is as efficient as using different base learners. But when more aggressiveness is needed, the Iterative-Partitioning Filter is outperformed by the Ensemble-Partitioning Filter and the Multiple-Partitioning Filter associated with a high conservative level ($\lambda \geqslant 17$).

$mpf$-$13$ is more efficient than $ef$-$13$ (# 44). $ef$-$20$ is more efficient than $mpfcv$-$17$ (# 10). $ef$-$20$ is as efficient as $mpfcv$-$13$ (# 11). Consequently, it is recommended to select the Ensemble Filter over the Multiple-Partitioning Filter when the filtering level is high (i.e., conservative scheme). On the other hand, the sets of instances removed by $mpf$ and $ef$ have more commonalities as the filtering level decreases (see Fig. 3) and that $mpf$-$13$ is more efficient than $ef$-$13$. When the filtering level is low, it is recommended to use the Multiple-Partitioning Filter.

# 6. Conclusion

This chapter presented the Ensemble-Partitioning Filter, a generic implementation of some commonly used noise filters described previously in the literature. The Ensemble-Partitioning Filter can be tuned by input parameters such as the number of partitions, the number of base classifiers or the iteration stopping criterion. Hence, by setting these parameters appropriately, it is possible to instantiate the Classification Filter, the Ensemble Filter, the Multiple-Partitioning Filter, and the Iterative-Partitioning Filter. Formalizing such a generic approach to noise filtering allows customizing a filtering scheme which best fits the needs of the practitioner.

In our empirical work no artificial noise is injected in the dataset because analyzing the effect of the filters on inherent noise is closer to a real-world scenario. However, there is no direct way to know which instances are noisy. In order to overcome this problem, a technique referred to as the efficiency paired comparison is formalized to assess the relative efficiency among filters.

It was observed that a conservative voting scheme with more iterations is recommended instead of an aggressive scheme with fewer iterations. Additionally, a filter combining different base classifiers with an aggressive voting scheme is as efficient as a filter with a conservative scheme using only one base learner through multiple iterations. We also confirmed that the Classification Filter performs the worst among all filters. In the case of conservative filtering, the combination of the Ensemble Filter with a high filtering level is more efficient than the Multiple-Partitioning Filter. However, for the same number of experts, it is recommended to use the Multiple-Partitioning Filter over the Ensemble Filter when the filtering level is low (i.e., aggressive filtering).

Table X summarizes our recommendations depending on the filtering requirements exposed in Section 3.6, i.e., efficiency, complexity, expertise and scalability. The recommendations differ depending on the nature of the filtering problem. If the fit dataset is large, an aggressive scheme is recommended. On the other hand, when

TABLE X
RECOMMENDATIONS FOR THE APPROPRIATE FILTER

| Filter | Efficiency when the filter is | | Complexity | Expertise | Scalability |
|--------|------------|--------------|------------|-----------|-------------|
|        | aggressive | conservative |            |           |             |
| ef     | +          | ++           | − −        | − − −     | −           |
| mpf    | ++         | +            | −          | − −       | +           |
| mpfcv  | +          | +            | −          | − −       | +           |
| ipfcons | +         | +++          | − −[a]     | +         | +           |
| ipfmaj | −          | −            | − −[a]     | +         | +           |
| cf     | − −        | − −          | +          | +         | −           |

[a] The complexity may vary depending on the required number of iterations.

the amount of training instances is limited, a conservative filter is more appropriate. For each criterion, the less/more attractive the filter, the more '−'/'+' symbols are used.

Future work will continue to explore other algorithms for both attribute and class-noise detection. For example, combining the filtering experts can rely on a more sophisticated voting scheme such as weighted voting, plurality voting or instance runoff voting [25]. Furthermore, additional case studies with other software quality and software measurement datasets will further validate the findings of this study.

ACKNOWLEDGEMENTS

We are grateful to all the current and previous members of the Empirical Software Engineering Laboratory at Florida Atlantic University for their patient reviews. We also thank the staff of the NASA Metrics Data Program for making the software measurement data available.

REFERENCES

[1] Fenton N.E., Pfleeger S.L., *Software Metrics: A Rigorous and Practical Approach*, second ed., PWS Publishing, Boston, MA, 1997.
[2] DeMarco T., *Controlling Software Projects*, Yourdon Press, New York, 1982.
[3] Munson J.C., Khoshgoftaar T.M., "The detection of fault-prone programs", *IEEE Trans. Software Engrg.* **18** (5) (1992) 423–433.
[4] Wendell J.D., Hedepohl J.P., Khoshgoftaar T.M., Allen E.B., "Application of a usage profile in software quality models", in: *Proceedings of the 3rd European Conference on Software Maintenance and Reengineering, Amsterdam, Netherlands*, 1999, pp. 148–157.
[5] Khoshgoftaar T.M., Allen E.B., "Logistic regression modeling of software quality", *Internat. J. Reliability Quality Safety Engrg.* **6** (4) (1999) 303–317.

[6] Witten I.H., Frank E., *Data Mining, Practical Machine Learning Tools and Techniques with Java Implementations*, Morgan Kaufmann, San Francisco, CA, 2000.

[7] Khoshgoftaar T.M., Seliya N., "Analogy-based practical classification rules for software quality estimation", *Empirical Software Engrg.* **8** (4) (2003) 325–350.

[8] Evett M.P., Khoshgoftaar T.M., Chien P.-D., Allen E.B., "Modelling software quality with GP", in: *Proceedings: Genetic and Evolutionary Computation Conference*, Morgan Kaufman, Orlando, FL, 1999.

[9] Khoshgoftaar T.M., Allen E.B., Naik A., Jones W.D., Hudepohl J.P., "Using classification trees for software quality models: Lessons learned", *Internat. J. Software Engrg. Knowledge Engrg.* **9** (2) (1999) 217–231.

[10] Gamberger D., Lavrač N., Grošelj C., "Experiments with noise filtering in a medical domain", in: *Proceedings of the 16th International Conference on Machine Learning*, Morgan Kaufmann, San Francisco, CA, 1999, pp. 143–151.

[11] Teng C.M., "Evaluating noise correction", in: *Proceedings of the 6th Pacific Rim International Conference on Artificial Intelligence, Melbourne, Australia*, in: *Lecture Notes in Artificial Intelligence*, Springer-Verlag, 2000, pp. 188–198.

[12] Khoshgoftaar T.M., Seliya N., "The necessity of assuring quality in software measurement data", in: *Proceedings of the 10th International Symposium on Software Metrics*, IEEE Comput. Soc. Press, Chicago, IL, 2004, pp. 119–130.

[13] Redman T.C., "The impact of poor data quality on the typical enterprise", *Commun. ACM* **41** (1998) 79–82.

[14] Wang R.Y., Strong D.M., "Beyond accuracy: What data quality means to data consumers", *J. Management Information Systems* **12** (4) (1996) 5–34.

[15] Laudon K.C., "Data quality and the due process in large interorganizational record systems", *Commun. ACM* **29** (1) (1986) 4–11.

[16] Orr K., "Data quality and systems theory", *Commun. ACM* **41** (2) (1998) 66–71.

[17] Zhu X., Wu X., Chen Q., "Eliminating class noise in large datasets", in: *Proceedings of the 20th International Conference on Machine Learning*, AAAI Press, Washington, DC, 2003, pp. 920–927.

[18] Yang Y., Wu X., Zhu X., "Dealing with predictive-but-unpredictable attributes in noisy data sources", in: *Proceeding of the 15th European Conference on Machine Learning, Pisa, Italy*, Springer-Verlag, 2004, pp. 471–483.

[19] Quinlan J.R., "Induction of decision trees", *Machine Learning* **1** (1) (1986) 81–106.

[20] Brodley C.E., Friedl M.A., "Identifying mislabeled training data", *J. Artificial Res.* **11** (1999) 131–167.

[21] Khoshgoftaar T.M., Joshi V., "Noise elimination with ensemble-classifier filtering: A case-study in software quality engineering", in: *Proceedings of the 16th International Conference on Software Engineering and Knowledge Engineering, Banff AB, Canada*, 2004, pp. 226–231.

[22] Khoshgoftaar T.M., Rebours P., "Noise elimination with partitioning filter for software quality estimation", *Internat. J. Comput. Appl. Technol.*, special issue on Data Mining Applications, in press.

[23] Khoshgoftaar T.M., Zhong S., Joshi V., "Noise elimination with ensemble-classifier filtering for software quality estimation", *Intelligent Data Analysis: Internat. J.* **6** (1) (2005) 3–27.

[24] Ho T.K., Hull J.J., Srihari S.N., "Decision combination in multiple classifier systems", *IEEE Trans. Pattern Anal. Machine Intelligence* **16** (1) (1994) 66–75.

[25] Alpaydin E., "Voting over multiple condensed nearest neighbors", *Artificial Intelligence Rev.* **11** (1–5) (1997) 115–132.

[26] Ali K.M., Pazzani M.J., "Error reduction through learning multiple descriptions", *Machine Learning* **24** (1996) 173–202.

[27] Kwok S.W., Carter C., "Multiple decision trees", in: *Uncertainty in Artificial Intelligence*, vol. 4, Elsevier Science Publishers, Amsterdam, 1990, pp. 327–335.

[28] Sakakibara Y., "Noise-tolerant Occam algorithms and their applications to learning decision trees", *Machine Learning* **11** (1993) 37–62.

[29] John G.H., "Robust decision tree: Removing outliers from databases", in: *Proceedings of the 1st International Conference on Knowledge Discovery and Data Mining*, AAAI Press, Menlo Park, CA, 1995, pp. 174–179.

[30] Fürnkranz J., Widmer G., "Incremental reduced error pruning", in: *Machine Learning: Proceedings of the 11th Annual Conference, New Brunswick, NJ*, Morgan Kaufmann, 1994, pp. 70–77.

[31] Freund Y., Schapire R., "A short introduction to boosting", *Japan. Soc. Artificial Intelligence* **14** (1999) 771–780.

[32] Breiman L., "Bagging predictors", *Machine Learning* **24** (2) (1996) 123–140.

[33] Wilson D.R., Martinez T.R., "Reduction techniques for exemplar-based learning algorithms", *Machine Learning* **38** (2000) 257–286.

[34] Tomek I., "An experiment with edited nearest-neighbor rule", *IEEE Trans. Systems, Man and Cybernetics* **6** (6) (1976) 448–452.

[35] Aha D., Kibler D., Albert M., "Instance-based learning algorithms", *Machine Learning* **6** (1) (1991) 37–66.

[36] Winston P.H., "The psychology of computer vision", in: *Learning Structural Descriptions from Examples*, McGraw–Hill, New York, 1975, pp. 157–206.

[37] Tang W., Khoshgoftaar T.M., "Noise identification with the $k$-means algorithm", in: *Proceedings of the 16th IEEE International Conference on Tools with Artificial Intelligence, Boca Raton, FL*, 2004, pp. 373–378.

[38] Lorena A.C., de Carvalho A.C., "Evaluation of noise reduction techniques in the splice junction recognition problem", *Genetics and Molecular Biology* **27** (4) (2004) 665–672.

[39] Teng C.M., "Correcting noisy data", in: *Proceedings of the 16th International Conference on Machine Learning*, 1999, pp. 239–248.

[40] Gamberger D., Lavrač N., "Conditions for Occam's Razor applicability and noise elimination", in: *European Conference on Machine Learning, Prague, Czech Republic*, 1997, pp. 108–123.

[41] Zhao Q., Nishida T., "Using qualitative hypotheses to identify inaccurate data", *J. Artificial Intelligence Res.* **3** (1995) 119–145.

[42] Guyon I., Matic N., Vapnik V., "Discovering informative patterns and data cleansing", *Adv. Knowledge Discovery and Data Mining* (1996) 181–203.

[43] Lawrence N.D., Schölkopf B., "Estimating a Kernel Fisher discriminant in the presence of label noise", in: *Proceedings of the 18th International Conference on Machine Learning, Williamstown, MA*, 2001, pp. 306–313.

[44] Muhlenbach F., Lallich S., Zighed D.A., "Identifying and handling mislabelled instances", *J. Intelligent Inform. Systems* **22** (1) (2004) 89–109.

[45] Kittler J., Illingworth J., "Relaxation labelling algorithms—a review", *Image and Vision Comput.* **3** (4) (1985) 206–216.

[46] Zhu X., Wu X., "Cost-guided class noise handling for effective cost-sensitive learning", in: *Proceedings of the 4th IEEE International Conference on Data Mining, Brighton, UK*, IEEE Press, 2004, pp. 297–304.

[47] Hipp J., Güntzer U., Grimmer U., "Data quality mining—making a virtue of necessity", in: *Proceedings of the 6th ACM SIGMOD Workshop on Research Issues in Data Mining and Knowledge Discovery, Santa Barbara, CA*, 2001, pp. 52–57.

[48] Marcus A., Maletic J.I., Lin K.I., "Ordinal association rules for error identification in data sets", in: *Proceedings of the 10th ACM International Conference on Information and Knowledge Management, Atlanta, GA*, 2001, pp. 589–591.

[49] Khoshgoftaar T.M., Seliya N., Gao K., "Detecting noisy instances with the rule-based classification model", *Intelligent Data Analysis: Internat. J.* **9** (4) (2005) 347–364.

[50] Hulse J.V., Khoshgoftaar T.M., Huang H., "The pairwise attribute noise detection algorithm", Tech. Rep., Department of Computer Science, Florida Atlantic University, Boca Raton, FL (November 2004).

[51] Khoshgoftaar T.M., Rebours P., "Evaluating noise elimination techniques for software quality", *Intelligent Data Analysis: Internat. J.* **9** (5) (2005) 487–508.

[52] Hickey R.J., "Noise modeling and evaluating learning from examples", *Artificial Intelligence* **82** (1996) 157–179.

[53] Angluin D., Laird P., "Learning from noisy examples", *Machine Learning* **2** (1988) 343–370.

[54] Zhu X., Wu X., "Class noise vs. attribute noise: a quantitative study of their impacts", *Artificial Intelligence Rev.* **22** (2004) 177–210.

[55] Berenson M.L., Levine D.M., Goldstein M., *Intermediate Statistical Methods and Applications: A Computer Package Approach*, Prentice Hall, Englewood Cliffs, NJ, 1983.

[56] Quinlan J.R., *C4.5: Programs for Machine Learning*, Morgan Kaufmann, San Mateo, CA, 1993.

[57] Khoshgoftaar T.M., Yuan X., Allen E.B., Jones W.D., Hudepohl J.P., "Uncertain classification of fault-prone software modules", *Empirical Software Engrg.* **7** (4) (2002) 297–318.

[58] Friedman J., Stochastic J., Hastie T., Tibshirani R., "Additive logistic regression: A statistical view of boosting", *Ann. of Statist.* **28** (2) (2000) 337–374.

[59] Lin C.T., Lee C.S.G., *Neural Fuzzy Systems: A Neuro-Fuzzy Synergism to Intelligent Systems*, Prentice Hall, Upper Saddle River, NJ, 1996.

[60] Koza J.R., *Genetic Programming*, vol. 1, MIT Press, New York, 1992.

[61] Khoshgoftaar T.M., Seliya N., "Software quality classification modeling using the SPRINT decision tree algorithm", in: *Proceedings of the 14th International Conference on Tools with Artificial Intelligence, Washington, DC*, 2002, pp. 365–374.

[62] Komorowski J., Polkowski L., Skowron A., *Rough Set: A Tutorial*, Springer-Verlag, Berlin/New York, 1998.

[63] Domingos P., "Metacost: A general method for making classifiers cost-sensitive", in: *Knowledge Discovery and Data Mining*, 1999, pp. 155–164.

[64] Kohavi R., "The power of decision tables", in: Lavrač N., Wrobel S. (Eds.), *Proceedings of the 8th European Conference on Machine Learning, Heraclion, Crete, Greece*, in: *Lecture Notes in Artificial Intelligence*, Springer-Verlag, 1995, pp. 174–189.

[65] Freund Y., Mason L., "The alternating decision tree learning algorithm", in: *Proceedings of 16th International Conference on Machine Learning, Bled, Slovenia*, Morgan Kaufmann, 1999, pp. 124–133.

[66] Platt J.C., *Advances in Kernel Methods—Support Vector Training*, MIT Press, Cambridge, MA, 1999, pp. 185–208 (Chapter 12).

[67] Kolodner J., *Case-Based Reasoning*, Morgan Kaufmann, San Mateo, CA, 1993.

[68] Frank E., Witten I.H., "Generating accurate rule sets without global optimization", in: *Proceedings of the 15th International Conference on Machine Learning, Madison, WI*, Morgan Kaufmann, 1998, pp. 144–151.

[69] Holte R.C., "Very simple classification rules perform well on most commonly used datasets", *Machine Learning* **11** (1993) 63–91.

[70] Cohen W.W., "Fast effective rule induction", in: Prieditis A., Russell S. (Eds.), *Proceedings of the 12th International Conference on Machine Learning, Tahoe City, CA*, Morgan Kaufmann, 1995, pp. 115–123.

[71] Gaines B.R., Compton P., "Induction of ripple-down rules applied to modeling large databases", *J. Intelligent Inform. Systems* **5** (3) (1995) 211–228.

[72] Frank E., Trigg L., Holmes G., Witten I.H., "Naive Bayes for regression", *Machine Learning* **41** (1) (2000) 5–25.

[73] Peng J., Ertl F., Bhagotra S., Mosam A., Vijayaratnam N., Kanwal I., "Classification of U.S. census data, data Mining Project CS4TF3", http://www.census.gov.

[74] Atkeson C.G., Moore A.W., Schaal S., "Locally weighted learning", *Artificial Intelligence Rev.* **11** (1–5) (1997) 11–73.

[75] Khoshgoftaar T.M., Rebours P., "Generating multiple noise elimination filters with the ensemble-partitioning filter", in: *Proceedings of the 2004 IEEE International Conference on Information Reuse and Integration, Las Vegas, NV*, 2004, pp. 369–375.

[76] Jain R., *The Art of Computer Systems Performance Analysis: Techniques for Experimental Design, Measurement, Simulation, and Modeling*, John Wiley & Sons, New York, 1991.

# Requirements Management for Dependable Software Systems

## WILLIAM G. BAIL

*Software Engineering Center*
*The MITRE Corporation*
*McLean, VA*
*USA*

**Abstract**

Achieving dependable behavior from complex software systems requires careful adherence to best software practice. Experience gained over years of both failed development and successful efforts has clearly demonstrated that one essential key to developing systems is proper engineering of the requirements for that system. Systems that are mission and/or safety critical are especially vulnerable to shortcomings in the requirements specifications. What may be acceptable anomalies in the behaviors of non-critical systems become unacceptable and dangerous for systems on which high levels of trust are placed. Just as a good foundation is important for a building, requirements are important for software systems. This chapter provides an overview of the nature of requirements, presents some typical challenges that are frequently encountered, and provide some recommendations for how to avoid or overcome problems that may occur.

ADVANCES IN COMPUTERS, VOL. 66
ISSN: 0065-2458/DOI 10.1016/S0065-2458(05)66003-2

# 1.  Introduction

Over the past two decades, the size and complexity of software systems have grown significantly. Within large systems, more and more functionality is being allocated to the software portion, in recognition of its flexibility and power [22]. Many of these systems are being placed into service where, should failure occur, the potential for damage is significant. This damage may result in loss of service, financial losses, harm to property, and even loss of life. Recognizing this risk, the software engineering community has placed a great deal of emphasis on developing techniques aimed at minimizing the number of defects that are introduced into the system (*defect avoidance*), at detecting and removing latent defects (*defect removal*), and at tolerating the presence of defects (*fault tolerance*), with the overall goal of reducing our risks, and at the same time, making development more cost efficient.

Detecting and removing defects early is important. Industry experience shows that the effort and associated cost of removing defects from systems is significantly higher the later in the life cycle they are discovered. Metrics that support this experience were reported as early as 1981 [4]. This data indicated that the cost of removing defects after delivery was often 100 times more expensive than removing defects during the requirements or design phase. In a more recent article [5], the authors refined this observation somewhat, stating that the cost increase for small, non-critical systems to be about 5 times, although for large, complex systems, the multiplier was still about 100 times.

Davis [9] reported similar findings based on additional evidence, providing the values in Table I for relative costs to repair based on life cycle phase:

The lesson here is to avoid defects early in the development process. However, in a recent report for NASA, [3] described the results of a root-cause analysis performed in 1994 [23] of 387 software defects discovered during the integration test phase of the Voyager and Galileo spacecraft development efforts. The distribution of the defects is shown in Table II.

The analysis found that 74% of the defects were functional in nature. Of these, between 69% and 79% were "directly attributable to errors in understanding & implementing requirements" allocated to the system [3]. These numbers indicate that fully half of the system defects found during integration were due to requirements. Requirements, of course, are defined right at the beginning of development. Ref. [20]

TABLE I
RELATIVE COST TO REPAIR DEFECTS

| Phase when defect is detected | Relative cost to repair |
| --- | --- |
| Requirements analysis | 1 |
| Design | 5 |
| Coding | 10 |
| Unit test | 20 |
| Acceptance test | 50 |
| Operational/maintenance | 200 |

TABLE II
ROOT CAUSE OF DEFECTS

| Defect classification | Percentage of defects |
| --- | --- |
| Functional | 74% |
| Interface | 24% |
| Internal | 2% |

TABLE III
COST OF REPAIRING DEFECT BY PHASE

| | | Phase when defect introduced into system | | | | | |
|---|---|---|---|---|---|---|---|
| | | Req Anl | Design | Code | Test | Int | Operations |
| Phase when defect repaired | Req Anl | 1 | | | | | |
| | Design | 5 | 1 | | | | |
| | Code | 10 | 2 | 1 | | | |
| | Test | 50 | 10 | 5 | 1 | | |
| | Int | 130 | 26 | 13 | 3 | 1 | |
| | Operations | 368 | 64 | 37 | 7 | 3 | N.A. |

reports that more than half of the requirements defects discovered were due to tacit requirements, those that had not been written down.

The report also provided some more detailed metrics on the cost required to correct defects based on the life cycle phase they entered the software, and the phase when they were discovered and removed (see Table III). According to their results, a requirements defect costs 130 times more to remove during integration than it would cost if it were detected and removed during the requirements analysis phase. This is consistent with earlier results. Since half of the defects found during integration were due to requirements errors, the cost of not discovering them earlier represents a significant contribution to the overall project cost.

The results also indicate that the cost of removing a requirements defect during integration is ten times more costly than removing a coding defect during integration. These findings and others strongly suggest that minimizing defects in requirements is a key step in being able to affordably develop systems with low numbers of defects.

Over the years we have grown to recognize that despite our creating and applying more and more techniques, we simply do not have the ability to develop large, complex software systems that are completely free of defects [21]. We can neither develop them without defects, nor can we discover and remove all defects prior to placing the system into service. The sheer cost of finding and removing all defects is far more than we can afford. That means the system could fail at any time.

One of the most popular techniques is the use of extensive testing. We follow a process of "build-test-fix"—we test to find problems, fix the problems, and then test again, repeating this cycle until the application behaves the way we think it should. In this way, we hope to test quality in, as opposed to building quality in from the beginning. Much of this type of testing is focused on system-level tests, just prior to acceptance testing. The problem with this approach is that we are reacting to embedded defects in the system rather than proactively removing them prior to the testing phases. Such an approach tends to be expensive and time-consuming.

In this chapter we focus on the development of high-quality requirements as a way of improving the quality of our software systems. Some practitioners might say that while the requirements are important, a more important aspect is how the system is built. That is, the development processes are more crucial than the requirements, since without them, the requirements cannot be implemented. This observation is certainly valid—processes are indeed crucial. In fact, in this chapter we emphasize the importance of sound processes for developing requirements.

An important observation is that requirements form the foundation of all (software) system development. If we don't handle requirements properly, we incur significant risk. Many historical examples demonstrate this. If you do not clearly define what you want your system to do, you will have some (often unpleasant) surprises:

*"You get what you spec, not what you expect"*

The intent of this chapter is to describe the role of requirements, and how they should be managed, for dependable systems. Specifically, we will examine:

- *Requirements*—What is system is supposed to do, and to not-do (besides splitting infinitives).
- *Management*—The disciplined and planned process of control.
- *Dependable*—Predictable, confidence inspiring, satisfies a need with no sweat.
- *Software*—Programmable logic used to achieve behavior.
- *System(s)*—A device that satisfies a need or delivers a service.

Note that there is a large body of related work on this topic. Requirements development, requirements documentation, requirements management, dependability modeling, and other related topics have been documented many times in books, articles, journals, tutorial, and other papers. The references section of this chapter lists many of these. This chapter will not cover specific approaches to requirements definition (such as specific tools and techniques)—this is beyond our scope, and would duplicate the material that already exists on this topic. Instead we will characterize classes of these techniques, and provide recommendations for how to select the appropriate ones for projects of interest, specifically dependable systems.

In this chapter we focus on software system requirements. We presents a overview of requirements engineering with a particular focus on requirements for dependable systems. We emphasize the concepts behind "requirements" (as opposed to specific techniques) to provide a basis for whatever specific approaches may be selected by development teams. If the reader wishes to explore further, please refer to the references for additional material.

Specifically, this chapter contains eight sections:

- *Introduction*—the purpose and goals of this chapter, and an overview of what will be covered.
- *Dependability*—an introduction to the concept of and motivation behind dependability.
- *Nature of Requirements*—an introduction to system and software requirements, and how they are created. The various types of requirements, their role in development, and their impact on system success.
- *Categories of Requirements*—a description of the various categories of requirements.
- *Handling of Requirements*—a description of how each of the various types of requirements need to be handled.
- *Requirements Quality Attributes*—a description of criteria that can be used to determine the quality of a set of requirements for a system.
- *Requirements and Dependability*—an analysis of how the development and handling of requirements relates to the dependability needs of users.
- *Common Requirements Challenges*—an analysis of some common challenges to developing high-quality requirements.

## 2.  Dependability

Dependability is a quality of a system that is generally considered to be an important attribute of a high-quality system. We don't buy an application for our PC if we know that it is undependable. To help decide whether to buy a software package or not, we may depend on word of mouth or on reviews of software products published in magazines. If we are building a new system, we don't hire someone to develop it for us and state as a requirement that it needs to be undependable (*The system shall be undependable*). Yet, when defining the requirements for our new systems, we frequently do not directly address the desired (or expected) levels of dependability that we want and need. We define what we want it to do, its user interfaces, its functionality, and so on, but except for an occasional sentence stating that it needs to be "reliable," we generally associate "dependability" with the system's meeting its requirements, and leave any specific guidance unstated.

But as we observed in Section 1, no software system is perfect, that is, defect-free. There will always be embedded defects that may cause a system failure at some point, usually at the worst possible time. [8] observed that

> "debugging removes the minimum possible number of bugs that must be removed in order to pass the test sequence. For example, bugs outside the area of

test focus are not removed. This property appears to correspond with the informal principle called 'Murphy's law'."

If we were exceptionally cautious, no software system would ever be used in practice, especially for use in safety-critical activities. Yet we do use such systems. The Airbus A320 and the Boeing 777 are controlled by software. Despite appearances, we are neither foolish (at least, not all the time) nor exceptionally courageous. Rather, we rely on such systems only after we have become convinced that they serve our purposes with an acceptable level of risk. To do so, we establish mechanisms that allow us to make an informed judgment to place trust in the system, and base this judgment on evidence.

A primary aspect of this decision process is to clearly identify and define what we expect in terms of "dependability." We generally tolerate a certain level of "rough edges" as long as the services that we really care about are delivered. But we have to tell someone what we care about.

## 2.1   IFIP WG 10.4

But exactly what would a dependability requirement look like? There has been significant effort in the technical community directed at formalizing the concept of dependability, and at expanding the underlying concepts. Many organizations view dependability as being a combination of three common product attributes—reliability, maintainability, and maintainability (RMA). NASA, for example, initially adopted this view for the EOSDIS (Earth Observing System Data and Information System) project.

In 1980, the International Federation for Information Processing (IFIP) established within its Computer Systems Technology Technical Committee (TC 10) a new working group named "Dependable Computing and Fault Tolerance." WG 10.4 has defined *dependability* as:

> "The trustworthiness of a computing system which allows reliance to be justifiably placed on the service it delivers" http://www.dependability.org/wg10.4/

There are some key words in this definition:

- *trustworthiness*—the level of trust we can place on the system;
- *reliance*—the dependence on the system to perform a service;
- *justifiably*—substantiation that the reliance is appropriate, based on evidence;
- *service it delivers*—the specific services on which we place trust.

In other words, dependability is related to the level of trust we can place on a system that it will deliver a specific set of services. The definition implies that some form of justification is necessary to warrant placing this trust. Blind optimism is not sufficient.

This definition leaves out any specific reference to the nature of the services, how the reliance is to be justified, and how levels of trust can be determined. Subsequent work has expanded on this aspect.

## 2.2  The Dependability Tree

To provide more clarity, additional refinements of the concept of computer system dependability have been made, notably [1,16,18,19]. They define what they call the *Dependability Tree*, as depicted in Fig. 1.

In this model, dependability consists of three parts:

- The *dependability attributes* of the computing systems—these are defined by the system's requirements and are the factors that make up the level of trust that can be placed.

- The *means* or *mechanisms* to be used to achieve these attributes—these are addressed by the design features of the system.

- The *threats* to the systems that would compromise their achieving the desired attributes—these are the defects in the system that would cause failure.

The model defines the six dependability attributes as follows:

- *Availability*—the ability of the system to be ready for operation at any point in time. This is usually defined as the proportion of time that the system is ready

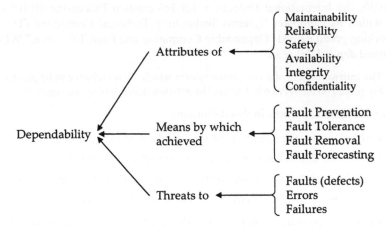

FIG. 1.  The dependability tree.

for use, to the total time period of interest. If, for example, the goal is for the system to be available for use for all but 4 seconds per year, then the availability is 0.9999999 over the year.

- *Reliability*—the ability of the system to operate for a period of time without failure. This is defined as either the failure rate (average failures per time period) or as the average operational time between failures, also referred to as the *mean time between failures* (MTBF). A typical reliability requirement would be a failure rate of 0.01 failures/hour, or, equivalently, a MTBF of 100 hours. Both specify that the system is required to operate continuously for 100 hours on the average before failing.

- *Safety*—the ability of the system to avoid actions that result in catastrophic actions that result in human injury, large financial loss, or damage to important assets. This includes actions that are required as well as actions that must be avoided.

- *Confidentiality*—the ability of the system to avoid disclosure of information to unauthorized recipients.

- *Integrity*—the ability of the system to avoid being corrupted. This attribute covers the correctness and consistency of the software code and the data structures that contain the information being processed, as well as the system's ability to avoid corruption while it is executing. It includes protection against unauthorized modification or destruction of the information and the code.

- *Maintainability*—the ability of the system to be easily repaired, enhanced, or modernized.

Note that reliability and availability are interrelated concepts that are not necessarily in synchronization. That is, a system could have high levels of availability yet have high failure rates. This would occur whenever the system is able to recover quickly from each failure. A system could also have low failure rates and low levels of availability. This would be the case if the recovery times are long yet infrequent.

## 2.3   Information Assurance (IA)

There is a related framework that has recently been developed by the United States Department of Defense called Information Assurance (IA) [11]. IA consists of five system attributes [24] that are designed to characterize the ability of the system to protect and defend information and information systems. Of these five, three are the same as in the Dependability Tree: availability, integrity, and confidentiality. There are two attributes that have been added:

- *Authentication*—A security measure designed to establish the validity of a transmission, message, or originator, or a means of verifying an individual's authorization to receive specific categories of information.
- *Non-repudiation*—An assurance that the sender of data is provided with proof of delivery and the recipient is provided with proof of the sender's identity, so neither can later deny having processed the data.

The IA model is one aspect of dependability that focuses totally on the security of the information being processed by a system. These two attributes are definable as specific behavioral requirements that can be addressed with functional requirements.

## 2.4  Acceptability

The Dependability Tree model provides a useful context in which system dependability can be viewed. Since its introduction, there have been various refinements and extensions proposed, including the creation of a System Acceptability Model [10, 27]. In these refinements, the concept of stakeholder acceptance was added to reflect the roles of the customers and users in the operation of the system. Figure 2 shows this model.

Consideration of stakeholders is an important facet, since acceptance of a system is often based on more than its simple dependability. Stakeholders want a high-quality system that meets their needs, but that can be made available when they need it and at a price they can afford (*practical acceptability*). Rather than having a single set of fixed expectations, stakeholders frequently trade-off various features: functionality versus delivery of system, reliability versus ease-of use, etc., based on their needs. For example, lower levels of reliability might be acceptable if the availability of the

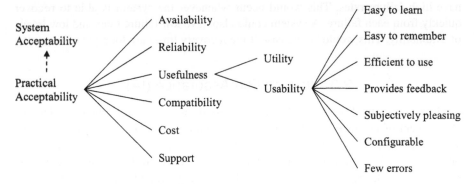

FIG. 2. Sandhu's system acceptability model.

system is enhanced. A higher priced system might be acceptable if it is of higher quality.

When deciding whether to accept a system, there are multiple factors that stakeholders take into account. They are concerned with how well the system conforms to the requirements that were imposed. They also want the system to be suitable for use. That is, the requirements for the system need to appropriate for how the system will be used. Part of this consideration is how easy the system is to use. Another part is whether the specific capabilities and functions provided smoothly fit into the way that the users expect to operate once the system is placed into service. They also want the cost to be controlled and affordable, and they want the system delivered and placed into service in a timely manner so that they may gain utility from it.

All of these factors are considered by customers when they decide whether to accept a system or not. Using Sandhu's Acceptability Model as a basis, we added these other factors, and defined the following framework for defining and evaluating the acceptability of a system based on its dependability. See Fig. 3.

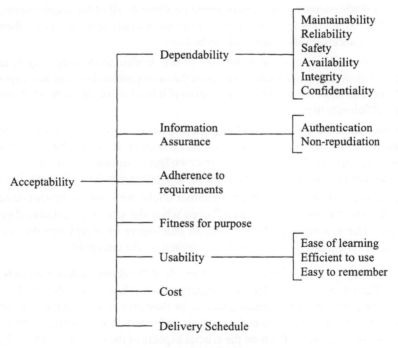

FIG. 3.  Acceptability framework.

In this framework, a customer or user's acceptance of a system depends on several interrelated factors, not just purely on dependability. Several dependability-specific attributes as well as IA were added to Sandhu's model to reflect the nature of the trade-offs that customers need to make. This being the case, when defining dependability requirements, all relevant factors need to be considered as contributors to the decision of whether to buy or build a system or not.

Factors that contribute to the decision, in addition to the dependability attributes discussed previously, include:

- *Adherence to requirements*—this attribute addresses the proportion of the requirements that the system successfully supports. Because not all requirements are generally equally important or critical, users are willing to accept products that do not deliver all of the services that the requirements define. Any limitations to the use of the product can be offset by the utility actually delivered. A similar situation may occur if the services that are delivered do not correspond to those defined in the requirements. If the services can satisfy the users' needs, then the system might still be acceptable.

- *Fitness for purpose*—the system might conform to all of the requirements, but if they do not define the services that the users really want and need, then the level of acceptability is not likely to be high.

- *Usability*—the system has to be easy to use. It also needs to be easy to learn. Limitations in usability can render even the most powerful system unacceptable. Users can however accept a system, even if it hard to use, if the level of service is sufficiently high.

- *Cost*—the cost to develop and acquire a system, as well as the cost to operate the system, must be within the customer's budget. It is a cliché that software development projects are usually over budget. Customers may be willing to accept the additional cost if the value of the system is sufficiently high for them.

- *Delivery and schedule*—There is another cliché for software system development: the "software is 90% done," even when the scheduled delivery date has past. The flexibility in the schedule is one aspect of acceptance that can be traded off against the other attributes desired by the customer.

When defining the requirements for a system, all of the above factors need to be addressed. Each needs to be defined as accurately as possible to ensure that the developers are able to perform appropriate tradeoffs as they progress through development. Knowing this emphasis, developers can make informed design and implementation decisions, focusing their efforts on the crucial aspects of the system as defined by the future users of the system.

In addition, the nature of the reliance must be defined. The need is based on the re-alization that dependability has several interpretations. The precise nature of what is expected, and the allowable variations, must be described. For example, do the users require total conformance to specification, or will they tolerate degraded levels? Will they accept optional back-up features to provide recovery operations, or is the prime feature the what they require? The reliance will be characterized by an *acceptability function* which captures the customer's perception of value and willingness to accept degradation in various capabilities.

## 2.5    System Quality

As described in the previous section, stakeholders want a high-quality system that meets their needs, but that can be made available when they need it and at a price they can afford. With this view, acceptability has four major components:

- *Quality*—the system possesses attributes of sufficient quality.
- *Meets stakeholder needs*—the system provides services that the stakeholders need.
- *Schedule*—the system will be available for use when needed by the stakehold-ers.
- *Cost*—acquiring the system is affordable.

In this context, we can refine our general concept of system quality, by recogniz-ing that the quality attributes of a system are a subset of the overall acceptability attributes, as shown in the shaded area of Fig. 4. Quality is an attribute of a system that can be determined independently of cost and schedule, although achieving high levels of quality generally requires larger budgets and more time for development. The quality of a system is also independent of whether the system is suited for any specific user's needs. A stakeholder may decide to purchase a system of less over-all quality if that system is more suitable for how the stakeholder plans to use the system.

## 2.6    Types of Failure

There are several different ways that our systems can fail. These are addressed by [1] as the failure modes. Perhaps the most obvious and visible form is the system's crashing, requiring a reboot. On a personal computer, for example, this could be identified by a frozen screen, a non-responsive cursor, and the inability of a Control–Alt–Delete (for Windows-based PCs) to regain control. For a PC, pressing the power

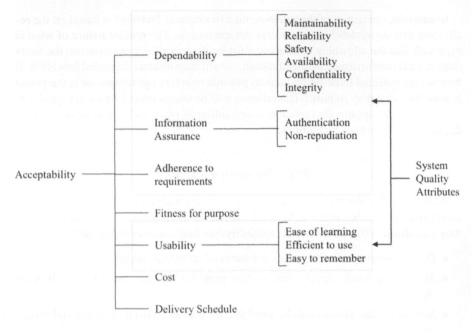

FIG. 4. System quality attributes.

button and forcing a complete reboot is a potential recovery strategy. For an embedded system, the failure may be observed by the system's no longer being operational.

There are other types of failure, some of which may be more subtle and harder to spot. These include (but are not limited to):

- The currently-active application hangs—in this situation, the application that is being used becomes non-responsive but the system continues to operate. For a Window-based PC, for example, the recovery techniques involves pressing Control, Alt, and Delete keys, allowing the user to abort the application and return control to the operating system.

- The currently-active application crashes—in this situation, the application that is being used aborts, returning control to the operating system. For an embedded system that has no operating system, the system will become non-operational.

- An application produces an incorrect result—when asking an application for information, the answers provided are incorrect—that is, do not satisfy the requirements. One effect of incorrect result would be the system's performing an incorrect action, potentially threatening safety or the compromise of information. Another effect is providing incorrect results as information to the users of the system, who may use the information to perform actions that could also threaten safety.

– Responds too slowly or too quickly—an application responds too slowly or perhaps too quickly. An example would be a program that on an assembly line controls part placement on a series of products. If the program is too fast, the assembly has not yet arrived and the part drops unused. If the part is too slow, the partially-assembled product continues down the assembly line without the part that it needs.

For many, the system's crashing is the most obvious form of failure. More subtle, and often more damaging, is when the system delivers an incorrect result. Incorrect information or actions on the part of the system could be innocuous, annoying, or dangerous.

When a system fails, it is often unable to deliver its services until it is corrected in some way, such as by rebooting. The proportion of time that the system is able to provide services is known as its *availability*.

When a system fails by producing an incorrect result, the concept of recovery is complex—it may appear to outside observers that the system is still operational. However, the incorrect result may be a one time effect based on input data, indicating that it indeed may be operational, or it could be an indication that the system has entered an erroneous program state, and that all future actions are suspect and potentially incorrect.

Two types of failure associated with erroneous results that present particularly hard challenges to developers are those that are *intermittent* and those that are caused by *Heisenbugs*. Intermittent failures are those that occur seemingly randomly. Recreating them in order to correct them can at times be time consuming and expensive, since determining and recreating the exact state in which the failures occur is not always possible. Such failures, until their root cause is determined, present a continuing risk of system failure when using the system.

*Heisenbugs* [7] are defects in a system that cause observable failures, such as erroneous output values. However, when developers attempt to identify their location using instrumentation, inserting logging statement, or turning on debugging, the failures disappear. They are called Heisenbugs after the Heisenberg Uncertainty Principle used in quantum physics because of their ability to disappear when being examined. Note that the term is commonly misused to refer to defects that cause random failures.

Software users, selfishly so, expect the systems they use to be completely dependable. But users may be unwilling to pay the cost of developing such systems. In practice, experienced users learn the various behaviors of the programs that they work with, including those areas that are not dependable. When using the program, they simply avoid those unreliable features, and work their way around them. Sometimes this is unacceptable however when those features are critical to what the users need.

It is important to note that in a formal sense, a failure of a software system is a observable variation from its required behavior, given the state of the system. If however the requirements do not define the behavior that is needed and appropriate, to the user the system has failed even if the requirements are fully met. If the requirements are not complete, and fail to describe all of the needed capabilities, the system can be, in a strict sense, correct but unusable. Safety-related behaviors often fall into this category. Many safety requirements are stated in terms of actions to avoid (*the system shall not allow the car to move forward when a passenger door is open*). If not all of these behaviors are described, that is, if there is a failure mode that was unanticipated, then the system could pass all of its requirements tests, yet still be unusable.

## 3. Nature of Requirements

In this section we will introduce the concept of a "requirement." Understanding what requirements are, where they come from, and how they mature through the system development process, is crucial so that we can effectively capture and document the customers expectations and needs. Knowing the range of criteria with which the customer will base their acceptance of the system provides a clear roadmap for development, and allows us to balance engineering decisions. Core to this, of course, is understanding what the customer expects as a dependable system. Regardless of how much functionality the system provides, if the customer does not view the system as being "dependable," they will simply not use it.

### 3.1  IEEE Definition of Requirement

Requirements form the foundation of all software development. They tell the developers what to build. They guide the design and implementation by providing to the developers the "form, fit, and function" of the product. They provide a means of communications between the customers, users, and developers to ensure that the resulting product is what the users need and the customers want. They provide a basis for defining criteria to be used for acceptance of the final product by the customer. Finally, they support product maintenance and enhancements by documenting the final "as-built" product.

Despite this central role, however, there are many different views about what a system or software requirement is. The effect of this disparity of views is a lack of consistency in how requirements and defined and managed across industry. In this section, we will try to establish a baselines of definitions to assist in achieving a common, coordinated view.

The term "requirement" is defined in IEEE Std. 610.12-1990, IEEE Standard Glossary of Software Engineering Terminology [14] as:

> "(1) A condition or capability needed by a user to solve a problem or achieve an objective.
> (2) A condition or capability that must be met or possessed by a system or system component to satisfy a contract, standard, specification, or other formally imposed documents.
> (3) A documented representation of a condition or capability as in (1) or (2).
> See also: design requirement; functional requirement; implementation requirement; interface requirement; performance requirement; physical requirement."

This definition is necessarily broad since it has to cover the many variations of popular usage. Unfortunately, as a result, the term is often used carelessly to refer to several different concepts. Drawing on its definition within English, popular use is to apply the term to refer to anything that is "required" for a project. Often items referred to as requirements include hopes, dreams, budgets, schedules ("This schedule is required". . ."This budget is required". . ."These software (SW) components must be used". . ."These algorithms must be used". . .)

As we shall see, while each of the statements refers to a requirement, each refers to a different *type* of requirement. Each type needs to be handled differently since each has a different role and affects software development in different ways. In the next section we focus on differentiating the different types of requirements and on providing recommendations on how to handle them appropriately. All requirements (in any sense of the word) are important in some way—they just need to be understand in the context of their meaning. When working with critical and dependable systems, careful management of these different types of requirements is crucial, since each influences dependability in different ways.

For additional clarification, let us refer to IEEE Std. 830-1998—*IEEE Recommended Practice for Software Requirements Specifications* [15]:

> "A requirement specifies an externally visible function or attribute of a system."

This definition narrows the scope considerably. Instead of using the term "requirement" to refer to anything that is "required," IEEE Std. 830-1998 defines it to be a specification of externally-visible behavior. That is, requirements deal with the inputs and the outputs of the system, but not what happens inside the system. We need to be clear about how we use this term however, since the word actually refers to several different concepts.

For the context of this chapter, we assert that for any specific product, the behavioral requirements for that product specify its externally visible behavior, that is, behavior as seen by other systems outside of the system of interest.

## 3.2   Derivation of Requirements

In understanding how we need to manage requirements, it is important to understand where requirements come from and how they evolve from general concepts to clearly defined behaviors.

Overall there are six types of activities that are involved in creating requirements. These are not sequential but rather interdependent. Not all of these would be performed for every system. Some may have been completed, either explicitly or implicitly, beforehand. This may be the case for systems with clearly defined needs where a lot of rationale and trade studies would be wasted effort. Many systems however need a complete requirements analysis to ensure that the system is appropriate and dependable.

The six activities are:

- Identify the need for the system.
- Characterize the operational environment.
- Select a strategy to satisfy the needs.
- Define the capabilities.
- Define the way the system will be used.
- Define the requirements.

### 3.2.1   Identify the Need for the System

The purpose of this activity is to determine why a system is required. Systems are built in order to provide automated services that cannot easily or efficiently be satisfied by other means. These needs can range from being very simple (a thermostat to regulate temperature in a room) to very complicated (avionics wing surface controls for aircraft). As a first step, it is important to identify the benefits of relying on a system as balanced against the risks associated with any potential failures of the system. If the benefits are not clear and compelling, the decision to buy or build a system might not be appropriate. In many situations this decision is easy—an author would simply buy a word processing system in order to write the next great novel. In other cases, however, the decision might not be as straightforward. The cost of either building or buying a system might exceed the benefits that would be realized from using it. When completing this activity, either the need for the system has been identified and justified, or there is no need, and no further action is required. Note that there is no decision yet regarding whether a system should be built, an existing system should be purchased, or an existing system should be modified. The strategy for how to achieve the services has not yet been defined.

As an example, suppose that a manager for a particular building is being required to keep a record of the environmental conditions in his building. He may already have a computerized building environmental control system, but this system might not provide for keeping records. He therefore has a need to collect the appropriate information regarding the building's environment.

### 3.2.2   Characterize the Operational Environment

The purpose of this activity is to identify and define the characteristics of the environment in which the system will operate. This includes other systems with which the system will interact, physical attributes (temperature, weather, sensors, control devices, ...), and any human operators and users. This information is crucial since systems rarely exist in a vacuum (unless they are on spacecraft). As such, it is important to understand the environment so that the role of the system and how it will interoperate with other parts of the environment can be more clearly defined. Once developed, the characterization will assist in understanding the roles of the various elements in the environment, will support devising a strategy to provide the needed services, and will assist in developing the user scenarios. In many situations, the environment will already be well understood. In others, the environment will contain many unknowns, especially if the system is to be used in a new environment. Developing requirements in the presence of many unknowns is a risky activity.

Continuing the example of the building manager, the result of characterizing the relevant elements of the operational environment may look like Fig. 5. Note that this picture only illustrates the major items in the environment. A full description of the environment would include the operational characteristics of each item, including input/output descriptions, formats of messages, patterns of activity, etc.

### 3.2.3   Select a Strategy to Satisfy the Needs

This activity could be also described as defining the overall systems architecture. The goal is to describe the various software and hardware assets, as well as the people who will compose the system, that will, as a whole, satisfy the needs that had been identified. There will generally be several alternative approaches to how the system can be designed. The developers will perform tradeoffs among the alternatives, weighing the benefits and weaknesses of each relative to fulfilling the users' needs.

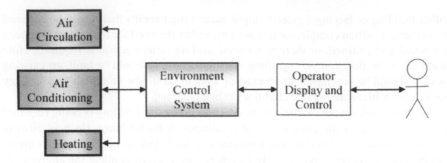

FIG. 5. Example of an operational environment.

Some alternatives may take advantage of assets already present in the operational environment. If existing systems can provide some or all of the services directly, there is no sense in developing a new system. Other alternatives may require that one or more new systems may have to be built that will provide the needed services. The strategy needs to be closely coordinated with the operational environment to ensure that all viable solutions are identified and considered.

Revisiting our building manager, after considering the possible alternatives for satisfying the need for a way to collect the history of, and create reports for, the building environment, he may decide to augment the existing systems with two new systems, one to record the environmental data, the other to create reports based on the histories. This system design is shown in Fig. 6.

### 3.2.4   Define the Capabilities

Once the overall strategy has been formulated, the next step is to identify the specific capabilities that will have to be provided by each part of the system environment. At this point, the requirements have not yet been refined to the point where they can be viewed as actual requirements. Rather, they are most commonly described in general terms that can be referred to as *capabilities*. Based on the strategy developed previously, this assignment can take different forms. If the strategy involves using existing systems, the capabilities can be assigned to the existing systems. If the strategy requires modifying existing systems, the nature of these changes needs to be defined. Finally, if one or more new systems are needed, then the necessary newly-defined capabilities need to be allocated to these systems. The product of this stage is a definition of a set of capabilities and a mapping of these capabilities to various assets, both old and new, in the overall operational environment. This stage is an additional refinement of the systems design, since it expands on the initial design by more precisely describing the individual systems that form the architecture and the

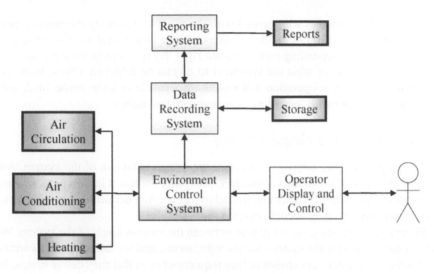

FIG. 6. Overall strategy (system design).

relationships between the systems. Just as with the previous activity, this stage will involve performing tradeoffs among the various alternatives.

Continuing our example, our building manager may have defined the capabilities as follows:

- The Data Recording System will be capable of sampling the environmental data as measured by the Environment Control System, and saving this information for future use.

- The Reporting System will be capable of creating reports based on the historic data, and printing these for the building manager.

- The Environment Control System will retain its current capabilities, which will be augmented by the capability of providing its real-time environmental data to the Data Recording System.

### 3.2.5  Define the Operational Scenarios

This activity captures and describes the different ways that the system will operate, including how the users will interact with it. Various alternative situations will be identified, with the goal of describing as many possible modes of operations as feasible. These descriptions will form the basis for more detailed operational scenarios. The product of this activity is a characterization of the expected ways that the users (including other systems) will interact with the product, to satisfy the needs identified previously. The form of the descriptions may be in a formal notation [25], or it may be in English, depending on the desired rigor. By developing these scenarios, a better understanding of what the system is to do can be achieved. Often, such scenarios reveal modes of operation that would otherwise have gone unspecified, only to occur during operation, potentially causing a system failure.

### 3.2.6  Define the Requirements

The purpose of this activity is to define the actual behaviors of the system. Additional detail is added to the capabilities, providing sufficient information to allow development to proceed. Generally, the behaviors are first defined in a general form, and are refined until they become exact definitions.

There is an interesting interplay here between the various levels of the system. We have requirements for the system, for the subsystems, and for the components within each subsystem. Each set consists of true requirements, in that they define externally visible behavior. But the items for which the requirements are allocated differ. This observation is further analyzed in the next section. At this stage, there needs to be a great deal of detail in the descriptions of the behaviors. The building manager, for example, will know the exact key strokes needed to create a report, and will know the various options for the format of the reports.

## 3.3   Hierarchies of Requirements

One important feature of this process is the prominent role played by trade-off analyses. As each stage is completed, the degrees of freedom available to the developer are narrowed as they analyze each alternative and weigh the advantages and disadvantages of each alternative. The general flow of this process can be illustrated as shown in Fig. 7.

As this process flows from the system level down to the system design level, we are creating different levels of requirements. The first set defined are those for the overall system. Next we define requirements for each subsystem, and then for each of the components within that subsystem (if there are subsystems). The requirements for the system define the behavior visible to observers outside of the system. At this level, the behaviors of each of the subsystems are essentially hidden, although some of these subsystems may have interfaces directly to the "outside." Figure 8 illustrates this concept.

For any specific system/subsystem/component, its design consists of two closely related items:

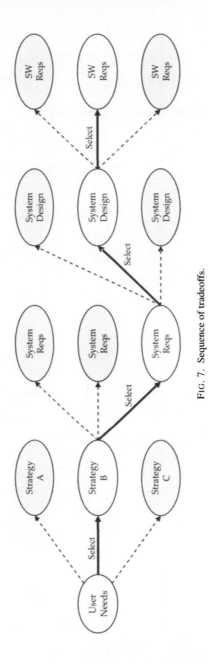

FIG. 7.  Sequence of tradeoffs.

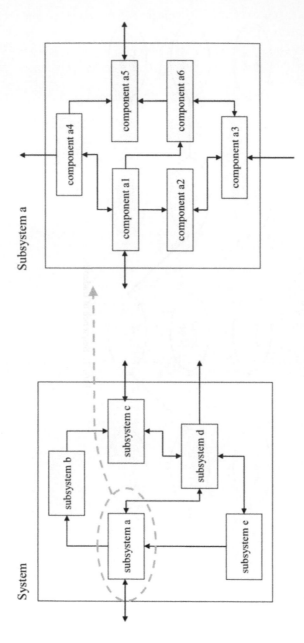

FIG. 8. Components within a system.

- the *requirements* for each of its constituent components (defining the behavior of the components);
- the *interrelationships* between the components. That is, the way that the components interact to fulfill the behaviors required for the component.

In particular, at the system level, the interaction of its subsystems produces the behavior of parent component as a composition.

At each level, we will produce a set of requirements that describe the behavior at that level. We will then end up with requirements at the system level, at each subsystem level, and at each component level, as seen in Fig. 9.

When systems are developed, one common effect is that the system requirements are typically defined at a less-precise level than the software requirements, particularly for those behaviors that will be produced by the software. As development proceeds, these requirements will become more precise. Unfortunately, it is not a common practice to maintain the system requirements documentation up to date to reflect this refinement.

When we document requirements, we need to be clear about to which level and to which component each requirement applies. Failure to do so is likely to cause confusion when the system is being developed. For large, complex systems, the activities described above (particularly steps 4, 5, and 6) are repeated several times as each successive layer of the system is defined. It is crucial to allow sufficient time for each requirement analysis activity to operate. For example, attempts to short-circuit development schedule by providing system requirements directly to software developers and skipping the software-level requirements analysis, is a false savings. Generally, the system-level requirements are not in a form or level of maturity appropriate for initiating implementation. Figure 10 illustrates a sequence that supports this concept.

For the purpose of this chapter, we will focus primarily on two different levels of requirements:

- the *system requirements*, defined for the entire system to be produced including hardware, software, and perhaps human operators;
- the *software requirements*, defined for the software components that are part of the overall system.

## 4.  Categories of Requirements

As suggested by IEEE Std. 610.12-1990, there are several different categories of requirements. The identification of these categories vary across industry (for example [12]). However, the categories most commonly used are:

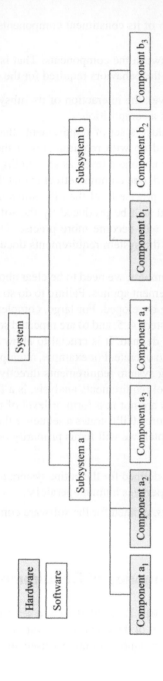

FIG. 9. Levels of requirements.

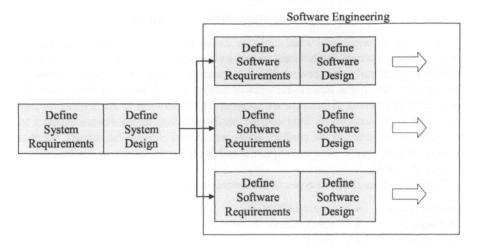

FIG. 10. Relationship of system requirements analysis to software requirements analysis.

- *Behavioral requirements*—these are associated with externally visible behaviors of a system. They are also referred to as functional specifications or functional requirements.

- *Quality of construction requirements*—these address those characteristics of a system that are associated with the system's construction. They are qualitative attributes of an item, such as usability and portability. As such, they are often not directly observable, and usually deal with how the product can be handled.

- *Implementation requirements*—these are also called *implementation constraints* and *design constraints*—they consist of restrictions placed on developers that constrain the form and style of how they built the system, thereby limiting their design space. For example, the developers may be required to use a specific algorithm, a customer-preferred design style, or specific reusable components, both COTS and others.

- *Programmatic requirements*—these deal with the terms and conditions imposed as a part of a contract and are exclusive of behavioral requirements. They generally deal with items like cost, schedule, and organizational structures. These are also often called *programmatic requirements*.

We will look at each of these categories in more detail in the following sections.

## 4.1    Behavioral Requirements

This category represents what might be called the core of requirements that we work with for systems. Behavioral requirements define the visible behavior of the products, specifically the services that the system is to deliver. These requirements specify behavior that is observable without having to look inside of the system. As such, all requirements of this type are (potentially) observable or measurable by testing. That is, we can verify their correct implementation in a software product by testing them. We execute the product, apply inputs, and observe the outputs. We then compare the outputs to what was expected as defined by the requirements themselves such as an oracle.

There are seven different types of behavioral requirements:

- Functional
- Interface
- Temporal
- Capacity
- Resource utilization
- Trustworthiness
- Usability

### 4.1.1   Functional Requirements

This type of requirement addresses functional input-output behavior that can be expressed in terms of responses to stimuli. That is, for every input that is applied to a component, a specific output is defined

$$output = fn \ (input)$$

For example, the functional requirements for a module could be defined as a table of values (see Table IV).

Usually the function to be performed is more complicated than this example, and cannot expressed simply as a table of inputs and outputs. In some cases, the function can be expressed in mathematical terms:

$$output = 5 * square\text{-}root \ (input)$$

The table format can be combined with mathematical expressions (see Table V).

| TABLE IV |  |
|----------|--|
| EXAMPLE—TABLE OF VALUES | |
| Input | Output |
| 1 | 5 |
| 2 | 3 |
| 3 | 7 |
| otherwise | 0 |

| TABLE V |  |
|---------|--|
| EXAMPLE—TABLE WITH FUNCTIONS | |
| Input | Output |
| $< 0$ | 0 |
| $\geqslant 0$ | square-root (input) |

Often, the required behavior is too complex to be defined in terms of just input/output. In the examples above, the behavior is memory-less. That is, the output is strictly a function of the current input. However, many interesting behaviors depend not just on the current inputs, but also on the history of inputs. Such behaviors can be described using more sophisticated techniques such as state transition tables, formal methods, etc. They can also be defined using less sophisticated techniques, such as English. The less precisely they are defined, the more the likelihood for misinterpretation.

The key aspect of a functional requirement is that as a result of an input, there is an observable output. Consider the following statement:

> "Whenever a new temperature input is received, the software will compute a running average of the temperatures received."

This statement describes no externally visible behavior. As such it cannot be directly tested. This statement therefore is not a functional requirement, but rather an implementation constraint (see Section 4.3).

### 4.1.2   Interface Requirements

Requirements of this type deal with the characteristics of system's interfaces, that is, the windows through which the outside world views the system (and vice versa). Interfaces fall into three broad types, as illustrated in Fig. 11:

- *Peer-to-peer interfaces*—through which the system interacts and exchanges information with other systems.
- *User interfaces*—that interact with human operators. This type includes design of user interface displays.
- *Computing infrastructure interfaces*—that deal with capabilities provided by lower-level elements, needed by the system for operation. Examples include messaging middleware APIs and operating system interfaces.

Interfaces are particularly important. Failure to adequately define system interfaces has resulted at times in rather dramatic and expensive failures. For example, NASA's Mars Polar Orbiter crashed onto the surface of Mars partially because of an interface error.

### 4.1.3   Temporal Requirements

Temporal requirements deal with observable behaviors that are associated with time. They are usually associated with specific functional requirements by establishing bounds on the latency of the responses and actions taken by the system. Sample requirements of this type include those that focus on *speed*, *latency*, and *throughput* of functional behaviors. Examples include:

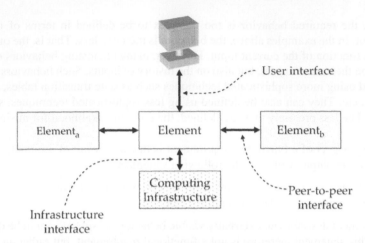

FIG. 11. Types of interfaces.

- *Speed*—how quickly functions are performed, e.g., "Display refreshed screen every 0.5 sec."
- *Latency*—how long processing takes for functions, e.g., "Transmit filtered data within 2 sec of receiving unfiltered data."
- *Throughput*—how much processing can take place in a specific period of time, e.g., "Process 10,000 database requests per hour."

### 4.1.4   Capacity Requirements

Capacity requirements deal with the amount of information or services that can be handled by the component or system. These are important since they establish the way that the system can be used. If the capacity needs are not clearly defined, developers might underestimate what is needed and the users will find the system unusable. On the other hand, developers might provide too many resources, making the system expensive and resource-intensive. Examples include:

- "The system shall be able to support 25 simultaneous users."
- "The system shall be able to manage up to 20,000 employee records."

### 4.1.5   Resource Utilization

This type of requirement addresses the infrastructure resources needed by the system as it is operating. In many cases, a product may be introduced into an existing environment and must share resources with other systems. In other cases, due to constraints on budget, hardware availability, etc., there may be limitations on computer resources that are available and can be used. When buying a shrink-wrapped software application at a store, the boxes containing the application usually describe the expected operating environment. A product might state that it can operate on Microsoft® Windows®[1] 2000 or Microsoft® Windows® XP, on an Intel® Pentium®[2]-based computer with a minimum of 250 MB memory and 10 MB available disk storage. Typical requirements of this type include:

- *Memory usage*—e.g., "The system may use no more than 250 MB core memory during execution." (also known as *main* memory or *RAM* memory).

- *Processor usage*—e.g., "The system has a limit of 20% of total processor cycles (loading) average over 24 hours, and a limit of 60% of total processor cycles peak."

- *Storage usage*—e.g., "The system shall use no more than 5 GB disk storage for logging data."

- *Communication usage*—e.g., "The system shall use no more than 50% of the available channel capacity at any time during operation."

## 4.1.6   Trustworthiness

Trustworthiness requirements describe the desired levels of confidence that users can place on the product's ability to provide their required services. There requirements are sometimes referred to as "dependability" requirements, but to avoid confusion with the dependability attributes described earlier, we will use a different term. In general requirements of this type cannot be verified directly despite their being externally visible. This is because they express levels of confidence that are not directly measurable, and in order to verify that they have been successfully implemented, a collection of observations must be made that, taken as a whole, is used to form an argument of success. No single test can verify the presence of the requirement.

For some products, the level of trustworthiness might not be a significant concern, either because the impact of failure might not be significant, or because the environment in which the product is being used can tolerate failures. For other products however, being able to trust the delivery of service is of significant concern because of the role that the system plays. Whenever the services provided by the system are critically needed, the requirements become more critical.

---

[1] Microsoft® and Windows® are registered trademarks of Microsoft Inc. in the United States and/or other countries.

[2] Intel® and Pentium® are registered trademarks of Intel Corporation or its subsidiaries in the United States and other countries.

Of the dependability attributes described in Section 2 (Dependability and Information Assurance) five are associated with trustworthiness:

- *Reliability.*
- *Availability.*
- *Safety.*
- *Confidentiality.*
- *Integrity* (partial association).

The remaining dependability attributes (maintainability, authentication, and non-repudiation) are not considered to be trustworthiness requirements.

- *Maintainability* is a quality requirement. This type is described in Section 4.2.
- *Authentication* and *non-repudiation* are functional requirements since they address specific behaviors.

*Integrity* has a mixed relationship since it covers two aspects of a system:

- *Integrity of operation* is a feature of a system that protects it from being corrupted while it is operational. With the rise of viruses, worms, spyware, and other insidious software that target operational systems, systems must have protection against being infiltrated by such threats. Systems must also be able to detect and counter attempts to modify data used by the system for operation. This aspect of integrity is a trustworthiness requirement, because the negative effects are visible externally, but the ability to resist such attacks cannot be proven with certainty through testing.
- *Integrity of construction* is a feature of a system's design and construction that deals with the ability of the system's resources to be protected from unauthorized modification. Such resources include its source code, its executable modules, its internal databases, and other artifacts that form the system itself. This aspect of integrity is quality requirement (Section 4.2).

When we work with systems that are expected to evidence high levels of dependability, trustworthiness requirements are of primary importance.

### 4.1.7 Usability

Usability requirements deal with how easy it is for an operator to make use of the system. Because there are two basic types of operators (humans and other systems), there are different approaches to expressing these requirements. In general, usability when applied to system-to-system interfaces deals with the complexity of the interfaces, their ease of implementation, and their efficiency of operation. When applied to human operators, usability deals with the complexity of the interfaces relative to the how operators can operate with them, the ease of learning, and the efficiencies with which operators can exploit the services provided by the system.

Usability requirements cannot be directed verified, since they involve subjective behaviors that often have to be collected over time.

## 4.2 Quality of Construction Requirements

The second major category of requirements are those that address the quality of the construction of the software (as opposed to the quality of any of the associated work products, such as the requirements documents). These requirements do not specifically address behavioral attributes of the product, but rather, they deal with how the product can be handled. They are affected by the design and code patterns used to develop the system, since these patterns influence how we can work with the product. Quality of construction requirements are not directly measurable and in order to gain insight into their implementation, we need to rely on indirect measures that help us infer the level of quality of the component. These measures typically focus on identifying patterns within the code. Evaluation of how well a specific system achieves these requirements tends to be based on subjective and heuristic criteria.

In the literature you may see many different kinds of factors included in this category. However, many of the popular ones belong in other categories because they focus on different aspects of the system. For example, *usability* is often viewed as a quality requirement. In fact, it is better associated with the behavioral requirements since it deals with externally visible behaviors of the system. It is important to correctly categorize requirements so that they can be managed appropriately throughout development, test, and operation.

Some examples of quality requirements include:

- *Portability*—the ease with which a product can be ported from one platform to another. An example would be moving a product that executes on a Windows® XP / Intel® Pentium® platform, to run on an Apple® Macintosh® platform running OS®[3] X. Companies who develop and sell personal computer applications often need to provide their products on both platforms. To make this porting easier, they design their software to minimize dependencies on the underlying computer and operating system. These companies define a portability requirement for their products. The degree to which this factor is achieved in a system affects the effort required to move the product from one platform to another.

- *Maintainability*—the ease with which a product can be fixed when defects are discovered. Since complex software systems always have defects, requirements

---

[3] Apple®, Macintosh®, and Mac OS® are trademarks of Apple Computer, Inc. registered in the U.S. and other countries.

are placed on the system that they be maintainable. This places a need on the developers to design the system in such a way that repairs are facilitated. This is often known as design for repair (DFR). Developer of hardware products, such as irons, toasters, and automobiles have another approach known as design for assembly (DFA). In this latter approach, the focus is on designing the product to make it easier to build. DFA and DFR are often opposing goals. In software, since the system is complete once it is designed, DFA has traditionally not been an issue. The degree to which a system is maintainable affects the effort required to correct defects.

- *Extensibility*—the ease with which product can be enhanced with new functionality. Systems are rarely static. Once delivered and placed into service, users typically make suggestions for improvements. The environments in which systems operate are seldom static. Changes in the environment usually require changes to the system. Commercial products add new features in order to stay competitive with other products. If a system is designed to be extensible, such changes can be achieved cost effectively. If a system is not extensible, at times it may be more cost effective to build a new system from scratch than to attempt to extend the current one.

- *Reusability*—the ease with which the product or portions of the product can be reused in the development of other systems. Note that the focus is on the ease with which the code can be borrowed and adapted. Reusability associated with the selection of functional capabilities is a behavioral requirement.

- *Integrity* (partial association)—as described in Section 4.1.6 (Trustworthiness Requirements), integrity has a mixed relationship since it covers two aspects of a system: integrity of operation and integrity of construction. When the focus is on the second category, integrity is a quality requirement since it addresses the design and construction of the product itself.

## 4.3   Implementation Requirements

This category deals with restrictions that are placed on developers. These restrictions focus on activities that take place during the design and development of the software system, and serve to limit the degrees of freedom available for product development. Such restrictions fall into two broad categories:

- restrictions on the *product design and implementation*;
- restrictions on the *processes and development approaches* used.

The requirements in this category are also referred to as *design constraints* or *implementation constraints*.

Requirements that fall into this category do not directly address externally visible behavior, although they have at times a profound influence on product behavior. Rather, they focus on restricting the design space, limiting the alternatives available to the developers. Generally, for any specific set of requirements, there are many different ways that they could be implemented. The design process performs tradeoffs on these alternatives and selects the designs that make the most sense. By providing implementation requirements, this design space is reduced. Often, such constraints are defined in order to enhance the quality of construction of the product.

For restrictions on the product design and implementation, there are two main types:

- *Design constraints*—restrictions on design styles that can be used.
- *Implementation constraints*—restrictions on coding or construction.

Some examples of common types of implementation requirements are:

- *Use of specific software components*—a customer may require that a specific software package be used as a part of the system, based on previous experience with that product or based on a desire to standardize. Note however that requiring some types of components might not fall into this category. For example, if a customer requires the use of the VxWorks®[4] operating system as part of the computing infrastructure, this requirement may be an interface requirement, since it enforces a specific external interface.

- *Imposition of specific algorithms*—at times, the customer may require that specific algorithms be used to certain functions. For example, the customer may have developed their own algorithm for speech recognition, and desires to have this algorithm used in the system. Note that at times, a customer may provide an algorithm as a means of defining behavior. If it is not mandated that the algorithm be used as is, but rather be used as a model of the functional behavior, then providing an algorithm is a behavioral requirement.

- *Required use of specific designs and design patterns*—customers may require that specific architecture styles be followed, or that specific design patterns be used. This constraint may range from a statement that the system is to have a "layered design," to a statement that the system shall employ fault tolerant features. This latter example typically occurs when the system needs to have high levels of dependability. Another example is the constraint that the developers need to define a global error handling policy for the system. This too is typically employed for dependable system development.

---

[4]  VxWorks® is a registered trademark of Wind River Systems, Inc.

- *Imposition of specific coding styles*—customers may require that specific coding styles be used. This constraint may arise from experience in similar systems where certain coding styles were proved to have advantages. It may also be based on the desire to avoid error-prone constructs in the code. Often, this type of constraint is specified using a coding style manual.

Constraints on the processes and development approaches usually take the form of specifying the process model to be followed, specific development techniques to be applied, and certain tools that need to be employed.

## 4.4   Programmatic Requirements

The fourth major category of requirements address the mechanics of developing the product. These requirements are often expressed as terms and conditions (T&Cs) imposed as a part of a contract, and define available resources as well as logistical restrictions. Some typical examples include:

- *Costs*—e.g., the project has $10,000,000 to cover costs for developing the product.
- *Schedules*—e.g., the product will be delivered in 18 months from the date of signing the contract.
- *Organizational structures*—e.g., the project will be managed from the software engineering branch of the home office.
- *Key people*—e.g.,
  - the chief scientist of the developing organization shall serve as the lead software engineer.
  - the nephew of the procurer's wife shall serve as the lead tester.
- *Locations*—e.g., the development work shall be performed at the San Diego facilities, proximate to the customer's main office.

While these are required characteristics of development effort, they are not characteristics of the product. In particular, while such requirements do not directly address desired levels of dependability, they often directly affect the ability of the development effort to achieve those levels. For example, if not enough time or budget is provided, the ability of the development team to achieve high levels of dependability, or even to deliver the product, may be affected to the detriment of the system. A clear description of programmatic requirements is essential for a project to ensure that they are able to trade-off expected requirements and product quality against resources available.

## 5.  Handling Requirements

Each of the different categories of requirements defined in the previous section has a different role in the development process. Because their roles vary, the way that each requirement is handled needs to vary. Failure to recognize these differences generally results in wasted effort and the potential for embedded defects. Understanding the nature of how the categories affect the different activities in the development process is therefore key to planning and managing projects.

### 5.1   Overview of Development Processes

As a general view, software development consists of six different kinds of activities: requirements development, design, code, construction, verification, and validation (V&V). These can be characterized as follows:

- *Requirements development*—the activity which defines the requirements for the product to be built.
- *Design*—the activity which creates the structure of the system, from the architectural-level design of the product, through the detailed design down to the code units. The product of this phase is a structure consisting of components and interactions between these components.
- *Coding*—development of the source code.
- *Construction*—also known as integration. This is the activity that involves putting the various pieces (components) together, forming larger and larger aggregates, until the entire system has been formed.
- *Verification*—the activities that examine the various intermediate and final products that are created during development to determine if they meet the criteria established for them, such as required behavior, adherence to standards, and so on. This is also called *developmental test*.
- *Validation*—the activities that ensure the entire completed product is performing as required, based on its behavior as seen through its external interfaces. This is also called *product/acceptance test*.

Verification and validation are very similar activities. They differ principally where they focus their attention. Verification focuses on the intermediate products that are created during development, while validation focuses on the final product itself.

There are several different techniques used for V&V. The applicability of these techniques vary according to the category of requirement that needs to be verified. We will not examine these to any detail since there are ample resources on the topic, but we will describe them at a high level. V&V techniques fall into five general categories:

- *Testing*—an activity in which the product is executed and challenged with various stimuli to determine its behavior. The responses are then compared to expected responses to determine degree of adherence to requirements. In some cases, the responses of the system may be examined directly. In other cases, a detailed analysis of the results may have to be performed, perhaps over the course of several tests. The execution environment may include the actual operational environment in which the system will be deployed, or it may include simulations of other systems in the environment. There are two flavors to testing based on the ability to determine behavioral conformance:
  - *Definitive*—the results are quantitative and can be compared directly to the requirements. The results can be stated as pass/fail.
  - *Analytic*—used to address requirements that cannot be definitively verified, but for which mathematical and other forms of analysis can be applied to make an argument for compliance. The results of testing, perhaps over the span of many tests, provide data that support an argument for either pass or fail, but do not provide an absolute determination of conformance. Such arguments, generally made with mathematical analyses, serve to establish the levels of trust that can be placed on the system's performance. For example, to verify that a system has the required levels of reliability, the system is executed, the results collected and analyzed to infer the achieved level of reliability.
- *Analysis*—an activity in which attributes of the system are examined analytically, often supported mathematically, and the results used to support an argument of compliance and to establish levels of trust. Techniques in this category do not rely on testing because the requirements that are addressed generally cannot be verified, either efficiently or at all, with testing. The system attributes generally used for analysis include the system design, its code, and system models.
- *Demonstration*—an activity in which the product itself is manipulated in some way to demonstrate that it satisfies a qualitative requirement. To show that a product is portable, for example, a demonstration of rehosting the product from one computer to another may be performed.
- *Inspection*—a visual examination of the product, its documentation, and other associated artifacts to verify conformance to requirements. For example, a software component may be inspected to verify that makes no operating calls other than to a POSIX®-compliant[5] interface.

---

[5] POSIX® is an acronym for the Portable Operating System Interface. POSIX® is a registered trademark of the IEEE®.

- *Process analysis*—the activity that examines the techniques and processes used by the developers to determine if they are adhering to the project standards and plans. This may involve examination of the various intermediate and final products as well as programmatic artifacts and records.

## 5.2 Effect of Requirements on Development Processes

Each of the different categories and types of requirements affect the development activities in different ways. They affect the development processes selected by the developers, the design, the coding styles, and the way that the system is tested. It is important to identify the type of each requirement so that its handling by the development team can be more easily identified.

Behavioral requirements are provided as input to the design and code activities. They exert indirect control over these activities, but do not directly control the way the developers build the product. That is, these requirements do not restrict the degrees of freedom available to the developers. Most behavioral requirements are generally verified using definitive and analytic testing approaches, because they are defined as observable behaviors. The exceptions are for trustworthiness and usability requirements which generally need to be verified using analytic testing strategies. For example, a system's usability may be measured by performing time-and-motion studies while operators work with the system as it is operating.

The behavioral requirements have a direct effect on the test activities. Each such requirement has a defined input/output pattern that can be directly tested. In many cases, the testers may have to employ sophisticated tools, such as data extraction devices, to perform the tests. It is important to note that any data that is extracted is obtained from observing the inputs to, and the outputs from, the product under test. If it is necessary to extract data that is internal to the product under test, then the requirement is not easily testable and needs to be rewritten. In some cases, the verification of correct operation requires post-test analysis. Again, the exceptions are associated with the trustworthiness and the usability requirements.

Quality requirements are verified using demonstrations and inspections. These approaches are necessary because this type of requirement deals with how the system product can be handled. For example, a developer may demonstrate a system's degree of portability by demonstrating how the source code can be modified to run on a different host. The portability may also be verified by inspecting the design and code for the presence of design patterns that enhance the portability aspects of the system.

Implementation requirements are verified using both inspection techniques and process analyses. They cannot be verified by system testing, although they can be verified using lower-level testing of the components within the system.

Programmatic requirements are verified by inspection and process analysis.

TABLE VI
TYPES OF REQUIREMENTS AND THEIR VERIFICATION APPROACHES

| Type of requirement | Verification approach | | | | | |
|---|---|---|---|---|---|---|
| | Definitive testing | Analytic testing | Analysis | Demon-stration | Inspection | Process analysis |
| Behavioral | | | | | | |
|   Functional | ✓ | ✓ | ✓ | | ✓ | |
|   Interface | ✓ | | | | ✓ | |
|   Temporal | ✓ | ✓ | ✓ | | ✓ | |
|   Capacity | ✓ | ✓ | ✓ | | ✓ | |
|   Resource utilization | ✓ | ✓ | ✓ | | ✓ | |
|   Trustworthiness | | ✓ | ✓ | ✓ | ✓ | |
|   Usability | | ✓ | ✓ | | | |
| Quality | | | | ✓ | ✓ | ✓ |
| Implementation constraints | | | | | | |
|   Product constraint | | | | | ✓ | |
|   Process constraint | | | | | ✓ | ✓ |
| Programmatic | | | | | ✓ | ✓ |

Table VI summarizes the effect of each type of requirement on how verification is to be performed.

# 6. Requirements Quality Attributes

How do we know that our system requirements are good enough? What guidance is there to help us define our requirements to ensure that they will be adequate to develop the system, and will avoid problems later on in the development process?

To start, we should listen to the collected advice of those who have had experience in developing requirements for projects. Especially valuable is the advice of those who encountered problems—their lessons-learned can help us avoid problems in the future. This advice is reported in various journals and conferences, and forms the basis for industry best practice. One good additional source of advice is the IEEE Recommended Practice for Software Requirements Specifications, IEEE Std. 830-1998 [15]. This publication provides a set of quality factors for requirements specifications for systems. These factors are based on industry experiences, and provide a sound basis for evaluating the requirements for any project. If we fail to infuse our requirements with these qualities, we run a severe risk of encountering significant difficulties during development. For dependable systems, this risk is even more substantial since the effect of failure for such systems is likely to be severe.

The IEEE Recommended Practice lists nine criteria against which a requirements package can be assessed. While they may seem obvious, it is important to apply them to requirements specifications, such as when performing peer reviews. Systems that need to be highly dependable are especially sensitive to the quality of their requirements. As such, understanding these attributes and properly applying them is crucial. Some of these attributes are to be evaluated against the entire requirements specification as a whole, while others are to be evaluated against individual requirements.

The nine attributes are:

- Complete
- Unambiguous
- Correct
- Consistent
- Verifiable

- Modifiable
- Traceable
- Ranked for importance
- Ranked for stability

Each of these factors is briefly described below.

## 6.1  Complete

For any specific product (system, subsystem, component, . . .), its set of requirements is considered to be complete if the requirements, taken as a whole, describe all aspects of the system to be built. Note that this does not say that all important requirements are defined, or all behavioral requirements, but rather *all* requirements.

It is generally not possible, just from an engineering analysis, to determine if all required behaviors are described (Fig. 12). We cannot envision requirements that the user has forgotten or hidden. New ideas for behaviors may be thought of at almost any point in development. This situation is common for many projects, driving developers crazy as they try to keep up with the new requirements being provided. The generation of previously-undefined functions is a key driver of requirements volatility.

One strategy is to engage in extensive dialog with the customers and future users of the system. *Requirements elicitation* is one technique that helps in ensuring that the requirements identify everything that is needed. We may also need to understand the domain for which the system will be used, and to analyze the environment in which the system will be used. The users and customers may be simply unaware of some requirements that are needed.

While it is impossible to imagine all possible requirements that are "out-of-the box," if the requirements categories described in Section 4 are used as a checklist, it is possible to reduce the likelihood that some requirements will be missed. Applying Section 4 allows us to ensure that all categories of requirements have been consid-

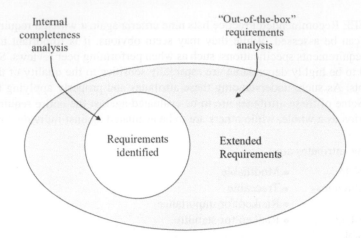

FIG. 12. Two aspects of completeness.

ered. For example, by stepping through the categories, we may discover through elicitation that the customer had not included programmatic requirements (*"Forgot to mention that you have 6 weeks for this project"*). Or we may discover that no interface requirements had been defined.

An easier task is to analyze the requirements already identified and determine if they are internally complete.

One way to judge completeness is to determine if all ranges and combinations of inputs have been accounted for, including illegal and low probability inputs. For dependable systems, this is particularly important since such systems need to maintain control even in the face of unexpected inputs from the environment.

For example, consider the sample functional requirement that was presented in Table V. It may appear to be complete, but what is the required behavior should the input value be greater than the maximum value that can be represented by the host computer?

Note that it is possible, and in fact likely, that during the beginning stages of development, the requirements will not be complete in the sense described here. This will occur because not all aspects of all requirements will have been determined. While this is the case, it is important to explicitly acknowledge the levels of incompleteness in the requirements specification to ensure that the developers have an expectation of more information to be supplied, and can design defensively to account for future changes.

## 6.2   Unambiguous

This attribute applies primarily to individual requirements but also can include two or more closely-related requirements. A requirement is unambiguous if it has one and only one interpretation. By reading such a requirement, if any two knowledgeable reviewers arrive at different conclusions about what the requirement says, then it is likely to be ambiguous.

The risk of ambiguity is that it is likely to lead multiple designers in different directions during design and implementation. It is also likely to cause developers to interpret the requirement in a way that is different from the writers of the requirements. The overall result it that the system, once complete may produce incorrect behavior. Or it may result in excessive effort being expended during system integration to discover and correct the discrepancies. This raises the risk of unintended side-effects, anomalies in behavior, and even failures of the system.

Some examples of ambiguous requirements are:

- "The user interface shall be easy to use"—the word "easy" is not clear, and could interpreted differently by different developers and testers.

- "If channel 1 and channel 2 or channel 3 are active, then the panel light will be illuminated"—the absence of parentheses does not make it clear whether the correct interpretation is "(channel 1 and channel 2) or channel 3," or "channel 1 and (channel 2 or channel 3)."

Some viable strategies that help in reducing ambiguity include

- Use of formal notations.
- Avoidance (or minimization) of natural language.
- Disciplined peer reviews and Fagan inspections.
- Independent review of requirements documents.
- Creation of system models to demonstrate understanding and reveal misunderstanding.

## 6.3   Correct

A requirements specification is correct if every requirement stated in the specification is one that the software shall meet. There should be no requirements that are inessential and beyond what is needed to implement the needed capabilities. Correctness ensures consistency with the underlying user needs. A system could be developed with complete adherence to its assigned requirements, but if these requirements do not match the user's needs, then the system is likely to be worthless [10].

Correctness for software specifications also implies agreement with the system specification, if there is a separate set of system requirements. Often, however, the system specification does not provide the level of detail that the software specifications provide. As such, the system requirements could be compliant with the user's needs, but the software requirements could contains variances. If this is the case, then those requirements are not correct.

## 6.4    Consistent

A requirements specification is consistent if no subset of requirements within the specification conflict with each other. If there are inconsistencies in the requirements specification, it is likely that unless detected and corrected, the design of the product will itself contain inconsistencies. Hopefully, such an inconsistency will be discovered during integration testing, but if it is not, then it represents a latent defect that may cause failure during operation. As an example of an inconsistency, consider the following two requirements:

- When the fluid level is $\leqslant$ two meters, the pump will operate at 1 gallons per minute.
- When the fluid level is $\geqslant$ two meters, the pump will operate at 5 gallons per minute.

These two statements conflict regarding what needs to happen when the fluid level equals exactly two meters.

Some viable strategies that help in ensuring consistency include:

- The use of formal notations that assist in performing consistency checks.
- The use of tools that can automatically perform some levels of verification.
- The use of executable models to demonstrate consistency.

## 6.5    Verifiable

A requirements specification is verifiable if every requirement contained in the specification can be verified. In turn, a requirement can be verified if a cost-effective finite process exists to show that each requirement has been successfully implemented. This means that the behavior defined by the requirement can be observed by challenging the system with stimuli during execution, and observing the responses, comparing them with the requirements to determine whether the system conforms to the requirements.

A common reason why a requirement would not be verifiable is if its description were ambiguous, vague, or poorly stated. Another common reason is if the behavior cannot be observed. For example, creating a requirement such as:

"The program will execute for 1,000 years without failure."

is not likely to be verified, unless the tester gets paid by the hour. For requirements of this type, arguments can be formed that support a positive verification, but such acceptance is by inference rather than by direct verification.

One strategy that is used is to include with each requirement a specific test case that will directly verify that requirement when the test case is provided to the system. If it is not possible to create such a test case, it is reasonable to conclude that the requirement is not verifiable.

## 6.6   Modifiable

A requirements specification is modifiable if changes can be made to the requirements without major disruption of the structure of the specification. This quality attribute is associated with how the requirements document is organized. If developers use an automated tool, the tool should have features that allow changing individual requirements, and notifying which other requirements are affected.

Of course, changes can always be made to a requirements document. The key is that these changes can be made efficiently, without a lot of effort and without disrupting a large proportion of the requirements document itself. There are several ways that a requirements specification can be hard to modify:

- If a requirement is described in several places in the document, changes made to this requirement will necessitate making changes in several places at once. This raises the likelihood of mistakes being made.

- If several requirements are combined in text, perhaps in a single paragraph or section, making changes to any one is going to be more difficult.

- If the specification does not have a clear and well-organized structure, it will be difficult to safely make changes with the assurance that all relevant areas have been successfully modified.

- If the requirements themselves are intertwined and not clearly differentiated, it may be difficult to describe them clearly and in a structured manner. This situation relates to the level of coupling and cohesion between the requirements, where coupling between requirements is a measure of the degree of interdependence between them, and cohesion is a measure of how "single-purpose" each requirement is.

Some viable strategies that help in enhancing the modifiability of a set of requirements include

- Use of automated tools to manage the structure and content of the document.
- Applying the concepts of low coupling and high cohesion to the structure of the specification.

## 6.7   Traceable

A requirements specification is traceable if the origin of each requirement is clear, and the structure of the specification facilitates the referencing each requirement within lower-level documentation. Traceability is crucial for a dependable system since it ensures that the requirements as they are developed are consistent with the higher-level requirements that serve as the basis for the system. For software requirements, this quality indicates that every software requirement must be traceable back to one of more system requirements. For system requirements, this quality indicates that every system requirement must be traceable back to a defined capability as expressed by a user.

When attempting to perform a trace on some software requirements, it is at times difficult to pinpoint exactly what the precedent system-level requirement is. In some cases, the mapping is clear and one-to-one. In other cases, however a software requirement may seen to be out of the blue. At the software level, many requirements are defined in order to provide support for a system-level requirement. The system level requirement is achieved through the composition of multiple software-level requirements. Overall there are four flavors to this relationship:

- *One-to-one*—the software requirement is in direct support of the system requirement, defining the same behavior.
- *One-to-many*—the system requirement is supported by multiple software requirements, and all of the software requirements must be successfully implemented for the system requirement to be satisfied.
- *Many to one*—the software requirement supports multiple system level requirements. If the software requirement were to be incorrectly implemented, all of the system requirements would fail.
- *Many-to-many*—multiple software requirements support multiple system requirements. If any one of the software requirements were to fail, all of the mapped systems requirements would also fail.

One way of determining the relationship is to hypothesize the effect should any specific software requirement were to fail. Whichever system requirements fail as a result are those that depend on that software requirement.

It is not unusual to have a software requirement that seems to bear no relationship to any specific system requirement. Often, these requirements have a utility basis, in that they perform some lower-level functions that are needed to support the execution of higher-level requirements. For example, a *heart-beat* function would fall into this category. A component might have a requirement to emit a heart-beat signal every 5 seconds to a controller component. The use of such a signal is one approach to determining if all components in a system are still active. Normally, this function could not be mapped directly to a specific higher-level component, yet it is essential if the system is to operate successfully.

## 6.8  Ranked for Importance

A requirement is ranked for importance if it is assigned a rating of its criticality to the system, based on the needs of the users. In any system, not all requirements have the same level of importance. There are usually a set of core behaviors that are key to supporting the users, and a set of others that have varying levels of utility.

One criterion that is often used is the level of negative impact should the requirement not be correctly implemented and fail during execution. Safety-related requirements, for example, should be explicitly tagged in a specification to ensure that the developers can easily identify them. Another useful criterion is expressing the requirement in terms of a range of acceptable behaviors. One way of providing a range is to explicitly define it, such as: "The system will provide the geographic position of the car to within an accuracy of between 10 and 15 meters." Another approach is to define a goal for the behavior and also provide a minimum acceptance behavior, such as: "The system will respond to users' requests for their bank account balances within 5 seconds (objective) but at most 10 seconds (threshold)." In this example, the objective value is the "hoped for" behavior, while the threshold value is the minimum acceptable.

This attribute is especially important for a dependable system for several reasons:

- It provides a means to characterize the overall desired acceptability of the system by ranking the requirements. By weighting the requirements, including those associated with the dependability attributes, it facilitates the tradeoffs needed to allow assessing the level of trust to be placed on a specific system, based on observed behaviors during acceptance testing.

- It allows prioritization of the requirements thereby facilitating the designers ability to perform tradeoffs during design and development.

- It provides a framework for selecting degraded modes of operation.
- It supports selecting areas of focus for investment of developers' time and effort to apply more rigorous processes.
- It explicitly allows developers to rank the priority of any defects found during testing. When systems are tested, anomalies are usually ranked according to a scheme of priority, with the highest priority failures being corrected first. If the requirements provide such information, the assignment of priority becomes an easier, less subjective task.

## 6.9   Ranked for Stability

A requirement is ranked for stability if its likelihood to change is identified, based on changing expectations or level of uncertainty in its description.

When defining requirements for a system, it is exceedingly rare for the requirements to be complete and final at the beginning of the project. On the contrary, it is common for requirements to change through the development cycle, with some changing more rapidly than others. Even when the product is complete, there will be changes requested, either based on subjective preferences or based on objective motivations. Typically, users will know in general which requirements are most likely to change, and which are less likely to change. They will also be able to have a general idea regarding the extent of possible change that the requirement may undergo.

It is a significant help for developers to have this information. By knowing the areas where changes are most likely, and knowing where requirements will be most stable, they can tune the design to be able to accommodate these changes. For example, there might be a requirement that states a response to a user input needs to be within 5 seconds of the operator's pressing a key. If in addition, the developers were also told that this latency may change to somewhere between 3 and 7 seconds, they would be better able to prepare for such a change in the design. If they were not aware of the likelihood of such a change, they might hard code a dependency making any changes difficult if the time latency were to be altered.

## 7.   Requirements and Dependability

As described in Section 2, the trust placed on a system is based on the expected delivery of services and the confidence of the user that the system will deliver the services. The nature of these services need to be defined in the requirements for that system. Confidence is rarely based on a single factor in the set of requirements. Typically, it is based on a combination of the factors. Overall customer acceptance

TABLE VII
ACCEPTABILITY FRAMEWORK

| Acceptability Factor | | Requirement Category | |
|---|---|---|---|
| Factors | Subfactors | Category | Subcategory |
| Dependability attributes | Availability | Behavioral | Dependability |
| | Reliability | Behavioral | Dependability |
| | Safety | Behavioral | Functional |
| | Confidentiality | Behavioral | Functional |
| | Integrity | Behavioral | Functional |
| | Maintainability | Quality | |
| Information assurance | | Behavioral | Authentication non-repudiation |
| Dependability means | Fault prevention | Implementation | Product |
| | Fault tolerance | Implementation | Product |
| | Fault removal | Implementation | Process |
| | Fault forecasting | Implementation | Process |
| Adherence to requirements (correct behavior) | | Behavioral | |
| Fitness for purpose | | *Correlation of behavior to user needs* | |
| Usability | | Behavioral | Dependability |
| Cost | | Programmatic | |
| Delivery schedule | | Programmatic | |

*(Acceptability)*

is achieved by weighting the various factors, and evaluating the system against the weighted combination. The combination of items that contribute to the decision to accept is summarized in Table VII. Note that each factor is strongly associated with a specific type of requirement as defined in Section 4. With this structure, we can effectively manage the various components of acceptance and handle each factor appropriately, based on its requirement category.

With this framework, customers can explicitly define what they expect in terms of services, including the levels of reliance that can be placed on these services. Overall, each project needs to decide whether the expense and effort involved in infusing high levels of dependability into a system is justified.

# 8.   Common Requirements Challenges

Within the overall context of developing requirements, projects often face unforeseen challenges that affect their ability to completely define the requirements and to develop a system. Even with the goal of satisfying the IEEE quality factors, it is not always possible to achieve the full set. Technical challenges and limitations of budget and schedule prevent a full exercise of these concept, even for critical systems that are required to have high levels of dependability. In addition, even a direct adherence to the principles does not guarantee that the requirements will be sound. The realities of large system engineering place many challenges to our ability to infuse our requirements with these attributes. Also, it is not always obvious how to achieve these qualities. In this section we describe some common challenges that projects typically encounter and provide some recommendations on how to overcome them as their requirements are created and applied.

In spite of accumulated experience and maturing expertise, the practice of developing software systems has encountered many bumps in the road. Rather than seeing a continual improvement in our abilities, we have been struggling to maintain system qualities. One of the key contributors to this problem is our practices of managing requirements.

In spite of our advancements and incremental progress, we do not understand the fundamental theories that drive requirements. We cannot reliably perform forward engineering and predict system behaviors based on requirements that have been developed. The state of practice is still hit and miss, poke and probe, code and test. Yet more and more functionality is being placed into systems. The systems are becoming more complex and being placed in positions of trust, including autonomous systems, medical devices, full digital avionics, and others which, if they fail, might inflict harm on institutions and individuals.

This situation is especially dire for systems that must be dependable. We must invest large amounts of effort and time to provide confidence that critical systems operate as they should. As such, we need to carefully and studiously apply what we do know.

In this section we discuss several common challenges that projects encounter, together with some effective solutions that have proven to be effective:

- Requirements not matching users' real needs.
- Volatile and late-defined requirements.
- Unknown "physics" for embedded systems.
- Fear of excessive detail.
- Test environment does not match operational environment.
- Ineffective and unusable human computer interfaces.
- Over-specified/over-constrained/unbounded.

## 8.1  Requirements Not Matching Users' Real Needs

In this situation, the system and software requirements are defined. They are provided to the developers who then proceed to build the system described in the requirements. When complete, the system is presented to the users who discover that it is not usable or does not satisfy all or some of their needs.

An alternate scenario is when the requirements are provided to the users prior to implementation, but for one reason or another, they did not fully understand what the requirements actually said. The end effect is the same.

There are several causes for this situation.

- The developers decided that involving the users would not be useful or would take too much time. Or perhaps they simply forgot.

- The requirements were defined in a form that was not easily understandable to the user community, perhaps in a formal notation.

- The requirements were presented to the users in an incomplete state. Perhaps the developers presented to the users the proposed user screens in a static Microsoft® Powerpoint®[6] slide format, and did not proceed into a dynamic simulation to provide more of an operational flavor.

- The operational environment in which the system was to be used was not adequately analyzed and modeled.

- The modes of use to be followed by the users were not adequately modeled and analyzed.

The key to acceptance of a dependable system is the awareness of the user community of the actual behaviors of the system. Users (should) recognize that all systems contain faults and evidence anomalous behaviors, and should base acceptance on whether the system is dependable enough for their specific needs. Likewise, developers need to understand the basis by which the users make these tradeoffs.

Some recommended solutions include:

- Directly involve users in requirements development.
- Create prototypes and allow users to play with various capabilities.
- Create models of usage patterns.
- Correlate requirements against models of user operations (user scenarios).

## 8.2   Volatile and Late-Defined Requirements

Rarely for any development project are the system or software requirements fully defined up front, before development starts. Even for projects which establish such a goal, requirements typically change over time as new ones creep in, existing ones

---

[6] Microsoft® and Powerpoint® are registered trademarks of Microsoft Inc. in the United States and/or other countries.

are modified, and old ones are removed. This situation is the reality of developing modern, complex, software-intensive systems. In fact, for most systems, the final requirements are not fully defined until the product is ready for operation. It is not until this point when all of the detailed behaviors are fully refined. Of course, most of these behaviors are typically documented by the code itself, since the requirements documents are rarely kept up to date at a detailed level.

A typical profile of the completeness of requirements definition is shown in Fig. 13.

Rather than waste energy and resources in resisting this situation, much like the force of gravity, we need to understand the reasons why this is the case, and plan our development projects accordingly to take advantage of it.

In general there are four types of requirements changes that typically take place:

- New requirements are *added*—these requirements represent new capabilities and functions.

- Existing requirements are *modified*—no new capabilities result, but there are changes to the ones already defined.

- Existing requirements are *deleted*—representing functions or capabilities no longer needed.

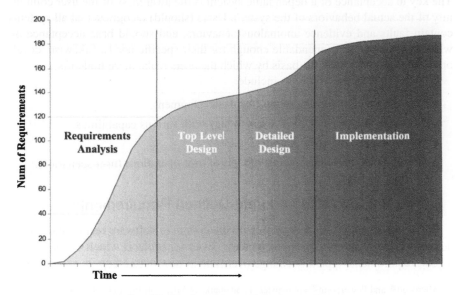

FIG. 13. Requirements completeness over time.

- Existing incomplete requirements are *refined*—details are added to provide more information about what the expected behavior should be.

The downside of requirements changes is the impact on the developers who will have to perform rework in order to bring the design and code up to date. As such, projects must plan for change, and expect that some proportion of changes will take place. Part of the planning needs to focus on applying appropriate techniques to minimize the amount of change that will take place.

The actual level of risk to a project for late-changing requirements depends on the requirement attributes, and the lineage of the requirement to the emerging (or completed) design. In fact,

- Some requirements *can* be defined either early or late.
- Some requirements *must* be defined early.
- Some requirements *should* be defined later.

The criteria that can be used to determine this spectrum can be summarized as follows:

- If the *level of understanding of the desired behavior* is low (exact behaviors not well understood or unknown), a delay in fully defining the requirements may reduce risk. This is because for certain requirements, if the requirement is defined and frozen early, later changes may impact design and cause rework to design and code that was created to address the prematurely defined behavior.
- If there is a *high likelihood that the requirement will change*, a delay in definition may reduce risk by avoiding later rework, for similar reasons as above.
- If a requirement has high or complex *external component dependencies*, early resolution and definition are likely to reduce risk. This is because late changes will affect not only the component in question but also other external components which have dependencies on that requirement.
- If a requirement has *strong internal design dependencies*, early resolution and definition are likely to reduce risk. This is because late changes will require extensive rework caused by the extensive and strong dependencies internal to the component in question.

These criteria are summarized in Fig. 14 which defines the situations where early definition and late definition are favored.

One type of requirement that is often defined late and is subject to continual change is that of human-computer interfaces. Individual users each seem to have their own preferences for what they want their screens to look like.

There are several different strategies for minimizing the risk presented by volatile requirements. These include:

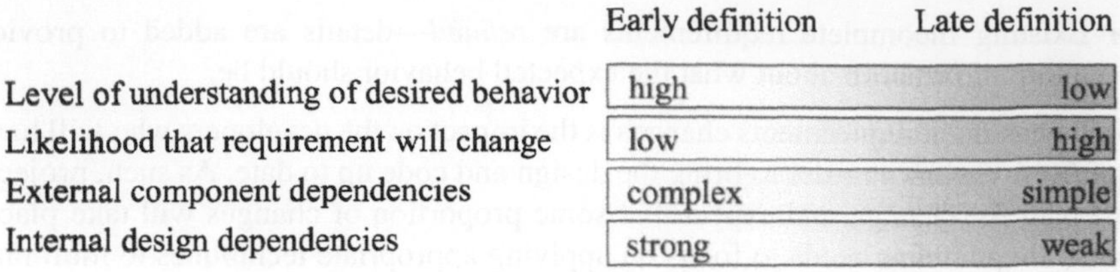

|                                              | Early definition | Late definition |
|----------------------------------------------|------------------|-----------------|
| Level of understanding of desired behavior   | high             | low             |
| Likelihood that requirement will change      | low              | high            |
| External component dependencies              | complex          | simple          |
| Internal design dependencies                 | strong           | weak            |

FIG. 14. Early and late definition of requirements.

- Ensure that all requirements are characterized with their expected stability and their relative importance (two of the IEEE 830-1998 [15] quality attributes).

- Where possible, design the system to allow for run-time reconfiguration. This approach will allow users to make limited changes in behavior themselves. Personal computer operating systems allow for a wide range of customization so that each user can tailor the appearance and functions to their own liking.

- Establish metrics to closely track the changing of requirements, particularly those that would cause significant rework effort. In particular, closely track immature requirements, undefined requirements, and changing requirements.

## 8.3   Unknown "Physics" for Embedded Systems

Many systems have a close connection and interaction with the outside "real-world." Effective operation of these systems often depends on a detailed and accurate knowledge of the characteristics of the physical environment. The system exercises control over physical entities by measuring the environment and based on knowledge of it, outputs signals that result in effective controls. For example, if we have a system that controls fluid levels in a holding tank, we need to know the characteristics of the fluids, the various pumps and controllers, the effect of the ambient temperature, the accuracies of the various sensors, and so on.

When developing the requirements for such a system, we often do not know the precise physical characteristics of the environment, and of the external entities with which the system, will interact. Perhaps we have some inaccurate models, perhaps also we have some measurements, but the information we have is often far from complete. Yet we need to develop a system that exercises the correct control, without knowing what the exact effect of our signals will be. For this reason we call this topic "physics."

In situations like this, developers will create an early version of the system and use this "prototype" as a way of exploring the universe in order to refine out concepts of what may be required. Rather than being a pure prototype, however, often these early versions will be incremental editions of the product, designed to probe the environment and extract the information needed. Often, as we learn more about the environment, we may have to make substantial changes to the internal structure of the system, perhaps by replacing entire algorithms and design structures. Sometimes, changes may be limited to fine grain discoveries that require changing constants in the code.

Many systems that need to be highly dependable are in this category. They often are safety-critical as well. Examples include avionics systems that control the surfaces on an aircraft as well as nuclear power plans controls that monitor operations. As such it is crucial that the requirements for these systems are handled appropriately. In particular, these requirements need to ranked for stability. In addition, the development process must explicitly acknowledge that some experimentation and discovery will take place. Likewise, the design needs to be developed in a manner that facilitates changes in the areas that need to be changed.

Some recommended mitigation strategies include:

- Use of executable models and prototypes.
- Use of simulations to depict external environment.
- Use of data logging functions to collect relevant data.
- Iterative development of system, and use of iterations to probe and explore the environment.

## 8.4   Fear of Excessive Detail

When developing a set of requirements for a system, developers often avoid describing too many details concerning the expected behaviors. This avoidance is justified under the rationale that such detail is really "part of design," and is not really needed. Instead, the details are left for the developers to fill in when they work through the system design. Examples of details that are avoided include items such as external system interfaces where the details of the interface are known and documented, as well user interfaces where the displays are pre-defined or must follow certain display and iconic formats and standards.

As we have seen however, regardless of the level of detail provided, requirements are never design. That is, you can describe the requirements to the smallest, most atomic level possible and still never enter the realm of design. Describing, for example, the exact formats of interfaces, the content of messages, even the order of the bits in each transmitted byte, is simply a part of describing externally visible behavior.

This is also the case when describing details about user interfaces and screens. If the specific features, formats, colors, fonts, etc. are described, the focus is still

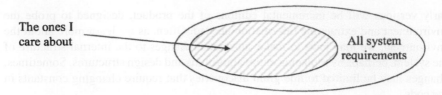

FIG. 15. Important requirements as a subset of all requirements.

on items that are externally visible. We may refer to this process as "user interface design," but we are simply providing details about externally-visible behaviors.

It is important to remember that providing such detail for all requirements is not always necessary. However, in some cases, specifically for critical requirements, this detail may be extremely important. Developers should never shy away from providing such information as requirements if the information is critical to properly understanding what the system is to do. It is not an irrelevant detail, for example, to specify that the units of measure being output from a specific subsystem are in meters, when another subsystem needs to use this data and might assume that the units would be in feet.

We need to remember that we often refine requirements as we proceed through development. Often we do simply not know the details as we start development. We need to start with a set of requirements based on what is known at project initiation time. This uncertainty needs to be explicitly defined in the requirements themselves. Then as we proceed through development and as the details for the requirements are better understood, we can augment the requirements to reflect this information. It is important however that as the details become known, they are documented. This is important information that needs to be captured. The result is that the requirements documents will change over time, but ensuring that they mature appropriately is an important task.

There are some requirements, particularly at the detailed level, that do not need to be defined in all their glory. The specific characteristics of the behaviors simply might not be important to the users (Fig. 15). There is no use in spending effort to address these requirements, but to avoid this effort, it is necessary that the user be clear about what requirements details are needed, and what are not. The exact behaviors can then be decided by the implementers based on their own design tradeoffs.

## 8.5   Test Environment Does Not Match Operational Environment

A key goal is to effectively test the system once it is built. To be able to determine how it will behave once placed into operation, the test process needs to challenge the system with tests that replicate the actual operational environment. Failure to do so often results in unpleasant surprises occurring once the system is released to the users. If the behavior is sufficiently annoying or dangerous, it is likely to be scrapped, or at best, not used.

There are three common causes for this situation

- The project does not have available a high-fidelity test environment that contains up-to-date models of the operational environment.
- The project has access to such a test environment, but the models are out-of-date and are low-fidelity.
- The project runs short on time and decides to cut out some "extra" steps.

In Section 3 we discussed the steps to be followed to develop requirements. Two steps are especially important to being able to create an effective test program. First, a model of the operational environment needs to be developed. If the system is to be used in an office setting, the characteristics of the office need to be captured. If the system is to operate in a boat, it may be necessary to model the ocean characteristics. If the system is to make use of signals received over radios, the models need to capture the nature of these signals. It is important to model not only the expected environment, such as a clear radio signal, but also abnormal and noisy aspects of the environment, such as radio signals when traveling through a tunnel. Otherwise, when placed into service, the system will encounter stimuli that it was not prepared for, and may experience failures.

Second, it is important to model how users will interact with the system by creating operational scenarios and usage models [25]. These models should be based on the overall purpose of the system, but should also include abnormal patterns of use, such as random keyboard inputs. These models help to verify that the user needs will be met, but will also facilitate the generation of automated tests.

## 8.6   Ineffective and Unusable Human–Computer Interfaces

The term Human–System Interface (HSI) is a general term that refers to the mechanism used for communications between users of a system and the system itself. HSIs are most commonly thought of as visual mechanisms, including both graphics-based and text-based displayed on computer screens. But they can also include other forms of interactions, including sound and movement (such as vibrations). Modern cellular phones, for example, employ multiple forms of HSI, including sound (for incoming calls and listening to conversations), vibration (for silent ringing), and visual (for number display and pictures).

There are several other common terms used to denote these interfaces, including MMI (man-machine interfaces), HCI (human–computer interfaces), HMI (human machine interface), GUI (graphical user interfaces), and OI (operator interface). Strictly speaking, GUIs refer to visual interfaces that display graphics, so any interface that relies solely on text would not fit into this category. Since HSIs are externally visible, their definition is part of the requirements development process.

A common and persistent challenge for developers is the creation of HSIs that are suitable for the users of the system. It is important that the users of a system are comfortable with and readily accept the "look-and-feel" of the displays presented to them. Unfortunately, with humans involved, there is a lot of personal taste and preference associated with acceptance of displays. Many large projects have spent extra resources to redesign the user interfaces after delivering what they thought was the completed system. Even with user acceptance, if the interfaces are not designed to display information efficiently and clearly so that the operators can assimilate the data, make appropriate decisions, and direct the system to perform appropriate actions, the system will be ineffective.

There are some important steps that should be taken when developing user interfaces to mitigate some of these risks.

- For systems where humans are an integral part of the system's operations, human performance must be defined and assessed as a part of system performance. This means that overall acceptance of the system needs to include humans as part of the process.

- Involve users early with design of user interfaces—ensure that the future users of the system are involved early with the design and operation of the user interface. This could involve creating dynamic prototypes of the system interfaces, allowing users the opportunity to experience alternate forms of operation prior to implementation and delivery. Experience has shown that static displays have a limited utility. Since they cannot demonstrate dynamic characteristics, the information provided to users is inadequate for overall evaluation.

- Perform usability analysis to determine how well users can learn and interact with the system. In association with providing early prototypes of the interfaces, it may be necessary for certain critical systems to perform detailed usability studies. In such studies, future users are asked to run through various scenarios and are closely monitored to observe their ability to assimilate and respond to the various displays. Their efficiency of motion and their reaction times can be measured as various alternative user interface designs are provided to them.

- Obtain formal agreement on HSIs once they are defined as part of requirements. One troublesome situation that has been experienced by projects is the dissatisfaction with the displays after development, even when there was initial concurrence that the displays were acceptable. This occurs for a couple of reasons:

- Users, being human, change their minds, or simply forget their earlier agreements.
- The user community changes between the time the HSIs are defined and the time that the system is ready to deploy. The new group of users has a different perspective on what the displays should look like.

If there is a formal agreement between the customer and the developers on a specific set of HSIs, then the process of requesting changes is made more difficult. This formality should not affect the ability to make critical changes, but will discourage the temptation to make changes just for change sake. Associated with this agreement, however, should be a formal analysis that verifies the HCI is sufficiently supportive of the systems operational requirements.

- Defer some HSI features as run-time configuration option. In general, many HSI features can be implemented late in the development process. Features such as text style, colors, and general appearance are usually parameter driven. If at all possible, one strategy may be to allow for the users to configure the displays in certain limited ways themselves, thereby avoiding much of the small-change syndrome. In some cases, such changes might be reserved for a "super-user," while in others, it may be provided as a general capability. Of course, this feature should be carefully defined as a system requirement.
- Rely on standards to help produce common views. Many operational domains have their own standards for displays. Relying on these standards can help in the design process, and can help to avoid the temptation to request changes later.
- Rely on standard tools to help produce the HSIs. The use of tools to generate displays is a common practice these days. Such tools make developing and changing HSIs a much easier task that in the past.

## 8.7  Over-Specified/Over-Constrained/Unbounded

At times, a project may discover that the requirements it has defined cannot be implemented, either due to technical reasons (*don't know how to implement*) or due to programmatic reasons (*not enough time and money*). One possible cause for this situation is an inappropriate selection and definition of the requirements themselves.

If the requirements are too ambitious, too restrictive, or too general, developers will find that their implementation may be difficult. Ambitious requirements tend to push the state-of-the-art and may be impossible to satisfy in a given schedule. At times, such requirements may represent a "gold plating" of the system—features that are not really needed either at all, or to the level described in the requirements. They may also result in capabilities that are not needed, yet, if implemented, could potentially affect the performance of the system.

Other times, some requirements may be defined that are too restrictive, resulting in narrow, point solutions. Systems with such requirements tend to inflexible, unable to grow and extend over time, and become outdated when their mission changes.

Requirements that are too general have the opposite problem—they tend to be flexible, but often extremely inefficient. They are able to support many capabilities, but none efficiently.

The overall result of these requirements is a wasting of resources, and potentially, an inability to develop the system at all. There are some very general recommendations that can help to mitigate these risks:

- Focus on prioritization of requirements. Apply the IEEE 830-1998 [15] Quality Factor "Ranked for Importance" when developing and reviewing the requirements. Ensure that not all are marked as *important*, and that the spread of importance levels is acceptable to the users.
- Build system in a series of increments. Plan for completing the most important capabilities in the earlier builds, so that if the project has to be stopped for any reason, there will exist an operational version of the system available for use.

## 9. Summary

Requirements form the foundation for all of software development. While it is easy to develop software systems without requirements, it is not easy to gain any utility out of systems built that way, except by accident. Requirements allow us to develop systems that are useful since requirements provide a focus for the development of these systems. To increase our trust in software systems, we need to clearly define what we expect from them, and use these documented expectations to assess the nature of the reliance we can place on them. We can trust systems that have defects and failure modes, as long as these are contained and controllable. Mapping our expectations to what the systems actually deliver is a large component of determining the appropriate level of confidence. By characterizing our expectations into an assessment framework, we provide a way of deciding whether to accept any particular system, and whether to place that system into service at a given level of trust and confidence. We know that every complex software system has embedded defects, but if we follow a careful and deliberate process, we can be assured that we can use that system with an acceptable level of risk.

There is a large body of work that has focused on the need for being able to build highly-dependable systems. One valuable source of information is the High Dependability Computing Project (HDCP), a joint initiative supported by NASA and several universities. This effort has resulted in several products, including the Unified Model of Dependability [2] that can be used to capture users' expectations of what they want for a system's dependability, an attribute-utility based model using Kiviat graphs to represent dependability [13], an approach to assess high dependable software [26], and the iDAVE model [6] which provides a framework for assessing the return on investment, supporting the trade offs necessary when projects have limited resources yet need dependable systems.

For systems which we need to trust, a careful requirements development process will produce five essential items:

- A clearly stated description of the need for the system.

- A description of the environment in which the system will operate, including models of the behaviors of other systems with which the system will interoperate.

- Usage models that capture the various ways that the users will operate the system, including both likely modes of operation as well as infrequently used operations.

- A set of requirements specifications that describe the behaviors of the system and its primary components, down to the major software elements. These specifications are kept up-to-date as requirements changes take place, and as imprecise requirements descriptions are refined throughout the development activity (including the system specification).

- A clear description of what the customer will accept, covering the items in the acceptability framework.

In addition, when writing our requirements, we need to ensure clarity of description. There are many guides (e.g., [17]) that provide advice regarding style. Understanding these and applying them appropriately is crucial. We can never eliminate the chance that something will go wrong, but we can achieve a high level of confidence that the system will behave as we want it to. Careful attention to understanding and documenting what the users want is a first step to achieving this confidence.

## REFERENCES

[1] Avižienis A., Laprie J.-C., Randell B., "Fundamental concepts of computer system dependability", in: *IARP/IEEE-RAS Workshop on Robot Dependability: Technological Challenge of Dependable Robots on Human Environments*, May 21–22, 2001.

[2] Basili V., Donzelli P., Asgari S., "High dependability computing program", Computer Science Department, University of Maryland, Technical Report CS-TR-4601, UMIACS-TR-2004-43, June 2004.

[3] Bennett T., Wennberg P., "The use of a virtual system simulator and executable specifications to enhance software validation, verification, and safety assurance". Final Report for the NASA Office of Safety and Mission Assurance, Software Assurance Research Program, Research Initiative 583, May 2004.

[4] Boehm B.W., *Software Engineering Economics*, Prentice Hall, New York, 1981.

[5] Boehm B., Basili V.R., "Software defect reduction top 10 list", *IEEE Computer* (January 2001).

[6] Boehm B., Huang L., Jain A., Madachy R., "The ROI of software dependability: The iDave model", *IEEE Software* **12** (3) (May/June 2004) 54–61.

[7] Bourne S., "A conversation with Bruce Lindsay. Error recovery", *ACM Queue* **2** (8) (November 2004).

[8] Brady R.M., Anderson R.J., Ball R.C., "Murphy's law, the fitness of evolving species, and the limits of software reliability", Cambridge University Computer Laboratory Technical Report no. 471, September 1999.

[9] Davis A.M., *Software Requirements: Objects, Functions, & States*, Prentice Hall, Englewood Cliffs, NJ, 1993.

[10] Dewsbury G., Sommerville I., Clarke K., Rouncefield M., "A dependability model for domestic systems", in: *Proceedings of Safecomp 2003*, Edinburgh.

[11] Department of Defense, "Information assurance—DoD directive", 8500.1, October 2002.

[12] European Space Agency, "Guide to the software requirements definition phase", ESA Planet. Space Sci.-05-03 Issue 1 Revision 1, March 1995.

[13] Huynh D., Zelkowitz M.V., Basili V.R., Rus I., "Modeling dependability for a diverse set of stakeholders", in: *The International Conference on Dependable Systems and Networks*, University of Maryland, 2003.

[14] "IEEE Std. 610.12-1990, IEEE Standard Glossary of Software Engineering Terminology".

[15] IEEE Computer Society, "IEEE Recommended Practice for Software Requirements Specifications, IEEE Std. 830-1998".

[16] Knight J.C., "An introduction to computing system dependability", in: *Proceedings of the 26th International Conference on Software Engineering (ICSE '04)*.

[17] Kovitz B.L., *Practical Software Requirements: A Manual of Content & Style*, Manning Publications, Inc., Greenwich, CT, 1998.

[18] Laprie J.-C., "Dependable computing and fault tolerance: basic concepts and terminology", in: *Proc. of the 15th IEEE International Symposium on Fault-Tolerant Computing (FTCS-15)*, Ann Arbor, Michigan, June 1985, pp. 2–11.

[19] Laprie J.-C., "Dependability: Basic concepts and terminology", in: *Dependable Computing and Fault Tolerant Systems*, vol. 5, Springer-Verlag, Vienna, 1992, pp. 257–282.

[20] Lauesen S., Vinter O., "Preventing requirement defects", in: *Proceedings of the Sixth International Workshop on Requirements Engineering: Foundations for Software Quality (REFSQ'2000)*, Stockholm, June 2000.

[21] Littlewood B., "Learning to live with uncertainty in our software", in: *Proceedings of the 2nd International Software Metrics Symposium*, London, IEEE Computer Society Press, October 1994.

[22] Littlewood B., "Software reliability and dependability: a roadmap", in: *The Future of Software Engineering, 22nd International Conference on Software Engineering*, Limerick, ACM Press, June 2000.

[23] Lutz R.R., "Analyzing software errors in safety-critical, embedded systems", Jet Propulsion Laboratory, California Institute of Technology, Pasadena, CA, 1994.

[24] McKnight W.L., "What is information assurance?", *CrossTalk—The Journal of Defense Software Engineering* **15** (7) (April 2002).

[25] Prowell S.J., Poore J.H., "Computing system reliability using Markov chain usage models", *Journal of Systems and Software* **73** (2) (2004) 219–225.

[26] Rus I., Basili V., Zelkowitz M., Boehm B., "Empirical evaluation of techniques and methods used for achieving and assessing software high dependability", in: *DSN Workshop on Dependability Benchmarking*, June 25, 2002.

[27] Sandhu J., "Multi-dimensional evaluation as a tool in teaching universal design", in: Christopherson J. (Ed.), *Universal Design*, Hausbanken, Norway, 2002.

# Mechanics of Managing Software Risk

## WILLIAM G. BAIL

*7900 Cypress Place*
*Chevy Chase, MD 20815*
*USA*

**Abstract**
Developing large, software-intensive systems is a significant challenge. Completing such developments on time and within budget requires careful attention by both management and technical staff. It seems that almost every project is faced with unexpected events and situations that directly affect the chances for success. When combined with the inaccuracies inherent in our estimation techniques which provide only approximations to actual cost and budget, the chances for successful completion seem extremely small. One technique that has been shown to be helpful is that of continuous risk assessment and management. With this technique, projects take a proactive approach to potential pitfalls, and plan for the unexpected. Unfortunately, many projects do not realize the full advantages of risk management because of shortcomings in how they apply risk management techniques. This chapter provides an short overview of risk management, and then describes two key processes that are often inadequately implemented: documenting risk and planning for risk mitigation.

ADVANCES IN COMPUTERS, VOL. 66
ISSN: 0065-2458/DOI 10.1016/S0065-2458(05)66004-4

**143**

# 1. Introduction

The general concept of risk is familiar to most software developers. Nearly every day they come face-to-face with the limitations of their techniques, and see their software projects fail to meet their budgets and schedules. As a result, today most large software projects have established formal risk management as a part of their common practice. In many cases, particularly for Government contracts, such processes are mandatory, and are intended to be an integral part of the development process. To ensure conformance, projects develop formal risk plans which define the processes and activities to be used by the project in identifying, tracking, handling, and reporting risks that arise during development.

There have been many papers and books written about software risk, e.g., [7,10–12,22,24]. These works describe the various types of risk typically found in software-intensive projects and the different types of impact that result. They also describe how to plan for effective risk management. In many cases, however, the application of these risk management principles has been somewhat less effective than it should be. One key reason is that the fundamental characteristics of risk and how risk affects software development are not fully understood.

Additionally, on many such programs, risk management is often seen as a box to check, a pro-forma action to take just to keep the boss happy and the QA (quality assurance) people off your back. The proper motions are followed but the integration of risk management into the everyday life of the developers is often lacking. Even when followed, risk management tends to be applied loosely, without sufficient attention placed on the mechanics. This laxity results in a less-than-effective process, reinforcing the impression that risk management is not an important activity.

In this chapter, we will review some key elements of software risk, explain the mechanics of describing and reporting risks, and provide some motivation for projects to take the process more seriously and effectively apply the practice. We will not repeat the extensive advice provided in the many articles on this topic. Rather we will emphasize these core concepts, and refer to other articles for additional material.

Overall, risks are closely tied to the plans that are created for a project [6]. Project plans describe the activities to be performed as well as the processes to be used. These plans also define the budgets and the amount of time available for completion of the project. Correlating the details in the plans with the likelihood of being able to successfully follow the plan is a key part of risk management. Once we accept that a particular plan is adequate, and we start work on the project, we implicitly trust that the plan will carry us through to a successful conclusion. Of course, knowing that we will always have limited resources (not enough time, not enough money, not enough technology), we did not infuse the plan with the most intensive set of processes. That is, the plan, by necessity, contains compromises needed in order to meet these constraints. These tradeoffs create the environment in which risks tend to occur. If a project is able to adhere to its plan, then any risk have been either avoided or mitigated. In essence, risk management deals with ensuring that the plans are executable.

In this chapter, we will start by examining how projects are planned. We will then present a formal definition of risk, and discuss the various aspects of risk, including risk levels. Afterwards, we will present approaches that can be taken for mitigation of these risks. We will also discuss how risks can be reported and tracked.

## 2. Project Planning

Every software project creates a plan that describes how the system and the software will be developed. Sometimes this plan is informal and maintained in the minds of the developers (hopefully only in the case of small projects). For larger projects, and those which are to develop critical systems, this plan is usually more formal and often consists of several documents, such as a Software Development Plan (SDP), a Configuration Management Plan (CMP), System Requirements Document (SRD), and others. Taken as a whole, these documents contain a detailed description of what is to be built and of all essential activities necessary to build the system. The descriptions cover what activities will be performed, when they will be performed (the development schedule), and how they will be performed (the process and techniques). As such, the project plan provides a roadmap for the developers to guide them through development. For management, it supports the acquisition of the resources needed for the project and the coordination of the various activities that will be performed. For the programmers, it describes the system to be developed as well as the tools and techniques that they will need to perform the development itself.

The plan also provides a framework to allow management and the project stakeholders to monitor progress as the project proceeds. An essential part of such planning is the definition of measures that allow monitoring of progress. Without such measures, management is flying blind—not a desirable situation to be in on a large software project. The actual metrics collected do not always have to be numeric (such as counting source lines of code), but they do have to be objective to ensure accuracy in assessment. Overall, project plans allow stakeholders to gain confidence that the system will be developed on-time, within budget, and with the capabilities that they need. By gaining confidence in the processes and techniques to be used, and in the way that the effort is organized, stakeholders can support the project. In a sense, the project plan is a contract between the stakeholders and the developers. Once the stakeholders have gained confidence, they can feel free to invest in the project, managers can gain confidence that the project can be successful, and the developers can willingly accept the responsibility.

There is some essential information that project plans need to contain. This information includes descriptions of the various external dependencies that the project has to external sources. These fall into three categories:

- *Materials*—that are used to build the system. These are received from other activities in a manner similar to a production line, manipulated by the activity, and provided to later activities. Materials can include intermediate products, information, and other items needed to develop the system. For example, for a software development project, customer requirements are necessary to build the system. For the coding phase of a software project, the detailed design description is needed. In general, any specific activity cannot be completed (and often cannot start) until its required materials are available.

- *Resources*—supplies required to perform the activity. These include staff, hardware, software and hardware tools, schedule, and budget. The resources need to be of adequate quantity to support the activity, as well as of sufficient quality.

- *Controls*—that guide and constrain the conduct of the activity in various ways. Examples include the software processes defined and the management structure which monitors and directs the staff. For software projects, a typical control is the Software Development Plan, which defines specific processes, tools, and techniques that the programmers are to use. For example, an SDP might specify that the developers are to use the IBM® Rational Rose®[1] development tool. The SDP might also specify that the developers need to develop specific types of documentation in specific formats. These control the way that the developers complete their tasks.

If any of these dependencies fail to be as expected and planned by the project, there is a chance that the project will fail to be successful. For example, a tool might prove to be inadequate, a needed design document might be late, or development technique might be inappropriate for the problem to be solved. Any of these variations from the expectations in the plan could threaten project success.

For a typical software project, we might show the relationship of the project to its environment as shown in Fig. 1.

Projects contain a set of interrelated and interdependent activities, each of which is similar to a mini-project. The cumulative result of these activities is the final software product. Each activity depends on others for intermediate products, and provides to others their own intermediate products. Each activity has its own set of resources

---

[1] IBM® and Rational Rose® are trademarks and registered trademarks of International Business Machines Corporation.

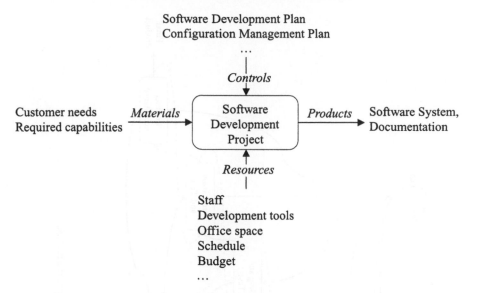

Software Development Plan
Configuration Management Plan
...
|
*Controls*
↓

Customer needs    *Materials* →   Software
Required capabilities       Development    *Products* →   Software System,
                    Project                       Documentation

↑
*Resources*
|
Staff
Development tools
Office space
Schedule
Budget
...

FIG. 1. Typical software development project dependencies.

which are needed to carry out their phase of development, and its own processes that define how the activity is to be performed. The project plan describes the activities, their interdependencies, and their processes, and provide the roadmap for development to proceed.

This structure also provides a framework with which project progress measures can be defined. If the activities (and subactivities) are clearly described, projects can track progress by observing when activities are started and completed. These metrics are sometimes called *inchstones* (as opposed to milestones) since they are tracked at a much smaller level of granularity than major project milestones. Monitoring inchstones achieved versus inchstones planned is one of the most effective measures in monitoring risk.

For software development, we generally have a set of well known activities or "phases," consisting of requirements analysis, design, coding, and test, in various forms. We could depict such a project in Fig. 2.

This diagram is considerably simplified, since there are many complex interdependencies that are not illustrated. Not surprisingly, the diagram has the general appearance of the Waterfall process model, where each phase or activity flows into the next [1].

Within the context of the overall project, each constituent activity has a set of expectations about what will be available for its use. It expects that it will receive

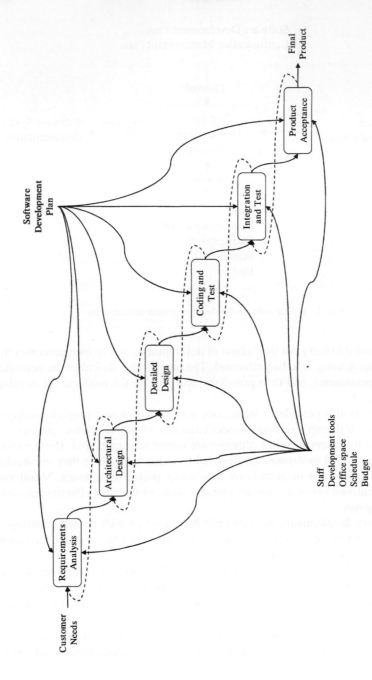

FIG. 2. Typical software development activities.

the necessary intermediate products from other activities at a particular time and at a defined level of quality, and to have available the processes, techniques, and tools needed to complete their job. All of these expectations are defined in the project plan. If everything goes as planned, the final product will be delivered on time, within budget, and with the necessary functionality and quality.

If we were to compare plans of today with those of even ten years ago, we would see many improvements. The current state of software development planning has gained from years of experiences where problems occurred during the development of software systems. We have made many changes in how we develop software, many at a low level. For example, it is now commonplace to perform peer reviews [19] of intermediate products to minimize the potential for defect leakage from one development phase to the next. Such improvements have been incorporated into project planning specifically to address common-place risks, and have improved overall industry best practice. Peer reviews also appear as a mandatory process activity in the Software Engineering Institute's CMMI (Capability Maturity Model Integrated) [20].

However, despite our improvements, there is always the potential for problems to occur during development. Any number of events could occur (and usually do) that could change the condition of the project and potentially disturb the planned activity sequence. Well-written plans typically include consideration of such events and include mechanisms to monitor, detect, and mitigate such risks. Such activities include prototyping stages, backup plans, dual-path development, "off-ramps," and other strategies designed to avoid impacts caused by problems that may occur [2, 3,21,8]. In this sense, project planning emulates fault tolerant systems by including fault detection and handling features into their plans.

When defined, the assumption is made that the plan is adequate to successfully complete the development, and to produce the system that will emerge at the end. That is, there is an expected flow of events that culminates in product delivery. Of course, plans are rarely completed without some form of disruption, particularly for software projects. Undesired (sometimes unpredicted) events occur that perturb the plans. Predicting these events and planning to avoid any undesirable effects is the role of risk management.

## 3. Fundamentals of Risk

We use the word "risk" frequently in software development efforts, but it is important to have a precise understanding of what it means and how it affects the way we develop systems. In this section we will provide a formal definition of risk and then examine two key elements of risk: risk *likelihood* and risk *impact*.

## 3.1   Formal Definition of Risk

Formally defined, a risk is a potential change of some aspect of a project or of its environment that, should it occur, will adversely affect the project's likelihood of being successfully completed. The change is initiated by an event, called the *risk trigger* or *risk event*.

Why does change present such a problem? Because, as we discussed in Section 2, projects are based on project plans that define what has to be built, what is needed to build it, and how it needs to be built. These plans are based on specific assumptions about the state of the various resources and assets that are available. If one or more of these assumptions proves to be wrong, either because it was initially incorrect or because the situation has changed, then the result of the change may invalidate the plans that were prepared, and may adversely affect the project's chances for success.

Hence, a risk consists of three core elements [13,14]:

- A *potential change* to the state of the project or to its environment that, should it occur, will adversely affect the project. The change could be associated with the resources needed by a project, the staff assigned, the tools to be used, or any other aspect that will affect how the project will be conducted. Projects generally experience change continually, and plan for such change. At times, however, some changes may perturb the plans and affect how the project can be completed.

- The *likelihood* that the change will occur. While nearly all project assumptions might at some point be found to be invalid, some are more likely than others. Hence, correlated with the change of condition is a measure of the probability that the change will actually take place.

- The *impact* to the project should the change occur. When there is a change in a project, it is not necessarily true that it is for the worse. When we describe risks, however, we are referring specifically to those changes that threaten the success of the project.

Frequently in the literature, risks are defined as having two elements: the likelihood of occurrence and the resulting impact. However, it is crucial to include a description of the change that results in the negative impact. A clear identification of the change clarifies the origin of the risk, and assists in planning for mitigation.

Note that a risk is associated with a *potential* change in a project. At the time the risk is identified, the change to the project has not yet happened. Once the risk occurs, it is no longer potential. It becomes a *problem*. The key difference arises when mitigation strategies are formulated. One approach for mitigating risks involves reducing the likelihood of occurrence. With problems, this option is not available—mitigation must focus solely on reducing the impact.

To help to explain this definition, consider the following example.

A project has assigned a staff of five programmers for the development of the design and code. One of these programmers is an experienced veteran, while the others are relatively inexperienced. The project managers are planning for the experienced programmer to manage and train the others, and have allowed for some extra time in the schedule for this training to take place. There is a risk, however, that the experienced programmer may decide to leave his position, and take another job elsewhere.

In this situation, the project managers have defined a plan that they believe adequately covers the need for the inexperienced programmers to be trained. If however the experienced programmer quits, then the project would experience a change of condition—one of the plan's assumptions will have been invalidated, namely that the lead programmer would be available to direct and train the others. The likelihood of this happening is hard to say, but with the rising salaries in industry (before the dot-com bust), the managers feel that it is fairly likely.

The trigger event that activates the risk is the lead programmer's quitting. Subsequently, there is a chain of impacts that result from this event. First the immediate impact—the absence of a lead programmer to manage the other programmers. Work has to be accomplished every day, and without the lead programmer, this day-to-day coordination will not take place. Second, since the lead programmer was responsible for the design of the system, and since he had a good perspective of what the system should look like, when he leaves, he will bring this knowledge with him—the overall design of the system will be cast into doubt. Third, with his absence, there will no one to train the less experienced programmers.

Faced with this potential event, the project managers could choose among several alternative strategies to offset any negative effects. One alternative is to wait until the lead programmer leaves. The managers could then assign a new senior programmer to take over the position. This new programmer will need to learn about the system, understand its emerging design, get acquainted with his programming staff, and begin to train the junior programmers. All of this change will take time, potentially affecting the overall delivery schedule and costing more money. In addition, the quality of the system might be affected, since the lead programmer thoroughly understands the application domain and the requirements for the system that was to be built.

A second alternative is to "sweeten the deal" by providing incentives for the lead programmer to stay, such as raise his/her salary, provide additional vacation time, or given him/her a bigger office. As we will see, this approach is generally referred to as risk avoidance. While it will result in additional costs, it might be desirable since it will avoid disruptions in the development activities.

A third alternative is to assign an experienced programmer as deputy to the Lead. The Deputy could offload work from the Lead, such as focusing on peer reviewing intermediate products. Should either leave, the disruption would be minimal. The costs would be higher but this early investment might be worth the investment in terms of the added support of an experienced developer and the reduction in risk of a key staff member's leaving. This approach is referred to as risk mitigation.

## 3.2   Risk Likelihood

Because risks are potential, that is, have not yet happened, there is uncertainty associated with their occurrence. We refer to the level of uncertainty as the *likelihood* of the risk. More precisely, the uncertainty is characterized by the likelihood that the trigger event will take place, thereby altering the status of the project in some way that will result in an adverse effect.

When we estimate the likelihood of occurrence, obtaining a high degree of accuracy is generally not possible. Determining the likelihood is not a definitive process. Rather, it is a function of the nature of the risk as well as the features of the project plan. There have been many guidelines created to assist in estimating the likelihood of risks. These are generally based on environmental factors, personnel factors, and technical factors.

There are many variations of how risk likelihood is represented. In some cases, projects use a probability estimate, ranging from 0.0 for impossible events, to 1.0 for certain events. In others, a simple High, Medium, and Low estimate is used. In still others, a category-based layering is used, with the categories being something like:

- Very unlikely—very low probability of happening.
- Unlikely—low probability but possible.
- Possible—may occur but not guaranteed.
- Likely—will probably occur, but not guaranteed.
- Very likely—highly probable of occurring at some point.

It is generally not advisable to define a large number of likelihood levels. For example, projects that attempt to define the probabilities with two digits of accuracy generally discover that such fine grained differentiation is impossible to achieve, and often results in spending more time on deliberations estimating the probabilities than on addressing the risk itself (see *tetrapyloctomy*[2]). Based on collective experience, projects generally settle for somewhere between three and five levels of likelihood.

---

[2] *Tetrapyloctomy*—the act of splitting a hair four ways. From Eco, Umberto, *Foucault's Pendulum*, Ballantine Books; Reprint edition (November 13, 1990).

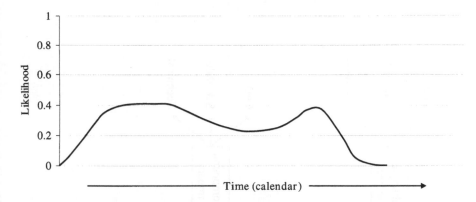

Fig. 3. Varying likelihood of risk.

In addition to the likelihood of occurrence, there is also the aspect of *frequency* of occurrence. In some cases, the risk might not be whether a specific event occurs, but rather how often the event occurs. Generally, such risks can be defined by the frequency levels. That is, instead of the risk event being "The developer's work station will fail, requiring a reboot," it would be stated as "The developer's work station will fail more than ten times per day, requiring multiple reboots."

It is important however to note that risks do not generally have a fixed likelihood of occurrence. Most risks have a varying likelihood that changes over time. Due to conditions inside of and external to the project, at times the risk may be more likely to occur, and at times it will be less likely to occur. Figure 3 illustrates this pattern.

## 3.3   Risk Impact

When the state of the project or its environment changes, there is often an effect on the project. At times, the effect may be beneficial, such as when the project is able to hire an exceptionally talented software engineer. Other times, however, the effect will be detrimental, such as when a project's top software engineer leaves. Risk management is by nature focused on the detrimental impacts and how they can be avoided or handled.

Whenever the risk event occurs, there may be an immediate impact, followed by a series of cascading impacts, each of which affects the conduct of the project. This chain reaction perturbs the expectations of various project activities, and may ultimately affect the project's cost and schedule, as well as the technical adequacy of the product itself. Figure 4 illustrates this effect.

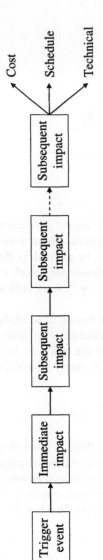

FIG. 4. Chain reaction of risk impacts.

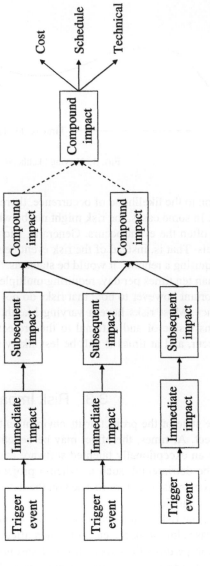

FIG. 5. Interaction of multiple risks.

This figure shows a simple model of the flow of impacts leading up to the overall effect on the project. In any complex project, however, there will be multiple risks and multiple impacts, causing a complex pattern of interactions. As a result, these interactions may raise the likelihood of other risks occurring, and increase the level of the impacts. This phenomenon is illustrated in Fig. 5.

For any project, it is important to have an understanding of how various risks affect the project's opportunity for success, including their multiple interactions.

However, not all risks have the same impact. As a result, the impacts expected from each risk are ranked according to the severity of the impact, based on the overall effect on the project's three acceptability criteria: cost, schedule, and technical sufficiency, and, consequently, to the acceptability tolerance of the stakeholders [4]. Risk impacts are typically classified into a small set of bins, such as shown in Table I.

The exact criteria in the table are typical examples, and will vary from project to project, and from organization to organization. However, this general approach to categorizing the impacts is commonly used. At times, a project might use a numerical value for the impact level, such as 1 to 5, corresponding to Low to Critical.

These figures show the effect of the risks on the project's cost, schedule, and technical adequacy. The effect of most importance, however, is the willingness of the customer and their stakeholders to accept the system. Most stakeholders are willing to accept some variation in these factors, even if the impact is large. For example, they may be willing to provide additional funds, accept a delayed delivery of the project, and even accept a less capable product. Every customer however has a limit beyond which perturbations in the final product exceed their needs. At some point they will decide that the product is no longer acceptable and will withdraw support. This effect is illustrated in Fig. 6.

In the context of balancing the impacts to cost, schedule, and technical adequacy, it is important for the developers to understand the nature of the tradeoffs that the customers will consider. If the customers are extremely intolerant of any variations in the plan, then the developing team must exercise exceptional discipline in developing the product. This discipline will end up costing additional resources, potentially making the project too expensive and causing the customers to lose interest. As mentioned, however, most customers have some degree of tolerance for varying levels of adverse impact. They may accept a somewhat higher cost and schedule if they can obtain all of the required functionality. Or they may be willing to accept lower utility from the system if they can get it delivered on time. This level of stakeholder tolerance has a direct influence on the level of the risk impact, since for less tolerant customers, even a small perturbation in cost, schedule, or technical content may result in cancellation.

TABLE I
SAMPLE RISK IMPACT CLASSIFICATION

|  | Low | Minor | Moderate | Serious | Critical |
|---|---|---|---|---|---|
| Cost |  |  |  |  |  |
| % of budget | <2% | 2–5% | 5–7% | 7–10% | >10% |
| Schedule |  |  |  |  |  |
| % of schedule | <5% | 5–10% | 10–15% | 15–20% | >20% |
| Technical | Missing | Missing | Missing | Missing large | Missing |
| effect on | minor | some | some | amount of | critical |
| functionality | functionality | functionality | important | important | functionality |
|  |  |  | functionality | functionality |  |

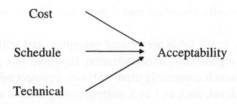

FIG. 6. Effect of Cost, Schedule, and Technical shortfalls on Acceptability.

The trade range for acceptability may appear something like the figure shown in Fig. 7. In this figure, the tradeoff range is indicated as a surface below which the customer will tolerate variations in cost, schedule, and technical content. Each axis is represented as a percentage of the original plan. For example, in this example the customer will accept the project if the 100% of technical content is achieved at 80% of the projected schedule, even if the cost rises to 140% of the budget. Each project and customer will have a different pattern for acceptability.

One key aspect of the risk impact is that they are often not static. That is, depending on when they occur during a project's conduct, the impact may have varying levels of severity, as shown in Fig. 8. This pattern is important when planning for risk mitigation activities.

## 4.  Sources of Risk

Every software development project faces risk. Many of these are common across all sofware projects [23], and hopefully, most of these are mitigated by the adoption of standard software development processes. Many are unique to the project and its specific characteristics. These should be addressed by the project plan. In spite of

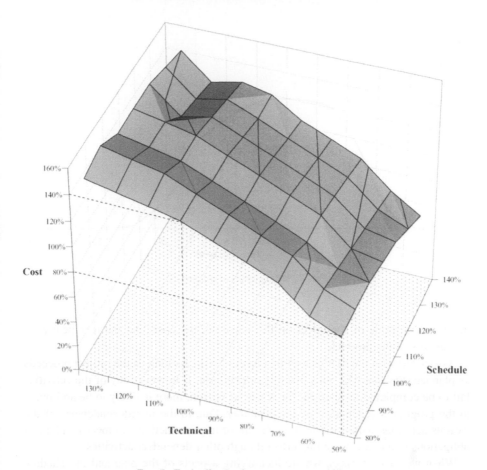

FIG. 7. Tradeoff range for customer acceptability.

best efforts however, projects still face risks and are likely to encounter various risk trigger events as they head towards completion of their products. One key to being able to successfully handle risks is to understand and clearly describe their source. Such understanding assist in monitoring for emerging risk situations as well as in preparing mitigation plans. Many models for risk prediction have been created to assist in the risk identification process. Briand [5] for example uses design metrics to identify potential areas in the system where problems may emerge.

The risks for the overall project roll up from the risks for each activity to be conducted for the project. The overall impact of the risks, at the project level, are

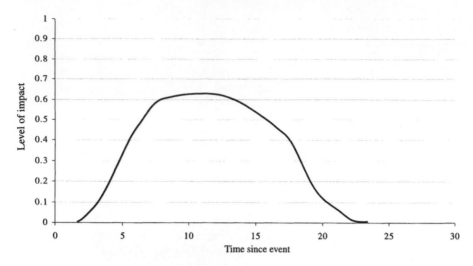

FIG. 8. Varying levels of risk impact.

described in terms of the effect on the schedule, the cost, and the technical content/quality of the product.

Associated with the SDP is a certain level of risk. As long as the project proceeds as planned, the risk will remain stable or decrease. If however any of the activities fail to be completed as planned, for whatever reason, there is likely to be an impact to the program's acceptance by the customer. Due to the interdependencies of the various activities within the project, failure of any one activity to meet its planned obligations will cause a rippling effect though other dependent activities.

When we identify risks, we are identifying aspects of the plan and its schedule where there is a possibility that some event may occur that will perturb the plans' proceeding as originally devised. When so disturbed, the effect may affect the system's performance, its development schedule, or its project cost. All three affect the willingness of the customer to accept the product in some way.

For software projects, risks are ever-present. Developing software is inherently risk prone because every time we develop a new system, we are creating something that is new, that is, unprecedented. If software were fabricated like hardware, where there is a design phase and then a production phase, we would have fewer risks. With hardware, production consists of replicating multiple copies of the same product, based on the design that was created. But software has no production phase—the design of the software is the final product. Note that we are treating software coding as design. It is the final step of detailed design where the smallest features of the design are finalized. Since the design is always new (particularly at the coding level), we are treading on uncharted territory. Being able to assess risk based on a system's design is an important activity. Ref. [16] describes one such approach.

The degree of newness of course varies widely. In some cases, the software system to be developed is based on an existing system, and as such, can borrow much of its overall design and even much of its code. But there is always some portion that must be created fresh, and this is where the risks originate. In other systems, most or all of the system is new. At times, the system is to implement requirements that have never been implemented before.

Risks therefore can arise from any aspect of the project plan's not being achieved. In fact, some authors assert that risk management is intrinsic to project management [17]. A development activity might not receive the intermediate products it needs on time. Or the intermediate products might not have the necessary characteristics that are needed, such as missing functionality. The tools used by the activity might not be adequate for the job. The problem to be solved might be beyond the capabilities of the staff. The process selected might not be appropriate for the problem. These are just a few items that could hamper achieving the project plan.

Boehm [2] has identified what he refers to as the top ten software risk items. These are listed in Table II, along with a short description. This list is based largely on

TABLE II
BARRY BOEHM'S TOP TEN SOFTWARE RISK ITEMS

| Risk item | Description |
| --- | --- |
| Personnel shortfalls | Not enough staff |
| | Staff with talents incompatible with core technologies |
| | Inexperienced staff |
| Unrealistic schedules and budgets | Schedule and/or budgets allocated insufficient for completion of project |
| Developing the wrong functions and properties | Developers produce system that is not what the users want or need |
| Developing the wrong user interface | User interface is not easy to use, fails to follow standards, and/or is not appropriate for user needs |
| Gold plating | Some requirements are more ambitious than what are needed |
| Continuing stream of requirements changes | Through development, the requirements continue to change, causing extensive rework |
| Shortfalls in externally performed tests | System testing falls short and fails to adequately test product prior to release |
| Real-time performance shortfalls | System fails to meet required latencies for critical functions |
| Straining computer-science capabilities | Required functionality is at or past state-of-the-practice, is unprecedented, and is forcing too much innovation |

TABLE III
CAPERS JONES' TOP TEN SOFTWARE RISK ITEMS

| Risk item | Description |
| --- | --- |
| Inaccurate metrics | If the metrics collected by the project do not reflect the actual condition and state of the project, the project may find itself in trouble too late in the process to recover. |
| Inadequate measurement | If insufficient metrics are collected for a project, the actual condition and state of the project might be unknown, and the project may find itself in trouble too late in the process to recover. |
| Excessive schedule pressure | If an unrealistic development schedule is provided to the developers, the project may be forced to take hazardous shortcuts that threaten project success. |
| Inaccurate cost estimating | If the initial estimation of the cost required for developing the software system is inaccurate, the project is likely to run out of funds prior to project completion. This usually results in the skipping of some required process steps thereby increasing the risk of realizing poor product quality. |
| Management malpractice (e.g., knowledge) | If project management does not understand the essentials of software development, they may make poor decisions that will undercut the ability of the developers to complete the project successfully. |
| Silver bullet syndrome (will save the project) | If the project has an unrealistic belief that a miracle tool or process will provide the productivity enhancement needed to complete the project, they may discover too late that the "silver bullet" will not save the project, and be unable to recover. |
| Creeping user requirements | If the requirements are changed continually late into the development process, the rework necessary to accommodate these changes are likely to delay progress and consume resources. |
| Low quality | This "risk" is actually an impact resulting from many risks, including those listed above. |
| Low productivity | If the actual productivity realized by the developers is less than that planned for, the project is in risk of being late. If shortcuts are taken to recover schedule, the final product's quality is threatened. |
| Cancelled projects | This "risk" is actually an impact resulting from many risks, including those listed above. |

Boehm's experiences with a large defense contractor and have a heavy management flavor. Another more software engineering view of the "top ten" risks is provided by Capers Jones [15]. These are listed in Table III. Note that in both cases, the risks are general terms and often stated as impacts. There are many other lists of top risks in addition to these (e.g., [6,9,18]).

## 5.  Handling Risks

In order to avoid the negative impacts associated with risk, projects employ various strategies for mitigation. Of course, since software development is a risk-abundant environment, projects cannot afford to handle every risk they identify. Resources are generally tight for projects, and so planning for risk mitigation needs to focus on those risks that are of higher importance, based on the characteristics of the project and the expectations of the stakeholders. In this section we describe how to determine the priorities of risks and then examine these concepts and provide some examples.

### 5.1  Risk Levels

Not all risks are at the same level of significance to a project. Some may present a catastrophic effect, while other may have only a minor impact. But some risks that have high likelihoods of occurring can be considered to be less threatening if their impacts are low. Likewise, risks that have significant impacts can be less of a problem if their likelihood of occurring is very low. Projects, therefore, need to be able tradeoff impact and likelihood to determine appropriate mitigation actions. To this end, the concept of *risk level* is defined.

Risk level is determined by combining the risk's likelihood with its impact. In general, this can be viewed as the *expected value* of the risk impact (risk impact times the risk likelihood). Because of the inaccuracies with which impacts and likelihoods are estimated, exact values for these terms is nearly impossible to determine. For example, deciding between 0.75 and 0.80 probability that your lead programmer will quit is a fruitless exercise. As such, we tend to use the large grain classification of impacts and likelihoods that we described in Sections 3.2 and 3.3.

Based on the impacts and likelihoods, we generally define three overall levels of risk: High, Moderate, and Low.

A sample mapping from impact and likelihood to risk level is shown in Fig. 9. This table is often called a *risk matrix*. Many other mappings are possible of course [25], but this table is typical. In this matrix, cells that contain an H are those that represent high risk levels, those that contain an M represent medium risk levels, and those that contain an L represent Low risk levels. When color printing is possible, the cells are filled in with red for high, yellow for medium, and green for low.

Some projects assign numeric values to likelihood and impact, and multiply them together to determine the overall risk level. As an example of this approach, if we assign the range of values from 1 to 5 for both likelihood and impact, we would have a risk matrix as shown in Fig. 10. In this scheme, the three risk level categories are generally defined as:

- *High risk*—for risk levels greater than or equal to 15.

| Likelihood \ Impact | Low | Minor | Moderate | Serious | Critical |
|---|---|---|---|---|---|
| Very Likely | M | M | H | H | H |
| Likely | L | M | M | H | H |
| Possible | L | M | M | M | H |
| Unlikely | L | L | M | M | M |
| Very Unlikely | L | L | L | M | M |

FIG. 9. Sample risk matrix.

| Likelihood \ Impact | 1 | 2 | 3 | 4 | 5 |
|---|---|---|---|---|---|
| 5 | M | M | H | H | H |
| 4 | L | M | M | H | H |
| 3 | L | M | M | M | H |
| 2 | L | L | M | M | M |
| 1 | L | L | L | M | M |

FIG. 10. Sample numeric risk levels.

- *Medium risk*—for risk levels greater than equal to 5, and less than 15.
- *Low risk* – for risk levels less than 5.

Note however that the assignment of risk level to cells does not correspond exactly to the computed values. A risk with a likelihood of 4 and an impact of 1 is generally considered to be a low risk, while a risk with a likelihood of 1 but with an impact of 4 is considered to be a moderate risk. This difference is based on the relative ease of mitigating risks with low impact versus those with higher impacts.

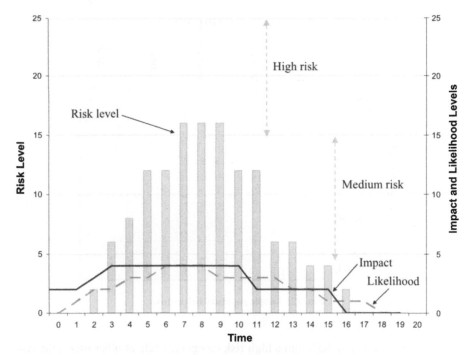

FIG. 11. Variation of level of risk over time.

Some projects may have a critical need for a system, to the point where any perturbation of its completion may have serious consequences. For such projects, even
very unlikely risks events would be considered being at a High risk level. This situation is analogous to the safety implications of a critical system. If a system were
to provide life support to a patient undergoing surgery, even a very unlikely chance
of a failure (once every 100 hours of operation perhaps) would be unacceptable. Of
course, project risks are associated with the development of systems, not necessarily
with their operation.

The relationship of risk likelihood and impact is somewhat more complex than
as shown in the matrix. Because each of the factors take effect at varying times
and at varying levels, the matrix can capture the risk only at a specific point in the
project. For any specific risk, the actual risk level can vary according to time, as
shown in Fig. 11. In this figure, we see how both the risk likelihood and the risk
impact vary over time (the two lines at the bottom of the figure). The risk level,
being a combination of risk impact and risk likelihood, reflects this variation over

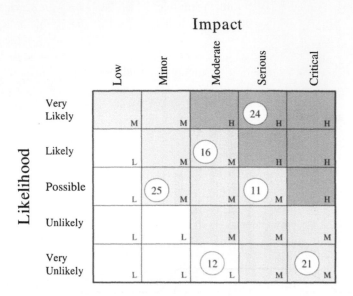

FIG. 12. Sample populated risk matrix.

time. At times, this risk falls into a high risk category, while at other times, the risk is in a low risk category.

Once identified, risks need to be reported regularly and predictably. By their nature, stale reports do not adequately keep stakeholders informed regarding the current status of the risks. Since many risks have the potential for falling apart quickly, or need rapid mitigation applied, timely reports are crucial. In addition, the reports need to convey their information as easily and clearly as possible to facilitate mitigation.

Figure 12 illustrates a sample risk matrix populated with project risks. Each risk is assigned a unique tracking number. This number is placed in the matrix in the cell corresponding to its risk level. In this example, there are six risks that are being tracked by the project, specifically risks 11, 12, 16, 21, 24, and 25. Based on the project's analysis, these risks range from low to high.

Alternately, some projects and organizations use what is called a "stop light chart," so named because of the use of red-yellow-green as a way of indicating the risk, reminiscent of a traffic stop light. A sample of such a chart is shown in Fig. 13. Note that in this chart, only those risks that are actively being monitored are listed. Any risks that have a risk level of Low, either inherently or because of mitigation, are often not listed. If mitigated, these risks are often referred to as being *retired*.

| Risk No | Risk Name | Likelihood | Impact | Risk Level |
|---|---|---|---|---|
| 1 | Defects in compiler | Likely | Serious | H |
| 5 | Late delivery of test hardware | Likely | Moderate | M |
| 8 | Inadequate training for new complier | Possible | Moderate | M |
| 13 | User indecision on GUI design | Likely | Critical | H |

(a)

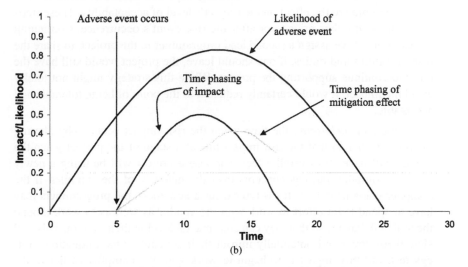

(b)

FIG. 13. (a) Sample stop light chart. (b) Effect of impact and mitigation timing on risk planning.

## 5.2 Risk Mitigation

When risks are identified, if they are of sufficient risk level, projects need to plan for mitigation activities to address any impacts that may result from the risks. There are four basic strategies associated with mitigation planning. These are applied to those risks which have been assessed as having sufficient levels of threat to justify investment of resources for mitigation. Because the risk levels vary over time based on varying conditions, it is important that the project perform continuous risk monitoring to ensure that the currently-important risks are addressed. The four strategies are:

- Reduce the *likelihood* of the risk's occurrence—by defining a set of activities to reduce the likelihood of the risk's occurrence. this strategy aims at avoiding the risk's turning into a problem, thereby avoiding the impact caused by the risk. Returning to our earlier example, suppose we have a project where we have a lead programmer who might desire to quit his job and move elsewhere. The strategy of providing additional incentives, such as raising the salary, providing more vacation time, or giving the lead a larger office with a river view, is one approach to reducing the likelihood of the lead programmer's leaving.

- Reduce the *impact* of the risk—by defining steps that absorb or avoid the impact, and minimize the effect on the project's level of acceptability. These steps can be applied either prior to or after the risk event's occurrence. Continuing our example, if we assign a second lead programmer to the project, to share the responsibilities and duties, if one should leave, the project would still have the other to continue supporting the project. While this strategy might not totally avoid the impact, it would certainly reduce it to the point of being tolerable and acceptable.

- *Deferring or accelerating* the time when the risk impact occurs—by altering the project plan so that the risk impact hits at a stage of the project when the impact will have less overall effect. Suppose a project will be using a newly released compiler, but has concerns over the maturity of the compiler. If the compiler contains defects (as is typical for a new tool), the programmers may have to spend extra effort to work with the vendor as well as to work around the tool deficiencies so that they can continue to develop their system. This will slow them down and potentially impact their schedule. One mitigation strategy to avoid this impact is to begin to work with the compiler earlier in the schedule than was originally planned. This shifts the impact of the risk, so that if extensive compiler fixes are needed, they can be accomplished before the programmers are heavily dependent on its correct operation.

- *Accepting and absorbing* the impact—by balancing the impact against other aspects of the project. If our lead programmer were to leave, we might decide that we could absorb the overall impact on cost and schedule.

In planning for mitigation, there are six steps:

(1) Identify the risks that have the most potential for disruption of the project (the greatest impact of overall acceptability). Use the risk levels as a basis for this identification, but not as the sole resource.

(2) Determine if there are any viable actions that can be taken to reduce the likelihood of these risks. If so, create a plan to initiate these actions.

(3) Define and monitor metrics designed to detect the risk event. In the case of the potentially immature compiler, a project might collect metrics on the error rate experienced by the programmers when using the compiler. If the error rate rises above a nominal level, it can be concluded that the risk has become a problem.

(4) Identify any viable actions that can either reduce or change the timing of the risk impact. If there are such actions, create a plan to activate these actions should the risk event occur. These actions include any strategies for absorbing the impact. The mitigation plan for each risk should define the schedule for each mitigation step as well as the project resources needed to accomplish the mitigation. Since the risk event has not yet occurred, the schedule is generally defined relative to the time when the risk event occurs.

(5) Define metrics designed to monitor the risk levels of each risk, addressing both the likelihood of occurrence and the level of impact. Continuously monitor these metrics. In the case of the immature compiler, monitoring the amount of effort needed to differentiate between a compiler bug and a bug ion the application code is one measure of the impact.

(6) Define metrics designed to track the effectiveness of the mitigation actions. Continuously monitor these metrics. Using the metric applied to the compiler in the above example, a continual monitoring of the error rate might indicate a maturation of the compiler as indicated by the error rate dropping over time.

Project plans created for projects generally contain activities designed for both product development as well as some level of risk mitigation. When a specific risk is identified, the risk mitigation actions may include elements of the project plan, but usually adds new steps tailored for the risk.

When planning for the mitigation of risks, it is important to consider the timing of the impacts and of the mitigation effects:

- *Impact timing*—the time period when the impact of the risk becomes noticeable or measurable.

- *Mitigation timing*—the time period when the effect of the mitigation activities take effect.

Even if a risk has a serious impact, if the impact has a delay before it has a noticeable effect, it may be prudent for projects to address risks with less serious impacts first. Likewise, if the mitigations steps have a delay before they can be fully effective, then projects need to plan for activating them as early as possible to ensure maximum effectiveness. The effect of timing on mitigation planning is illustrated in Fig. 13.

A project risk mitigation plan is therefore a dynamic, continuously changing document that contains a list of currently identified risks. For each risk, the plan defines:

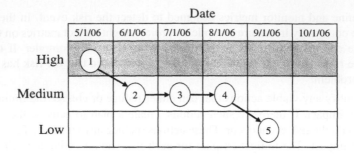

FIG. 14. Risk mitigation plan chart.

- Metrics for detecting the risk event.
- A set of scheduled mitigation steps designed to address the risk.
- Metrics designed to track the risk level as the mitigation steps are applied.
- Planned reduction of risk level correlated to each risk mitigation step.
- Resources required for implementing the risk mitigation steps.

Plans for mitigating risks can be reported using a chart such as shown in Fig. 14. In this chart, each risk mitigation step is uniquely identified. The date on which the step is performed is defined, and the expected effect on the risk level is described. This chart can be used to track the effectiveness of risk mitigation, since at each date, the risk metrics can be applied to ensure that the reduction in risk level was achieved as planned.

For each risk that needs to be tracked and mitigated, projects need to create a report that contains all the information concerning the risk. This report is periodically updated to reflect any changes in condition. A sample report is shown in Fig. 15.

## 6.  Conclusion

Software development projects are always risky. Because developing software involves innovation, the risk can never be eliminated. Some authors assert that any software project that has a low risk is not being aggressive enough in advancing capabilities. This judgment depends on the system to be developed of course. However, there are many steps that can be taken to manage software risk. Careful attention to the identification and monitoring of risks is crucial to avoid project failures. While most projects have some form of risk management in place, they do not always pay sufficient attention to some of the crucial aspects of risk management.

**Risk Number:** 24

**Risk Name:** Immature compiler

**Risk Description:** The compiler is a new product. As such, it may be immature and not work properly. It might abort, it might generate incorrect code, it might not properly process the programming language, or it might generate inefficient code.

**Likelihood:** Likely – the compiler is brand new.

**Impact:** Moderate – some extra work will be required, requiring more attention by the programmers. The vendor is usually reliable so the impact is probably not too severe, and will be corrected rather quickly.

**Acceptability** – It will probably raise the overall cost and increase the schedule by a couple of weeks.

**Mitigation:**

**Associated metric:** Number of defects per compiler test

| Step | Description | Expected Risk Level | Metric (m) |
|---|---|---|---|
| 1 | xxx | Remain at High | > 5 |
| 2 | xxx | Decrease to Medium | 2 < m < 5 |
| 3 | xxx | Remain at Medium | 2 < m < 5 |
| 4 | xxx | Remain at Medium | 2 < m < 5 |
| 5 | xxx | Drop to Low | m = 0 |

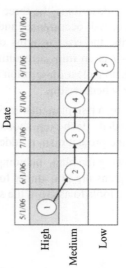

FIG. 15.  Sample risk summary report.

In this chapter, we emphasized the importance of three items:

- Clearly describing the three key components of risk: the risk event, the likelihood of risk occurrence, and the risk impact. A common mistake is to simply describe the risk in terms of its impact. For example, "schedule" is never a risk—it is an impact resulting from a risk event. Planning for mitigation depends on a clear description of the event itself and the chain of effects that lead to the schedule slip.

- Creating a risk plan that tracks risk levels, and applies effective mitigation steps as needed. Each step should be clearly identified as being either part of the baseline project plan or added specifically to address the risk.

- Following the plan, including the active use of risk metrics to monitor progress. Risk plans are not simply to keep management happy. They are extremely effective tools to assist in the success of the project.

## REFERENCES

[1] Boehm B.W., "A spiral model for software development and enhancement", *IEEE Computer* **21** (5) (1988) 61–72.
[2] Boehm B.W., "Software risk management: Principles and practices", *IEEE Software* (January 1991).
[3] Boehm B.W., DeMarco T., "Software risk management", *IEEE Software* (May/June 1997).
[4] Brekka L.T., Maksimovie V., Picardal C., Iftekharuddin K., "Risk management and systems engineering discipline", in: *IEEE 1996 National Aerospace and Electronics Conference—NAECON*, 1996.
[5] Briand L.C., Thomas W.M., Hetmanski C.J., "Modeling and managing risk early in software development", in: *Proceedings of the 15th International Conference on Software Engineering*, 1993.
[6] Chittister C., Haimes Y.Y., "Assessment and management of software technical risk", *IEEE Trans. Systems, Man, Cybernetics* **24** (2) (February 1994).
[7] DeMarco T., Lister T., "Risk management during requirements", *IEEE Software* (September 2003).
[8] Department of Defense, Defense Acquisition University, "Risk management guide for DoD acquisition", fourth ed., February 2001.
[9] Doernemann H., "Tool-based risk management made practical", in: *Proceedings of the IEEE Joint International Conference on Requirements Engineering (RE'02)*.
[10] Fairley R., "Risk management for software projects", *IEEE Software* (May 1994).
[11] Feather M.S., "Towards a unified approach to the representation of, and reasoning with probabilistic risk information about software and its system interface", in: *Proceedings of the 15th International Symposium on Software Reliability Engineering (ISSRE'04)*.

[12] Fenton N., Neil M., "Software metrics and risk", in: *FESMA 99—2nd European Software Measurement Conference*, 8 October, 1999.

[13] Gemmer A., "Risk management: Moving beyond process", *IEEE Computer* (May 1997).

[14] IEEE Std. 1540-2001, IEEE Standard for Software Life Cycle Processes—Risk Management.

[15] Jones C., *Assessment and Control of Software Risk, Yourdon Press Computing Series*, Prentice Hall, 1994.

[16] Kitchenham B., Linkman S., "Estimates, uncertainty, and risk", *IEEE Software* (May/June 1997).

[17] Lister T., "Risk management is project management for adults", *IEEE Software* (May/June 1997).

[18] Moynihan T., "How experienced project managers assess risk", *IEEE Software* (May/June 1997).

[19] NASA Software Policy, Directive NPD 2820.1C.

[20] Paulk M.C., Weber C.V., Garcia S., Chrissis M.B., Bush M., "Key practices of the capability maturity model, version 1.1", Software Engineering Institute, CMU/SEI-93-TR-25, February 1993.

[21] Ropponen J., Lyytinen K., "Components of software development risk: How to address them? A project manager survey", *IEEE Trans. Software Engrg.* **26** (2) (February 2000).

[22] Roy G.G., "A risk management framework for software engineering practice", in: *IEEE Proceedings of the 2004 Australian Software Engineering Conference (ASWEC'04)*.

[23] Sherer S.A., "The three dimensions of software risk: Technical, organizational, and environmental", in: *IEEE Proceedings of the 28th Annual Hawaii International Conference on System Sciences*, 1995.

[24] Williams R.C., Walker J.A., Dorofee A.J., "Putting risk management into practice", *IEEE Software* (May/June 1997).

[25] Yau C., "A quantitative methodology for software risk control", in: *Proceedings of the 1994 IEEE International Conference on Systems, Man, and Cybernetics*, 1994.

# The PERFECT Approach to Experience-Based Process Evolution

## BRIAN A. NEJMEH

*INSTEP Inc.*
*999 Chapel Forge Court*
*Lancaster, PA 17601*
*USA*

*Systems and Entrepreneurship*
*Messiah College*
*One College Avenue*
*Grantham, PA 17027*
*USA*

## WILLIAM E. RIDDLE

*Solution Deployment Affiliates*
*658 La Viveza Court*
*Santa Fe, NM 87501*
*USA*

*Fraunhofer Institut Experimentelles*
*Software Engineering*
*Fraunhofer-Platz 1*
*67663 Kaiserslautern*
*Germany*

**Abstract**

Improvement game plans—carefully defined, organized and managed sequences of process change activities based on standards, maturity models and best practices—are critical to a company's success. Also critical is the ability to evolve processes in response to precipitous, unpredictable changes to critical business-context factors such as financial goals, customer desires, personnel availability, and available process performance support technology. This chapter describes an approach—PERFECT—to process evolution resulting from many decades of experience in helping companies—of a variety of sizes and in many industry sectors—rationally, rapidly and incrementally evolve their processes, often but not necessarily in the context of an overall improvement game plan. The approach is based on a framework—PEDAL—identifying twelve categories of activities comprising process evolution. Three Case Studies introduce the framework and process evolution approach and show their application across a wide variety of situations to evolving a company's processes through narrowly focused, short, overlapping process evolution exercises each addressing a set of tightly inter-related processes. Several important lessons learned are discussed, followed by a description of a variety of simple techniques and tools allowing process change agents to rationally describe, understand, learn from, plan and manage process evolution exercises. The chapter ends with a discussion of various improvements that should be made to the PERFECT process evolution approach and its underlying PEDAL framework.

# 1. Introduction

A company's engineering, business and operational processes are major determiners of its success. It is through these processes that the company identifies customer needs, develops and delivers quality products, applies leading edge techniques and tools, competes within the marketplace, demonstrates conformance to regulatory and contractual constraints, manages its out-sourcing and subcontracting arrangements, and keeps its work force up-to-date professionally. Process deficiencies with respect to any of these business-context factors can lead to serious failures, including: reduced market-share; decreased profitability; increased time-to-market; insufficient work force capability and productivity; and non-effective, inefficient business performance. Any of these negative effects can "sound a company's death knell."

Companies fully understand that to prevent these potentially disastrous results they must rationally, incrementally, and agilely adjust their products in response to changes to customer desires, marketplace structure, personnel availability and capability, business goals, and available technology, as well as many other business-context factors. They know this requires developing near- and long-term product-related objectives, tracking the progress of projects against these objectives, and modifying the objectives in response to project performance difficulties and failures. They additionally know they must argue that their products are suitable with respect to their business context, for example, through their marketing literature and demonstrations of regulatory constraint satisfaction. They realize they must learn from the experiences gained in one project to improve the conduct of future projects. Finally, they know there will be precipitous, unpredictable changes to their business context and they must respond—as quickly as possible—by appropriately modifying their product-related objectives, projects, suitability arguments and experience interpretations. In short, successful companies understand that rational, incremental, agile *product evolution* is key to their success and survival.

Companies often fail to understand that rational, incremental, agile *process evolution* is equally key to their success and survival. Successful companies frequently improve their engineering processes, for example in response to a need to demonstrate some level of product development and project management capability. However, they often fail to address the improvement of their business and operational processes to the same degree, with the same care or with the same levels of effort. In addition, companies often fail to realize that maintaining the status quo, process-wise, in the face of change is often a more critical issue than is improvement. Finally, they often focus on relatively long-term improvement based on an assumption of business context stability and fail to realize that they must also be positioned to quickly change their processes in response to precipitous, unpredictable changes to their business context. As a result, companies are often surprised to find that while they have addressed process improvement with major efforts consuming extensive resources, they still fail in ways that can be traced to process deficiencies.

As a result of a collective five decades helping companies—of many sizes and in many industry sectors—successfully evolve their processes, we have concluded that a superior process evolution capability is *the* key factor in assuring a company's success. We have found that the capability *often* requires the ability to use standards, maturity models and best practices to continuously improve the company's processes over relatively long periods, measured in years. In addition, we have also found that the capability *always* requires the ability to rapidly—in a matter of weeks and months—adjust their processes in response to sudden, unforeseen events. The longer term focus allows the company to address business context requirements, for example, the need to periodically demonstrate conformance to regulatory constraints. The shorter term focus helps the company contend with precipitous, unpredictable changes to the company's business context, for example, an unexpected failure to demonstrate conformance because of seemingly ancillary factors such as an inferior training program.

Further, we have found that the basis for achieving and maintaining the shorter term focus is to understand the *dynamics* of process evolution, the ways in which process evolution can and must change to cope with new business contexts. Further, we have found that these changes can best be accommodated if process evolution is conducted through multiple, short, concurrent, iterative, mutually influential process change exercises, each narrowly focused on a small set of specific, highly interrelated, business-context issues.

Finally, we have found that this approach to process evolution can create a sense of confusing, unmanageable "chaos." We have developed a framework and an associated process evolution approach to help process change agents cope with this apparent chaos. The framework—which we call PEDAL (Process Evolution Dynamics Activity Landscape)—helps process change agents describe, understand, learn from, plan and manage process evolution exercises. The process evolution approach—which we call PERFECT (Process Evolution Rationalization through Flexible, Experience-based, Continuous Tailoring)—helps process change agents continuously, iteratively, and rapidly perfect the company's processes in response to sudden, unforeseen business-context changes.

The goal of this chapter is to help companies understand and effectively apply PEDAL and PERFECT. To set the stage, we first discuss *improvement game plans* supported by standards, maturity frameworks and best practices (Section 2) and then argue the need for a more expansive *process evolution* point-of-view (Section 3). We then describe the PEDAL framework (Section 4) and the PERFECT approach to process evolution (Section 5). This is followed by a discussion of a variety of techniques and tools developed to support the PERFECT process evolution approach (Section 6). The chapter ends with a discussion the value of the PEDAL framework and the PERFECT process evolution approach as well as several ways in which their value could, and should, be improved (Section 7).

## 2. Improvement Game Plans

Companies look to standards to understand *why* their processes should have various properties, maturity frameworks to understand *what* activities should be included in their processes, and best practices to understand *how* the activities might best be carried out. Successfully addressing all three of these concerns assures that a company's processes continuously match the company's needs and objectives by achieving more than merely satisfactory levels of process excellence (see Achieving Process Excellence sidebar).

Work-to-date on achieving high degrees of process excellence by addressing these *why*, *what* and *how* concerns has addressed several aspects of evolving a company's processes over time. Taken collectively, the results support the definition of *improvement game plans*: carefully defined, organized and managed sequences of process change activities based on standards, maturity models and best practices. We discuss improvement game plans in this Section using primarily software development process examples.

Standards—for example, the ISO 9001 Standard for product quality [25] and the Business Standards Institute's standard regarding the confidentiality, integrity, and availability of information [8]—identify goals and requirements for an improvement game plan. These standards do not directly identify activities, roles, artifacts or assets (see "Speaking of Processes" sidebar). Nor do they indicate operational aspects such as how the activities should be carried out or the responsibilities of specific roles. They do imply, and often explicitly state, major conditions that must be satisfied for the processes to be judged acceptable with respect to some area of concern such as product quality or information security. The standards contribute to achieving process excellence by focusing the attention of the company's process change agents upon critical business issues. They contribute to a company's success in many ways, most notably by highlighting regulatory or contractual constraints

Achieving Process Excellence

High levels of process excellence lead to engineering, business and operational processes which constantly satisfy the company's needs and are 'fit for use.' The key aspects of achieving process excellence are:

**Discipline:** process performance is orderly and steadily converges on an intended result; processes may be easily managed

**Maturity:** processes are consistently performed from project to project; processes are continuously improved based on experience

**Agility:** processes can be adjusted to both expected and unexpected changes in the use of their interfaces; interfaces may be changed in response to new requirements

**Efficiency:** process performance is rapid and cost-effective; time and effort are not wasted

"Speaking of Processes"

Clear process description requires the distinction of several different types of process entities:

**activity:** a unit of work performed in carrying out the process; for example, *Develop Project Plan*

**role:** a set of permissions and obligations which must be adhered to during activity performance; for example, *Project Manager*

**artifact:** a tangible object created or modified by activities; for example, *Project Plan*

**condition:** a situation occurring during process performance; for example, *Project Plan drafted*

**asset:** a resource supporting process performance; many relate to artifacts, for example a `template` provides an initial value for some artifact (the `template` itself is not manipulated during process performance but rather it is copied to provide an initial version of the artifact); other assets relate to activities, for example, a checklist, a policy statement, or a standard; still others are automated agents (i.e., tools) or human agents that support achieving a role's responsibilities.

See [48] for a more detailed discussion of the concepts useful in describing processes.

which affect the company's ability to sell its products as well as obtain and retain contracts.

Definitions of effective, efficient best practices provide descriptions of detailed, concrete activities and tasks within the processes. *Agile methods* [1,20] are one example. Each reflects its developer's philosophy regarding the purpose of agility and defines specific techniques for agile process performance. Another example is the *operational procedures* collected and promoted by the IEEE Computer Society for software development [22] and the Project Management Institute [43]. Best practices reflect—often merely by assumption or implication—process excellence-related requirements. For example, eXtreme programming [5] proposes that a Code Module activity be conducted by two programmers, one to create the module's code and the other to continuously assess whether or not the code is syntactically and semantically correct. This is intended to satisfy requirements such as: "the module's code satisfies its requirements" and "errors are caught as early as possible." Best practices contribute to a company's success because satisfying the practices' specific requirements contributes to satisfying success-related requirements regarding product quality, product development efficiency, project manageability, work force effectiveness, etc.

Maturity models provide a "bridge" between the requirements-oriented standards and the implementation-oriented practices. These models:

(1) identify key practices that contribute to meeting success-related requirements;
(2) organize the practices into coherent collections; and
(3) in terms of the collections, define a sequence of successively more mature levels of capability.

The definitions of the key practices imply the activities that are needed and often additionally identify relevant artifacts, roles, conditions and assets. Perhaps the most widely known maturity model is the Carnegie Mellon® Software Engineering Institute (SEI[SM]) *Capability Maturity Model®* (*CMM®*) [41]. This maturity model identifies a wide variety of software development practices, organizes them into five Process Areas, and uses the Process Areas to establish a sequence of increasing capability from *Level I: Ad Hoc*—at which process performance is somewhat random with little discipline or efficiency—to *Level V: Optimizing*—at which a company has unambiguously defined and fully integrated their management and engineering processes, conscientiously captures process-performance data, and uses the data to guide not only project management and conduct but also continuous process improvement. Other example maturity models are the SEI's *Capability Maturity Model Integration* (*CMMI®*) (*V1.1*) [11] which also addresses software development, the

---

[SM] SEI is a service mark of Carnegie Mellon University.
® Carnegie Mellon, Capability Maturity Model and CMM are registered in the U.S. Patent and Trademark Office by Carnegie Mellon University.

Information Systems Audit and Control Association's *Control OBjectives for Information and related Technology* (*COBIT*) framework [12] which addresses business as well as software development processes, and the *Six Sigma* approach [50], developed by General Electric, to achieving high levels of product quality. Maturity models assist in achieving process excellence in two ways: first, by focusing attention on the myriad concerns in a logical sequence, and secondly, by suggesting both an overall design for the company's collection of processes (along the lines delineated by the practice collections) and conceptual designs for the processes themselves (in terms of activities, roles, artifacts, conditions and assets identified in the process definitions).

The work-to-date on *why*, *what* and *how* concerns is quite complementary, addressing different aspects of improving a company's processes over time. For example, the maturity model work may be viewed as setting a context for establishing the requirements for applying agile methods [13]. As another example, agile methods can be considered as possible ways to accomplish many of the key practices established by maturity models [6].

Improvement game plans—carefully defined, organized and managed sequences of process change activities—are based on standards, maturity models and best practices. The standards provide overall requirements for the efforts. Maturity models establish a basis for overall, iterative, long-term improvement by establishing a logical sequencing for the work that has to be done. In addition, a maturity model's key practice definitions establish conceptual designs for the processes and establish specific requirements for these processes. Finally, best practice definitions support the definition of detailed, concrete approaches to carrying out the processes.

In many cases, improvement game plans are based on the CMM maturity model and move the company, step-by-step, from a primitive, ad hoc level of capability to a superior, optimizing level. The details of a variety of these efforts, and data demonstrating their cost-effectiveness and value, may be found in the SEI's Software Engineering Information Repository http://seir.sei.cmu.edu.

Over the past decade, significant improvements to the applicability and value of improvement game plans have come from them not being viewed as a strict, level-by-level "march" from the primitive to the superior level. This has included simultaneously addressing several levels [16], interleaving a concern for other standards, for example, [8] and the People Capability Maturity Model [14,51], and skipping levels and shifting among maturity models as the available standards, maturity models and best practices, as well as the company's process improvement goals, mature [37].

## 3.   Process Evolution

Improvement game plans are critical to a company achieving the levels of process excellence needed to successfully compete and survive. These game plans, however, are focused on relatively long timeframes (measured in years) and are based on an assumption of stability that is often precipitously disrupted, especially in today's highly dynamic business climate. Work forces may be reduced with little advance notice, mergers lead to a company suddenly having many ways of conducting their business, poor and good performance (in terms of profitability, sales, etc.) can radically change process improvement budgets (positively as well as negatively), competitors enter the marketplace with little warning and little advance knowledge of their market-niche focus or their "unique selling points," and product/service providers are continually introducing new capabilities that might, if adopted, significantly improve a company's engineering, business and operational processes.

The use of improvement games plans must therefore be augmented with a compatible approach to process improvement that allows the company to respond to sudden, unforeseen changes to their business context. We call this additional approach to process improvement *process evolution*. In this section we discuss the nature of process evolution and requirements for effectively and efficiently carrying it out. The rest of the chapter discusses an approach to process evolution, reflecting our experiences in many quite radically different process improvement situations, that meets these requirements.

### 3.1   Process Evolution Focus and Intent

Process evolution efforts, in contrast to improvement game plans, are focused on short timeframes (measured in weeks or months) and specifically intended to help companies cope with precipitous, unpredicted changes to their business context. They are intended to complement improvement game plan-based improvement efforts. They are also intended to provide an effective approach to process improvement for those companies that realize they must continuously improve their processes in response to business-context changes but decide, for whatever reasons, not to make the investment needed to use an improvement game plan-based approach. Finally, an important focus of process evolution efforts is upon maintaining the *status quo* in the face of change. In industry sectors not subject to regulatory constraints or sectors in which companies are not required to demonstrate specific levels of capability, maintaining the status quo in the face of business-context changes is often quite critical.

## 3.2    The Nature of Process Evolution

Process evolution involves a variety of parallel, inter-related streams of activities, each focused on specific objectives and collectively focused on achieving some goal. These streams are complimentary and must be coordinated, consistent, and mutually supportive. Further they must rapidly provide positive results. This is not only because they are focused on the short term. It is also because there is frequently not enough time to pre-arrange for the commitment of all the needed resources, and early positive results are needed to be able to obtain additional support.

During process evolution, the focusing business context can (and will) precipitously change in totally unpredictable ways. Process evolution must, therefore, not only rapidly provide near-term successes but simultaneously support the knowledge acquisition that supports the description, understanding, learning, planning and managing that allows companies to contend with future business-context changes. This requires a focus on making continuous, incremental, iterative change by concurrently performing many activity streams, each narrowly focused on one or a small number of specific business-context issues.

## 3.3    Process Evolution Requirements

Our view of process evolution implies a variety of specific objectives, among them:

- coordination among the many activity streams that are occurring in parallel; for example, the concurrent upgrading of a company's processes and the material it uses to retrain its work force and train new hires;

- coordinated and mutually influential concern for corporate-level requirements, needs, objectives, and constraints; for example, concern for the need to effectively compete in some new market segment when defining an activity stream's objectives (and vice versa);

- appropriate resource allocation decisions; for example, the funding and staffing of a workflow automation effort that would, if implemented, considerably reduce the cost of re-training the company's work force with respect to new versions of the company's processes; and

- rapid, timely distribution of effective process documentation that helps process performers understand what they should do, why, and how it differs from what they have been doing; for example, deploying the process documentation via the company's intranet with advice about how to tailor the processes to specific types of projects.

Meeting objectives such as these requires satisfying the following requirements for process evolution:

- recognition of multiple, parallel streams of process evolution activities,
- effective coordination among these activity streams,
- synergy across the activity streams with respect to business objectives,
- incremental accumulation of information about the company's processes, and
- support for improvement game plan activities.

## 4. The PEDAL Framework

After actively participating in more than a dozen process evolution efforts, and reviewing reports and detailed records from several dozen others, we have found that:

(1) most efforts—including the best planned ones—appear to be somewhat chaotic in nature,
(2) there is always an order underlying the apparent chaos, and
(3) this underlying order may be articulated in terms of interacting streams of activities.

We have created the PEDAL framework is to allow the "orderly chaos" to be clearly and succinctly articulated. One objective is to allow process change agents to discover and unambiguously describe complex, apparently chaotic, process evolution efforts. A second is to allow the change agents to transcend the details and gain a solid understanding of "What happened?" A third objective is to allow the change agents to identify lessons learned and guidance that may positively affect the company's future process evolution efforts. The fourth and final objective is to allow the change agents to successfully plan and manage future process evolution efforts.

In this section, we first describe a view of process evolution that fosters rational discussion. Then, we define the PEDAL framework, first in terms of general evolution stages, then in terms of three fundamentally different kinds of process-related information, and finally in terms of twelve fundamental activity categories. This section ends with a discussion of the framework's use in describing process evolution dynamics.

### 4.1 A General View of Process Evolution

Processes evolve incrementally over time, sometimes in formal, well-planned ways but often informally as a result of experiences gained during their performance.

Projects

> By "project" we do not mean merely the "official projects" a company uses to organize and track its work, the productivity of its work force, its profitability, etc. The project may be formally commissioned and actively managed, for example, a project commissioned to develop a new version of a product or maintain an existing product. Alternatively, the project may be neither formally commissioned—for example the "project" by which employees trade information, often around the water cooler, about their experiences in carrying out their work—nor fully, actively managed—for example, the "project" by which a team manages the evolution of techniques and tools supporting the company's operational processes.

Process evolution is therefore often perceived as chaotic with many activities being carried out in parallel, each activity changing not only the details of some specific process but also the interfaces among the processes. The apparent chaos is only an illusion, however, and there is an underlying order. Key to recognizing this order is to focus on a subset of the processes being evolved and describe the streams of activities that change the processes over time. Once these activity streams have been articulated, then coordination among them may be described in terms of the interactions among the activity streams.

A collection of processes is often comprised of sub-collections which have *strong process coherency*—by which we mean that changes to one process in the sub-collection lead to changes to many of the other processes in the sub-collection—but which have *loose process coupling*—by which we mean that changes to a process in one sub-collection leads to few, if any, changes to the processes in some other sub-collection.

A *process set* is a collection of processes to be performed during some project (see Projects sidebar). For example, a `Software Development` process set typically contains `Requirements Management`, `Software Design`, and `Walkthrough Review` processes as well as many other software development-related processes. A process set has strong process coherency because the processes share many artifacts and have many critical dependencies. For example, a `Requirements` document will be shared among most all of the processes in the `Software Development` process set and the `Software Design` process may not begin until the `Requirements` document has been developed by the `Requirements Management` process and been validated to some degree. On the other hand, the coupling among process sets is loose because document sharing and other dependencies among projects are typically minimized to allow effective, efficient progress as the projects proceed in parallel. For example, the document sharing and dependencies between a company's `Software Development` and `Human Resource Management` process sets will typically be limited to `Job Description` documents and satisfaction of a `Staffing Needs fulfilled` condition controlling the initiation of the project.

A *process evolution exercise* is the coordinated and managed performance of activities that results in new versions of the processes in a process set. A process evolution exercise may primarily focus on only one, or a small number, of the processes in a process set. However, because of a process set's strong coherency, it is often necessary to update many, perhaps all, of the processes in a process set to maintain their process-to-process consistency. Therefore, while the process evolution exercise may begin with a focus on only one process, it is not unusual for it to expand in scope to other processes in the process set.

In addition, a process evolution exercise identifies requirements for changes to processes in other process sets. The exercise will almost always reveal the need to change processes in other process sets, again to maintain consistency. Therefore, one process evolution exercise may lead to requirements for some other process evolution exercise that may be being performed concurrently or may be performed in the future. These requirements may be expressed in many ways. Most often the requirements are specified in terms of the definitions of artifacts shared among the process sets. Frequently, the requirements involve the definition of conditions that control coordination between processes in different process sets. These conditions identify the situations that the processes in one set expect will be established or reacted to by the processes in the other set.

It is certainly possible that the requirements resulting from one process evolution exercise cannot be satisfied. This leads to the trading of information about the requirements among the exercises in an attempt to concurrently change the processes in mutually satisfactory ways. This overlap of the process evolution exercises with the exchange of information about the necessity and satisfiability of requirements is what leads to the illusion of chaos.

## 4.2   Process Evolution Stages

We have found that twelve activity categories are both necessary and sufficient for describing, understanding, learning from, planning and managing process evolution exercises. The activity categories pertain to long-term efforts, lasting one or more years, and short-term ones, lasting only a few weeks or months. The categories are not only pertinent to process evolution efforts guided by well-defined plans but also to efforts that are relatively unplanned and unmanaged. Finally, the activity categories are pertinent to processes that govern a company's large-scale, engineering efforts—for example, its software development and maintenance processes—as well as to its more narrowly-focused operational procedures—for example, its travel-reimbursement and report-production processes. These activities form a "basis set" for process evolution—all process evolution efforts are comprised of a (perhaps complex) combination of activities, each belonging to one of the activity categories, and no process evolution efforts involve activities which do not belong to one of the categories.

We set the stage for defining and discussing the activity categories, and therefore defining and discussing the framework, by first indicating their general nature in terms of a four-stage process evolution model and the nature of the information the activities use, modify and produce in terms of a set of three databases. The four-stage process evolution model is discussed in this section. The databases are discussed in the following section.

The PEDAL framework is a variant of Shewhart's Plan-Do-Study-Act (PDSA) statistical quality-control model [49] underlying Deming's work on quality improvement [15]. Another process improvement-oriented variant of the PDSA model is the QIP software engineering-oriented improvement model [4] developed by the Fraunhofer Institute for Experimental Software Engineering in Kaiserslautern, Germany, and its sister organization, the Fraunhofer Center for Experimental Software Engineering, in College Park, Maryland. A third variant is the IDEAL CMM-oriented software development process-improvement model [31] developed at the SEI. In contrast to these other PDSA models, PEDAL concerns the objectives of process evolution efforts. These objectives reflect the goals of one (or, in some cases, two) of the process evolution stages depicted in Fig. 1.

### 4.2.1 Scope

The goal during this stage is to establish a process evolution exercise's context, requirements, progress-related metrics and plan. This includes determining the operating context for the processes as well as establishing requirements for the process evolution exercises. It also includes defining specific process evolution objectives and metrics for assessing progress during process evolution exercises. A *process architecture* is defined during this stage to allow process change agents and stakeholders clearly and unambiguously discuss the processes and argue their suitability. (See Process Architecture sidebar.) The concepts defined by the process architecture are used to record information about "as-is" versions of the processes, versions reflected by the current documentation and the ways the processes are actually carried out. The concepts are also used to define "should-be" versions of the processes, versions that reflect suggestions from process performers and other stakeholders about changes. The "as-is" and "should be" descriptions are used to make the process, process documentation and process evolution requirements concrete and well-defined. The descriptions are also used to establish concrete plans for process evolution exercises.

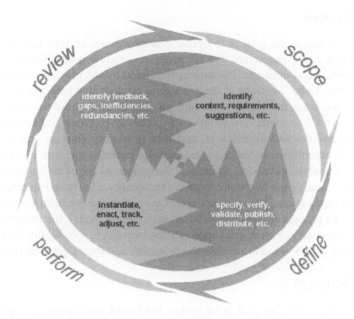

FIG. 1. Process evolution stages.

Process Architecture

A process architecture identifies the concepts that process change agents and stake-holders use to describe and evaluate a company's processes. Process architectures vary from company to company, and a company's process architecture will vary over time. A process architecture rigorously defines the process elements pertinent to describing and evaluating the process. This may be the full set of possible elements: activities, roles, artifacts, conditions and assets. Normally, however, it is just a subset of these elements. The process architecture also rigorously defines the elements' attributes and their inter-relationships. The major reasons for specifying a process architecture are:

**Clarification:** The process architecture identifies the concepts which are important in thinking about a company's processes.

**Discussion:** The process architecture facilitates discussion among process change agents and other stakeholders.

**Evaluation:** The process architecture facilitates checking the completeness, consistency and accuracy of the processes and their descriptions.

See [48] for a more detailed discussion of process architectures.

### 4.2.2  Define

During this stage, the goal is to define new processes, as well as new versions of current processes, and assure that the processes, and their descriptions, are complete, consistent and accurate. The concepts defined by the process architecture are used to define "to-be" versions of the processes, versions that help process performers understand what they need to do and provide them with advice and guidance about how to do their work, how to tailor the processes to group and individual preferences, capabilities and experiences, and how to modify their on-going work and update their capabilities in order to successfully perform the new processes. Pre-performance analysis is used to assure that the processes are of high quality and "fit for purpose." Analysis is also done to assure the quality, clarity and suitability of the process documentation. The analyses are often performed by informal and formal reviews. If the process architecture is based on a formal model, the analyses may be analytic or simulation-based. Trial applications, in projects specifically set up for the purpose, may also be used to validate the processes and their documentation.

### 4.2.3  Perform

During this stage, the goal is to gather use-based qualitative and quantitative information about the quality, clarity and suitability of the processes and their descriptions. The process documentation is distributed throughout the company. The defined processes are instantiated (as project plans) and performed. With respect to process evolution, this includes training company personnel, tailoring the processes to meet the needs of specific projects as well as the experiences and skills of project personnel, and creating project plans and refinements to plans for the company's projects. Process performance is actively monitored during this stage. Information is collected about performance failures (and successes); this includes information about any changes needed to successfully perform the processes. Information is also collected about the process documentation, including data about inconsistencies, its completeness and clarity, and customizations made by process performers to match their preferences, capabilities and experiences.

### 4.2.4  Review

The goal during this stage is to retrospectively, based on historical evidence, prepare advice affecting the definition of future process evolution exercises. The definitions of the processes and process evolution exercises, and information about their performance, are audited for conformance to constraints and the satisfaction of requirements. Information gathered during prior applications of the company's processes is examined to identify and prioritize changes to the processes and their documentation. Similar information gathered during process evolution exercises is examined to identify and prioritize potential changes to the definition or conduct of future exercises. With respect to both the processes and process evolution exercises, the information is examined to identify: new assets and improvements to existing assets; additional information to be gathered about standards and best practices; and other influences upon what happens during the other stages.

## 4.3 Process-Related Information

During a process evolution exercise, the activities in the various stages use, modify and produce process-related information relevant to some aspect of the process or its performance. Over time, this information creates a *repository* of all that is known about the company's processes and their effective, efficient, accurate performance. The repository also, over time, reflects all of the versions and variants of the processes that have been used for a company's projects. The repository is, in essence, a corporate knowledge base concerning the company's processes.

Conceptually, the repository is composed of three (logically) distinct databases, each holding a categorically different kind of information:

- a *Process Information* database holding descriptions of the various processes in terms of the process elements, attributes and relationships defined by the company's process architecture,

- a *Resource Information* database holding the assets (templates, checklists, policies, etc.) supporting performance of the company's processes, and

- a *Project Information* database holding the specific work products (designs, meeting minutes, white papers, etc.) produced during the course of a specific project.

A company's repository contains one Process Information database holding information about all of its process sets, several Resource Information databases each pertaining to one of the company's process sets, and many Project Information databases, one for each of the projects carried out by the company.

Activities in all of the categories create new information to be held in these databases based on the information held in previous versions of the databases. As such, the activities collectively mature the information in these databases over time. In many cases, this maturation involves updating the information in one of the databases by synopsizing or integrating information held in the other databases. For example, a new version of an asset (deposited into a Resource Information database) is often created by inspecting, and abstracting from, the various specific artifacts (held in Project Information databases) created from previous versions of the asset.

## 4.4  The PEDAL Framework

The PEDAL framework identifies twelve fundamental activity categories. Collectively, activities falling into these categories serve to mature the information held in the repository. Individually, the activities use, modify and produce information held in the repository in order to satisfy specific objectives.

The PEDAL framework is depicted in Fig. 2 using a "flower-petal" diagram first suggested by Kouichi Kishida [27]. The twelve activity categories are depicted as "flower petals" with an indication of their relationship to the four stages. Their production and use of information in the repository is indicated by the bi-direction arrows used to depict each category. The intended implication is that activities in all of the categories may proceed concurrently with their coordination achieved by the exchange of information through the repository.

The diagram implies a logical, clockwise, progression of activities in the various categories, starting with a Gather activity, and their use and production of informa-

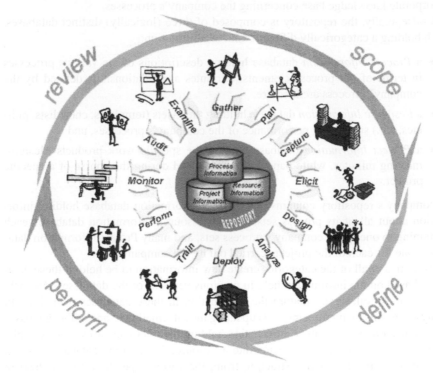

FIG. 2.  The PEDAL framework.

tion contained in the repository. The diagram, however, does not *prescribe* that an exercise starts with a Gather activity, that activities in all of the categories are performed during a process evolution exercise, or that activities are actually performed in the implied order. In fact, as demonstrated by the Case Studies in Section 5, a process evolution exercise will involve only a subset of the activities, performed as necessary to meet the exercise's objectives.

The order of activity performance is not, however, totally arbitrary. Major constraints come from the need to produce information before it is needed; these constraints are implied by the definitions of the activity categories appearing in the following sections. Other constraints are also important. Any number of business, technical, resource or schedule constraints may dictate that certain process evolution activities are performed or omitted to satisfy such constraints. For example, a need to quickly, under severe time constraints, define a process might lead to an initial Define stage activity without any preceding Plan stage activities.

The categories are discussed in this section; use of the diagram to describe and understand actual process evolution exercises is discussed in the following section.

### 4.4.1 Gather

Activities in this category establish requirements for a process evolution exercise and the processes it will address. They also collect assets that will facilitate performance of the processes and the process evolution exercise itself. The objective is to find, filter and organize information that either impacts the company's processes and the process evolution exercise or can be used to support performance of the processes or the process evolution exercise. Information obtained during these activities may include constraints upon the processes: maturation frameworks (e.g., CMM, CMMI, etc.), regulatory constraints, policies, standards (e.g., ISO 9001), etc. It may also include information about resources supporting both process and process evolution exercise performance: detailed procedures and techniques, best practices, templates, checklists, (good and bad) examples from prior performances, etc. The information might also concern other constraints such as budget and schedule limitations, market conditions and personnel availability and capability. As one result of activities in this category, the Process Information database contains information about constraints upon the processes being evolved, as well as their importance and their necessity. As another result, process change agents have information that affects the definition of a concrete process evolution exercise plan.

### 4.4.2 Plan

These activities develop a plan for a process evolution exercise and define the criteria used to measure progress and success. The objective is to identify requirements

Process Metrics

Process metrics define quantitative and qualitative measures related to a process, its performance and its evolution. Process metrics are relevant to a process entity (i.e., activity, role, artifact, condition, asset) or combination of entities.

**Static Process Metrics** relate to properties of the defined process (e.g., number of role types, artifact types, etc.).

**Dynamic Process Metrics** relate to process performance properties (e.g., elapsed time for the performance of an activity, number of activities performed, number of artifacts created, etc.).

**Process Evolution Metrics** relate to the process of making changes to a process over time (e.g., number of iterations within a process evolution exercise).

See [35] for a more detailed discussion of process metrics.

for the process evolution exercise and the processes resulting from the exercise. Essentially, these activities define the criteria that may be used to measure progress during the process evolution exercise to determine its success. The criteria concern the static or dynamic properties of the processes being evolved during the exercise and the properties of these processes' descriptions. They also concern the status of a process evolution exercise. A major task is to define the metrics (see Process Metrics sidebar) used to measure process evolution exercise progress. As a result of activities in this category, the Process Information database contains concrete exercise objectives defined in terms of process properties and process description properties.

### 4.4.3  Capture

These activities gather and organize information about the company's *should-be* processes—the processes as they should be performed, usually as described in the documentation for the processes. One objective is to establish a process architecture—process elements, their attributes and their inter-relationships facilitating process agent and stakeholder discussion and evaluation of the company's processes—and use it to organize information about the company's should-be processes. Another objective is to update the company's process documentation to use the terminology defined by the process architecture and remove any inconsistencies. A third objective is to gather suggestions from process performers and other stakeholders concerning improvements to the processes and their documentation. As a result of activities in this category, the Process Information database contains a definition of the process architecture and, in terms of it, information about not only the processes as they should be performed according to the current process documentation but also stakeholder thoughts about potential improvements.

### 4.4.4   Elicit

These activities gather and organize information about the company's *as-is* processes, the processes actually being performed. The objective is to understand how the processes are currently being performed in practice. In part, these activities capture the experiences of the company's work force as indicated by the ways personnel actually carry out the processes and have tailored and customized them to match the needs of specific projects or personnel. These activities involve interviews with process performers, trainers, appraisers and others having insight into process performance. The Process Information database is updated to reflect the "reality" of what really happens during process performance This may be done by changing the information about the should-be processes, or it may be done by developing a separate description so that comparisons may be made between the should-be and as-is processes. A side-effect of these activities may be to suggest changes to the process architecture. As a result of activities in this category, the Process Information database contains information about how process performers actually carry out the processes.

### 4.4.5   Design

These activities specify the company's *to-be* processes—the processes the company wishes to use in the future. The objective is to define the company's new or revised processes. The major task is to develop descriptions, expressed using the concepts defined in the process architecture, of processes that conform to any constraints, appropriately utilize the company's personnel, and reflect the personnel's experiences and expertise. This usually involves an intermixture of work focused on a process set and work devoted to defining the interactions among the process sets. A side-effect of these activities may be to suggest changes to the process architecture. As a result of activities in this category, the Process Information database contains information about the processes that are to be used, in the future, to conduct the company's business.

### 4.4.6   Analyze

Activities in this category focus on verifying and validating the processes and their descriptions. One objective is to analyze the processes and process descriptions (see Process Analysis sidebar). Another objective is to make appropriate change requests or suggestions. Activities in this category verify and validate the work

Process Analysis

---

Evaluation of the quantitative and qualitative characteristics of a process and its (should-be, as-is and to-be) descriptions.

**Purpose:** identify errors and anomalies, i.e., characteristics that might be errors depending on information beyond the scope of the analysis and requiring human interpretation.

**Properties:** suitability of a process or its description concerns:

- **clarity:** the degree to which performers will reach similar interpretations or results
- **completeness:** the degree to which performers' questions have been addressed
- **consistency:** the degree to which redundant statements are congruent
- **accuracy:** the degree to which the results of performance will be as specified
- **suitability:** the degree to which the results of performance are as required or needed

**Approaches:**

- **inspection:** informal and formal reviews; for example, a `Walk-through Review` or a `Desk Check Review`
- **formal analysis:** analysis based on a formal model's semantics; for example, analysis based on a state transition model of processes
- **simulation:** analysis based on the simulation of process dynamics; for example, use of a queuing theory model of system dynamics
- **trial use:** use of the process in a non critical-path exercise; for example, use of the process in an additional project specifically designed to evaluate the process rather than contribute to some project's success

---

done during Capture, Elicit and Design activities. Using process descriptions and reports generated from the information in the Process Information database, reviewers check the properties of the processes and their descriptions. The reviewers also check process-versus-process properties, description-versus-description properties, and process-versus-description properties. The reviews may involve consideration of process dynamics through, for example, the consideration of use cases. The reviews may also involve considering the differences between old, as-is processes and proposed, to-be processes. As one overall result of activities in this category, the Process Information database contains information about errors or anomalies in the processes or their descriptions, perhaps accompanied by change requests or suggestions.

### 4.4.7 Deploy

These activities disseminate descriptions of the processes throughout a company. The primary objective is to communicate the new or revised processes and help on-going projects migrate to the new processes as required and feasible. This leads to activities which define a look-and-feel for the company's process documentation, create documentation having this look-and-feel, and distribute the documentation to the company's work force. The means of distribution will determine the form that needs to be created; intranet distribution, for example, requires a web-based form. Multiple versions, with alternative look-and-feels or presented in alternative rendition media, may have to be created. The documentation may be accompanied by information about: how to best view the documentation or obtain hardcopy versions; the situations in which use is mandatory; how to migrate an on-going project to the processes; the ways in which the processes may be tailored; and how to couple the new processes to already-existing processes with which they interact. A second objective is to create and distribute addition descriptions, for example, material soliciting feedback about the quality and suitability of the processes and their documentation. A third objective is to collect information about any difficulties encountered in distributing the descriptions. As a result of activities in this category, the Process Information database contains versions of the descriptions accompanied by information regarding the ease or difficulty of introducing the process within the company.

### 4.4.8 Train

These activities provide on-the-job and course-based process education and training to new hires and the current work force. An objective is to establish the work force's ability to accurately, effectively and efficiently carry out the processes. This may involve educating the work force about the process architecture (as needed to understand the process descriptions). It may also involve developing the skills to use new resources (e.g., new tools) that support process performance. Another objective is to collect information about any difficulties encountered in educating and training the company's work force. As a result of activities in this category, the Process Information database contains material explaining the processes in terms supporting on-the-job and course-based training accompanied by information regarding the ease or difficulty of process-related education and training.

### 4.4.9 Perform

The goal of this category's activities is to assure that the processes can be, and are, performed accurately, effectively and efficiently. Support for assuring accuracy, effectiveness and efficiency may be provided by dedicated personnel ("process police") or electronically (i.e., via process workflow support). One objective with respect to process evolution is to adapt the company's processes to the specific needs of the company's projects and identify any problems in the processes or their documentation. An additional objective—again, with respect to process evolution—is to gain experience in using the processes and identify any additional problems that need to be addressed. A third objective is to modify the processes to address problems discovered during performance. As a result of activities in this category, the Process Information database contains information about how the processes are applied in the company's projects and any difficulties which were encountered.

### 4.4.10 Monitor

These activities track process performance with the intent of gathering information that will affect future process evolution exercises. The objective is to obtain quantitative data about the performance of the processes over many projects. Activities in this category gather the data that will be used in assessing the processes and improving them over time based on experiences in performing them in a variety of projects. Metrics defined during activities in other categories guide the data collection. Data collection may be manual, assisted by checklists or other assets. When workflow support is provided, data collection may be accomplished by instrumenting the process' workflow script. A secondary task, therefore, is to note any workflow support problems that impact data collection. As a result of activities in this category, the Process Information database contains quantitative, longitudinal data concerning the ease and difficulty of performing the processes.

### 4.4.11 Audit

During activities in this category, the processes, process performance information and process descriptions are reviewed with respect to their requirements. A major objective is to assess conformance to regulatory or contractual constraints. In part, this involves reviewing the processes' descriptions, perhaps by reviewing process documentation and perhaps by reviewing descriptions published in some review-oriented format. It also involves reviewing information about process performance to assure that it is consistent with the process descriptions. Review meetings will require special reports about the processes and their performance designed to assist in addressing review questions and issues. As a result of activities in this category, the Process Information database contains information about the conformance and non-conformance of the processes, their documentation and their performance to regulatory or contractual constraints.

## 4.4.12  Examine

These activities serve to organize and analyze information gathered during other activities and develop a prioritized list of potential process changes with an indication of their criticality. The objective is to collect and sort out feedback from the other activities to aid the definition of future process evolution exercises. This involves recording lessons learned, analyzing the results of audits, defining desirable and/or required changes, identifying desirable additional performance-support resources, specifying changes to the process architecture, defining new process and process description properties to be analyzed, specifying new process performance data to be collected, etc. It also involves identifying requirements for future versions of the process. In short, it involves:

(1) reviewing feedback from the previous activities;
(2) noting requirements for future process versions, and
(3) capturing valuable assets to support future process performance. As a result of activities in this category, the Process Information database contains a list of process evolution activities that should be carried out in future process evolution exercises. The primary result is a prioritized list of actions that could to be taken to satisfy the (new) requirements.

## 5.  Describing Process Evolution Dynamics

PEDAL identifies and defines a collection of fundamental process evolution activity categories. Because the framework is non-prescriptive, it admits a wide variety of process evolution exercises. In this Section, we first give three Case Studies indicating the broad range of process evolution exercises permitted by the PEDAL Framework. Following this, we make some general observations about process evolution as indicated by the Case Studies. Finally, we identify some important lessons learned from the Case Study applications as well as other applications.

### 5.1  Process Evolution Description Case Studies

We have applied the PEDAL framework and PERFECT approach to process evolution in a variety of situations. A representative sampling are discussed in this section including one application in which process evolution was carried out in the context of an improvement game plan, one that addressed the company's business—rather than its software development—processes, and one that involved the development—over several applications in a variety of companies—of a general process for business-driven product planning.

### 5.1.1 CMM-Based Development of Processes Conforming to Regulatory Constraints

This Case Study concerns a large, multi-national manufacturer of embedded software devices. The manufacturer had developed a set of processes governing the "birth-to-death" design, development, marketing, delivery and maintenance of their products' software components. Their products were subject to regulatory constraints levied by a Government organization. They had been appraised at CMM Level II and wished to move to Level III. Prior to a Level III appraisal, they would be audited with respect to the regulatory constraints. Their processes were described in several Word documents, roughly one per process set. For example, they had one document for their three different kinds of Peer Review processes and one for their Requirements Management processes. They were aware of many problems in their process documentation, ranging from simple inconsistencies (e.g., different names in different documents for a particular role) to process-logic errors (e.g., work products not produced before they are needed) to incompatibilities across their process sets (e.g., inconsistent definitions of the interfaces between processes in different sets). In addition, they were finding that manual maintenance of the documents was not only increasingly error prone but also starting to consume so much time that deployment of new versions could not be accomplished in a timely manner. Finally, they had received several requests for views better satisfying process performer needs (e.g., a table that describes document production and usage by activities) and had recognized the need to provide views that supported non-performance needs (e.g., views supporting work force training, conformance audits and capability appraisals).

**Evolution Effort Scope.** The company's Software Engineering Process Group (SEPG) decided to focus on their software development processes, simultaneously prepare for their regulatory-constraint audit and Level III appraisal, correct the noted inconsistencies and errors, move from their Word-based documentation to *WebGuides* (see WebGuides sidebar), and include new process performance-related views as much as possible. They consciously decided to delay work on related processes, for example, process training and process documentation deployment processes; before working on these other processes, they planned to gain experience by performing them in the context of the evolving software development processes. Additionally, they consciously decided to delay producing audit- or appraisal-oriented views; again, they planned to use experience during the upcoming audit and appraisal to guide development of these views.

**Evolution Effort Goals.** The SEPG launched a process evolution effort having the following goals:

WebGuides

---

A WebGuide is a website providing highly interlinked information regarding process elements (activities, roles, artifacts, conditions and assets) as well as their inter-relationships [28,47]. WebGuides are not narrative discussions of the process (as often found in process documentation). Rather they are stylized, structured presentations that describe each process element in terms of "information chunks." For example, for an activity the chunks include: a synopsis of the activity, the roles which have responsi-bility for successful activity performance, the other roles that participate in the activity, the activity's enabling and termination conditions, etc. [18]. WebGuides are typically quite large (4000-plus web pages are not unusual). They cannot, therefore, be success-fully maintained manually. General knowledge management technology, for example, Lotus Notes [21] may be used to maintain and generate them. It is more effective, however, to use specialized *WebGuide Generation Tool Suites* allowing the definition of a process-specific schema for the knowledge base and specialized view generators (examples include Dreamweaver [30], iNotion [24], IRIS [39], process Max [44], and Spearmint/PMC [23]. These tool suites provide a rich array of reports about the inter-relationships among the process elements; for example, artifact usage and production views, activity predecessor and successor views, views regarding role participation in activities, etc. Only a small number of these views are provided by manually main-tained process documentation because of the difficulty of establishing and maintaining them and their consistency.

---

- G1: Update *all* of the company's software development processes in preparation for the upcoming audit and appraisal.
- G2: Correct errors and inconsistencies noted to date as well as problems and inconsistencies uncovered by several levels of review (by the SEPG itself, by personnel from various divisions invited to review the new processes, and by the work force in general).
- G3: Convert the company's software process documentation to WebGuides de-ployed via the company's intranet.

### *Evolution Effort Strategy.*

The SEPG decided to initially focus on just two of its software process sets—Peer Review and Requirements Management. By initially addressing more than one process set, the SEPG intended to develop a process architecture appropriate for all of its software development processes. By simultaneously addressing two process sets, the SEPG intended to define a reasonable approach to evolving a process set as well as an understanding of the inter-play among the process evolution exercises addressing different process sets.

After completing some, but perhaps not all, of the work on these two process sets, the SEPG planned to move on to its other software development process sets—Quality Assurance, Design and Implementation, Maintenance, etc. Because of time pressures, the SEPG planned to move on to addressing other process sets as soon as they felt that their approach to working on a process set was reasonably well-defined and fairly stable. They were willing, in other words, to forego achieving an "ideal" process set evolution process in favor of achieving a reasonable process that would, itself, have to evolve over time.

### *Process Evolution Exercise.*

With respect to a process set, the SEPG planned to evolve its processes using a highly iterative steam of activities. This activity stream was:

1. Define a process architecture pertinent to the process set's processes. (Capture)
2. Import the information in existing Word documentation into a Process Information database. (Capture)
3. Generate an example WebGuide and review it to validate the process architecture and the WebGuide look-and-feel. (Analyze)

     Iterate activities 1-through-3 as necessary.

4. Improve the process definitions and correct errors and inconsistencies noted to date. (Design)
5. Generate WebGuides and have the full SEPG use them to identify errors and inconsistencies in the processes and process descriptions. (Analyze)

     Iterate activities 4-through-5 as necessary.

     Iterate activities 1 and 3-through-5 as necessary.

6. Disseminate a test version of the WebGuides for review by a select group of personnel with respect to the suitability of the processes in the process set. (Deploy)
7. Analyze the feedback from the review and identify issues that need to be addressed. (Analyze)

     Iterate activities 4-through-7 as necessary.

     Iterate activities 1 and 3-through-7 as necessary.

8. Assure that the processes, and their WebGuides, are ready for deployment throughout the company. (Analyze)

9. Make the WebGuides available via the company's intranet. (Deploy)

10. Tailor the processes to meet the needs of specific projects and the abilities and experiences of project personnel, noting not only the changes needed to tailor the processes but also any errors and inconsistencies in the processes or the WebGuides. (Train)

   Iterate activities 4-through-10 as necessary.

   Iterate activities 1 and 3-through-10 as necessary.

*Exercise-to-Exercise Influences.*   The SEPG recognized that changes to the processes within one process set would imply changes to processes in another process set. It planned to use changes to Requirements Management processes to understand the changes that might be needed to Peer Review processes, and *vice versa*. It also planned to address this cross-exercise influence by developing and evolving, through experience, a process for managing changes to inter-process interfaces. The SEPG recognized that this would introduce a "broader scope" activity stream that coordinated changes across multiple process evolution exercises.

## 5.1.2   Rationalization of Inventory-Control Processes and Development of Requirements for Process-Support Technology

This Case Study concerns a product service division within a large, Fortune-100 company. This division was responsible for receiving defective/damaged products and determining the most cost effective approach to repairing the defects, completing the repairs, and shipping the repaired product back to the customer. The division used straightforward, fairly standard, inventory control procedures not only to support the repair process but also to support identification of the "best" repair approach based on the current status of their parts inventory. The inventory control procedures were supported by an inventory control system.

For various reasons, the decision had been made to replace the current inventory control system in six months. The cut-over to the new system was scheduled to be done over a weekend; no overlapped operation of the old and new systems was planned. The division had established an Information Technology Infrastructure (ITI) Project to implement and test the new inventory control system to the degree needed to avoid a major disaster when the new inventory control system became operational.

The Manager of the ITI Project had found that the documentation for the current inventory control procedures was not only rather vague but also rather poorly understood and rarely consulted. She also predicted that, because of differences between the old and new inventory control systems' hardware (mostly its user-interface terminals), the current as-is procedures would have to be changed, mostly in minor ways but in some cases in rather significant ways. She was understandably worried that mismatches between the service personnel and her IT personnel understandings of the current and new procedures would lead to a failed implementation and a resultant inability to conduct business.

### Evolution Effort Scope.

The ITI Project Manager had decided to first document the procedures to the degree necessary:

(1) for service and IT personnel to mutually agree on the division's current procedures,

(2) to support describing changes to the procedures, and gaining rapid mutual agreement, as the IT personnel learned more about how best to apply the new inventory control system, and

(3) to support the definition of test cases. There was the conscious decision to not, initially at least, describe the procedures to the degree of detail and precision needed for a new Procedures Manual; the more immediate need was to prepare for the cut-over and it was felt that future work could mature the procedure documentation as needed for the Procedures Manual. There was also the conscious decision to not yet tackle the problem of how to validate the new procedures through controlled testing by service personnel. It was decided that a decision about how to do this should be delayed for two-to-three months until the decision could be made in the light of experience with implementing the new support capabilities.

### Evolution Effort Goals.

The ITI Project Manager established a single goal:

- G1: Precisely define the inventory control procedures to the degree needed for IT personnel to understand the current procedures, define and get approval for changes, and effectively test the implemented support prior to the change over.

### Evolution Effort Strategy.

This led to a rather straightforward approach: develop an initial set of descriptions in consultation with the service personnel, use modified descriptions to gain agreement by the service personnel on changes to the procedures, and develop and conduct tests to verify correct implementation. It was fully realized that critical to the success of this approach would be to use a description technique already familiar to both the service and IT personnel and, in addition, carry out activities in parallel as much as possible.

### Process Evolution Exercise.

The ITI group decided on the following approach:

1. Identify an appropriate approach to describing the procedures. (Capture)
2. Interview the service personnel and develop descriptions of the procedures currently in use. Iterate with the service personnel until there is agreement that the descriptions are accurate. (Elicit)
3. Consult with service personnel to explore and get approval for changes that implementation of the support indicates would be valuable or necessary. (Analyze)
4. Use the descriptions to define verification tests, conduct the tests and then iterate back to activity 2 as test results indicate is necessary. (Analyze)

*Exercise-to-Exercise Influences.* The first activity was easily (and rapidly) completed; the current documentation already used a transaction-based, state-machine, notation. The problem came at the start of the second activity. In preparing for the interviews, a list was made of the current as-is procedures so that they could be grouped into categories and the interviews could be prioritized and most efficiently conducted on a category-by-category basis using well-focused group interviews. The procedure list identified some 350-plus procedures, *many* more than anyone expected. It was quickly realized that time did not allow for all of them to be described, even to the somewhat minimal level of detail and precision needed.

This led to changing the second activity as follows:

2.1 Identify the 50-or-so "high-risk" or "critical path" procedures most critical to the division's success. (Plan)
2.2 Interview the service personnel and develop descriptions of these procedures. Iterate with the service personnel until there is agreement that the descriptions are accurate. (Elicit)

In addition, the third and fourth activities were changed to focus on the "high-risk" or "critical path" procedures.

This modified approach was quite successful for several weeks. The next problems arose when the IT personnel consulted with service personnel to get their approval for changes. A rather simple problem was that it was difficult for the service personnel to understand exactly what changes had been made. Most problematic was the difficulty, for both service and IT personnel, to understand the impact of the changes.

It was realized that the "change impact understanding" problem had to be solved by the service and IT personnel conducting "animation exercises," depicting the dynamics of process performance, when considering the changes. It was also realized that these exercises, as well as the problem of understanding the change being proposed, could be facilitated by some visualizations of the "delta" between the old and new procedures. This led to changing the first activity[1] as follows:

1.1 Identify an appropriate approach to describing the procedures. (Capture)
1.2 Develop an approach to describing the differences between the old version of a procedure and its new version. (Plan)

A technique, and some supporting tools, were rather quickly implemented to support the side-by-side description of old and new procedure versions with highlighting of the differences. This led to successful, on-time cut-over to the new inventory control system.

### 5.1.3 Business-Driven Product Planning

This Case Study concerns the development, over several process evolution exercises with several technology product companies, of a business-driven product planning approach [36] to address a common product planning problem within these companies. The common problem had to do with how to define and decide upon the range of possible product feature, cost, schedule combinations which were best and, in turn, how to define a product release plan that afforded some degree of release flexibility. Said another way, all of the companies wanted to avoid the "all or nothing" nature of traditional product release plans.

This Case Study focuses on solving a set of process-related problems that were common to a number of different companies. This required that the process we developed be robust enough to be applied in a myriad of diverse settings, including those companies that were small start-ups in the initial phases of product definition and release as well as those that were very mature, publicly-held software companies whose products had been in the marketplace for 15-plus years.

**Evolution Effort Scope.**  Unlike the other cases studies, this work was not birthed within the context of a single company. Rather, having seen a common product planning problem across a myriad of companies, we decided to scope out and define a business-driven product planning process that could be used in a variety of settings. The work began by providing a high-level process for defining a product release plan. Once the high-level—generic—product planning process was defined, use of it in subsequent applications incrementally expanded its activities based on lessons learned from applying the process in various commercial settings. We consciously

[1] This changed an "already completed" activity. This was not really a problem since the PERFECT view is that activities are done in parallel rather than in sequence. Introducing the new task within the first activity merely meant that it was "re-activated" and the new task was addressed, with influences upon the performance in the future, of the other activities.

decided to delay work on automation related to the product planning process. We also deferred any work on related processes, such as project management and version and configuration management, that would obviously be impacted.

*Evolution Effort Goals.*   We defined the following goals for the product planning process:

- G1: It must apply to technology product companies, regardless of their size, industry or state of product maturity.
- G2: It must provide a sound decision framework for assessing the range of possible feature, schedule, cost combinations and lead to the definition of release schedules with desirable content, predictable costs and firm schedules.
- G3: It must lead to a series of incremental release streams that preserve release flexibility.
- G4: It must provide a product planning process that could be used in the context of an agile development method.

*Evolution Effort Strategy.*   We initially focused on defining the high-level product planning process. We first performed a best practices literature search in the area of incremental product planning. We also researched the product planning disciplines of successful software product companies. This led to an initial product planning process that consisted of the following activities—Define Release Themes, Define Feature Areas, Analyze Feature Cost & Value and Plan Product Release. This allowed us to grasp the breadth of the planning process scope we were attempting to address without requiring us to define the details of the process. Clearly, however, such a high-level process definition was not ready for use by any company. The second iteration of the product planning process definition involved decomposing and defining, to the task-level, each of the activities. Only after completing the second stage of process definition evolution was the process ready for pilot deployment. In the third iteration, the product planning process was applied in a variety of diverse settings in parallel. This resulted in a number of keen insights about deficiencies, anomalies and opportunities for improving the product planning process definition. In turn, we continued to evolve the product planning process to the point where it was successfully deployed across a number of diverse companies.

*Process Evolution Exercise.*   We decided on the following approach:

1. Research and gather best practices related to product planning. (Gather)
2. Create a high-level process architecture and a preliminary high-level product planning process definition. (Capture)

3. Develop a task-oriented product planning process by decomposing the high-level product planning process definition. (Design)
4. Analyze the process definition for completeness, consistency and ease of application prior to pilot use of the process. (Analyze)
5. Apply the product planning process in a variety of different company settings. (Perform)

> Iterate activities 3 and 4 based on
>
> feedback and lessons learned from activity 5.

6. Package and distribute the product planning process within companies. (Deploy)

***Exercise-to-Exercise Influences.*** In this Case Study, the exercise-to-exercise influences concern the evolution of the product planning process. By design, our first exercise defined a high-level process; we needed, though a subsequent exercise, to define a process that was concrete enough to be applied in specific situations. Further iterations were driven by experiences gaining in using the process in a number of different situations.

## 5.2   Observations

Collectively, the Case Studies highlight a variety of aspects of the PEDAL framework and PERFECT approach to process evolution and the impacts of using them. These are discussed in this section.

The PEDAL framework is applicable to a wide variety of process evolution situations, pertaining not only to a company's software engineering processes but also to its business and operational processes. In addition, process evolution exercises may be in the context of an improvement game, but this is not necessary.

Every process evolution exercise has a specific focus and a well-articulated set of goals. At the start of every exercise, there is also an identification of what the exercise will not address. This clarifies what future exercises will have to address. Experiences in one exercise will, and should, prejudice subsequent exercises. The prejudice may be strong but that isn't always the case. For example, with respect to the first Case Study, in handling the evolution of non software development-related process sets (e.g., a `Conformance Demonstration` process set) the approach used for software development-related process sets *could* be used. In all likelihood, however, these exercises will be different, if only because they have different goals, are carried out by other personnel and are conducted in other timeframes (and therefore different business contexts).

In every process evolution exercise, the emphasis is upon evolving both the company's processes and its ability to conduct process evolution exercises without a large amount of "up front" work on either the company's process evolution process or a standard versions of its processes. Some advance work is needed in both regards, but it need not be extensive. To adjust for the lack of extensive advance work, the company's processes and its process evolution processes are evolved iteratively through the use of short, relatively well-focused, exercises that lead to the rapid definition of new versions based on actual experience. The company's standard processes and its ability to conduct process evolution exercises both evolve as a result of experience gained in a variety of exercises.

There is no "one size fits all" process evolution exercise; exercises will vary, often quite radically. A major reason is that an exercise's starting point—in terms of the category of its first activity—varies as needed to meet the situation that exists when the exercise begins. In addition, an exercise involves the activities needed to meet the exercise's objectives; in fact, mapping the activities to the categories highlights the activities' objectives by indicating the information they use and should produce. However, the activities included in an exercise and their sequencing depends on the results of previous exercises and varies as required to meet the exercise's focus and goals.

Exercises are performed concurrently. This raises the need to directly address the cross-flow of information from one exercise to a concurrently performed exercise. This cross flow of information reflects the fact that, to make progress, activities in one exercise will at various points need information produced by activities in other exercises. If the information is not available, the activities will have to wait. This means that a major challenge is to not only minimize the information-flow cross-dependencies among activities but also to manage activity performance in a way that reduces waiting time. We have found that general, fairly obvious, principles can help meet these challenges; for example, the principle "continuously monitor activity performance and watch for bottlenecks."

Another general observation is that use of the PERFECT process evolution approach and its underlying PEDAL framework tends to reveal the "order within the chaos." In practice, process evolution efforts involve hundreds of activities all proceeding concurrently. The overall effort will, without a doubt, appear to be chaotic; but there is an underlying order and this can be exposed by using the notions of process evolution exercises, with the PEDAL framework not only clarifying the nature and objectives of the activities within an exercise but also the information flow-based interactions among the activities within the exercises and between activities in concurrent exercises.

The final observation is that none of the exercises discussed in the Case Studies explicitly included the development of techniques and tools to support process evolution. This was the case in general over all of applications of the PEDAL framework. Their development and application is important, but we have found it best to have them follow from, rather than drive, the exercises. Several techniques and tools have, in fact, been developed and applied and these are discussed in Section 6. Their development and application, however, followed from actual needs identified during process evolution exercises rather than from some pre-conceived, hypothetical, need.

## 5.3  Lessons Learned

A major theme of the PERFECT process evolution approach is "learn from experience." The most important lessons learned from applying the approach to date are:

- Plans are important but "getting started earlier rather than later" is critical. A major reason is that the intent is to enable companies to rapidly respond to a precipitous, unpredicted change in their business context. This is, we found, better done in the context of on-going process evolution, when the focus and goals are well known, rather than in the context of process evolution planning. Plans are, of course, needed to obtain the necessary management commitment and the allocation of resources. But the "up front" value demonstration should be, first, narrowly focused on the initial exercises and, secondly, accompanied by an argument that process evolution will be a continuing, never ending, corporate endeavor.

A second major reason is that the emphasis of the approach is to capitalize on experience. When company's have no experience—such as in the second Case Study—then it can be gained by doing some actual exercises. Some experience can be obtained by involving a process evolution services provider, but these providers will not have the requisite knowledge of the company's culture, practices, and history. Getting started and responding to problems as they arise is, we found, best not only in gathering experience but also in establishing the "frame of mind" needed to respond to business context-change "problems."

- Do not automate too early. It is often easy, especially for technologists, to focus on developing supporting techniques and tools rather than on the job at hand, namely process evolution. For example, in the third Case Study, our early intuitions were to build a tool suite to support the automation of the product planning process. We resisted the temptation to do so, instead focusing on the real-world application of the product planning process and refining the process based on lessons learned during its application. This proved to be invaluable in rapidly evolving the product planning process to a point where it could be practically used in a diversity of product planning settings. In addition, by delaying the development of the tool suite we had a much understanding of the its requirements.

- Solving one process-related problem more often than not significantly contributes to the solution of other process-related problems. For example, in the situation discussed in the second Case Study, success required the development of ways to visualize the differences between the old and new procedure versions. This capability provided quite valuable support for the company's retraining of its work force.

- Develop and actively use a Process Architecture. The architecture establishes a basis for clear, crisp communication not only among the company's process change agents but also between these agents and stakeholders. It also establishes a basis for identifying confusions, inconsistencies and errors in the process and its documentation. In situations where the company already had process documentation, we found that the process architecture could be quickly articulated in an initial Capture activity specifically devoted to process architecture definition. When the company had no documentation, or their documentation was minimal or poorly explained their processes, we found it best to evolve the architecture over the first one-to-three process evolution exercises. In all cases, we found a process architecture critical to continued success and that the architecture itself should be continuously evolved by periodically performing an appropriate Capture activity (as part of some process evolution exercise).

- Work with, rather than, replace any existing graphical depictions of the company's processes. In almost all of the applications of the process evolution approach, we found that the company already had a graphical depiction of their processes showing, most usually, the flows of control and documents. These depictions were often quite detailed. They were also quite often complex and ambiguous (indicating that the company did not have a well-developed, mature, process architecture). They did, however, allow the process change agents and stakeholders to focus their attention and discuss problems and alternative solutions. Rather than take the top-down approach of first "cleaning up" the diagram (and its underlying process architecture) we found it best to delay this activity and, further, do it incrementally across several process evolution exercises.

## 5.4   Process Evolution Description

Narrative descriptions of process evolution efforts, such as used to describe the Case Studies, certainly help process change agents focus their efforts and understand the purposes of their actions. They also provide process change agents with insights into what happened during a process change exercise. In this section we discuss two representations we have additionally found useful in providing retrospective descriptions of process exercises.

An example of one of these representations appears in Fig. 3 which graphically depicts the exercise discussed in the first Case Study. In this description, the exercise's activities are mapped to the twelve activity categories defined by the framework with ordinal numbering used to indicate the order in which the activities are performed. Rather than merely duplicate the information in the narrative description, this graphical representation indicates additional information. First of all, it explicitly indicates which activity categories were *not* included in the exercise. This can help process change agents understand and articulate the reasons for whatever problems might have arisen. It can also help the agents understand the applicability of the exercise as a means of addressing a business-context change. Finally, by providing a checklist of sorts, it can help the agents focus on what might need to be done in future exercises.

Graphical descriptions such as appearing in Fig. 3 also better imply the information flow that takes place during a process evolution exercise. By explicitly indicating the databases in the repository, it allows process change agents, with additional annotations, to describe the flow of information among the process evolution activities.

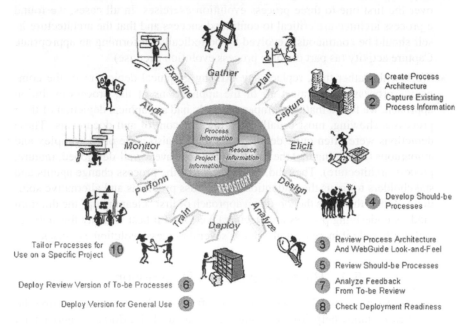

FIG. 3.  Process evolution exercise.

Because of the different intents of the databases, it helps the agents understand when the flow takes place—roughly: during process definition, during project planning, or during process performance. This in turn, can help the agents understand the source of problems (including inordinate wait times) and predict the feasibility of some future exercise either in continuing to address some business-context change or some change that precipitously occurs.

We have found that as process change agents become familiar and facile with using graphical descriptions such as appearing in Fig. 3 they can quickly articulate and discuss process evolution problems, potential solutions, lessons learned to consider in defining future exercises, and the potential value of an exercise with respect to some business-context change. In addition, the agents can use these descriptions to develop rough plans for process evolution exercises. This partially involves understanding the skills, knowledge and experience that will be needed and adjusting the plan to better match the capabilities of available personnel. It also involves first getting a sense of what will done before delving into the details and then developing, in parallel with developing the details, a better understanding of how the activities relate to each other. Finally, we have found that these descriptions are also a valuable management tool; they can be used to describe the status of an exercise, the potential sources of problems, and key conditions that need to be checked in the future.

However, we have also found that an additional representation is needed to fully support process change agents in understanding, learning from, planning and managing their process evolution exercises. This stems from the fact that descriptions such as in Fig. 3 can become quite complex and hard to understand when, as typically occurs, there are many iterations during a process evolution exercise. An approach to depicting iteration during process evolution exercises is shown in Fig. 4 which corresponds to the first Case Study but which, for the purposes of example, reflects a more complete accounting of the activities in the process evolution exercise.

Descriptions such as in Fig. 4 more clearly indicate the flow of control among iterations that are not evident from descriptions such as in Fig. 3 and are poorly depicted by annotating such descriptions. In addition, they reveal major phases that occur during the process evolution exercise. In Fig. 4, for example, the phases are:

(1) Commit: validate the approach and develop a plan,
(2) Convert, Correct and Update: iteratively develop and review versions,
(3) Launch: obtain additional reviews and prepare for application within projects, and
(4) Use: apply the processes within projects.

Note that the flow of activities is depicted in two ways in Fig. 4. First, there is a timeline that indicates membership of the activities in the various categories. Second, below the timeline presentation is a textual representation that uses a regular

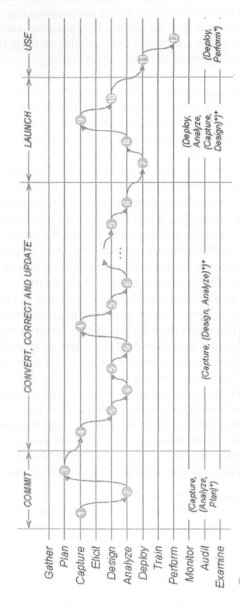

FIG. 4. Process evolution exercises—alternative depiction.

① convert two representative processes using the default architecture
② review the results to determine the value of moving to a WebGuide
③ plan conversion of the organization's existing process definitions and develop an initial organization-specific process architecture
④ convert several of the organization's processes to a WebGuide
⑤ improve the WebGuides to reflect "current thinking" about the processes that had not been reflected in the paper-based documentation
⑥ have the SEPG informally review the WebGuide to identify incompleteness and inconsistencies
⑦ deploy a test version for review by a select group of personnel outside the SEPG
⑧ analyze the feedback from the review personnel
⑨ redefine the process architecture and convert the WebGuide as needed to reflect the new architecture
⑩ do a "final review" in preparation for deploying the WebGuide on the organization's intranet
⑪ deploy the WebGuide via the organization's intranet
⑫ use the documentation in the organization's projects

expression-like notation to indicate the flow of activities with respect to the categories. Both highlight the extent to which the activities "cover" the activities as well as the iterative flow of the activities. Together they indicate that there are both graphical and textual ways to depict the iterative flow.

## 6.  Process Evolution Infrastructure

Many techniques and tools have been created to support developing and carrying out improvement games plans. Primary among them have been Process Asset Libraries [40] providing templates, examples, procedures, guidance checklists, etc., for both the process being working on and the improvement process itself. In addition, most improvement game plan-oriented service providers have developed their own set of proprietary techniques and tools.

All of these techniques and tools provide part of a process evolution infrastructure —a collection of techniques and tools supporting a company's process change agents' work in describing, understanding, learning from, planning and managing their process evolution exercises. In our work developing the PERFECT approach to process evolution, we have found it necessary to add additional techniques and tools to support process evolution exercises.

The techniques and tools we have developed result from our experiences in applying the PERFECT approach to process evolution. The need for them was "discovered" during on-going exercises, they were quickly defined and implemented as needed for that exercise, and then they were refined and improved as needed to support subsequent exercises. Tool suites can be, and often are, evolved over time, but this is generally within the context of some overall, rational plan [46]. In our experience, the overall plan is not necessarily needed.

### 6.1  Additional Assets

Several of the applications of the PERFECT approach to process evolution focused on software process improvement. Most of these were in the context of the company's improvement game plan effort. In these cases the assets developed over time by the improvement game plan community were generally sufficient; they sometimes had to be changed in relatively minor ways but that is a normal part of improvement game plans. In those applications that focused on software development processes but were not in the context of an overall improvement game plan, we found it most often sufficient to "re-use" assets from the improvement game plan community, changing them as necessary to fit the needs of the company.

We had to develop additional assets for three reasons. First, the PERFECT approach to process evolution concerns many activities that are not within the scope of many, if any, improvement game plan approaches. For example, the deployment of new versions is within the scope of the PERFECT approach to process evolution but not within the scope of the standards, maturity models and best practices underlying improvement game plans. We had to development assets to support these additional activities, for example, a "deployment checklist" to help rationalize and guide the deployment of new versions of the process.

Secondly, many of the applications concerned business and operational processes rather than software development processes. In these applications, we had to develop assets specific to these other process domains. These assets were analogous to those developed for software processes by the improvement game plan community. They were, however, quite often radically different from those found in this community for two reasons. First, in the software process improvement community, the processes being considered have a broad scope, for example, a Peer Review process. In business and operational processes, however, the processes generally have a considerably more narrow scope, for example, a Travel Request Approval process. Secondly, business and operational processes are most often thought of in terms of a transaction-based or state change-based model. Software processes are thought of in analogous terms—for example, in terms of information flow among activities—but not with the degree of detail and rigor afforded by transaction-based or state change-based models. For these reasons, the templates we developed for these non software process-oriented models were similar in function but almost always quite different in form from those developed by the improvement game plan community.

The third reason we had to develop new assets was that we needed assets that supported the PERFECT approach to process evolution itself.[2] For example, to support the applications described in the third Case Study, we needed to define a set of templates that corresponded to the product planning process' work products. It is not surprising that these assets are needed; the PERFECT approach to process evolution is, itself, a process and templates, examples, guidance, checklists, etc., are as much needed to support it as they are needed to support the process that is being evolved.

In summary, we needed to expand the contents and broaden the scope of the Process Asset Library in many directions. We did this with little—hardly any—advance thinking about what was needed. Rather, we developed new assets "just

---

[2] This type of asset appears to be largely absent from the set of assets developed by the improvement game plan community. It appears this community has focused on the assets needed for the processes that are being improved. Individual service providers have developed assets supporting their approach to improvement game plan development and conduct. But few assets, if any, have been developed, and made available, by the community at large.

in time," as the need for them became apparent during process evolution exercises, and then evolved them in the course of using them in subsequent exercises.

## 6.2   Process Information Gathering

In all of the process evolution exercises, there was the need to support the gathering of information about should-be, as-is and to-be processes. This often led to the development of "information gathering" assets, primarily forms that we could use for the efficient gathering of information about the process being evolved from process performers, process design experts, customers, and other stakeholders. We found, however, that these forms were hardly ever re-usable from exercise to exercise. Each company had evolved a somewhat unique way of thinking and talking about their processes. The information gathering forms had to reflect this and rarely were the forms developed for one application useful without considerable modification.

In addition, we found that it was generally better to gather information during working sessions with the stakeholders. Just as different companies view processes in different ways, different people having some "stake" in a process will view it in different ways. Forms-based information gathering, therefore, more often than not resulted in confused, sometimes seemingly contradictory, information about the process. Interactive sessions attended by a cross-section of stakeholders were more often the most effective way to understand the process from the collective point-of-view rather than from a variety of separate, hard to integrate, points of view. We ended up, therefore, developing several techniques for interactively gathering information about the company's processes. These were sometimes used to gather information about the company's as-is processes; they were much more often used to gather information about the should-be and to-be processes.

As much as possible we tried to gather information through forms since this was much more efficient than holding interactive sessions. But we found interactive, face-to-face working sessions to be the best way to get unambiguous, understandable information at least two-thirds of the time. Our use of forms and working sessions is explained in the remainder of this section.

- **Architecture Definition Interviews.** As indicated in the list of lessons learned, different companies, and different people connected with a company, think and talk about the company's processes in different ways. Therefore, we tended, over time, to start our engagements by interviewing a sampling of process performers, process change agents, project managers, and corporate executives as well as the company's "process experts," its customers and its investors. These interviews were very open-ended. After establishing the overall intent as being to understand the way stakeholders think and talk about the company's processes, the interviews commenced with the open-ended question: Tell me about your company's processes. The intents were many, from simple to complex. At the "simple" end of the spectrum was the intent to identify the way terms such as *process, procedure, activity, task, step, artifact, document, work product, role, team, condition, milestone,* etc. were commonly used by process change agents and stakeholders. At the "complex" end of the spectrum was the intent to understand the "views"—activity-based, artifact-based, role-based, etc.—that the different parts of the agent and stakeholder community used to understand and talk about the company's processes.

The result was a company-specific process architecture reflecting the company's process-related terminology and, more importantly, those aspects of a process—activities, roles, artifacts, conditions and assets—deemed important by the company's stakeholders. We have come to feel that it critical to start every engagement with this Capture category activity.

- **Patterns.** In some cases—but unfortunately not as many as we expected—the company-specific process architecture aligned with a pre-defined, well-defined architecture. For example, in two cases, it aligned with the ETVX process model [45] in which an activity is described in terms of its *E*ntry conditions, the *T*asks that must be performed, the additional tasks need to *V*erify activity performance, and the conditions that are true when its e*X*its. This led to the use of ETVX patterns in the assets we developed to gather information. It also led to the ETVX point-of-view in interactive sessions we held with stakeholders.

  As another example, in three other cases we found the use of a "phase gating" point of view—a process is comprised of several successive phases, the completion of each phase is "gated" by an activity that checks the validity of some conditions, and gating activities differ with respect to the documents that are considered and the conditions to be checked. Once again, this affected the assets we developed and the focus of interactive sessions.

- **Brainstorming Workshops.** Most often we found that the company's process architecture did not align with an established process model. In addition, we found there were variances, mostly minor, across the stakeholders in terms of their use of terms or their view of the company's processes. Among other things, this meant we were unable to develop effective information gathering forms. The result was that we developed a stylized approach to gathering information through focused, interactive, "brainstorming" workshops with eclectic groups of stakeholders.

  These workshops relied on tried-and-true, classic brainstorming techniques—such as the use of post-it notes, etc.—that have proven to be effective ways to elicit information during well-managed workshops. The sessions were organized into sequences that, collectively, addressed all the important aspects of a

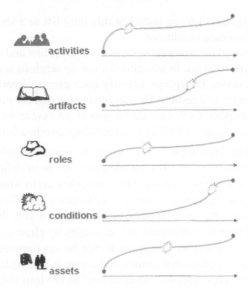

FIG. 5. Process brainstorming.

process. The sequence started with a focus on that aspect, typically activities, identified in the Architecture Definition Interviews as the primary concern of the stakeholders involved in the sessions. The sessions successively treated all of the aspects of a process; this meant that a side-effect was to help the company understand, and treat, aspects that they did not think were important.

In one exercise, three working groups were established, each focused on one of three inter-related processes and having order-of six participants. Over two weeks, each working group held half-day meetings three times a week. The first five sessions for two of the three working groups focused on process aspects in the order depicted in Fig. 5: 1st activities, 2nd roles, 3rd assets, 4th artifacts and 5th conditions. The third group started with a focus on conditions and then moved to a focus on assets, artifacts, roles and activities; this group had a preponderance of management-oriented, rather than performance-oriented participants and this was a more "natural" order for them to consider the various aspects of a process. As graphically illustrated in the figure, in each session comments inevitably arose regarding aspects that were not the session's focus. These were acknowledged and noted but either delayed to a future session or worked, offline, back into the results of a previous session. During each session, the emphasis was on determining "critical" process information. For example, it was easy to identify a large number of conditions gating the termination of an activity; the emphasis was on reducing this long list to a short one identifying the critical termination conditions.

The sixth session for every group was used to review and confirm the results from the first five sessions. In addition, follow-up sessions were used to homogenize the work across the groups, identify inter-process interactions, and verify and validate the overall results. The net result was that coherent descriptions of three of the company's software development processes were developed with about 4.5 person-months of effort (not including overhead effort).

- **Modified Delphi Technique.** Often, it can be quite difficult to get a group of stakeholders to reach a consensus on the goals, scope or definition of a process. We have found the use of a modified Delphi technique in which each participant is asked to respond to a specific question or to rate a list of issues to be a critical tool. Our approach has been to have each participant give their perspective on the matter and then to consolidate the responses by eliminating duplicates and other responses deemed by the group to not be appropriate. The participants then discuss the responses that remain and a vote is subsequently taken pertaining to the matter. This process continues until an obvious choice emerges or the group can reach some acceptable consensus on the matter.

## 6.3 Activity Category-Specific Support

We found it valuable to have tools providing automated support for various activities in the twelve activity categories. Some examples are:

- **Importer.** In many engagements, we used a WebGuide Generation Tool Suite [23] providing for the automated generation of large online process documentation websites (the website was often in excess of 4000 web pages). The tool suite generates the process documentation website from information contained in a Process Information database. The database holds "fundamental facts" about the process, for example, information about which artifacts are used or produced by an activity. The generated website provides views that combine these facts to provide more global summaries useful to process performers, for example, a chart showing the flow of artifacts among the activities in the process.

    Often, companies already had process documentation at the start of an engagement. To apply the WebGuide Generation Tool Suite, it was necessary to identify the "elementary facts" within the current documentation and import them into the tool suite's Process Information database; this was a quite common Capture activity. At first, we tackled this problem on a case-by-case basis and successfully imported Word- and Excel-based documentation as well as documentation held in Lotus databases. Over time we realized that while we could not develop a generalized Importer, we could develop a set of relatively simple transforms that we could mix and match to support what was inherently a "human intelligence needed" procedure. Over time, we automated about 60% of the importing activity.

- **Value vs. Return-on-Investment Analyzer.** In many engagements, it was also necessary to initially gain the support and commitment of senior management. In one case, we developed an Excel spreadsheet-based tool to support this Plan activity. The focus was on transaction-based business processes. We followed an approach used in a study of the Return on Investment (ROI) provided by providing automated support for transaction-based business processes [9]. In our variant of this approach, the independent variables were factors such as the number of performers, the frequency of transaction performance, the cost of automated support implementation, the cost of training, etc. The dependent variables—the results—were estimates of the ROI and the time to cost recovery. The rather spectacular results—ROIs on the order of 10 to 100, and cost recovery generally within four-to-five months—were instrumental in gaining the needed support and commitment. We used variants of this approach, but not always with the use of a tool, to gather support and commitment in several subsequent situations.

- **"Difference" Reports.** In the application discussed in the second Case Study, we developed a tool-supported approach to displaying the differences between the old versions of a process and its new versions. This was achieved by extending the WebGuide Generation Tool Suite to create these information displays. A major part of the extension was to have the database hold information about the old—as-is—and new—to-be—artifacts and activities as well as "same as" information about the relationship between the old and new artifacts and activities. A major part of the display of the differences was a report identifying artifact and activity differences—the inclusion of new artifacts and activities and the deletion of old artifacts and activities.

  We also included the display of differences in the "dynamics" of the new versus old processes. This display showed, given a scenario defined in a starting condition and a set of stopping conditions, how the old and new processes would differ with respect to performing activities to achieve the stopping conditions when beginning performance in the starting condition. To automate the generation of this display of the dynamics, we developed a means to define starting and stopping conditions, relied on previously developed techniques [3,7] for computing activity sequences, and developed a way of displaying the result in terms of flowcharts with the activity sequences highlighted. A sample dynamics display is shown in Fig. 6.

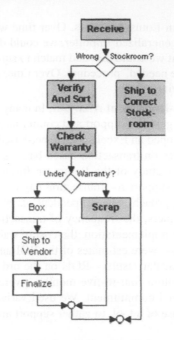

FIG. 6. Sample dynamics display.

## 6.4    Process Change Team Support

In all of our applications of the PERFECT approach to process evolution, we found it critical to provide support for teams of process change agents carrying out the process evolution exercises. This involved not only focusing their attention during meetings but also supporting their decision-making.

- **Team Meeting Support.** In those application in which we used the WebGuide Generation Tool Suite, the periodic team meetings generally had the intent of reviewing the process documentation resulting from the team's work to date, resolving issues as possible, and then moving on to address some additional aspects of the process. A major part of supporting the meeting was to generate a "fresh" version of the documentation to be reviewed in advance of the meeting or in real-time during the meeting.

  In the application discussed in the first study, we additionally extended the WebGuide Generation Tool Suite to incorporate meeting agendas and provide links to the parts of the documentation pertinent to each agenda item. For example, an agenda item might be "validate the association of roles with conditions."

This agenda item would be linked to the various summary reports regarding roles and conditions and, through them, to the role and condition descriptions themselves as well as the definitions of the activities that the roles participated in (to establish the conditions) and the artifacts (that were the process elements most usually used to define the conditions). Linking the agenda item to the role and condition summaries—and from there to the relevant information about roles, conditions, activities and artifacts—made it considerably easier to validate the association of roles with conditions.

In addition, we found it useful to further extend the WebGuide Generation Tool Suite to handle:

(1) a version of the agenda with annotations identifying the decisions made during the meeting and the meeting's results in general;

(2) a list of Action Items; and

(3) a list of Deferred Issues. All of this information could, in turn, be linked into the emerging process documentation. This provided a traceability of the team's work that was easy to use to review the team's work. It also facilitated future meetings. For example, it became rather simple to, as a part of every meeting, review the Deferred Issues, use the links embedded in the issue's description to view information that reminds everyone about the issue's details, and decide whether or not to continue to defer the issue. It was similarly easy to process the Action Item list to check status, raise issues and track progress.

- **Mentoring.** We also found it necessary to "gently" guide the focus and actions of process change agent teams outside of their team meetings. For example, in the situation described in the third Case Study, we had to work with teams, individually and collectively, in order to help them understand how to best apply and adapt the product planning process framework.

  As another example, in the situation described in the first Case Study, the team lead fully understood the importance of considering all five major aspects of a process—activities, roles, artifacts, conditions and assets—but individual team members did not understand the importance of some of these aspects. We had to help each member understand the importance of all of the aspects.

  We therefore found ourselves, in every application, working with process change agents to both broaden their view of a process and hone their ability to work with some particular approach to addressing their company's processes. We ended up using traditional mentoring techniques: "over the shoulder" observation, problem-driven interactions, the use of "hypothetical scenarios," etc.

- **Problem Reports.** From previous work based mostly on "first principles" rather than experience [33,42], we knew that process-evolution change agents would need reports such as a list of roles, a matrix indicating role/activity associations, and Work Breakdown Structure (WBS) descriptions of activities. These reports help process change agents quickly identify problems with the process or its documentation. For example, in one case a list of roles generated after importing the company's documentation revealed that they used some 350 names for only about 100 identifiable roles—the major problem was the appearance of "reasonable" name variants such as Project Manager and Project Leader, Tester and Checker, etc. As another example, review of the WBS for another company's processes indicated that they had many cases in which separately defined processes were actually variants of a "general" process and their documentation could be considerably simplified (and made much easier to maintain) if this were capitalized on.

In every application, however, we found that the groups needed additional reports. Further, these additional reports often concerned the dynamics of the process rather than the static nature of the process description. One of the most complex situations concerned a company having a process architecture that separated uses/produces from succeeds/precedes information. Uses/Produces information indicates activity/artifact relationships. Succeeds/precedes information indicates the time sequencing among activities. We extended the WebGuide Generation Tool Suite to generate reports about inconsistencies such as "this activity uses an artifact that no preceding activity produces." This might not be an error; the used artifact may be produced by some activity in some other process set. But it is an anomaly that must be considered, perhaps with the decision that "everything is OK."

- **Metrics.** Underlying every problem report is at least one factor pertinent to some goal. For example, the role list pertains to a "minimal role definition" factor—"the role list should contain only those roles necessary and sufficient to describe the process"—which, in turn, contributes to the goal of achieving clear, understandable documentation. As another example, a report identifying used artifacts that are not produced by some preceding activity pertains to a process logic factor—"every used artifact must be produced by some preceding activity"—which, in turn, contributes to a process-correctness goal.

Metrics are needed to be able to measure factors. Some metrics may be quite simple and quantitative, for example, the "number of redundant roles in the role list." Others may be equally simple but qualitative, for example, "the degree to which role responsibilities definitions overlap."

Most of the metrics we defined concerned the properties of the documentation, for example, the role list-related metrics just mentioned. However, to allow the PERFECT approach to process evolution to be adequately driven from a qualitative and quantitative perspective, we often had to define metrics reflecting the dynamics of the process. These metrics were often quite complex. The metrics concerning the degree to which used artifacts are or are not produced by a preceding activity is one example. As another example, in the application described in the third Case Study we needed to define a way to quantify the return-on-investment for development effort in terms of relative delivered market value.

- **Views.** A "process view" provides summary information about the process, usually indicating cross-correlations among process elements. For example, a table with rows for the artifacts, columns for the activities and uses/produces indications in each cell is a cross-correlation view. Another, more complex, cross-correlation view is one which identifies "communication obligations," each of which identifies an artifact that must be produced, the role responsible for producing it, the activity during which the artifact must be produced, the roles that will receive and review the artifact, and the activities during which the artifact will be reviewed by the receiving roles ("status reporting" is an example of a communication obligation).

  Problem reports are views of the process specifically intended to evaluate the factors resulting from the goals for a process evolution exercise. In addition we found it valuable to provide views not directly related to a factor. We found that these additional views provided insights that were helpful in assessing the process and facilitating a process evolution exercise but which did not concern some pre-identified factor. Many of these additional views were those that would be provided to process performers, for example, a WBS annotated with used and produced artifacts. We also found that while cross-correlations should be expressed in one way for process performers, process change agents were better served by inverting the correlations. As a simple example, process performers are usually most comfortable with an artifact/activity view that lists for each activity the artifacts it uses or produces. However, for many of the checks process change agents need to make, they are better served by a complimentary view that lists for each artifact the activities that use or produce it. In fact we generally found that change agents needed both of these complementary views to assess the accuracy, completeness and consistency of artifact flow during process performance.

  Finally, we often found it necessary to provide specialized views oriented towards specific evolution issues. For example, in applications within the context of a CMM-based improvement game plan, we found it was important to record and report the relationships between items in the defined process and the items defined by the CMM.

- **Decision Visualization.** In the application described in the third Case Study, we found it necessary to visualize the decisions that were being made about product planning during the performance of the process. We found it very valuable to take some key outputs of the product planning process, the relative effort and relative value estimates for each candidate product feature, and to plot them in a quartile matrix structure (i.e., the $x$-axis divided cost up into four cost quadrants (*very high*, *high*, *medium*, *low*) and the $y$-axis divided value up into four value quadrants (also named *very high*, *high*, *medium*, *low*). We would plot each feature in its proper $x-y$ coordinate matrix location. This visualization helped us to spot anomalies such as very high value and very low cost features, etc.

## 6.5    Process Evolution Infrastructure Summary

Over many applications and many years, we have gradually accumulated a large number of techniques and tools. The need for each was identified during an actual process evolution exercise; none were pre-identified in advance of an exercise. The initial implementation of each was simple, providing just what was needed at the time. Over time, we found that previously developed techniques and tools could be re-used to meet some need that arose during an exercise, sometimes without modification but most often with the addition of some features or capabilities required for the newly identified need.

We have, however, also identified many techniques and tools that we believe should be developed. These are discussed in the following Section in the course of indicating the ways in which the framework-based PERFECT approach to process evolution capability should be enhanced and improved.

## 7.    Value and Future Improvements

We have found that the PEDAL framework provides a solid, clarifying basis for the rapid, rational evolution of a company's process in response to precipitous, unpredicted changes to their business context. We have also found that, while the framework is important, its successful application requires the "philosophy"—embodied in the PERFECT approach to process evolution—of achieving long-term change through narrowly focused, short, overlapping process change exercises each addressing a specific business-context issue. Finally, we have found that positive effects can be obtained within the context of an improvement game plan but that such a plan is not necessary for positive effects to be achieved.

During the course of our applications, however, we have identified many improvements that would be beneficial. Some, as indicated in the previous section, involve the development of additional techniques and tools. Others involve addressing some quite difficult issues. In this section, we first discuss the value of the PEDAL framework and PERFECT approach to process evolution. We then discuss several significant enhancements and improvements we feel are particularly important.

## 7.1 Value of PEDAL and PERFECT

The PEDAL framework may be thought of as a combination of:

(1) a checklist of the activities that should be considered for inclusion in process evolution exercises;
(2) a specification of objectives for process evolution activities in terms of their exchange of information; and
(3) a means of describing the dynamics of process evolution exercises. As such it allows process change agents and stakeholders to crisply and succinctly discuss and evaluate what happened during past process evolution exercises, what is happening during on-going exercises, and what is planned for future exercises. By providing a structured, well-defined basis for canonically, normatively, describing and analyzing process evolution exercises, the PEDAL framework establishes a solid foundation for making process evolution highly experienced based.

Whereas the PEDAL framework focuses on individual process evolution exercises, the focus of the PERFECT approach to process evolution is upon the concurrent and longitudinal inter-relationships and interactions among process evolution exercises. The framework allows a separation of concerns; the improvement work being done on the company's processes can be understood in terms of concurrent work on the company's process sets. Work on a process set is tightly coupled and addressed via a process evolution exercise. The process evolution exercises themselves are loosely coupled, with the coupling following from the exchange of information about the processes being improved and, in addition, the exchange of information about the necessity and satisfiability of requirements. In sum, the PEDAL framework allows process change agents and stakeholders to focus on individual exercises whereas the PERFECT framework allows agents and stakeholders to continuously adapt process evolution efforts in response to problems, in particular precipitous and unpredicted changes to a company's business context.

The PEDAL framework and PERFECT approach emphasize the use of past experiences to influence future actions. This beneficially affects not only the conduct of process improvement efforts but also the implementation of techniques and tools to support process evolution. In keeping with the framework and approach's emphasis on experience, techniques and tools are: identified by concrete needs arising during process evolution exercises; implemented in a satisfying, "as needed," form; and evolved through their application in subsequent exercises. This not only makes it easier to rapidly start process evolution efforts, it also tends to control the effort and resources expended to provide the necessary techniques and tools.

The PERFECT approach to process evolution is not an alternative to using improvement game plans (and PEDAL is not an alternative framework to other PDSA-style frameworks). Rather this approach complements improvement game plan approaches by supporting rapid responses to precipitous, unpredicted events. The approach may be used in conjunction with improvement game plan approaches to add a short-term focus to the game plan's long-term focus. The approach may also be used in lieu of game plan approaches to support process evolution when a company does not have the inclination, need or means to take a longer range perspective. Therefore, the primary value of the PERFECT approach, and its underlying PEDAL framework, is to allow companies to enhance their long-term improvement efforts or make reasonable progress in improving their processes when they do not, for whatever reason, have a long-term improvement game plan.

## 7.2   Improvements

The PEDAL framework and PERFECT approach to process evolution are quite valuable, but they need to be improved in many ways. Several improvements are discussed in this section. In some cases, we are actively pursuing these improvements. In other cases, we have identified the improvement, and some of its critical issues, in the hope that we or others can pursue it in the future.

### 7.2.1   Process Evolution Agility

Our notion of process evolution has some similarities with agile methods [5,20]. Just as the agile methods community sees systems evolving into existence through a series of rapid iterations, so it is with our view of how processes should evolve over time. In alignment with the agile methods community, we see the world of process evolution as highly adaptive and typically not predictive.

We have proposed accommodating the adaptive nature of process evolution through a series of short, iterative exercises. Where we may differ from the agile methods community is that we believe we have defined a canonical process evolution framework within which any process evolution exercise can be defined. That is to say, we believe the range of process evolution activities one may perform is predictive, but the order and manner in which they are performed in sequence and in iteration over time is highly adaptive.

Specific issues include:

- To what extent would agile method practices (and their underlying philosophy) improve the conduct of process evolution exercises? For example, would the notion of "team programming" improve Design activities?
- Can patterns be developed for agile method practices so that they may be easily adopted for inclusion in a new version of a process?

## 7.2.2   Process Evolution Focusing

The PEDAL framework is non-prescriptive about the activities involved in a process evolution exercise and the order in which activities are performed. For example, process definition oriented exercises have their origins in activities in the Gather and Plan category while process measurement oriented exercises have their origins in activities in the Monitor, Audit and Examine categories.

Over time, we have developed several "default" approaches to initiating a process evolution exercise. We have developed an intuitive sense of when each of these is the "right" initial exercise based on the conditions holding when the effort begins. For example, if the company already has process documentation, the first exercise should involve an iteration of Capture and Analyze activities during which the existing documentation is analyzed to discover and verify/validate the process' "elementary facts" (and import them into a Process Information database if a WebGuide Generation Tool Suite is to be used). On the other hand, if the precipitating event is a failure to achieve a target maturity model level during an assessment, the first exercise should involve iterations of Elicit, Monitor, Analyze and Audit activities intended to understand the company's as-is processes in advance of planning the actions needed to make them compliant with the level's requirements.

In our applications we have noticed that some overall "theme" generally influences an effort's initial focus. For example, if the overall emphasis is upon conformance to regulatory constraints, then the effort tends to begin with Gather and Plan activities. On the other hand, if the overall emphasis is upon improving the company's training, then the effort tends to begin with Deploy and Train activities. Finally, if the overall emphasis is upon process performance efficiency, then the effort tends to begin with Perform, Monitor and Examine activities.

Clearly, there is the overall issue of how best to "get things going." Sometimes this is clear; often it is not. Further, we have not found a pre-defined, "one size fits all," exercise that should be used at the beginning of every improvement effort. In fact, we firmly believe that this universally applicable initial exercise does not exist.

Specific issues include:

- What factors help identify an effort's initial exercise?
- Which metrics are useful in evaluating these factors?

- What are the major themes influencing process evolution, how do they affect the definition of factors, and what are their metrics?

## 7.2.3  Process Evolution Guidance

Getting a process evolution exercise started is one thing. Keeping it going is quite a different matter. We often found that the activity categories emphasized in the initial exercise identify the activity categories needed in subsequent exercises. For example, process evolution exercises that began with Gather and Plan activities tended to be followed by exercises beginning with Train and Deploy activities. Equally often, we found that the focus of subsequent exercises was not at all clear. Further, we found that determining the focus became increasingly problematic as the effort proceeded.

The overall problem is guiding efforts through an appropriate sequence of exercises as a function of their overall process improvement objectives. Ideally, a set of questions could be defined related to process improvement goals and known information, such that when these questions are answered by process change agents, a set of recommended process evolution exercise sequences could be suggested along with their rationale. Process change agents would then be free to determine which of the potential exercise sequences make the most sense.

The overall issue is: Is it possible to rationally guide an effort through successive exercises? Believing that it is, the more specific issues are:

- What information is needed to guide a sequence of process evolution exercises?
- How can alternatives be comparatively judged and evaluated with respect to their efficiency, effectiveness and value?
- What does this imply with respect to an effort's initial exercise?

## 7.2.4  Process Evolution Support Capability

The previous topics imply the need to be able to collect and capitalize upon historical information. Deciding upon appropriate process evolution exercises in terms of questions to be answered, recommended activity sequences and the rationale for such recommendations all demand the collection of historical information (across companies as well as within a company). This suggests the necessity of automated support for collecting, organizing and interpreting the information. Having a repository of such information, one could begin to learn from past process evolution exercises to guide future process evolution exercises.

Specific issues include:

- What information should be collected regarding evolution activities/exercises and their success or failure?

- How can this information be used to guide future process evolution? [34,38]
- What techniques and tools can support the collection, analysis and use of the historical information? [38]
- How can alternative suites of techniques and tools be compared and the "best option" identified? [2]

## 7.2.5   Process Enactment Support

Process Enactment Support is generally understood to be proactive support for process performance based on retained knowledge about the status of the process. A commonly known example is workflow support [17,53] which has proven quite beneficial for business processes in which the status of the process can be encoded in terms of artifact states, the flow of artifacts from performer to performer can be automated based on the artifact state, and performers can be presented not only with the artifacts they need to work on but also links to appropriate tools and reminders of necessary conditions. A simple example is workflow support for expense form processing. The states that control the flow of a Reimbursement Request would be filled-out, approved, rejected and paid. Once a Reimbursement Request has been filled out by an Employee, it would be in state filled-out and automatically routed to the appropriate Manager who would also be provided Reimbursement Guidelines as a reminder the company's policies. After the Manager considered the request, the state would be approved or rejected. In the former case, it would be forwarded to the Accounting Office; in the later case it would be routed back to the Employee.

Analogous support can be provided when the activities are more general, and the states cannot be specified so concretely, through Role-Based Workspaces [29,19]. A Role-Based Workspace is an electronic context which provides access to the status information, artifacts and tools (and other assets) that an agent filling a role needs to carry out his/her work.[3] As the agent carries out his/her work, an underlying system can keep track of the agent's status. The system can use this status information to keep agents playing other roles appraised of the status of the work as it affects their work, for example, as it inhibits or enables their activities. When an agent has to switch his/her attention, the context can be saved, and the agent (or another agent) can re-start the work once he/she has the available time. Role-based workspaces therefore support an agent's context switching when he/she has to work concurrently on many assignments. They also support coordination among a group of agents who are collectively responsible for fulfilling a role's obligations, for example, a group of agents who cooperate to provide System Administration services. Finally, role-based workspaces support collaboration among the agents filling

---

[3]  A workspace may be generated from the same information used to generate WebGuides.

different roles within some process by providing the support for asynchronous and synchronous interactions, collaborative decision-making, etc., that is typically found in Computer Support Cooperative Work systems [10,32,52].

Process enactment support of either type—or anywhere along the spectrum of possibilities that they imply—is quite pertinent to process evolution exercises in two different ways. First, it should be considered when developing the new process. This leads to issues such as:

- What are the process enactment support-related factors that should be considered when defining a should-be or to-be process?
- How may process change agents decide whether a workflow style or a role-based workspace style is most applicable?
- What process enactment support-related issues should be considered at various points along a series of process evolution exercises?

The second reason that process enactment support is important with respect to process evolution is that it can support the process evolution exercises themselves. Process evolution is carried out by a team of process change agents, and this team's coordination and collaboration can be focus of the process enactment support. This leads to somewhat different issues, among them:

- What is the architecture for a process enactment support system and its constituent parts that allows the parts to be flexibly assembled in the variety of ways required to support the full spectrum of possible process evolution exercises?
- What constraints might this architecture and these constituent parts place on process evolution exercises and how can these constraints be minimized?

## 7.3   Game Plan Focusing

We feel that many long-range game plans might themselves be described in terms of the PEDAL framework as iterative performance of activities falling into the framework's activity categories. The framework can therefore be used to compare and contrast alternative approaches to improvement game plan-based process improvement. By using the framework to characterize alternative approaches, it could be used to decide among alternative service-provider or product-provider offerings. It could also be used by process service providers to articulate their range of service offerings or their approach as well as propose a particular process improvement effort. Similarly, a company could define their process improvement requirements in the form of an Request for Proposals that references specific PEDAL-defined process evolution exercises reflecting the requirements and scope of the work.

This use of the framework requires consideration of at least the following issues:

- In what ways does the PEDAL framework significantly differ from PDSA-style models—for example, QIP and IDEAL—which have been used to describe and characterize improvement game plan-based process improvement efforts?

- What are the decision-oriented factors regarding alternative approaches to improvement game plan-based process improvement and how are they reflected by the PEDAL framework?

- In what ways may the PEDAL framework support the estimation of "value delivered," "probability of success," "cost effectiveness," "return on investment," etc., for improvement game plan-based process improvement efforts?

## 7.4   Process Visualization

In Section 5.4, we provided two examples of graphically, visually, describing process evolution exercises. While we feel these are valuable, we also feel that considerably more is needed to allow the insights needed to rapidly adjust a process evolution exercise in response to problems or business-context changes.

The notion here is to define various representations—primarily graphical but also having other forms such as tables, indented textual lists, multi-dimensional graphs, etc.—that lead to a "deep" understanding of a process evolution exercise (or, for that matter, an improvement game plan and the process being improved/evolved). The goal is representations allowing insights leading to the articulation of problems and their solution. We note that the representations presented earlier reflect an activity-flow point of view, one that is quite commonly used in describing the dynamics of a process and quite easily understood by people having an interest in the process. These representations are based on activity-to-activity relationships, captured either directly through a *precedes/succeeds* relation or as implied by a *uses/produces* relation between activities and artifacts.

From our experience, and taking a cue from the emerging science of complex, adaptive networks [26], we have come to feel that other relations might lead to better representations providing enhanced visibility and insights. As an example, consider an *occupies* relation between agents and roles. A graphical representation based on this relation might show the strength of communication among roles as a function of role occupancy. The communication is stronger if the same agent occupies the two roles. This is because the communication when different agents occupy the role is limited to what one agent tells the other in response to questions whereas the communication in the case that the same agent occupies the two roles includes what the agent knows without being explicitly asked. Strong communication can lead to many effects: it can improve the accuracy of process performance; it can speed up process performance; it can lead to earlier discovery of problems; etc. All of these affect the conduct of improvement game plan-based improvement efforts and process evolution exercises. They can also affect the design of a process undergoing improvement or evolution.

Some of the issues are:

- What are the relations that provide insights into a process undergoing improvement or evolution or the effort effecting the improvement or evolution?
- How should information about these relations best be depicted to maximize the insights that can be gained?
- How do these representations affect the design and conduct of improvement game plans and process evolution exercises?

## 7.5   Process Evolution Planning and Management

To date, our work has had a decidedly "retrospective" emphasis. We have emphasized making progress by frequently "taking stock" of what has happened and adjusting activities as needed to correct problems or accommodate changes to the business context. Process change agents also need support in "looking forward" to plan the overall effort in general and the next exercise in particular. We sense that many of the techniques and tools we have developed to date are valuable in planning, and managing, the overall effort and individual efforts. We also sense that much more is needed.

One necessary capability is basically retrospective but decidedly "forward looking." This is the determination of lessons learned. The most important issue is:

- What information should be collected, and how should it be processed, to maximize the discovery of "lessons learned" that quickly and efficiently lead to adjustments to an improvement game plan or future process evolution exercises?

More generally, there is the need to use historical information to make plans for the future and manage the execution of these plans. Example issues are:

- What planning and management-oriented information needs to be collected during the activities in the various activity categories?
- How should traditional information collection and management technology (for example, version and configuration management technology) be applied to support the collection, consideration and application of historical information?

Finally, there is the need to address planning and management directly. An example issue is:

- How should plans be developed and managed in the highly dynamic context presented by precipitous, unpredictable changes to a company's business context.

In several applications, we found the need to give special attention to specific management issues stemming from the nature of the process domain itself. For example, in our product planning process work (described in the third Case Study), the process had to be modified to accommodate the fact that complex products can often have dozens of different feature categories and hundreds of different features within those categories. The product planning framework had to scale to manage such complexity in a form that could be used by product planning personnel. The issues here are process domain-specific, and we therefore do not list them and let the example indicate their nature.

## 8.  Summary

The overall intent of this chapter is to describe an experience-based framework and process evolution approach that help companies rationally, rapidly and incrementally perfect their processes in response to changes in market pressures, personnel availability, available technology and other business-context factors.

We first discussed the nature and considerable value of long-range improvement game plans based on standards, maturity frameworks and best practices. These game plans address a company's business-context factors such as conformance to regulatory constraints, the company's marketplace and financial goals, its work force's capabilities, and its use of techniques and tools supporting performance of its product development, project management, business and operational processes.

We then argued the additional need for a company being able to rapidly adapt their processes in response to precipitous, unpredicted changes to its business context. Improvement game plans are based on an assumption of business context stability and establish relatively long-term goals. In addition, there is the need to rapidly adapt process improvement efforts to address the challenges of perturbations that occur suddenly and without warning. Games plans have timeframes measured in years. Precipitous, unexpected perturbations to a company's business context require an additional ability to focus on timeframes measured in weeks and months.

Following this, we described a framework—PEDAL—which allows process change agents and stakeholders to crisply and succinctly discuss and evaluate what happened during past process evolution exercises, what is happening during on-going exercises, and what is planned for future exercises. The framework is based on an accounting of process evolution-related activities we have found to be critical. It not only identifies the activities but also organizes them in terms of process evolution exercises highlighting their dependencies. By providing a structured, well-defined basis for canonically, normatively, describing and analyzing process evolution exercises, the framework establishes a solid foundation for making process evolution highly experienced based.

We then discussed several example applications of an approach to process evolution—PERFECT—which allows process change agents and stakeholders to continuously adapt process evolution efforts in response to problems, in particular precipitous and unpredicted changes to a company's business context. Whereas the PEDAL framework focuses on individual process evolution exercises, the focus of the PERFECT approach to process evolution is upon the concurrent and longitudinal inter-relationships and interactions among process evolution exercises. PERFECT is specifically designed to allow process change agents and stakeholders to co-evolve an understanding of the problems they encounter when improving the company's processes and a definition of appropriate solutions (new processes) and effective process evolution exercises to achieving them. This discussion of the PERFECT approach ended with an indication of several ways the PEDAL framework may be used to visualize process evolution exercises constituting a process improvement effort.

Following the discussion of the PERFECT approach to process evolution, we described the techniques and tools we developed to support describing, understanding, learning from, planning and managing process evolution exercises. These techniques and tools were neither preconceived nor implemented in advance of carrying out process evolution exercises. Rather, the need for the techniques and tools devolved from conducting the exercises, they were implemented to meet the needs of the on-going exercise, and they were evolved over time as a result of their use in various, subsequent process evolution exercises.

We then discussed the value of the PEDAL framework and PERFECT approach to process evolution. We believe that co-evolution of an understanding of process evolution problems and appropriate solutions is extremely important. We feel that long-range improvement game plans provide critically necessary solutions to these problems. We also feel it is additionally necessary for companies to have a short-range, experience-based focus, particularly when they do not have the inclination, need or means to take a longer range perspective. We feel that the PERFECT approach to process evolution and its underlying PEDAL framework meet this need by, among many reasons, making it much easier to:

(1) provide the value demonstrations needed to gain personnel support,
(2) maintain management attention and support in times of resource restrictions,
(3) match the pace of current-day business context changes, and
(4) gather the lessons-learned experience and process performer insights needed to make additional changes.

Finally, we identified a wide variety of ways in which PEDAL framework and PERFECT approach to process evolution should be improved. We are actively working on some of these improvements. We identify the others to suggest the ways in which future work in the process improvement community could advance the capabilities of a company's process change agents.

## ACKNOWLEDGEMENTS

This work has been influenced—directly and indirectly—through most-interesting, delightful, rewarding collaborations with many people during a wide variety of projects in many organizations. Those who have had a major impact include: Niniek Angkasaputra, Ove Armbrust, Denis Avrilionis, Dave Barstow, Ulrike Becker-Kornstaedt, Fabio Bella, Jorge Boria, Alan Christie, Bill Curtis, Mark Dowson, Pat Ferguson, Jens Heidrich, Marc Kellner, Sally Miller, Tom Miller, Jürgen Münch, Alexis Ocampo, Don Oxley, Dick Phillips, Marilyn Phillips, John Sayler, Henry Schneider, Martin Soto, Joyce Statz, Vencat Subramanyam, Ian Thomas, Lyn Uzzle, Shawn Wietstock and Jack Wileden.

## REFERENCES

[1] Abrahamsson P., Salo O., Ronkainen J., Warsta J., *Agile Software Development Methods: Review and Analysis, VTT Publications*, vol. 478, VTT Technical Research Centre of Finland, Vuorimiehentie, Finland, 2002, http://www.vtt.fi/inf/pdf/publications/2002/P478.pdf.

[2] Angkasaputra N., Bella F., Riddle W., "Perspective-based evaluation of software process management tool suites", in: *Proc. of the Third World Congress for Software Quality (WCSQ), Munich, Germany*, 2005, http://www.iese.fhg.de/Products_Services/vincent/publications/spm_tool.

[3] Avrunin G., Dillon L., Wileden J., Riddle W., "Constrained expressions: Adding analysis capabilities to design methods for concurrent software systems", *IEEE Trans. Software Engrg.* **SE-12** (2) (February 1986) 278–292.

[4] Basili V., Caldiera G., Rombach D., "The experience factory", in: Marciniak J. (Ed.), *Encyclopedia of Software Engineering*, vol. 1, John Wiley & Sons Inc., Hoboken, NJ, 1994, pp. 469–476.

[5] Beck K., Andres C., *Extreme Programming Explained: Embrace Change*, Addison–Wesley, Boston, MA, 2004.

[6] Boehm B., Turner R., *Balancing Agility and Discipline: A Guide for the Perplexed*, Pearson Education, Inc., Boston, MA, 2004.

[7] Bristow G., Drey C., Edwards B., Riddle W., "Anomaly detection in concurrent programs", in: Gehani N., McGettrick A. (Eds.), *Concurrent Programming*, Addison–Wesley, Boston, MA, 1988, pp. 567–585.

[8] "Information security management—specification for information security management systems", BS 7799-2, Business Standards Institution (BSI) Group, London, United Kingdom, 2002, http://www.bsi-global.com/Information+Security/Standards+Publications/bs7799-2.xalter.

[9] Campbell I., "The Internet: Slashing the cost of business", Netscape Communications Corp., 1997, http://netcenter.netscape.com/netcenter.

[10] Christie A., Grana-Dominguez S., Gujran N., Riddle W., Rixey A., "SIS: An exploratory synthesis of workflow and collaborative technologies", Carnegie Mellon University, Software Engineering Institute, Pittsburgh, PA, July 1998.

[11] CMMI Product Team, "CMMI for Systems Engineering/Software Engineering/Integrated Product and Process Development, V1.1", CMU/SEI-2002-TR-004, Carnegie Mellon University, Software Engineering Institute, Pittsburgh, PA, 2002, http://www.sei.cmu.edu/publications/documents/02.reports/02tr004.html.

[12] "Control Objectives for Information and related Technology (COBIT)—Release 3.1", Information Systems Audit and Control Association, Rolling Meadows, IL, 2004, http://www.isaca.org.

[13] Curtis B., Nejmeh B., Riddle W., "Achieving process agility", in: *Proc. SEPG, New Orleans, Louisiana*, March 2001, Carnegie Mellon University, Software Engineering Institute, Pittsburgh, PA, 2001.

[14] Curtis B., Hefley W., Miller S., *People Capability Maturity Model*, Addison–Wesley Publishing Co., Boston, MA, 2001.

[15] Deming E., *Out of the Crisis*, MIT Center for Advanced Engineering Study, Cambridge, MA, 1986.

[16] Ferguson P., Leman G., Perini P., Renner S., Seshagiri G., "Software process improvement works!", CMU/SEI-99-TR-027, ESC-TR-99-026, Carnegie Mellon University, Software Engineering Institute, Pittsburgh, PA, 2002, November 1999, http://www.sei.cmu.edu/publications/documents/99.reports/99tr027/99tr027abstract.html.

[17] Fernström C., "ProcessWEAVER: Adding process support to UNIX," in: *Proc. Second International Conference on the Software Process: Continuous Software Process Improvement, Berlin, Germany*, 1993, pp. 12–26.

[18] Gates L., Goncharoff K., Kellner M., "An example process guide: Process guide for a descriptive modeling process", CMU/SEI-97-HB, Carnegie Mellon University, Software Engineering Institute, Pittsburgh, PA, 1997.

[19] Heidrich J., Münch J., Riddle W., Rombach D., "People-oriented capture, display, and use of process information", in: *Peopleware and the Software Process*, 2005, in press, http://www.computer.org/cspress/CATALOG/st01121.htm.

[20] Highsmith J., Cockburn A., "Agile software development: The business of innovation", *IEEE Computer* (September 2001) 120–122.

[21] "Lotus Notes", IBM Corporation, White Plains, NY, 10604, http://www.lotus.com/products/product4.nsf/wdocs/noteshomepage.

[22] IEEE Computer Society, "IEEE Software Engineering Standards Collection", CD-ROM (IEEE Computer Society Press, Los Alamitos, CA, 2003, http://www.computer.org/cspress/CATALOG/st01121.htm.

[23] "Spearmint/PMC Tool Suites", Fraunhofer Institut Experimentelles Software Engineering, Kaiserslautern, Germany, http://www.iese.fhg.de/Products_Services/vincent/technology.

[24] "iNotion", I-Logix, Andover, MA, http://www.ilogix.com/inotion/inotion.cfm.

[25] International Standards Organization (ISO), "Quality management systems: Requirements", ISO 9001, International Standards Organization, Geneva, Switzerland, http://www.iso.org/iso/en/iso9000-14000/iso9000/iso9000index.html.

[26] Jain S., Krishna S., "A model for the emergence of cooperation, interdependence and structure in evolving networks", *Proc. Nat. Acad. Sci.* **98** (2000) 543, http://arXiv.org/abs/nlin.AO/0005039.

[27] Kishida K., "Remarks during Second International Software Process Workshop, Coto de Caza, California, March 1985", *Software Engineering Notes* (August 1986).

[28] Kellner M., Becker-Kornstaedt U., Riddle W., Tomal J., Verlage M., "Process guides: Effective guidance for process participants", in: *Proceedings of the Fifth International Conference on the Software Process: Computer Supported Organizational Work, Chicago, IL*, 1998, pp. 11–25, http://www.iese.fhg.de/Products_Services/vincent/publications/EPGs.pdf.

[29] Krementz M., "Personal workspaces for Electronic Process Guide (EPG) users", Project Thesis, Fraunhofer Institut Experimentelles Software Engineering, Kaiserslautern, Germany, 1999.

[30] "Dreamweaver", Macromedia, San Francisco, CA, http://www.macromedia.com/software/dreamweaver.

[31] McFeeley R., "IDEAL: A user's guide for software process improvement", CMU/SEI-1996-HB-001, Carnegie Mellon University, Software Engineering Institute, Pittsburgh, PA, 1996, http://www.sei.cmu.edu/publications/documents/96.reports/96.hb.001.html.

[32] "NetMeeting", Microsoft Corporation, Redmond, WA 98052-6399, USA, http://www.microsoft.com/windows/netmeeting.

[33] MSP User's Manual, Ref. No. 23-34-5, SDA Inc. and INSTEP Inc. (March 1994).

[34] Münch J., Ocampo A., "Software process variability: Concepts and approaches", Report No. 124.04/E, Fraunhofer Institut Experimentelles Software Engineering, Kaiserslautern, Germany, December 2004.

[35] Nejmeh B., "Process cost and value analysis", *Comm. ACM* **38** (6) (1995) 19–24.

[36] Nejmeh B., Thomas I., "Business-driven product planning using Feature vectors and increments", *IEEE Software* **19** (6) (2002) 34–42.

[37] Nichols R., Connaughton C., "Software process improvement journey: IBM Australia application management services", CMU/SEI-2005-TE-002, Carnegie Mellon University, Software Engineering Institute, Pittsburgh, Pennsylvania, March 2005, http://www.sei.cmu.edu/publications/documents/05.reports/05tr002.html.

[38] Ocampo A., Bella F., Münch J., "Software process commonality analysis", *Software Process Improvement and Practice* (2005) 10.

[39] "IRIS", Osellus, Toronto, Canada, http://www.osellus.com/products/irispas.html.

[40] "Integrated Process Asset Library", Federal Aviation Administration (FAA), Washington, DC, USA, http://www.faa.gov/ipg/pimat/ipal.

[41] Paulk M., Curtis B., Chrissis M., Weber C., "Capability maturity model for software, version 1.1", CMU/SEI-93-TR-024, ADA 263403, Carnegie Mellon University, Software Engineering Institute, Pittsburgh, PA, 1993, http://www.sei.cmu.edu/publications/documents/93.reports/93.tr.024.html.

[42] PM User's Manual, Ref. No. 23-46-3, SDA Inc. and INSTEP Inc. (March 1994).

[43] "A Guide to the Project Management Body of Knowledge (PMBOK® Guide)", Project Management Institute (PMI), Four Campus Boulevard, Newtown Square, PA, 2000, http://www.pmi.org/info/PP_CurrentStandardsProjects.asp.

[44] Pragma Systems Corporation, Reston, VA, http://www.pragmasystems.com.

[45] Radice R., Phillips R., *Software Engineering, An Industrial Approach*, Prentice Hall, Englewood Cliffs, NJ, 1988.

[46] Riddle W., "The evolutionary approach to building the Joseph software development environment," in: *Proc. Softfair: A Conf. on Software Development Tools, Techniques, and Alternatives, Crystal City, VA*, July 1983, pp. 317–325.

[47] Riddle W., "Just-in-time process documentation", in: *Proceedings of the Argentine Symposium in Software Engineering, Santa Fe, Argentina*, 9–13 September 2002 (Astrophys. Space Sci. E 2002), http://www.iese.fhg.de/Products_Services/vincent/publications/JIT_ProcDoc.pdf.

[48] Riddle W., "Coping with process specification", in: *Proceedings 2003 Integrated Design and Process Technology Conference, IDPT-2003, Austin, TX*, Society for Design and Process Technology, Austin, TX, December 2003, http://www.iese.fhg.de/Products_Services/vincent/publications/COPEing.pdf.

[49] Shewhart W.A., *Economic Control of Quality of Manufactured Product*, original publication: 1931. Re-issue edition: American Society for Quality, Milwaukee, WI, December 1980.

[50] "What is Six Sigma?", General Electric, Fairfield, CT, 2004, http://www.ge.com/sixsigma/.

[51] Subramanyam V., Deb S., Krishnaswamy P., Ghosh R., "An integrated approach to software process improvement at wipro technologies: Veloci-Q", CMU/SEI-2004-TR-006, Carnegie Mellon University, Software Engineering Institute, Pittsburgh, PA, 2004, http://www.sei.cmu.edu/publications/documents/04.reports/04tr006.html.

[52] "Teamware Pl@za", Teamware Group Oy, Helsinki, Finland, http://www.teamware.net/Resource.phx/twplaza/index.htx.

[53] "Workflow Management Coalition, The Workflow Reference Model", http://www.wfmc.org/standards/doc/tc003v11.pdf.

# The Opportunities, Challenges, and Risks of High Performance Computing in Computational Science and Engineering

## DOUGLASS E. POST

*DoD High Performance Computing Modernization Office*
*Arlington, VA*
*and Carnegie Mellon University Software Engineering Institute*
*Pittsburgh, PA*
*USA*

## RICHARD P. KENDALL

*Los Alamos National Laboratory*
*Los Alamos, NM*
*USA*

## ROBERT F. LUCAS

*University of Southern California Information Sciences Institute*
*Marina del Rey, CA*
*USA*

ADVANCES IN COMPUTERS, VOL. 66
ISSN: 0065-2458/DOI 10.1016/S0065-2458(05)66006-8

**239**

# 1.  Introduction

The exponential growth in microchip processing power described by "Moore's Law" [1], the concomitant increase in memory and disk size, and the advent of massively parallel platform architectures have resulted in a factor of $10^{13}$ improvement in computer processing power since 1945 [2]. This expansion of raw computing power is enabling computational science and engineering to address many important problems with a degree of realism that was unimaginable twenty years ago. It is even becoming credible to envision computational science and engineering as a problem solving and research methodology that can stand along side experimental and theoretical science and engineering analysis. The continued growth of this computing power depends on continued improvements in processor speed, network bandwidth, memory size, computer architecture, and other aspects of computer technology. In particular the introduction of massive parallelization has been one of the biggest reasons for recent improvements in computer performance, but it has also resulted in much more complex platform architectures.

The increased complexity has made programming high performance computing applications more difficult and has increased the time required to develop application codes. Optimizing code performance has also become more difficult. Performance analysis and debugging tools for massively parallel platforms are still relatively immature. Programming models and language extensions (e.g., MPI, OpenMP, HPF, etc.) have evolved, but vary among platform vendors and architectures and often involve very low levels of abstraction. At the same time that developing even "simple" codes for high performance computers is becoming more difficult and challenging, developers are striving to develop very ambitious programs. While computational simulations are proving to be useful tools for scientific discovery and engineering design and analysis, their effectiveness at this time is limited by the available computer power and memory. These limit the spatial and temporal resolution, the accuracy of solution algorithms, the number of effects that can be included, and the range of time and distance scales that can be treated. The growth in computer processing power and memory is beginning to allow us to remedy these shortcomings. The newest application codes employ more grid points in multiple dimensions for better resolution, include many more effects that span orders of magnitude of distance and time scales, and utilize extensive and detailed sets of physical data from tables and models for greater realism. The size and complexity of the codes has become very large. The additional work associated with the increased programming challenges and the tasks involved with including more complete (and complex) models make code development much more difficult than was the case ten or twenty years ago.

The unparalleled complexity and scale of the applications, and the difficulty of developing them, leads to the challenge of developing complicated applications that can produce reliable and accurate answers. Finding errors in large, complicated codes running on massively parallel platforms is extremely difficult. The newest codes include models for many competing effects. Determining if the models are accurate and complete is essential for accurate predictive capability. Developing these applications in a timely and efficient manner is also crucial. The time scales for the development of many large-scale simulation projects extends to ten years or more for the largest and most ambitious applications [3] and involve teams of 15 or more highly trained and multi-disciplinary staff. The team leadership must include competent scientists, computer scientists, managers and leaders. An extensive validation program is required. The project must have strong, continuous support from sponsors, stakeholders and users throughout the lengthy development. Often this support is lacking, and the applications that could address strategic problems and issues are never successfully developed [4]. This defines another challenge—"The Development Challenge."

Together, these developments define four distinct challenges:

1. "The Performance Challenge:" Designing and building high performance computers.
2. "The Programming Challenge:" Programming for complex computers.
3. "The Prediction Challenge:" Developing codes with complex physical models that are truly predictive.
4. "The Development Challenge:" Supporting the development of application programs for Computational Science and Engineering.

We first briefly explore the promise of using high performance computers to address the strategic problems facing society. Next we characterize some of the key properties and characteristics of some important high performance computing applications. Then we address the four challenges highlighted above. We initially describe the scope of these four challenges, identify the risks involved with each challenge, and then suggest ways to mitigate the risks. Our descriptions and solutions rely heavily on case studies of a number of large computational science projects and stress the importance of continued case studies as an essential element of the maturing process for computational science and engineering.

## 2. Computational Science and Engineering Analysis

Computational science and engineering based on the use of high performance computers is growing exponentially. It pervades many disciplines (Table I). Several recent books present surveys of high performance computing applications [2,5] and descriptions of individual projects abound (see the references in Table I).

These applications and others that can be addressed with high performance computing literally span the fields of human knowledge and endeavor. High performance computing offers society the opportunity to address strategic problems of immense importance. During the first few decades of supercomputers (1960–1980), they were applied chiefly to national defense-related problems. As computers grew more powerful, it became possible to address a much broader range of problems. The number of such fields is growing. Even the social sciences are becoming more quantitative. Serious work in political science now involves supporting conclusions with analyzed data.

TABLE I

EXAMPLES OF HIGH PERFORMANCE COMPUTING APPLICATIONS (WITH ILLUSTRATIVE REFERENCES)

| | |
|---|---|
| Astrophysics [6] | Fracture Analysis [21] |
| Atomic and Molecular Physics [7] | Genetics [22] |
| Bioengineering and Biophysics [8] | Groundwater and Contaminant Flow [23] |
| Chemistry [9] | Inertial Confinement Fusion [24] |
| Climate and Weather Prediction [10] | Magnetic Fusion Energy [25] |
| Computational Biology [11] | Materials Science [26] |
| Computational Fluid Dynamics [12] | Medicine [27] |
| Cosmology [13] | Nanotechnology and Nanoscience [28] |
| Cryptography [14] | Optics [29] |
| Data Mining [15] | Scientific Databases [30] |
| Earth Systems [16,17] | Shock Hydrodynamics [31] |
| Earthquakes [17] and Volcanoes [18] | Space weather [32] |
| Engineering Design and Analysis [19] | Weather Prediction [33] |
| Finance [20] | Wild Fire analysis [34] |

## 3. General Characteristics of a Large Scale Computational Simulation

As illustrated in Table I, computational science and engineering addresses many problem domains. They fall into general classes based on the models and solution techniques used in the simulation (Table II).

These approaches are summarized in Dongarra et al. [2]. There are many categories of problems and solution techniques (Table III). Problems can be time-dependent (e.g., predicting the weather), static (e.g., stress levels in load bearing structure), or unsteady (turbulent flow). The partial differential equations can be either parabolic (e.g., diffusion or conduction), elliptic (e.g., many steady-state problems), or hyperbolic (e.g., wave equation [35]). While a few problems are linear, almost all real problems are nonlinear. They involve nonlinear equations with complicated, non-analytic coefficients and source terms that are expressed either as tables of data or calculated from in-line models.

Many different numerical schemes are employed. Many time-dependent problems use finite difference or finite volume techniques. These schemes can be made conservative (i.e., the numerical scheme obeys conservation laws at the level of machine accuracy), and are usually fairly simple to implement. Finite element techniques are used for many engineering problems, particularly time-independent problems involving complex geometries. Other problems can be formulated as integral equations, which can be solved as minimization problems (including finite element formulations), or with stochastic techniques like the Monte Carlo [36] method.

Dimensionality, the number of dimensions included in a calculation, also varies among codes. Generally the larger the dimensionality, the larger the number of calculations that must be performed, so there is a substantial incentive to use as few

TABLE II
EXAMPLES OF GENERAL PROBLEM FORMULATION AND SOLUTION
TECHNIQUES

- Initial value partial differential equations—explicit and implicit
- Static partial differential equations—eigenvalue and steady-state solutions
- Ordinary differential equations
- Integral equations
- Data search and mining
- Data analysis
- Particle simulation
- Number theory and integer processing
- Signal processing
- "Event" simulation

TABLE III

SAMPLE DISTINGUISHING FEATURES FOR PARTIAL DIFFERENTIAL EQUATION APPLICATIONS

- Initial value-time dependent, non-steady state, unsteady/steady state/eigenvalue
- Deterministic/probabilistic
- Parabolic/hyperbolic/elliptic partial differential equations
- Linear/non-linear
- Problem formulation
  - Finite difference/finite volume/finite element/integral/Monte Carlo/spectral elements. . .
- Dimensionality:
  - Spatial dimensions: 1, 2 or 3
  - Velocity dimensions: 1, 2 or 3
  - Total number of dimensions: 1-D to 6-D plus time, or
  - degrees of freedom (e.g., quantum mechanical systems): 1 to thousands
- Mesh and Grid
  - Structured/unstructured spatial mesh
  - Degree of complexity (see [37])
  - Adaptive mesh refinement/static mesh
  - Single material/property or multi-material/multi-property
- Single physics/Multi-physics → weakly/strongly coupled
- Degree of Multi-scale (largest distance or time / smallest distance or time = $10^n$); $n > 3$ or 4 requires sub-grid models and/or implicit techniques
- Solution approach
  - Operator splitting, coupled solutions
  - Implicit/explicit
  - Direct solution, iterative solutions
  - Data: Physical data models/physical data tables/no data

dimensions as possible. Some problems have inherent symmetries that allow reductions in the dimensionality. For many, the distribution of particles in a system can generally be described by the Boltzmann equation (1). The distribution function is a function of velocity, space, time, and particle type. $\mathbf{r}$ is the position vector, $\mathbf{v}$ is the velocity, $\mathbf{E}$ and $\mathbf{B}$ are the electric and magnetic fields, and $C$ is the collision operator. For each particle type, there are seven dimensions in full generality (3 space, 3 velocity and 1 time). Due to the nonlinearity and large size of the resulting grids, few calculations include the full distribution function. The dimensionality in velocity space is often reduced by using moments over the distribution function and truncating the moments after the second moment [38]. The total number of grid points scales as $n^m$, where $n$ is the number of grid points in one dimension, and $m$ is the sum of the number of spatial dimensions (0 to 3), velocity dimensions (0 to 3) and time dimensions (0 to 1). Since $m$ can be as high as 7, the models in most codes have reduced dimensionality

$$\frac{\partial f(\vec{r}, \vec{v}, t)}{\partial t} + \vec{v} \cdot \nabla f + \left(\vec{E} + \vec{v} \times \vec{B}\right) \cdot \nabla_{\vec{v}} f = C(f). \tag{1}$$

Computations are carried out at discrete points laid out in a "mesh" or "grid" [37]. Physical space is usually divided into cells. The cells can either be "fixed" in space (Eulerian) or tied to the material and move with it (Lagrangian) [39]. The meshes can either be structured or unstructured. With structured meshes, the information for adjoining mesh cells is stored in the order that the cells are arranged in real space. The cell information is indexed by location of the cell. The information for zone with indices $(i_x, j_y, k_z)$ is between zones $(i_x - 1, j_y, k_z)$ and $(i_x + 1, j_y, k_z)$, and so on. The location of a mesh cell in a structured mesh is identified from the zone indices. An unstructured mesh is more complex in that the information about the location of the cell and the location of adjacent cells is part of the information stored with each cell. This requires more work, and more storage, but splitting and combining cells is much easier.

A key limitation to accuracy is the lack of adequate spatial resolution in regions where high accuracy is required. The spatial resolution is limited by available memory and computer speed. It is possible to increase the resolution locally by "adaptive mesh refinement," that is, refining a mesh locally where higher accuracy is desired. This has the potential to increase the local resolution without major increases in the total number of zones in the whole problem. This is much easier for unstructured meshes since only the information for the affected zones needs to be changed. New zones can be tacked onto the end of the list of zones, a much easier task than inserting zones into a multi-dimensional list.

Some codes treat only one material. However, there is greater interest in multi-material codes that can treat a number of different materials simultaneously. Such multi-material codes have additional complexity due to the need to maintain material interfaces. This is straightforward for Lagrangian codes where the mesh moves with the material and the material interfaces can be located at the mesh boundary. It is more challenging for Eulerian codes since the mesh is fixed in space and the material moves through the mesh. The challenge is especially acute when the material interface moves through many cells during a timestep.

Application codes vary in the complexity of the models they include. Codes that include many strongly interacting effects are more difficult to develop than codes with fewer effects. This is particularly true if the effects happen on different time or distance scales. An example of these "multi-scale" problems is the turbulent flow of water down a pipe. The bulk flow of the water occurs with a distance scale on the order of the diameter of the pipe, and may require 10 to 50 zones across a one cm diameter pipe to resolve important features at the millimeter scale ($\sim 10^{-3}$ m).

Turbulence occurs at much smaller distance scales, down to the distance between molecules ($\sim 10^{-10}$ m). The ratio of the largest distance scale to the smallest is thus about $10^7$. For a two or three dimensional calculation $10^{18}$ to $10^{27}$ mesh cells would be required, a size that is completely impractical in the foreseeable future. In addition, since most fluid flow calculations are limited by a time step that is roughly the transit time of a sound wave across a zone, it would take $10^9$ time steps for information to propagate across the mesh, far too many time steps for a practical calculation. This translates into a measure of the degree of the multi-scale nature of the problem, Eq. (2). If $n$ in Eq. (2) is greater than 3 or 4, then it is basically impossible to treat both the smallest and largest time or distance scales with a single method

$$\frac{\lambda_{\text{large}}}{\lambda_{\text{small}}} \approx 10^n \quad \text{or} \quad \frac{\tau_{\text{large}}}{\tau_{\text{small}}} \approx 10^n. \tag{2}$$

If the same equations describe both the large and small time scale events, then implicit techniques can often be used to solve the system. These often involve ignoring the small scale effects and averaging over them. This can only be done if one has access to all of the values of the whole problem, and requires fast communication. If the equations are different for small and large scale effects, then methods that capture the essential features of the small scale phenomena need to be developed and coupled to the treatments of the larger scale events.

If the different effects in a simulation affect each other weakly, then each model can be solved independently and the results combined after each iteration or timestep (Eq. (3)) (operator splitting). Suppose the change in $f$ is due to two simultaneous effects, 1 and 2. For operator splitting the change in $f$ due to each effect is computed separately, then the two changes are added. If the time step is small and the effects are weakly coupled this may be sufficiently accurate. If the effects are strongly coupled, the change in $f$ due to both effects will need to be computed simultaneously and operator splitting cannot be used

$$\frac{\partial f}{\partial t} = \left.\frac{\partial f}{\partial t}\right|_1 + \left.\frac{\partial f}{\partial t}\right|_2, \qquad \left.\frac{\partial f}{\partial t}\right|_1 = O_1(f),$$

$$\left.\frac{\partial f}{\partial t}\right|_2 = O_2(f), \qquad \frac{\partial f}{\partial t} = O_1(f) + O_2(f). \tag{3}$$

Some codes do not require physical data. But more often, codes that treat physical phenomena must include real data for the source terms and coefficients in the equations. Examples of data include yield strengths, opacity, equations of state, conductivity, collision cross sections, reaction rates, oscillator strengths, energy levels, enthalpy, viscosity, magnetic susceptibility, etc. This data can be either collected and used in tabular format or computed by inline models or both. Construction of efficient

TABLE IV
CODE SIZE AND TIME SCALES

| |
|---|
| Number of zones or mesh cells $<10^{10}$ |
| Production run time per problem $<1$ to 2 weeks |
| Time steps or iterations $<10^6$ cycles |
| Development time $\sim$5 to 10 years |

and accurate methods for incorporating data and physical models into simulations is often challenging.

We can derive some estimates of the scale of large scientific and engineering codes from simple considerations. The size of practical problems and the time required to run them is determined by available memory and processor and memory access time. The time to develop a code is determined by the size of the code and both its capability and complexity (Table IV).

The present memory of a high performance computer is usually of order 1 GByte per processor. Present high performance computers have between 1000 and 100,000 processors. With expected growth, this will soon yield memories in the range of 10 to 100 TBytes. A typical application requires between 1 and 10 kBytes of information per cell, so this limits the number of mesh cells to the order of $10^{10}$.

For a variety of reasons, it is impractical to envision many large-scale problems that take more than a week or two for one run. A typical parameter scan with large scale code runs will require a few runs, almost never less than five to ten, and preferably more. There are only 45 or so usable weeks in a year. It is generally impractical for a single large problem to get more than 20% of the total time on a platform. Thus ten runs will take about 1/2 of a year, and more runs longer. Only in rare cases will a single problem be allocated more than about 10% of the total machine available for a year. Thus for almost all cases a few weeks is the limit for practical single runs.

The typical run time required for a time step is a few seconds for many common codes that solve initial value problems [3]. Since the maximum time per problem is about a week or two ($10^6$ s), this leads to an estimate of around $10^6$ for the maximum number of cycles, iterations or time steps. Similar estimates arise from round-off error accumulations. While we have discussed these issues in terms of initial value codes, similar conclusions exist for other types of codes, including signal processing codes, event simulation, data mining, pattern recognition, data analysis, etc.

Large-scale codes take a long time to develop to the point where they can be used with credibility. A typical scaling for the development time for large scale scientific codes is

$$\tau_{dev} \sim FP^{0.47} \times \text{contingency [40]}, \tag{4}$$

where $\tau_{dev}$ is the development time in months, the contingency factor is about 1.6 for scientific codes compared to the information technology industry [40], and FP is the number of equivalent function points for the code [41]. For typical scientific codes, FP $\sim$ SLOC/100, where SLOC is the source lines of code. For typical large scientific codes, the SLOC count ranges from 300,000 to 1,000,000. To put this in perspective [42], if the SLOC count is $\sim$450,000, FP $\sim$4500, and a contingency of $\sim$1.6 is assumed, then the development time $\tau_{dev}$ is $\sim$85 months, or $\sim$7 years.

# 4.  FALCON: An Example of a Large-Scale Scientific Code Project

## 4.1  FALCON Characteristics

Now that we have set the general context for large scale scientific codes, it is useful to describe a specific example. Two of the present authors (Post and Kendall) recently conducted a detailed case of study of one such code, the ongoing FALCON project. The actual subject of the case study is anonymous to encourage complete disclosure of all the important aspects of the project history and issues [43]. FALCON is larger and more ambitious than most current applications, but is prototypical of many of the next generation of high performance computing applications. It models many strongly coupled effects that span distance and time scales of 5 to 10 orders of magnitude. This case study allowed us to characterize the issues that the developers and users of large scientific codes face, including the programming and prediction issues highlighted earlier. Key points that emerged from the study were the importance of good software engineering and verification and validation. Verification is ensuring that the code has no errors, that it solves the equations correctly. Validation is ensuring that the models in the code are accurate representations of what occurs in nature. It usually involves comparing code results with the results of experiments and observations.

The goal of the FALCON code project is to develop a predictive capability for a product whose performance involves the trade-off of many strongly coupled physical effects with time and distance scales that span ten orders of magnitude or more. An accurate predictive capability is needed to reduce the dependence of the sponsoring institution on large, expensive and potentially dangerous empirical tests to certify the product.

The FALCON code project is based on an innovative and potentially very powerful method for solving a set of initial value partial differential equations for the conservation of particles, momentum and energy. These equations are non-linear and have non-linear source terms and coefficients that are calculated with analytic, computational and table look-up schemes. The coupled set of equations is solved with operator splitting with some degree of time and spatial error correction. A mixture of explicit and implicit techniques is used. The FALCON code was designed to run on massively parallel Symmetric Multi-Processor (SMP) platforms [2]. The product to be simulated is a multi-material object with a complicated geometry. The equations are solved on an unstructured two or three-dimensional mesh that captures the major features of the object. Generating a reliable mesh from CAD-CAM files and other descriptions of the problem is a highly challenging task in itself, often consuming several months of an expert's time to set up each new type of problem [37]. The unstructured mesh allows flexibility for incorporating adaptive mesh refinement and adding resolution for capturing fine-scale features where necessary.

Parallelization for computation with SMP architectures is accomplished with domain decomposition of the mesh using ParMetis [2]. The parallel programming model for distributed memory architectures is the Message Passing Interface (MPI) [2]. As noted before, the target platforms are SMP clusters with thousands processors.

The approach to performance optimization has been pragmatic. The team uses several optimization tools (e.g., PIXIE, DCPI, SpeedShop and prof [2]) to identify roadblocks. The team then works on minimizing the impact of the roadblocks. The emphasis during the early stages of development was to maximize performance through reasonable choices for the code architecture, and then to work on optimization after the basic capability of the code had been established. This approach was a response to the pressures to develop the basic capability necessary for demonstrating the actual and potential utility of the code as soon as possible, even if the initial performance efficiency was low. If the required capability had not been demonstrated in a timely fashion, the project would have been canceled. A substantial investment in optimization was thus a luxury to be addressed at a later time. This is not atypical of large-scale scientific code development projects.

The FALCON code project uses nine different languages and a set of external libraries including: Fortran, C, Perl, Python, Unix shells, SCHEME, MAKE, and external libraries. Most of the code is an object-oriented instantiation of Fortran 77. The team has successfully captured many of the advantages of low level object-oriented capability, such as polymorphism and inheritance, while avoiding the pitfalls of many levels of inheritance and excessive use of templates. The reliability of Fortran outweighed its limitations in the massively parallel hardware environment. The major blocks of code are about 410,000 SLOC of Fortran, 50,000 SLOC of C, 200,000 SLOC of library code, and about total 30,000 SLOC of Perl, Python and Unix scripts. Perl and Python are primarily used for build and test scripts.

The FALCON project computational tools are being used by a team of approximately 50 engineers to assess the behavior of new and existing product designs. The users are highly knowledgeable and experienced. They do most of the validation of the code by comparing the code results with data from past experiments and a few new experiments. Their level of experience and expertise is sufficiently high that they can not only identify bugs and model deficiencies but can often identify the source of the bug or the needed model improvements. The users participate very constructively and effectively in the development, verification and validation of the code. The code is extensively documented on an internal web-site (approximately 400 Mbytes of HTML files). The documentation consists of descriptions of the physics in the code, the algorithms and models in the code, the input and output, and instructions for how to run the code. This has proved highly useful for the users and has been a key contributor to the success of the project.

The level of maturity of the code project was judged to be somewhere between CMM Level 2 and Level 3 based on the processes and practices followed [44] by the FALCON code team.

## 4.2  FALCON Life Cycle

Based on the experience with similar projects at their institution, the FALCON code project lifetime is expected to be on the order of 30 years (Fig. 1). Indeed, some projects like FALCON have had lifetimes of up to 45 years. The first part of the life cycle was dedicated to development of an initial capability to solve the conservation equations without accurate source terms or coefficients. This took about five years.

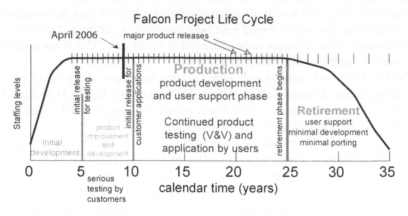

FIG. 1. FALCON project projected life cycle.

Now that capability is being tested and accurate models and data are being added. Further development will continue until a production capability has been achieved with more accurate source terms and coefficients. The production phase involves heavy use and testing by the user community. During the production phase, the code team will support the use of the code, maintain the code, port it to new platforms, and develop and add new capability as required by product engineers.

For similar projects at this institution, the ultimate life span of the code is determined by user demand and the difficulty of successively porting the code to new platforms. When a successor can replace the older code, and the product engineers have made the transition from the older code to the successor code, support for the older code ceases and it is "retired." The development of new capability then shifts to the successor code. The FALCON project is in the process of displacing an older code project with less capability. The life-time of these projects (20 to 30 years) is much longer than the time between new platforms (4 to 6 years). Thus, porting to new platforms is much more important than extensive performance optimization for any particular platform.

Like many computational simulations, the FALCON code project has a strong element of research and development to ensure that new algorithms and models are developed and successfully implemented. The users also have needs that must be met if the code project is to be successful. The adequacy of the models in the code can only be determined as part of an intensive validation program. It was impossible to draft a detailed list of requirements before the project was begun or to specify a detailed schedule.

In the case of the FALCON project, senior institutional management and the sponsor specified a set of requirements that would allow them to "sell" the program to the funding sources. This is similar to experiences in the Information Technology (IT) industry where a marketing department identifies market opportunities, and then signs up customers by promising the level of code capability necessary to outbid the competition. Then the software engineers are required to deliver the promised capability. This approach contributes to over-promising the capability that can be delivered within the defined schedule and resource level [45,46].

In the case of the Falcon project, the detailed schedule initially specified by the sponsor and senior institutional management was not based on the prior experience with similar codes or quantitative estimates (see Eq. (4)). Instead the schedule was based on when the capability was desired. In addition, the sponsor and institutional management chose a set of goals that appealed to the funding agency but were not the highest priority for the ultimate customers, the product engineers. The customers needed and wanted a different set of capabilities. They thus had little interest in the initial code project. Once it became clear that the schedule was almost a factor of three too optimistic and that the initial goals were not appropriate, the project goals were changed to match the needs of the customers and a more realistic schedule was developed.

## 4.3   Workflows and Tasks

The institution that managed the Falcon project has had decades of experience developing and using similar (but less ambitious) simulations. However, that experience was in serial development (i.e., develop one capability and test it, then develop a second capability and add it to the first, etc.) (Fig. 2). Serial code development would have taken 20 years or more to achieve the desired capability. The FALCON code project and others begun at the same time planned to develop the major components in parallel to speed up the overall development process (Fig. 3). Component development in parallel placed new and much greater demands on project management skills since the code teams were four to five times larger than in the past. It also called for better risk management techniques. If many components requiring similar development times are needed for the full capability, one failure would double the overall development time (see Fig. 3). This risk was realized for the FALCON project. A contract support group did not deliver a key component. The FALCON team has had to develop it internally. This subtracted from the resources available for other tasks and delayed realization of the full project capability. The institution that developed FALCON has had to learn how to organize and manage this new kind of code development process.

The tasks that the FALCON code development project and their users carry out can be grouped into seven categories (Fig. 4; Table V). Ideally, these tasks would

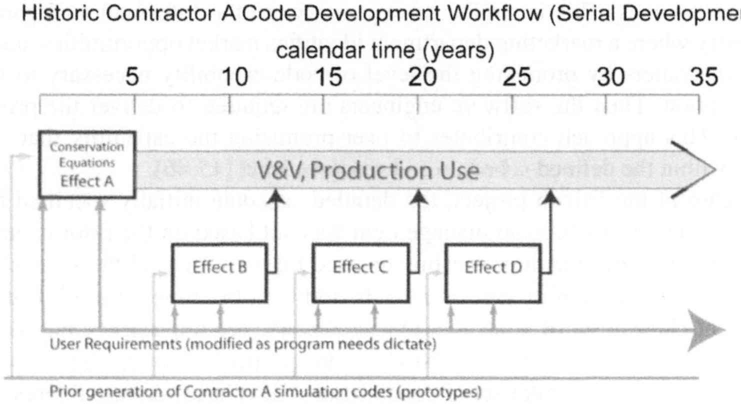

FIG. 2.   Legacy serial code development model.

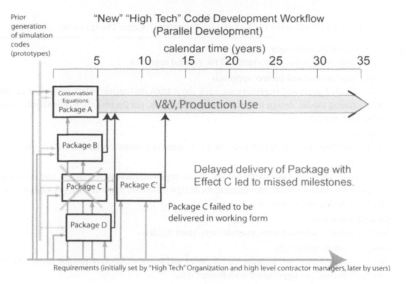

FIG. 3. FALCON parallel code development plan.

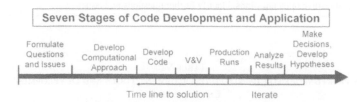

FIG. 4. Computational science and engineering code project workflow.

be carried out in a linear fashion (e.g., the classic "waterfall" model) [47]. In reality, they are nested, and iterative (Fig. 5). For instance, a candidate solver might be selected during the design phase. Then it might be discovered during the testing phase or during production runs that it does not provide the needed capability. Then the team has to go back, identify a new candidate solver, develop it, test it, etc., until a satisfactory solver has been found. One might discover in the V&V phase that the models miss an important effect that has to be included, and so on. Nonetheless, the use of these categories has been useful for ensuring that all of the tasks are identified for the hardware and software vendors (Table VI). Improved tools to accomplish these tasks would improve the ability of code teams like the FALCON code team to develop scientific codes more quickly with fewer defects and better performance.

TABLE V

SEVEN CATEGORIES OF TASKS FOR SCIENTIFIC CODE DEVELOPMENT

1. Formulate questions and issues
   Identify high level goals, customers and the general approach
2. Develop computational and project approach
   Define detailed goals and requirements, seek input from customers, select numerical algorithms
   and programming model, design the project, recruit the team, get the resources, identify the expected
   computing environment
3. Develop code
   Write and debug code, including code modules, input and output, code controllers, etc.
4. Perform V&V
   Define verification tests and methodology, utilize regression test suites, define unit tests and execute them, define useful validation experiments, design validation experiments, get validation results
   and compare with code results, etc.
5. Make production runs
   Setup problems, schedule runs, execute runs, store results
6. Analyze computational results
   Begin analysis during run to optimize run, store and visualize/analyze results, document results,
   develop hypotheses, test hypotheses with further runs
7. Make decisions
   Make decisions based on results, document and justify decisions, develop plan to reduce uncertainties and resolve open questions, identify further questions and issues

TABLE VI

OPPORTUNITIES FOR IMPROVED DEVELOPMENT TOOLS AND DEVELOPMENT
ENVIRONMENTS

- Problem set-up tools (mesh generation, etc.)
- Data storage and retrieval, especially over distributed networks
- Smoother upgrades for operating systems and tools
- Better and easier-to-use compilers and parallel programming models for massively
  parallel computers (now Fortran with MPI)
- Linkers and loaders with ability to link many languages
- Better parallel debuggers
- Performance analysis tools (hardware and software)
- Better run schedulers
- Visualization (office, small workroom, theater)
- Data analysis tools (V&V and analysis of runs)
- Testing tools (coverage analysis, software quality, . . .)
- Production run configuration and problem logs

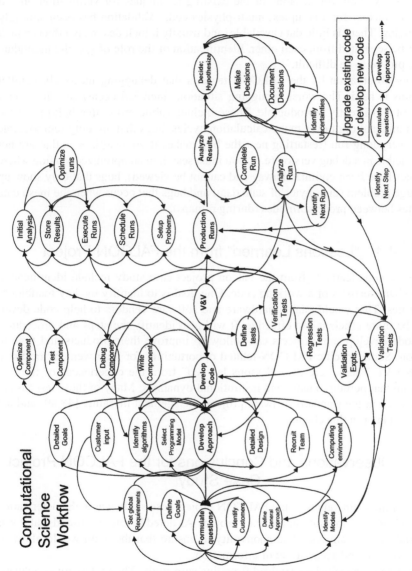

FIG. 5. Code development and application task categories.

The FALCON project also focused on verification and validation, but found it to be extremely challenging. None of the existing techniques for verification proved to be satisfactory for a complex, multi-physics code. Validation has been similarly challenging. There is little data available, and usually it includes many effects which cannot be separated from each other. Identification of the role of specific individual effects proved to be difficult.

A key observation by the FALCON team is that debugging massively parallel programs is hard. The worst debugging situations included occasions where bugs were not consistently reproducible. These include subtle errors that build from the least significant digit over many calculation cycles, bugs that are only reproducible after a very long run (restarting near the bug makes it go away), bugs that are not reproducible in a debug version (e.g., you must search in an optimized version where variables have been optimized away and cannot be viewed), bugs that only show up in a huge problem (giga-bytes of state data) and bugs that occur when the mesh data migrates between processor/nodes (during remaps).

## 4.4 "Lessons Learned" from the FALCON Project

The "lessons learned" from the Falcon project case study include identification of the characteristics of a working code. One goal is to identify the key roadblocks and issues. That would enable hardware and software vendors to help code developers be more efficient and effective. It will also identify the steps and procedures that code development projects can follow to improve their products and time to solution. Some specific FALCON-related opportunities for improvement are listed in Table VI. There were also "lessons learned" from the experiences of the Falcon team that pertain to team and institutional dynamics. Many of these lessons are emphasized in the standard software project management literature [48,49] and are addressed later in this chapter.

## 4.5 Observations and Conclusions for the FALCON Project Case Study

One of the main values of the FALCON project case study was a characterization of a large-scale computational science project. As noted before, we found that it was essential to maintain complete anonymity to ensure that the team would allow us access to a full and accurate set of information.

Three major conclusions evolved from this case study. The first major conclusion is that the life time for this project is expected to be around 30 years, much longer than smaller computational science projects such as are found in academia, and much longer than most projects in the Information Technology industry. This has driven the development team to be conservative in its approach and increases the importance of minimizing risks. As a consequence, the FALCON team has avoided using new and untried computer languages, compilers, code development methodologies, libraries, etc., especially those targeted to a single platform. Performance optimization has been much less important than being able to port the code to successive generations of platforms and to different types of existing platforms. Evidence that many projects have life cycles of many machine generations has had an impact on computer vendors. The vendors now have a better understanding of the need for stability and incremental steps for software development infrastructure and tools.

Secondly, the specification of the workflow steps has been useful for identifying the areas where hardware and software vendors can improve productivity by eliminating bottlenecks and improving programming efficiency. Specifying the development steps has helped computer vendors focus on the most productive areas for improvement.

Thirdly, this study demonstrated that, while it is impossible to set down specific detailed requirements for a scientific code project, it is important to outline them in enough detail to allow estimation of needed resources and the development of implementation time lines.

## 5. The Challenges Facing Computational Science and Engineering

### 5.1 The Performance Challenge

Computer power measured in Floating Point Operations per second (FLOP/s) has grown exponentially from about 10 FLOP/s in 1945 to about $35 \times 10^{12}$ FLOP/s in 2004 [2]. This expansion in capability has been achieved by a combination of increased processor speed (characterized by "Moore's Law" [50]) and improvements in computer architecture, networks and data storage. Greater processor speed has been achieved partially by technological innovation with electronic switches, progressing from relatively slow mechanical relays to vacuum tubes to discrete component transistors to integrated circuits. Present processors have millions of transistors and other components on a single chip with multiple arithmetic units. The clock speeds already are in the Giga-Hertz range. The feature size is a fraction of a micron. At some point within the next 40 to 50 years, Moore's law will saturate due to the finite size of atoms and molecules, the irreducible thermodynamic minimum heat associated with a bit of information, quantum interference between adjacent components, etc. Although there are indications that the rate of increase of processor speed is slowing, it is likely that processor speed will continue to increase for the next couple of decades [51].

Data storage capability has kept pace with processor speed. Mechanical relays and vacuum tubes were replaced by magnetic cores followed by transistors and capacitors. Now Gigabyte memories with access rates of hundreds of nanoseconds are common. As for persistent data storage, 10,000 rpm rotating disks are approaching a terabyte per disk. On the other hand, communication bandwidth between processors has increased much more slowly than processor speed, with the result that remote memory access and communication between processors are increasingly important factors limiting application speed.

Exponential performance growth appears likely to continue for the near term, largely because processing capability has also been accelerated by the use of many processors operating in parallel. Computers with as many as 50,000 processors are now in operation, and ones with 100,000 to 1,000,000 processors are under development. It is reasonable to expect a 100 TeraFLOP/s computer by the end of 2005 and a PetaFLOP/s computer in the 2010 time-frame. While the capability of computer platforms has been increasing exponentially, the cost per FLOP/s has been dropping rapidly. Indeed the cost of the largest supercomputer has remained in the $50M to $150M range (in 2000 $) for over 40 years.

These achievements have been remarkable and possibly unique in the history of technology. One can buy computers at a local office supply store for around $500 that are as powerful as the biggest and most capable computer available for any amount of money in 1990. In 2006, the PlayStation 3 will contain a TeraFLOP/s computer and cost about $200.

Although each significant advance in computer power involves technological innovation, it appears to everyone that computer capability will continue to grow exponentially, at least for the next 10 to 20 years. Predictions beyond that are hard to make. Many new technologies offer promise, including advanced materials, optical logic units, superconducting elements, and ultimately—the "Holy Grail"—quantum computers. Although no technology grows exponentially forever, there appear to be no near-term limits for computer capability.

This technological innovation has strong economic drivers. The market for faster processors and networks and larger memory is immense and diverse. High Performance Computing is a very small part of that market, but will continue to benefit from the progress driven by the whole computer market.

The "Performance Challenge" is thus being met. The capability it provides for addressing the important technical problems humanity faces is tremendous. But the increased capability comes at the price of increasing architectural complexity. It is becoming increasingly more difficult to develop programs for the increasingly more complex platforms. Realizing the capability of the new platforms leads to the second and third challenges: "The Programming Challenge" and "The Prediction Challenge."

The nature of the programming challenge becomes evident when one considers the kinds of computers code developers and production users want. They want fast integer and floating point arithmetic (with divides); fast, globally addressable, reliable memory and data storage; stable, long-lived and reliable platforms and architectures; and stable, long-lived and reliable software development and production tools that provide the needed capability and are simple to use. Basically they want something that looks like the UNIX workstation development and production environment they enjoyed 10 and 20 years ago. They want systems that are simple to use, and are reliable.

This is not what they are getting. Industry is delivering distributed memory systems with very slowly improving memory bandwidth. As noted, the rate of performance growth for individual processors is slowing. The new computers have an ever increasing number of processors linked together in ever more complex networks. The new machines and machine architectures are turning over every 3 to 5 years. Parallel file systems are generally complex and often unreliable. The development and production environment is often unstable, especially for the early life of a platform. The complexity of the platform architectures and memory layout make programming very complex. The performance of their codes is often only a few percent of the peak performance, which subjects them to pressure to optimize for particular platforms that have only a 3 to 5 year life span. The turnover in platforms and platform architectures means that code developers must port their codes to new platforms and architectures every 3 to 5 years. Production users face similar scale changes in the production environment.

An overview of the types of existing supercomputers sets the stage for the challenges that programmers face when developing codes for supercomputers or porting existing codes to them [52]. Progress in supercomputing is rapid, making any description of the landscape rapidly obsolete. Today, there two main types of high performance computers [2]. They are all clusters of Symmetric Multi-Processor (SMP) machines that employ either many cache-based commodity processors or a tightly integrated set of SMPs that process data in vectors. With rare exceptions, they are all Distributed Memory-Multiple Instruction Multiple Data (DM-MIMD) architectures in the nomenclature of D. Kuck [53]. Each "node" of the system is an SMP machine with its own, uniquely addressable, shared memory, employing anywhere from one to 512 processors. These processors are typically the same ones used in desktop PCs but can also include sophisticated RISC processors such as IBM's Power 5 or even custom vector processors as in Cray's X-1. The nodes of the supercomputer communicate with each other through high speed interconnects. Processors located in any given node can generally only access the memory at other nodes only through message passing protocols such as MPI (the standard message passing interface) [54] that are generally slower than direct memory access inside the node. As a result, access to program state distributed across global memory is now a major limitation for high speed computing. Fetching and storing data, especially on remote nodes, often takes 100 to 1000 times longer than performing integer or floating point arithmetic on a set of numbers. Programming for these complex architectures is much more difficult than for simpler architectures.

Today, most supercomputers are Linux clusters, often assembled by their owners. Larger supercomputers tend to be clusters of powerful SMPs sold by large, vertically integrated system vendors. The most powerful of all, for the moment, is IBM's Blue Gene/L, which is a custom integrated cluster of processors originally designed for embedded systems. We will discuss each of these in turn.

Generic Linux clusters are very cheap and very popular. They are generally built from commodity parts (processors, interconnects, memory, storage disks, etc.). The operating system software is usually some sort of open source LINUX. The cluster can be assembled and maintained either by the owner (cheapest) or by a contractor. Its interconnects are often nearly as fast as the ones available on the vendor platforms where more effort can be spent on optimization. The purchase price of a generic LINUX cluster can be quite low, and if cheap labor (e.g., graduate students) is available, they can be an attractive way to get computing cycles. There are many small clusters, ranging up to a few 100 processors, and larger systems are beginning to appear more frequently. One major drawback with such "homemade" systems is that there is no single vendor putting the whole system together and supporting it. When things don't work, there is often a lot of finger pointing among the various hardware and software suppliers, and no single party is responsible for fixing the problem. The required labor to support homemade LINUX clusters is thus a hidden, long-term cost that is often overlooked.

There are also many clusters integrated by system vendors. These companies range from small companies that specialize in LINUX clusters to the largest computer manufactures. The purchase price of such clusters is higher than the price of the components, but they are advantageous when an organization does not the indigenous talent to assemble clusters themselves. For one thing, the vendor is responsible for ensuring that the system works. Furthermore, the system integrator can include unique, proprietary technology not available to those building their own clusters. Red Storm located at Sandia and built by Cray is an example of such a machine. The operating system software for Red Storm is actually a joint Cray–Sandia development project, but Cray is responsible for ensuring that the entire system works. In addition, the vendor is responsible for ensuring that the common tool set of compilers, etc. work on the platform. Proprietary interconnects like that used in Red Storm are generally faster and more highly optimized than those used on generic clusters.

Most larger-scale systems are clusters of SMPs. Examples include the ASCI Q and Purple systems. These machines are built out of systems designed to be large servers, with multiple processors sharing the memory of each node. Users are thus tempted to use a shared memory programming model for communication and synchronization within nodes and message passing between nodes. Most such machines have multiple-issue RISC processors, but some systems delivered by Cray and NEC can have vector processors instead. The famous Earth Simulator built by NEC is an example of a cluster of vector SMPs. While the performance efficiency of vector machines often exceeds that of standard, multi-issue RISC processors, the price per TeraFLOP/s is much higher. Furthermore, most application codes need to be rewritten substantially to use vector computers. These factors have limited the attractiveness of vector processors in recent years.

The IBM Blue Gene is presently the world's fastest computer. It uses up to 128k very cheap and simple 700 MHz PowerPC processors. It locates two processors on a single chip, and puts two chips on a single circuit board along with 512 Mbytes of memory. Each board is a node. This is a very cheap and effective design, and a 360 Tera-FLOP/s computer costs approximately $70M. It is between 7 and 27 times cheaper per TFLOP/s than super computers of just two years ago. The cost reduction comes at the cost of slower interconnect speeds, and the memory per processor is somewhat lower than other supercomputers. Nonetheless, many applications, particularly those not requiring extremely fast memory access times, run very well on this machine. In its use of massive numbers of embedded processors, rather than PC or server CPUs, Blue Gene may very well be a harbinger of things to come in supercomputing.

Most of today's massively parallel platforms are designed for speed, sometimes specifically designed to place high on the top 500 list [52] by running LINPACK [2] efficiently. Unfortunately, few applications exercise massively parallel computers the same way as LINPACK. Benchmarks and "synthetic workloads" are needed so that vendors can test their platforms with software that places the same demands on the platform as "real" applications. Otherwise, the highest performing systems will be useful for only an increasingly small number of applications.

Looking to the near future, the supercomputing world can continue to expect rapid changes. A number of vendors are now marketing systems that include new components such as Graphics Processors (GPUs) or Field Programmable Gate Arrays (FPGAs). These components have the potential for greatly increasing the throughput of some aspects of codes such as single-precision, dense matrix operations in the case of GPUs.

Looking towards the end of the decade, a new generation of systems with a goal of 4 PetaFlops/s is being developed in the United States with support from DARPA's High Productivity Computing Systems program [55]. Three system vendors, Cray,

IBM, and SUN, are developing systems specifically designed to be more productive in measurable ways than today's systems. They will likely have globally addressable memories. They may even have new programming languages that will increase the productivity of scientific code developers. Details of the machines, as well as others such as the recently announced 10 PetaFlops/s follow-on to the Earth Simulator in Japan, are still closely held.

Vector processor symmetric multiprocessor machines are being developed and sold by Cray and NEC. The Japanese Earth Simulator with a peak speed of 35 TeraFLOP/s was built by NEC. While the performance can be very good, the price per TeraFLOP/s is much higher than other SMPs. Most application codes need to be rewritten substantially to use vector computers.

## 5.2 The Programming Challenge

The challenge of programming for the complicated and diverse architectures described above is daunting and continues to grow. As noted, modern computers can contain hundreds, thousands, even tens-of-thousands of processors linked together in complicated networks, with both local and distributed data storage hierarchies. The next generation of high performance computers could exceed 1,000,000 processors. Success requires that we be able to rapidly develop codes that will run efficiently on these complex platforms. A modern application code will often have millions, even billions, of computational cells. It can contain several million lines of code. It consists of dozens of complex, strongly interacting components and modules. The code can produce PetaBytes of output data, and require hours, days, or even weeks of run time to complete a problem. The programming challenges include: problem setup and mesh or cell generation, domain decomposition, load balancing, job scheduling and run-time problem management, check pointing and restart, debugging on thousands of processors, configuration management, output and storage for many terabytes of data, and finally the analysis and perhaps visualization of said data. Achieving good performance requires performance analysis tools to identify communication between processors, race conditions, data transmission inconsistencies and errors, cache use efficiency, etc. All of this is staggeringly complex compared to code development requirements only twenty years ago.

MPI and OpenMP have become the standard parallel programming models, but higher level languages such as Unified Parallel C (UPC) and Co-Array Fortran (CAF) are emerging [2]. The Message Passing Interface (MPI) is a programming model with a relatively low level of abstraction that allows the programmer to store and fetch data across a distributed memory architecture platform. OpenMP is a model for writing threaded programs for platforms that have a centrally and globally addressable memory architecture. While the programming challenge for large complicated codes is immense, it is often not much less for short, simple codes that need high speed processing of large data sets. In the latter case, the parallel version of a serial processing code that took a few days in the 1990s to develop may take weeks to months to address with massively parallel architectures due largely to the complications of writing and debugging the program. P-threads and OpenMP allow programmers to decompose applications on SMP systems (or SMP nodes of large clusters) into multiple threads which can share access to the same program state. Standard sequential applications can evolve to exploit concurrency on SMPs one construct at a time, making this an evolutionary and thus very attractive model for developing parallel codes. Unfortunately, performance for such codes tends to often lag expectations. Users tend to add directives to parallelize only a subset of the application, leaving large portions to run sequentially. Parallel regions under-perform because synchronization overheads are necessary to protect shared data and false-sharing can thrash the memory system. The net result is often disappointing performance on SMPs, especially when users do not invest the time and labor to restructure and hence parallelize entire codes.

For prior generations of computers, the development of operating systems, performance tools, debuggers, compilers, visualization tools, etc., was the responsibility of the platform vendor. Now, this software is often developed through Open Source venues, small development companies and university and national laboratory groups. MPI is the communication library used for most large-scale parallel applications. It provides a fairly low level programming methodology, not too far removed from assembly language. The programmer must determine what operations can be performed in parallel, and explicitly choreograph inter-processor synchronization and the exchange of data. This is a tedious and often error prone process which has remained largely unchanged during the twenty years since the delivery of the first hypercubes by Intel and NCube. On the bright side, message passing requires the programmer to decompose an application into multiple, independent programs with no shared state. When successful, this often heroic labor can be rewarded with applications that scale well on even the largest of today's supercomputers.

UPC and CAF are relatively new languages that have been specifically designed to facilitate the problem of programming large-scale parallel systems [2]. Both extend familiar programming languages (C and Fortran) with a global address space abstraction. The user must still explicitly identify concurrency in the application, but no longer has to explicitly manage the movement of data between processors. Instead, the user writes what looks like a standard C or Fortran program and the transmission of data between processors is implemented by the compiler. Unfortunately, acceptance of these new languages has been very slow. Users are loath to risk using programming languages or libraries that they are not confident will exist decades in the future. In turn, computer vendors don't want to support software that is not widely used, and progress with respect to programming environments stagnates.

As large-scale scientific and engineering problems become increasingly complicated, users also find it increasingly challenging to maximize the performance of
each individual processor. The performance growth of individual processors has long
outstripped the ability of memory systems to supply the necessary operands for applications whose working sets exceed the size of a CPU's cache. Furthermore, few
applications yield the breadth of instruction-level parallelism needed to approach
peak performance on processors that issue as many as eight instructions per cycle. High-quality optimizing compilers are needed as well as highly tuned libraries
for common operations such as linear algebra kernels. Sadly, the government agencies sponsoring research in computer science largely disinvested in this area in the
mid-1990s, and progress has been excruciatingly slow. Developers concerned about
performance find themselves doing tedious experiments in code restructuring that
have to be revisited each time the application is ported to a new system.

All of the difficulties discussed above exist for small codes as well as large ones.
Many small codes are developed to solve specific problems or test hypotheses, often
only being run to completion once. Even though the code itself may be small, the
programmer must still tackle the complexity of parallelizing the application. The
net result is that problem that could have been addressed and solved in a few days
in the 1990s may take weeks or even months to address with massively parallel
architectures, due largely to the complications of writing the program.

All of the above problems suggest that there is a second "More's Law" for programming to complement the conventional "Moore's Law" for semiconductors. As
the speed of computers increases each year, it takes "More" time to develop codes
that can run efficiently on the "Moore" complex platforms. Perhaps the only truly
viable approach to addressing the complexity of programming is to raise the level of
abstraction by using tools such as MATLAB™. While MATLAB™ is a proprietary
code, and massively parallel versions exist only as research projects, MATLAB™
does allow many code developers to develop powerful and complex codes much
more quickly than they could using Fortran, C or C++. The code performance with
MATLAB™ and other higher level programming abstractions is generally not as
good as with Fortran or C, but developing accurate codes rapidly is often much easier and faster.

As daunting as the programming challenge is today, it may become larger in
the near future. For prior generations of computers, the development of operating
systems, performance tools, debuggers, compilers, visualization tools, etc. was the
responsibility of the platform vendor. Now, this software is often developed through
Open Source venues, small development companies, or university and national laboratory groups. This is leading to problems with the availability and reliability of the
software [56]. Who is going to develop the next generation of tools to take the place

of CVS, MAKE, Vampir™, Ensight™, Totalview™, etc., for the next generation of supercomputers?

If high performance computers are to be useful tools for solving real problems, programmer productivity must improve at least as rapidly as the difficulty of programming for new computer platforms increases. This programming challenge has not been met over the course of the past twenty years, as supercomputers have evolved from vector mainframes to massively parallel, distributed memory MIMD systems. Given the relatively small research investments being made in programming models, languages, compilers, and other tools, it's hard to be optimistic that any real progress will be made in the near future.

When considering the programming challenge, one bright spot is the recent work by DARPA and DOE sponsored HPCS Development Time researchers to begin attempting to quantify the relative difficulty of using various programming models and tools. This in turn will allow developers to weigh the merits of adopting new technology based on more than just anecdotal evidence of its efficacy. Ultimately, it is hoped that quantifying the cost savings associated with new programming technology will accelerate its acceptance and hence overcome the programming challenge.

## 5.3   The Prediction Challenge

While "The Programming Challenge" is daunting, "The Prediction Challenge" may be even greater. The difficulty of programming massively parallel computers is largely a question of efficiency. It may take more time and be more difficult to develop such codes, but more resources and time will generally result in a working code. However, without reasonable assurance that the predictions of a code are accurate and can be trusted or, at a minimum, some idea of how reliable the predictions are, the predictions are largely worthless. There is then no reason to invest the resources to run the code, to develop the code or even to develop the computer to run it on.

A key part of the problem is that it is often very difficult to judge whether a code result is correct. For experiments or theory, the peer review process for published papers is the filter that separates the wheat from the chaff. However, for computational science, the existing peer review process doesn't necessarily work well. When a scientist receives a computational science paper from a journal to referee, he has no definitive way to determine if the paper is correct. He cannot reproduce the results in the paper, and generally he cannot check the important results with experimental data. The most important results typically make predictions for situations for which there is no data. That's often the purpose of the calculation. Even if the referee had a listing of the code—and he almost never does—the listing is not enough to determine the validity of a very complex and large calculation. All that the referee can do is to subject the paper to a series of "plausibility" checks:

- Is the paper consistent with known physical laws?
- Is the author a reputable scientist, known for careful work?
- Are the results consistent with other work in the field?
- Is the simulation validated with data as close as possible the regimes of application?
- Do the computational methods seem sound and applicable to the problem?
- Are the original models and fundamental equations correct?

Tragically, these criteria discriminate against new and exciting results, since such results usually cannot be thoroughly checked, and may be wrong. Major new contributions are thus less likely to survive the refereeing process in favor of more modest extensions of previously accepted work.

These criteria are not nearly as reliable and solid as the criteria used for theoretical or experimental papers. A knowledgeable reviewer can re-derive many of the important formulae in a theoretical paper. Experimental science is a well-established methodology, and important experiments are duplicated fairly quickly. In fact, important experimental results are usually not accepted by the general scientific community until they are confirmed by independent experiments. A similar practice will probably be necessary for computational science. "Discoveries" like cold fusion have their moment of fame then fade into infamy as "irreproducible" results. Reproducibility and the professional integrity of the scientist and engineer are the cornerstones of sound science.

Many things could be wrong with the computational science paper that the referee could not detect. The code could have errors in the way it was written such as bugs, the wrong use of computer or mathematical algorithms, inadequate resolution in time or space, non-converged solutions, etc. Even if the code had few errors, the models and equations in the code could be inadequate or wrong. As Robert Laughlin [57] points out, "One generally can't get the right answer with the wrong equations." The physical data used in the code may not have adequate resolution or may be inaccurate. The scientist or engineer running the code may not know how to set up or run the problem correctly. He may not know how to interpret the results of the code accurately. Yet the community relies upon referees to judge the correctness of published papers. It is a challenge the community must address if computational science is to become a mature field.

Important scientific, engineering design and public policy questions are beginning to be decided using predictions by computational scientists. As a community, it is our responsibility to ensure that computational science achieves the same level of reliability as theoretical and experimental science and engineering design. It is a question of professional integrity. If we do not meet our professional responsibilities, computational science will not become a credible methodology, and its potential for contributing to the betterment of the human condition will not be realized. If a significant number of computer predictions and analysis are wrong, and there is no way to determine which ones are right and which are wrong, people will not rely on them and will not support the development of our field.

What steps have other fields gone through as they matured? In "Design Paradigms," Henry Petroski traces the history of a number of technology fields as they mature. From his history, we have identified four stages needed for an engineering technology to reach maturity [58]. These stages can be illustrated using his example of suspension bridges. The first stage involved the design and construction of early suspension bridges. The designers and construction crews did not know the design limits and were deeply afraid of failures. The designs therefore were very conservative and extensively over-engineered. Although there were some initial failures, the early suspension bridges generally worked. An example is the Széchenyi chain bridge over the Danube joining Buda and Pest constructed in 1840. It stood for 105 years until the Germans damaged it in World War II. It was rebuilt in the 1980s and stands today.

The second stage involved cautious design improvement and optimization based on the first generation of bridges. The Brooklyn Bridge was constructed by John and Washington Roebling in 1880. It is still standing and carrying a modern traffic load after 120 years.

The third stage involved the development of continually more ambitious designs that pushed the limits of the existing technologies until large-scale failures occurred. The cautious approaches and the deep fear of failure of the prior generations of designers were often forgotten in the enthusiasm to go beyond the achievements of the past. The Tacoma Narrows bridge, constructed in 1940, failed catastrophically due to the excitation of wind-driven harmonic oscillations. Such bridge failures are spectacular. Almost everyone who reads this paper has seen the short movie of the galloping Tacoma Bridge as it bucked and pitched in the wind until it collapsed into the water. The civil engineering community studied and analyzed the causes for the failures, then developed solutions that became part of the design methodology for all future suspension bridges.

Advancement to the fourth stage—that of a mature field—is based on the development and adoption of the "lessons learned" from the failures and successes of that field. The field of suspension bridge design and construction is today a mature field. Very large suspension bridges are being built, such as the 2 kilometer span Akashi Kaikyo Bridge in 1998. A measure of the maturity of a field is the level of professional integrity of people in the field. Consider the case when a government agency puts a prospective new bridge out for bid with the hope that it can spend $50M and have a bridge in 2 years. Let us suppose that when the bids come in, the lowest bid is $100M with a construction time of 4 years. If the agency tries to convince the lowest bidder to do the job for $50M in 2 years, the bidder will walk away from the job, rather than build a bridge that will almost certainly fail. The industry knows how to build safe bridges. It can predict how long it will take and what it will cost to build a bridge. When was the last time a technical software project manager walked away from a scientific code project he thought would take 4 years for 15 developers to complete after the sponsor told him that the project had to be completed in 2 years with only 9 staff? When that happens, the field will be mature.

Another criterion is insurability. If one can buy insurance for reasonable rates that insure you for liability in case your product fails, that means that there is a reliable track record of success in your industry. Do any of us know of an insurance company that will insure the correctness of a new piece of scientific software? Other areas of software (e.g., embedded systems in automobiles, airplanes, etc.) are beginning to reach this level of maturity, but not scientific software.

We assert that computational science is in the midst of the third step on the path to maturity. The first generation of computational scientists used the supercomputers of the 1950s, 1960s and 1970s. They developed and used codes to analyze data, design nuclear weapons, model supernovae, conduct engineering analyses, etc. Computational science was a new field and everyone was very aware that it had limitations. Due to restrictions in memory and processing speed, the problems generally did not have adequate spatial or temporal resolution and the solutions were often not converged. Often only very approximate models were employed for the problems being addressed. Nonetheless, computational tools were a step forward over existing analysis tools, and—used with caution and careful verification and validation—produced better answers than other methodologies.

As computers became more powerful, the DOE and the NSF established "supercomputer" centers in the US between 1975 and 1985 to provide supercomputer capability to the academic and general national laboratory community. The DoD used supercomputers to address important national security issues. Industrial companies such as Boeing and General Motors used supercomputers for engineering analyses of aircraft, engine and automobile components. There was still generally a strong component of skepticism about computational results and as a consequence, computational predictions were usually thoroughly checked and validated.

By the 1990s, computing power had reached the point where some of the prior limitations on resolution and the ability to solve complex mathematical systems had been overcome. Computational techniques began to have the potential to seriously address difficult and important problems such as climate change and weather prediction, nuclear weapons design, astrophysics, non-linear turbulence, chemistry, biology and human event simulation. This coincided with the advent of a new generation of scientists and engineers specifically trained as computational scientists. They began to use computational techniques to tackle many very difficult and complex problems. While these scientists and engineers were highly skilled at using computers, many have not had the inherent skepticism about computational results that was characteristic of prior generations. Although they know that computational models are only incomplete models of nature, they have sometimes placed an unwarranted faith in the validity of the computational results.

## 5.4   Scientific Software Characteristics and Issues

A perspective on the maturity level of computational science and engineering can be gained from experiences in other problem solving methodologies. Large-scale simulation projects face similar challenges and are following a history similar to large-scale experimental projects [59]. Both:

(1)  require project planning and strong, effective leadership;
(2)  require a large well-coordinated, knowledgeable and effective team;
(3)  require a clear and consistent set of goals, resources and schedule;
(4)  have ambitious technical goals that push the frontier of known technologies;
(5)  must meet budget and schedule constraints;
(6)  need adequate flexibility and contingency to adjust to changing requirements and unexpected events;
(7)  must continually test their systems to detect and fix errors and faults; and
(8)  have to verify and validate their tools.

Using a code to address a technical issue is similar to conducting an experiment on an experimental facility. Computational scientists set up problems, run the code and monitor its performance, collect and analyze the results, draw conclusions and test hypotheses, and then document their conclusions and the basis of those conclusions, activities analogous to those of experimental scientists. A computational scientist must get computer time and use it effectively, just as an experimentalist must get time on the experimental facility. The computational scientist usually needs the support and help of the code development group and computer facility staff just as an experimentalist will need the support of the experimental facility staff.

The continual increase in computing power is allowing scientists to tackle more challenging problems. As a result computational science is making a transition from individuals and small teams of scientists modeling problems with only a few effects to large-scale teams modeling problems with many effects that link many disparate time and distance scales. Most of the physicists making this transition have backgrounds in theoretical physics and have had little or no experience planning, coordinating and leading, and managing technical software projects. Experimental scientists initially made the paradigm shift from individuals or small teams carrying out small-scale experiments in a one or two room laboratory ("the good old days") to much larger groups carrying out "big science" experiments on large scale facilities in the 1930s, 40s and 50s.

Computational scientists will need to make the transition from small-scale projects to large-scale projects, but it may be a more difficult step for them than it was for experimentalists. Code projects involving only one or two scientists can be accomplished fairly efficiently with little or no formal planning, especially if the project involves research and development of new physics or mathematical algorithms. Informal communication between two professionals is usually very efficient. Small-scale experiments usually require substantially more planning, organization and interaction with other staff than small code projects. Equipment must be designed and built, or procured and delivered, and integrated. Support is needed from machinists, electrical and electronic technicians, administrators, health and safety personnel, etc. Supplies must be ordered and delivered. There are well-established standards for the safety and quality of components and instruments. These require much more interaction with the outside world than does code development by small teams.

In addition, the experimental community had twenty or thirty years to make this transition. Computational scientists are trying to make the transition in only a few years. It is noteworthy that many successful scientific code projects have been led by scientists with experimental rather than theoretical backgrounds. Successful technical project leaders must combine many different talents. They must have a good technical overview of all aspects of the project, a coherent vision for the project, and a good sense for what is practical and achievable. They must be competent in the key individual technical areas being integrated. They must be able to command the personal and professional respect of their team, and the trust of their management. They need to make the right technical decisions, decisions whose correctness may not be apparent for years. They must be able to estimate the needed resources and schedule; ensure that all elements of the project succeed; guide, develop and nurture their team; anticipate the changing needs of their customers; and shield their team from unreasonable requests and requirements.

This is a heroic vision that is seldom encountered in practice. Nevertheless, few code projects are successful without leadership approaching this caliber. The 50 year history of simulation programs at a large federal contractor bears this out. That contractor has successfully developed over 15 major physics simulation codes for a specific mission during the last 50 years. Each project was led by one or two scientists during the development phase. The success of these code projects was largely due to the competence, vision and leadership of the code team leaders and the development of cohesive code teams. That contractor started many code projects over the last 50 years, but only about 15 were truly successful in the sense that they had long, useful lives. Those 15 code team leaders and their teams were one of the major reasons that contractor has produced most of the successful physics simulation codes used by the US for the mission of the contractor over the last 50 years. The contractor management recognized, supported and nurtured the team leaders and the teams.

Successful code development teams include staff with many talents. First there must be scientists with domain expertise. The purpose of the code is to solve a technical problem. Key members of the development team must be experts in the relevant domain. These experts are needed to define the models that must be solved by the code, and are needed to judge the validity of the results. The team must include staff knowledgeable in computational algorithms, the techniques used to solve the models. Without them, the code can be very inefficient in the use of computer time, often leading to long running times that are impractical or inaccurate solutions to the models. Computer scientists and scientific programmers are needed to devise the code architecture and implement programming techniques needed to run on today's complex, massively parallel computer platforms. As noted in the FALCON study, many large codes employ five to ten separate computer languages. Code librarians are needed to keep track of all of the pieces of the code being developed simultaneously by a large team. Experts in verification techniques and software quality are required. Technical writers are needed to produce documentation for the code team and users. In addition to these skills, the code team must receive institutional support to help it use development tools including compilers, debuggers, visualization tools, performance profilers, optimizers, configuration management tools, etc. [2,56]. Code validation requires detailed knowledge of experimental data from the application domain. Experimentalists and experienced users are normally required for this. In practice, each team member acquires some expertise in many of these issues, but the collective knowledge required for modern codes usually exceeds the capacity of one or two people so that a multi-disciplinary team is needed.

## 5.5   Success Is not Guaranteed!

There are many documented failures of computational science. The Columbia Space Shuttle Accident was caused by a piece of foam that broke off from the main fuel tank of the shuttle and struck the wing. The foam damaged the wing enough that hot gases entered the wing body during re-entry and destroyed the wing [60]. Very shortly after the foam was observed to have fallen off during launch, the potential wing damage was assessed computationally. The computational analysis results were ultimately interpreted as indicating that significant wing damage was unlikely. There were, however, many problems with the analysis. The analysis was carried out by an inexperienced engineer. The foam-wing collision conditions were outside the range of validation for the computational model, CRATER. The engineer's management didn't pass along all of the engineer's analysis to the upper level NASA engineers making the crucial decisions on what to do about the rest of the flight of the Columbia.

CRATER was intended to model the impact of small objects, such as meteorites, on the shuttle tiles. The piece of foam was more than 400 times the size of the impacting objects used in the CRATER validation tests. In addition, CRATER did not treat the strength of multiple layers of the shuttle tiles correctly. A more capable tool, such as LS-DYNA™—used by the aeronautics, defense and automobile communities to study the effects of the impact of large size objects (e.g., cars, projectiles, etc.) [61]—generally was not used by NASA because of the detailed setup required. Although CRATER was a much simpler and less appropriate tool than LS-DYNA for this problem, results could be obtained much more quickly. While most of the CRATER code results indicated that the damage would be minimal, some of the CRATER analyses did indicate that there might be a problem. The senior engineering managers discounted the negative results because the CRATER model had generally given conservative results for the smaller scale validation experiments. For calculating the impact of a large piece of foam on the shuttle wing, the code was, in fact, not conservative. Upper level NASA management was misled into believing that it was unlikely that wing was fatally damaged. As the NASA accident report stated, it may not have been possible to avoid the loss of the shuttle even if it had been apparent that the wing was seriously damaged. However no effort was made to look for damage or to fix it, partially because the CRATER [60] analysis suggested that the damage was likely insignificant.

A second example recently occurred in the field of sonoluminescence. In early 2002, scientists at the Oak Ridge National Laboratory formed sound bubbles in deuterated acetone that collapsed and produced light [62]. They reported tritium decay and the emission of 14 MeV neutrons. This could only be true if the temperature achieved in the collapse was in the range of $10^6$ to $10^7$ K, far higher than the $10^3$ K range normally produced in similar experiments. If such a high temperature was real, this would possibly be the most important scientific result of the 21st century. Nuclear fusion energy production might be achievable with tabletop conditions. These results were "confirmed" by computational modeling. "Hydrodynamic shock code simulations supported the observed data and indicated highly compressed, hot ($10^6$ to $10^7$ degrees Kelvin) bubble implosion conditions, as required for nuclear fusion reactions." Unfortunately the authors employed an arbitrary factor of ten enhancement in the driving pressure and assumed that the implosion was perfectly spherically symmetric to achieve agreement with the reported tritium and neutron results. The general physics experimental community quickly rushed to confirm such important results. No one else, including another group at Oak Ridge [63], found significant levels of either tritium or 14 MeV neutrons as reported by scientists. The final conclusion has been that the reported experimental results were erroneous, and that the assumption that the driving force should be enhanced by a factor of ten was unwarranted. The fact that the original code results could be interpreted as confirming the erroneous experimental results gave the experimentalists additional encouragement to proceed with publication. In reality the code was misapplied, and an erroneous result was reported to the scientific community.

A third case involved theoretical predictions of the performance of the International Experimental Tokamak Reactor (ITER) [64]. Based on extensive analysis of the results of smaller facilities by the international fusion community [65], the governments of the US, USSR, Japan and the European Community proposed to build a "next step" large experiment [66] as a joint project. Just at the time that the design of this large experiment was being completed by the international design team, and approval was being sought for construction, three theorists at the University of Texas and Princeton University completed a computer simulation of the expected performance of the proposed facility using a new code they had just developed. The new results indicated that the proposed experiment would not meet its performance objectives [64]. The new results and the implications of those results for the proposed international project were widely reported in the popular media [67]. The publicity strongly contributed to the US withdrawing from the project. The rest of the ITER partners stayed in the project, and, now, eight years later, the US is attempting to rejoin the project. Extensive analysis by the international fusion community, especially the American, Japanese, Russian and European scientific communities, during the following year led to the realization that the three theorists had neglected important effects with the result that the performance levels they had predicted were much lower than the most complete and most thoroughly validated theories would predict. The theorists had overstated the accuracy of their preliminary results. The more complete results of other groups indicated that the expected performance would be roughly what the original design team had predicted. In this case, a computational prediction that was later proven to be wrong had an important impact, and negative, on an international scientific policy issue [68].

Many other examples are also available. They illustrate that computational science is beginning to play an important role in society, but not always a constructive one. If this role is to be a positive one, computational scientists and engineers, as a community, must work to achieve a higher level of maturity—one which embraces accuracy and reliability. As in the case of evolution of suspension bridges, they must start analyzing their failures and successes, and learn from them. Professional integrity demands no less. To illustrate some of the kinds of "lessons learned" analyses that will be needed, we later describe the analysis that two of the authors (R. Kendall and D. Post) carried out for six computer simulation projects in a large federal program [69]. This analysis emphasizes both the importance of the code development process and the validity of the results of the computations. Both points are important because reliable answers require a mature methodology for development of the analysis tools.

## 5.6   The Development Challenge

As the FALCON case study and many surveys of computational science and engineering applications indicate, the development of such applications requires time and resources, and the attention and support of institutional and programmatic management. As noted above (Table V, Figs. 4 and 5), the development process involves at least seven different types of activities. However, the development process will be not begin unless an organization decides that a computational approach to solving its important problems is sufficiently promising that it is willing to commit the resources to developing and applying computational tools. There are at least six elements of a successful computational project.

1. Identification of an important problem to which computational techniques can contribute.
2. A long term commitment by an institution to initiate and support the required code development project.
3. Formation of a well-led, highly competent, and cohesive multi-disciplinary code development team.
4. Endorsement of the potential role that computational tools can play in the scientific analysis and discovery and engineering design process by experimental and theoretical scientists and design engineers.
5. Adequate computer resources and support for code development and production runs together with knowledgeable and experienced users.
6. Adequate validation data.

All of these elements are essential. The first issue is that decision makers at an institution or a program recognize areas that large scale computational science and engineering can facilitate. This requires a level of vision and expertise that not all institutions and programs possess. In many cases, they may not be aware that computational science can help contribute to the solution of their problems. In other cases, they may not know how to structure a computational science and engineering program to address their problems.

Successful computational science and engineering projects may take many years to develop the required code and to apply it to problems of interest. The institution or programs must thus recognize the opportunity and launch the project years before the solution will be necessary. Long-term commitments are becoming less common in industry, especially for methodologies that involve significant risk such as computational science and engineering. Since many scientific code development projects require continuous support over a development and production cycle that may last as long as five to ten years, the support of several generations of management is often required. This has been identified in the literature as a major risk factor.

It is challenging to form and sustain large, successful code development teams. Many institutional cultures do not recognize the value of such teams with the result that even if project teams are formed, they do not receive the continuous support necessary for success. A multi-disciplinary team is difficult to form and to sustain. Team members from different disciplines have different career goals and values. Maintaining an appropriate level of professional and personal respect among team members is often challenging. Domain scientists sometimes do not appreciate the contributions of other disciplines. Good team leaders are difficult to find.

Even if a good computational tool has been developed, it may not be applied to problems of interest unless the engineering or scientific community appreciates the value of the tool. Mature engineering communities have established methods for design and testing, and may be reluctant to use a "new" tool. It is important to work with potential users to establish the value of the computational tool. If it is clear that the tool will not be used, then the project should not be started. It is also important that the project have sufficient flexibility to follow the evolution of the domain field. Solving the problem of five years ago is not success. The code needs to solve today's problems. This is a point that is not widely appreciated in scientific code development.

Adequate computer resources and computer support are also essential. It must be possible for scientists and engineers to obtain results in a timely and convenient fashion. Usually many production runs are necessary to do parameter studies, validate the code for the problem of interest, and answer "what if" questions. If it takes too long to complete production runs or requires heroic efforts on the part of the user, the scientist or engineer will rely on other techniques to get the answers they need. As the Columbia Space shuttle experience indicates, knowledgeable, experienced users are essential.

If the code has not been validated for the problem of interest, then the scientist or engineer cannot rely on the code results for making decisions. Thus there must be adequate validation data and sufficient attention given to validating the code for the problem of interest. As we discuss later, it is an area that seldom receives adequate emphasis. The information technology industry spends more resources on testing than on code development, and their problems are usually conceptually simpler than those of computational science and engineering. Validation is all too often an afterthought in computational science and engineering.

These issues define the "Development Challenge," overcoming the risk that the scientific and engineering community will not launch code development projects to develop the computational tools that could help them address their important problems.

## 6. A Comparative Case Study

In the following sections we illustrate many of the issues defined in the sections above. Our approach has been to examine existing code projects, and develop "lessons learned" from their successes and failures. This approach has been followed successfully in other fields [43], and, to some extent, in the IT industry [48].

In 2002, two of us (Kendall and Post) analyzed and developed a set of "lessons learned" from a computational physics program launched and supported by a large federal agency [69]. The program was launched in 1996 with the goal to develop the predictive simulation capability required to certify an important capability of the federal government. If the simulations could be used to make accurate predictions, then the US would not have to carry out an expensive, lengthy and dangerous experimental program to empirically certify the required capability.

This situation provided us with an almost unique opportunity to do a comparative case study of six code projects with the same goals, level of resources and computing environments, but with different organizational, computational science and technical approaches. We were able to compare the effectiveness of the different approaches and environments and draw conclusions on the most effective approaches. Most other potential case study opportunities involve single projects with unique goals, requirements, and institutional environments. Drawing general "lessons learned" is thus more challenging in these cases.

The program included the development of large-scale, massively-parallel computer platforms, the associated operating systems and code development tools, application codes and supporting algorithms and models. At the time we conducted our study, some of the applications development projects had been successful in meeting their objectives and some had not. We analyzed the application projects utilizing metrics and case studies that focused on the history, organization and institutional support of the code projects. By identifying the common elements that led to success or failure to achieve objectives and comparing them to the experience of the information technology (IT) community (e.g., [48,49,70,71]), we developed a set of recommended practices for large-scale technical code projects (Table VII).

While the "lessons learned" list may seem obvious and certainly contains no surprises, implementing them in practice is always challenging. Every code project

TABLE VII
CODE DEVELOPMENT "LESSONS LEARNED" FROM THE COMPARATIVE CASE STUDY

**1. Identify the things your organization or institution does well and build on them.** Introduce change with clearly defined goals in an evolutionary fashion. Even though you may think that the ideal structure for effective code development might be radically different from the existing organization and culture, radical, changes imposed too rapidly will disrupt whatever is working, and likely will not lead to success. Successful change takes time and requires that the people in the institution feel "safe" and trust the management to treat them fairly.

**2. Teams, not organizations or processes, develop software.** Form the best team you can, support it, and help it "jell." A good team is the strongest asset an institution can have. Developing good teams is the key to developing good software. The teams need to have a balanced skill mix of scientists, programmers, mathematicians and computer scientists. A good team is also a crucial deliverable for a successful project because all further progress must build on the team.

**3. Run the code project like the project that it is, with requirements, deliverables, a sound plan, realistic schedules and adequate resources.** Align authority with responsibility. The project manager must be able to control the resources and the team, and have the active support of senior management. Otherwise, he is a project "cheerleader," not a project leader, and the project will fail. Detailed requirements are difficult to develop for scientific codes, but it is crucial to develop *some* requirements to anchor schedules and requirements.

**4. The development of large, complex technical codes is inherently very risky.** Many, if not most, code development efforts fail to meet their initial objectives, and many fail completely. It is essential to identify the major risks, minimize them and provide contingency and mitigation. The major risk factors for software projects are [72]:

- Uncertain goals, objectives and requirements;
- Inadequate resources and support, including an overly ambitious schedule;
- Institutional turmoil, including too much employee turnover;
- Requirements and goals that change too rapidly or increase too fast; and
- Poor team performance.

Two additional risk factors specific to technical software are:

- Non-delivery of essential components from outside contract organizations
- Poor judgment about the technical feasibility of candidate approaches and methods for meeting the requirements (cf. [45]).

Poor team performance was the smallest risk factor for the these code projects [69] as well as for the Information Technology (IT) software industry in general [73]. The other risk factors strongly dominate. Most code project failures (for the general IT community and this program [49,73]) are due to the failure of senior management to fulfill its responsibility to provide proper sponsorship, guidance, oversight and support for the code projects.

*(continued on next page)*

TABLE VII — *Continued*

**5. If adequate resources and schedule are not provided, the project will fail to meet its objectives on time.** The failure to meet the initial objectives on time is regrettable but not fatal. However, this failure may cause management to take actions that punish rather than help the code team, and thus contribute to the failure of the entire project. If the resource levels continue to be inadequate, and the schedule continues to be too ambitious, the project will fail. For resources and schedule, there is even less flexibility for software development than for conventional projects where one can fix two, but not three of: objectives, resources and schedule. For software, one can only fix the objectives. The objectives and goals determine the resources and schedule [48,49,74]. The rate limiting process for code development is the rate at which people can analyze problems and develop solutions. The ability to increase the schedule is severely limited. As Tim Lister states: "People don't think faster under pressure." Similarly, the maximum size of a code team is limited by the ability of people to communicate complicated information with each other. This is reflected in the quantitative analysis that follows in the next section. The standard estimation techniques indicate that the optimal schedule and team size are a function only of the size and complexity of the code [74]. Frederick Brooks put it another way: "Adding more staff to a late project will only make it later [75]." Ed Yourdon wrote a book entitled "Death March" about the disastrous consequences of overly ambitious code project schedules [76].

**6. Codes that customers, especially the users, do not want to use are like experiments that do not take data or equipment that people do not use.** Such codes are a waste of resources and the efforts of creative people. The code team and management must focus on providing what the customer both needs and wants. If the code cannot provide the user with a needed capability, the user cannot solve the problem that justified the code development project. If the customer does not want or like the product, the code will fail even if it is what is really required. The satisfaction and support of the users is the key success factor in long-lived codes.

**7. The value of the code to the user is the physics capability of the code.** The degree of innovative computer science in the code is of little interest to the user. The most successful codes concentrated on improved physics and have been very conservative in their use of cutting edge computer science. By computer science, we mean methodologies for code development and programming techniques. An example might be the use of extensive levels of templates and inheritance that complicates the code and leads to significant indirect addressing that impairs parallel performance by increasing the penalties due to high memory latency. We do not mean the development of more powerful mathematical techniques and algorithms. Indeed, many of the most significant improvements in the physics have been due to the development and use of new and more powerful computational mathematics techniques and algorithms that, together with increased computer power, enable the scientist to solve problems that couldn't be addressed with prior generations of computers.

**8. Computer science research within the context of an application project greatly adds to the risks and often results in code project failure.** Use modern, but proven techniques. Improving the physics is risky enough. Leave computer science experiments to those who can afford to fail a few times. Developing improved code development methods is very important and deserves support and emphasis. Such development should be carried out as an independent activity. The new methodologies should be tested in a way that does not add to the risks of important projects, and be adopted only when the methods have proved their worth.

(*continued on next page*)

TABLE VII — *Continued*

**9. Invest in the team members through training and professional development.** They will become more capable as they acquire new skills and will be more productive. It is a good way to encourage change and to get the team members to see how other groups and industries tackle their problems. In addition, their morale will increase in proportion to the support of their management. Training also provides an opportunity for code team members to share experiences with the rest of the team and with other teams.

**10. Software quality is important.** High quality software has fewer defects, is more reliable and is easier to develop, maintain and use. However, research-oriented staff will not take a series of processes defined in a book and follow them blindly because someone in authority tells them to. They will apply the same standard to software development methods that they apply to their science. They have to be able to convince themselves that any proposed new process adds value to their work. For improving software quality, it is more successful to convince the teams that each individual practice adds value (configuration management, etc.) than to try to convince them to blindly embrace on faith a large system of processes just because the management orders it. Software quality, however, can't be ignored. If you don't give it sufficient emphasis, your sponsor may impose software quality procedures that will very likely be much more onerous and less effective than the ones you would identify yourself.

**11. Physics codes are an incomplete representation of reality.** All models have shortcomings and often exhibit mistakes in their implementation. Without a verification and validation program for the codes and their applications, there is no reason to believe that the code results have any validity at all.

---

we studied violated at least a few. Almost all were violated for the least successful projects. These lessons are generally not new. Indeed, many of these lessons can be found in Fred Brooks' 1975 classic: "The Mythical Man-Month" [75] as well as a host of IT industry books and courses. Also, many of these principles apply to almost every organized human activity (e.g., F. Brooks [77]).

## 6.1  Quantitative Estimation

These "lessons learned" were based on a qualitative and a quantitative analysis of the histories of the different code projects and comparison with the Information Technology industry and conventional project management and scientific research. The quantitative analysis was a key element in establishing that these code projects had not been given a consistent set of requirements, resources and schedules. While our analysis [69] was relatively simple compared to the methods often employed in the Information Technology (IT) community [74], the conclusions are very clear. We found that the key predictor of success was the age of the code project and the amount of time allocated to complete the project and meet milestones. Our analysis of the historical data indicated that it takes about 8 years to develop a code with the initial level of capability needed to meet the requirements. The projects that had 8 years of development often succeeded, and all those that did not have 8 years of development time failed to meet their initial milestones. This result emphasized the crucial need for a consistent set of requirements, resources and schedule.

The case studies included metrics (code size, team size, age, etc.). To see if this experience was consistent with the Information Technology (IT) community experience, an analysis was performed on the case studies using a generic "function point" model [74] widely used by the IT industry. We calibrated this model for scientific code projects using the comparative case study data. Function points are a weighted total of inputs, outputs, inquiries, logical files and interfaces [74,78]. Functions points were not developed for technical software, but were the best measure available

$$FP = \left( \frac{C++ \text{ SLOC}}{53} + \frac{C \text{ SLOC}}{128} + \frac{F77 \text{ SLOC}}{107} \right), \tag{5}$$

$$Schedule \ (months) = FP^x, \quad 0.4 < x < 0.5; \quad use \ x = 0.47, \tag{6}$$

$$Schedule = Contingency \times Function \ Point \ schedule + Delays, \tag{7}$$

$$Team \ Size = 3 + 0.6\frac{FP}{150}. \tag{8}$$

Equation (5) converts the single lines of code, available for all of the projects, to Function points (FP). T. Capers Jones lists the equivalent single lines of code (SLOC) per function point (FP) for the common computer languages [74] since computer languages have different information densities.

In this model, the required schedule and average team size are determined by the Function Point (FP) count (Eqs. (6)–(8)). These general scalings were modified to account for the added complexity and viscosity associated with developing scientific codes specifically for the nuclear weapons complex. The schedule was lengthened by 1.5 years to account for the additional time it takes to recruit, hire, train and obtain security clearances for code development staff (the last step has no analogue in the commercial IT world). Using a methodology developed by the Lawrence Livermore National Laboratory Engineering Department [71], a contingency factor of 1.6 was calculated to account for the additional risks, uncertainties, and complexities for the restrictive computing environments that these projects shared (Eq. (7)). The standard FP scaling for the size of the code team (Eq. (8)) [74] was modified to match the comparative case study data. This included a correction for small code teams.

Seven code projects were analyzed (Table VIII). For reasons of anonymity, we have identified the projects with birds [43]. Table VIII lists the size of the code in function points, the time estimated by Eq. (4) to develop the initial capability of the code project, the actual age of the code at the point it was expected to accomplish its first milestone, whether or not the project succeeded, the optimal code team size estimated from Eq. (8) and the actual size of the team. The sizes of the codes (e.g., lines of code, loc) were approximate estimates by the code teams. Establishing the

TABLE VIII
SOFTWARE RESOURCE ESTIMATES FOR THE COMPARATIVE CASE STUDY PROJECTS[*]

| | Kite | Egret | Tern | Finch | Puffin | Gull | Jabiru |
|---|---|---|---|---|---|---|---|
| Single Lines of Code ($k$) | 184 | 640 | 410 | 300 | 500 | 200 | 314 |
| Function Points (Eq. (4)) | 4800 | 6100 | 5400 | 2900 | 4800 | 3800 | 2900 |
| Estimated schedule (Eq. (6)) | 8.7 | 9.0 | 6.9 | 6.6 | 8.1 | 7.4 | 6.7 |
| Project age (at initial milestone date) | 3 | 9 | N/A | 4 | 3.5 | 8 | 8 |
| Successful in achieving initial program milestone | No | Yes | N/A | No | No | No | Yes |
| Estimated staff requirements (Eq. (7)) | 22 | 27 | 24 | 14 | 22 | 18 | 14 |
| Real team size | 20 | 22 | 8 | 17 | 8 | 35 | 12 |

[*] Shading denotes historical data; white background denotes computed estimates (Eqs. (4)–(7)).

size of the code teams was challenging. In general, good records were not available. Thus the code team sizes were generally estimated by the code team leaders. Because good records were not kept, it was also difficult to account for staff who worked on the code project but were part of other organizations. More than one-half of the Gull code project team, for instance, was part of other organizations. Where this was an issue, we used conservative estimates. For example, the Gull code project staff probably had a staffing level of about 50 for the first 4 or 5 years of its life instead of the 35 we assumed. We used a smaller number based on the actual number of people we could definitely identify as having worked on the project.

The case histories and the estimation procedures indicate that it generally takes a minimum of 8 years for a code team to develop an initial capability for a weapons code project. The requirements for a weapons code are determined by the physics necessary to simulate a nuclear weapon. The contractors had over 50 years of experience in this area, and know these requirements in detail. Codes of this type have between 3000 and 6000 function points (Fig. 6).

Some of these codes were started well before the federal program began in 1996 (the Egret, Jabiru, Gull and Tern projects). The Egret project was started roughly in 1992 and had a working prototype in 1994. The Jabiru code project was started before 1992. The Kite, Puffin and Finch code projects were started around early 1997. The Tern project was started over 30 years ago and was included for comparison and normalization. Since the history of these code project can be matched with scalings derived from the experience of the commercial software industry, it is reasonable to conclude that the constraints, computer science practices and management issues that generally apply to the IT industry generally apply to the development of

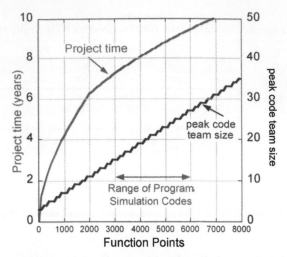

FIG. 6. Time required to complete a project and average code team size as a function of code capability measured in function points.

weapons codes as well (i.e., there is no "Silver Bullet" that can radically reduce the development time [79]).

The dominant factor for success is the age of the code project (see line 5 of Table VIII). The code projects that did not have sufficient time (8 years—see Fig. 7) failed to meet their milestones. The two projects (Egret and Jabiru) that successfully met the initial milestone were at least 8 years old. Three other projects (Kite, Finch and Puffin) were less than 8 years old and didn't meet their initial milestone. The Gull project was eight years old but didn't meet its initial milestone. Two of the projects eventually were successful in meeting later milestones after they had more development time. The other two did not meet their milestones and were eventually abandoned. The Gull project was successful in meeting a different set of milestones, but not the initial set. This is clear evidence that schedules and requirements must be consistent. The schedule cannot be fixed independently of the requirements, a fact long appreciated by the IT industry [48,74] but not adequately taken into account in the early planning for the whole program. The program set the milestone for demonstrating the capability of each code project to be three and a half years (December 1999) after the beginning of the program (~mid 1996) and three years after the date that many of the code projects were launched (~January 1997).

Adequate development time is necessary—but not sufficient—for success. Several code projects failed in spite of having adequate time. Poor practices and inadequate support—implicitly included in the contingency factor—hurt some of the projects as

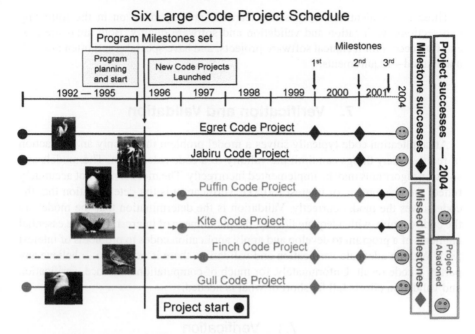

FIG. 7. Project schedule for six large-scale computational science code projects.

well. The Gull code project failed to meet its milestones even with adequate time and ample resources.

Another point is that it is clear from the function point scaling relations (Eqs. (5)–(8)) is that the code requirements determine both the schedule and resources needed for success. This estimating analysis indicates the importance of a realistic set of requirements, schedule and resources. Without them, projects will fail and the needed applications will not be developed.

These case studies helped persuade the program's senior management that the "younger" code teams (those started less than 8 years before the milestone) deserved a second chance. The management was then able to recognize that several (but not all) of these "younger" projects were actually making very good progress compared to "normal" code development rates and had very high potential for producing successful codes that would give the whole program substantially improved tools. Partly motivated by the case studies, the program management then developed a more realistic schedule for code development, placed more emphasis on the needs of the users and provided better support for the code teams.

Three issues identified as "lessons learned" are expanded on in the following two sections: verification and validation and software quality. Both areas are crucial for success for technical software projects, and have special—and often not well understood—requirements.

## 7.   Verification and Validation

An application code typically solves a model problem that is only an abstraction of reality. Many things can limit the validity of a code calculation. The models and solution algorithms may be implemented incorrectly. The models may not accurately reflect the phenomena of interest [80,81]. Verification is the determination that the code solves the model correctly. Validation is the determination that the models in the code capture, with adequate fidelity, the phenomena of interest. Both are essential elements of a program to develop and apply application codes to problems of interest [81]. Without adequate verification and validation, there is no reason to believe any part of a code result. Unfortunately, for much of computational science, verification and validation efforts fall far short of what is needed.

### 7.1   Verification

The code could have faults, use computer or mathematical algorithms incorrectly, have inadequate resolution in time or space, etc. The few existing studies of defect levels in scientific codes indicate that the error rate is often as large as 6 faults per 1000 lines of Fortran [82]. Even if the code has few faults, the models and equations in the code could be inadequate or incorrect. "One generally can't get the right answer with the wrong equations" [57]. The physical data used in the code may not have adequate resolution or may be inaccurate. The scientist or engineer running the code may not know how to set up or run the problem or how to interpret the results of the code accurately.

Both verification and validation become more difficult as codes become more complicated. A typical application might have many different components. A sophisticated climate modeling code might include models for ocean evaporation, ocean currents, ocean salinity, atmospheric flow, clouds, precipitation, $CO_2$ sequestration, radiation transport, atmospheric chemistry, ground water flow, vegetation growth, ice formation, etc. The code might predict many observables, such as average surface temperature, precipitation levels, etc. The accuracy of these observables depends on the accuracy of each component model, the completeness of the set of all the models (i.e., does the code treat all of the important phenomena), the accuracy of the solution method for the model including its interaction with the other models, the physical data used in the models, the adequacy of the problem generation and the ability of the user to correctly set up the problem, run it and interpret the results. Verifying and validating all of these is a major challenge.

The accuracy of a multi-model code depends first on the accuracy of each component, as well as the accuracy of their interactions. In practice, first one has to verify each component, then validate each component for the relevant regimes, then verify and validate progressively larger collections of interacting components, until the entire integrated code has been "verified" and "validated" for the problem regimes of interest.

There are at least five common verification techniques, all with serious shortcomings (Table IX).

Comparison with analytic results is worthwhile, but extremely limited in practice. There are usually few, if any, relevant problems with exact answers, especially with realistic boundary conditions, realistic geometries, realistic data, non-linear conditions, or multiple-component systems. The computational fluid dynamics community widely uses the convergence rate of the truncation error to verify programs [81,84]. This technique, too, is limited in applicability. It works best when the expected truncation rate can be determined from the basic difference equations and boundary conditions. That is often impossible. Convergence rates often are not useful to check two or more interacting modules. The third technique, the Method of Manufactured Solutions, is, in principle, very powerful [81,83,85]. It works for almost arbitrarily complicated and strongly coupled models, and almost arbitrarily complicated boundary conditions. However, problems with real data, moving or adaptive meshes, non-analytic (and non-differentiable) terms and real physical data are difficult to treat. These challenges, as well as the complexity of implementing the manufactured solutions, seem to prevent its wide-spread use. A fourth technique is monitoring properties the developers know have to be correct. Examples of such properties include "conserved" quantities (e.g., total energy, momentum, mass, etc.), quantities whose evolution can be estimated (e.g., entropy) to check

TABLE IX
TYPES OF VERIFICATION TECHNIQUES

1. Comparison of the code results with the analytic results for a problem with an exact answer;
2. Establishing that the convergence rate of the truncation error is consistent with the expected convergence rate;
3. Comparison of the observed results with the expected results for a problem specially manufactured to test the model (or models) [83];
4. Computation and monitoring "conserved" quantities and parameters that should be constant or are predictable; and
5. Comparison of the code results with the results from similar codes ("Code Benchmarking").

the accuracy of individual components and of the whole code, symmetry properties that should be preserved with symmetric initial conditions and boundary conditions, or procedures that can be predicted (e.g., procedural behaviors designed into the code). Comparing the results of a problem for two different codes (Benchmarking) can increase the likelihood of detecting errors, but only to a limited degree. Both codes could have compensating defects. Two codes usually have different ways of solving a problem and sorting those effects can be time-consuming and potentially impossible. Benchmarking is worthwhile because it can catch errors, but it isn't a substitute for a mathematically rigorous verification procedure. These are all necessary, but not sufficient, tests to verify that the code is correctly solving the equations.

In spite of all these limitations, verification must be done as thoroughly as possible. If a code is not solving the models correctly, then the answers are worthless. Any correspondence of the answers with reality is completely fortuitous. Verification needs to be performed every time the code or operating system (compilers, etc.) changes. This is often accomplished by running a set of test problems (a "regression suite") periodically (often every evening) and identifying when the answers change unexpectedly. A code has to be verified before it can be validated. Validating an unverified code is generally a waste of time. Given the deficiencies of existing practices, better verification techniques are desperately needed.

As a practical matter, diligent code developers do as much verification as they judge feasible, and then keep their eyes open for suspicious behavior by the code. However, this is far from a guarantee that the code is free of errors. Also, not all code developers (and users) are sufficiently diligent or knowledgeable.

## 7.2  Validation

Once a code has been verified as much as possible, the code must be validated for the problem regimes of interest. A code is never a valid tool for all conceivable problems. It can only be validated for specific regimes, and the validity in adjacent regimes estimated (Fig. 8). The entire calculational system including the user, computer system, problem set-up, problem running and results analysis for each user and computer system must be validated because all elements are important. An inexperienced or non-expert user can easily get incorrect answers using a good code in a validated regime.

Validation has a number of challenges. Each individual component and all important combinations of the components must be validated. Validation data and experiments come in a variety of forms (Table X).

Each type of experiment can be done before or after the code prediction has been completed and can address single-effect issues or integrated phenomena.

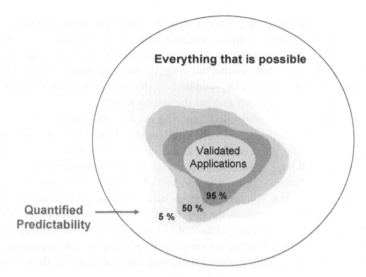

FIG. 8. Schematic illustration of code and problem validation and predictive validity range (Courtesy, D. Tubbs).

TABLE X

FOUR TYPES OF EXPERIMENTS USED TO VALIDATE CODES

1. Passive observations of physical events (e.g., supernovae explosions or the weather);
2. Experiments designed to certify a physical component or physical system (tests of an engineering component such a scaled airplane wing, car crash, etc.);
3. Experiments designed to elucidate a general physics or engineering principle or law (e.g., wind tunnel studies of turbulent eddies around airfoils); and
4. Experiments specifically designed to validate a code application (e.g., wind tunnel tests designed to provide data to validate a code calculation).

The best validation consists of the comparison of predictions made before an experiment with data from experiments designed specifically for validation. Successful prediction of experimental results is a better test than successful reproduction of existing experiments. Since few codes have no uncertainties, "tuning" a code for an application is usually necessary to get reasonable answers. The experienced user has learned how to set up an appropriately zoned mesh, how to vary the physical data within the known uncertainties to get reasonable answers, which effects are essential for the application and which are inappropriate, how to interpret the results, when the code is outside the region of validity, etc. With this freedom, it is thus often feasible to tune a code to match many of the salient points of an existing experiment. It is a much more rigorous test of the application to predict experimental results before the experiment has been conducted. This is also of course, the ultimate purpose of the code and computer system, to make accurate predictions of unknown events using known data before the events occur. An additional benefit of the validation process is that it trains the users how to use the code to get reasonable results. The entire computational system needs to be validated (code, user, computer system). As we have seen, an inexperienced user can get the wrong result.

For many applications, controlled experiments are not feasible or are impractical. For them validation is especially challenging. Models of astrophysical and large-scale geophysical phenomena (weather, climate, volcanoes, asteroid impact, watersheds, etc.) and large scale economic and political systems, must rely on historical data and current observations. The conduct of controlled supernovae explosions or scheduled earthquakes, volcano eruptions or asteroid impacts is not likely in the near future. For these phenomena, the best that can be done is to collect as extensive sets of data as possible, especially data that is fundamental to the correctness of the code. For these systems it is often not possible to get data for all conditions, a complete time history, adequately resolved data, and data for many of the quantities of interest.

However, many, if not most, applications can be validated with data from controlled experiments. Key issues include adequate coverage in space and time of the appropriate experimental initial conditions and the behavior of the important variables. An accurate description of the initial and boundary conditions is essential.

The types of experiments used for validation listed in Table X are also listed in order of their utility for validation. Aeronautical Computational Fluid Dynamics (CFD) codes were first validated using wind tunnel tests of scaled aircraft parts (Experiment Type 2, Table X). The object of the experiment was to test the aircraft part. The use of the data for validation was largely incidental and occurred after the experiment. Most of experiments of Type 2 were integral, in that they gave data that reflected the behavior of the trade-offs of a number of competing effects. Code developers have recognized that data for specific effects is needed to validate each component in their codes. They therefore have used data from single effect experiments designed to study a single, isolated phenomenon as much as possible. Such data might be yield strength data for metal components, thermal conductivity measurements, etc. Again, validation of a code was usually not the primary purpose of the experiment, although such experiments were often cheap enough that they could have been used for explicit validation experiments. The fourth type of experiment is one designed explicitly for code validation. The purpose of those experiments is to test the models in the code. The code is often used to design the experiment. Some of these points are illustrated in Fig. 9. An airfoil moving through the air sees a plane front of air rushing toward it. Fifty years ago, wind tunnels were used to faithfully reproduce the plane air front conditions to test aircraft components. Achievement of a plane front

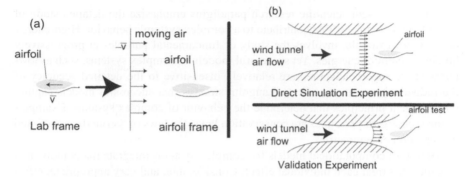

FIG. 9. (a) Wind tunnel matching planar air flow conditions of an airfoil moving through free space air to test aircraft components. (b) Comparison of large wind tunnel for testing aircraft components and small wind tunnel experiments designed to validate CFD codes.

required a large wind tunnel to minimize the effects of drag by the wall. Now, much smaller wind tunnels are used to validate the codes that are used to design airfoils. Once the requirement for a planar air front was removed, a much smaller and cheaper wind tunnel could be used. The validation wind tunnel facility can also have shorter set-up and experimental turnaround times and be more easily and thoroughly diagnosed. The idea is to test the code, not the component. A final test of the component may be advisable, but a CFD code validated for the appropriate conditions can be used for most, if not all, of the design studies.

In fact, data from experiments not designed for validation can sometimes be misleading or inaccurate for validation. The experiment may have been designed to measure a particular effect. The data for other effects may not have been checked sufficiently and may be inaccurate, misleading or wrong. As noted in the sonoluminescence example earlier, codes can be, and have been, forced to match incorrect experimental data.

A paradigm shift with regard to the value and importance of validation experiments is needed in the experimental community. Experimentalists and funding agencies understand the value of experiments designed to explore new scientific phenomena, test theories or certify and test the performance of a design component. Few appreciate the value of experiments explicitly conducted solely for the purpose of code validation. No mechanisms generally exist to get validation experiments funded even if experimentalists are interested.

Validation assumes an even more important role if one realizes a truly predictive model for a natural system—physical, chemical, biological, and so forth—may be much more than the sum of the individual components. For physical systems, Robert Laughlin recently pointed out that much of science today is inherently reductionist [86]. Present scientific research paradigms emphasize the detailed study of the individual elements that contribute to a complex system's behavior. High-energy physics, for example, involves the study of fundamental particles at progressively higher accelerator energies. Yet successful models of complex systems, such as low-temperature superconductors, are relatively insensitive to the detailed accuracy of the individual constituent effects. Laughlin stresses that successful models capture the emergent principles that determine the behavior of complex systems. Examples of these emergent principles are conservation laws, the laws of thermodynamics, and preservation of symmetries.

Almost all computational models for complex systems integrate many individual modules that treat each individual effect. Considerable, and very appropriate, effort is spent on validating each individual module. Yet if the "emergent" phenomena are not captured by the integration, the whole modeling system will be incorrect. Since a computational simulation is only a model of nature, not nature itself, there is no assurance that a collection of highly accurate individual components will capture the emergent effects. Yet most computational simulations implicitly assume that if each component is accurate, the integrated code will be accurate. Nature includes all of the emergent phenomena, but a computational modeling system may not. Accurately integrating many strongly competing effects is challenging for multi-scale phenomena even when the underlying "emergent" principles are explicitly known. For phenomena where the "emergent" principles are not known and built into the integration scheme, accurate calculations may not be possible. This perspective underscores the importance of validation of both the integrated code and the individual models.

Finally, since the value of verification and validation is to ensure that the code can give accurate predictions for the phenomena of interest, a written record of the verification and validation of the code is extremely important. That record is necessary to establish the credibility of the code predictions with the code project sponsors and customers. In fact, validation needs to be organized like a project, with goals and requirements, a plan, resources, a schedule, and deliverables including a documented record of the validation project.

Few existing computational science projects practice systematic verification or validation. Almost none have dedicated experimental validation programs with dedicated validation experiments. Yet, without such programs, computational science will never achieve credibility.

## 8.  Software Quality and Software Project Management

Software quality and software project management are very important issues. Improvements in quality offer the promise of greater longevity and easier maintenance.

Attention to quality will likely improve the code. Inattention to quality will almost certainly contribute to poor quality (high defect rates, and code that is hard to maintain and upgrade). It can also leave the code project vulnerable to the Software Quality Assurance (SQA) mafia employed by some organizations. If poor quality becomes an issue, the sponsors and customers will take action. The DoD and other sponsors have developed fairly rigid processes for code development and software quality assurance in response to disasters caused by buggy aircraft and satellite control software. Bugs in embedded control software have caused airplane and rocket crashes. To reduce the defect rate, the DoD and other organizations have established rigorous procedures for vendors to follow in the development of such software [44].

Similarly, sound software project management can do a lot to speed code development, increase the likelihood of a successful success and minimize the defect rate. Quality was an issue for the US automobile industry in the 1970s and 1980s [87]. The American automobile industry in general produced cars of relatively poor quality and lost market share to their Japanese competitors. A basic difference was that the US automobile industry did not emphasize quality on the assembly line and in the externally supplied components. They mostly tested the cars after they came off the assembly line and tried to fix the worst ones. The Japanese, on the other hand, emphasized quality at every step of the assembly process and for components. They tested the cars at many points along the assembly line and tested components before installation. The result was that Japanese cars had much higher quality, and the American automobile industry lost many customers.

Similarly, software quality engineering is most effective when it is applied at each step of the software development process. This is much better than the all too common practice of waiting until the code is nearly complete to begin testing the code. However, just as on the assembly line, different development processes require different methods. No one size fits all. Also, just as the Japanese auto makers emphasized input from the assembly line workers, the code developers themselves are often the best judges of how to implement quality improvements. A process rigidly imposed by senior management will likely get the same type of token (and sometimes malicious) compliance that was observed in the US auto industry.

Quality assurance for technical software has an important sociological dimension. Technical software is developed by teams of scientists and engineers. Scientists and engineers are trained to question everything, and accept nothing purely on the basis of authority. After all, even though he might want to, your boss cannot change the laws of nature—and that is what you are trying to model. That is why scientists are hired to develop scientific software. The models in the codes have to be correct. If the models do not reflect reality, the code results are worthless. Wrong models lead to incorrect results and to decisions that will be wrong, often with tragic consequences. Giving scientists a "bible" that describes an elaborate, rigid process for developing software, but which provides little in the way of justification is counter-productive. We have observed that it is more successful to work with the individual team to identify the "practices" that they judge add value to the scientific code development process, and encourage the teams to implement the practices they helped to identify [47]. It is also necessary to provide support to carry out some of the more routine practices. For large projects, it is better to hire a "code librarian" to implement and maintain the configuration management system and a dedicated "tester" to design, implement and run regression test suites than to default these activities to the team. Without additional resources, the team will have to drop other tasks to complete newly assigned software quality steps. The practices that technical software development groups have found useful include configuration management, requirements definition, sound software project management, regression testing, adequate documentation, design and code reviews, etc.

Various government agencies sponsor the development of technical software and its use to solve problems their problems. Often the contracting officers for these agencies are not very knowledgeable about the challenges of developing large, technical software projects. They are, however, accountable for delivery of their programs and projects their agencies sponsor. Large technical software projects usually have substantial risks. They are often behind schedule, over-budget, do not deliver exactly what was promised, and even fail entirely. To succeed, sponsors must hold the code development organizations accountable to deliver the promised codes. Government agencies are tempted to require that the organizations they sponsor follow a "process" model like the Capability Maturity Model (CMM) developed by the Software Engineering Institute at Carnegie–Mellon University [44]. After all, the data that indicates that code development organizations that follow the CMM processes produce "better" code, meet milestones more often, and deliver products within budgets. Who can be against these benefits?

This kind of quality for scientific software, however, comes with a severe price. An analysis of the Software Engineering Institute CMM processes indicates that it is most successful for software that must have no bugs (e.g., the airplane control software mentioned above). Implementing the CMM process, is expensive and lengthy. History shows that several years and substantial resources are required to move from one of the five CMM levels to the next. The strong emphasis on "process" limits the agility of the code team to explore new solution techniques and test different models to find the ones that best solve the problem of interest.

Computational science has different goals and requirements than embedded control or analysis software. For computational science, it is much more important that flexibility to improve the physics or chemistry and incorporate the best solution algorithms exist than to require that every last defect be eliminated. Developing the right physics or chemistry package usually requires experimentation and creativity.

It is impossible to plan every detailed facet of a large complex code with scientific and mathematical challenges—primarily because it is impossible to anticipate them due to the inherent research nature of scientific code development. The code development team must be very creative. It must develop and test many new algorithms and models to find ones that succeed. A rigid code development process impedes the flexibility and creativity needed to develop new codes. This is not only the case for scientific codes, but also for most really innovative software development. There is a running debate on this issue in the software literature between the "rigid process" community and the "agile software" community. The "agile software" community stresses the importance of innovation and the difficulty of being innovative if one is constrained by rigid processes [88]. The "rigid process" community stresses the importance of reduced defects and efficient code development [89]. Both positions have valid points, but the reality is that there is no "one size fits all" solution. Just as there is no "one way" to do laboratory experiments in physics, chemistry or biology, theoretical work in chemistry, physics or biology, or engineering design and analysis, there is no "one way" to develop technical software. There is no "fool proof" way to develop codes, or as Frederick Brooks states: "There is no silver bullet for software development" [75]. Just as in other scientific methodologies, one has to do the intellectually difficult work of examining and testing candidate practices and then using the ones that work for the problem at hand. But this does not mean that "any old method" is acceptable and will work. It only means that not every development problem has the same answer. While we cannot blindly accept what people hand us, we do have an obligation to find something that works well.

A constant theme that seems to always emerge from case studies is that good software project management is essential. It is usually more important than any set of externally imposed processes. The Software Engineering Institute stresses the importance of software project management in its "Team Software Process," [90] which captures many of the software project management methods long advocated in the general IT industry, especially in the non-government IT industry (e.g., [48,49,71, 75]). The Software Engineering Institute data shows that introducing sound software project management can often achieve as large a reduction in the defect rate as moving many levels up in CMM process.

The burden of identifying code development methods that work well falls on every code team. As noted before, if the team does not find methods that work, the sponsor will dictate the processes and methods to be used. The processes are unlikely to be the ones that the team would have selected. Developing a good set of practices and implementing them is the beginning of a good defense against being forced to follow externally-imposed practices. The code development team also has to be able to explain its practices and be able to demonstrate to management and, in some cases, to auditors from the sponsoring agency (DoD, DOE, NASA, etc.). that the team's practices work. There is no single solution ("silver bullet") for this problem either [75]. The team has to make the effort to establish credibility with its management so management will trust the team to do things right.

While the technical software community has many unique issues, it nonetheless can learn much from the general IT industry. The IT community has had to address the problem of how to plan and coordinate the activities of large numbers of programmers writing fairly complex software. In the authors' experience few of even the simplest well-known and proven methods for organizing and managing code development teams and projects are being employed by the technical software community. The most common approach seems to be to independently rediscover the IT industry "lessons." This unfortunately leads to wasted effort, delayed schedules, and, all too often, failure of the project.

Several of these "lessons" are worth highlighting. It is very important to learn how to develop specifications and requirements for technical projects. Most technical projects start out with a vision of what the code team leaders want to accomplish. Unfortunately, the leaders do not develop requirements and specifications at the level of detail that the other members of a large team can follow to produce an integrated code. This often leads to overly ambitious goals and unrealistic schedules, missed milestones, and sometimes to project failure. While good estimation is difficult, one commonly recommended technique is to develop a prototype that requires 5 to 10% of the full project resources, and use it for estimation [91]. Another technique is to look at similar projects and scale from them. In fact, most technical code projects do not appear to follow very many of the "lessons learned" from the program code projects listed in Table VII.

A related issue is the need to balance the need to improve the computer science techniques and methodologies used for code development while using conservative and reliable practices for the development of essential applications. A good example of this is the effort to develop the Common Components Architecture as a way to standardize component development [2]. In principle, this is a great idea. If one develops a module, it would be wonderful if it could be used in many applications. The core of the idea is to develop interface specifications for modules. Where this is possible, it should greatly help code development. Unfortunately, modules are the building blocks of applications and every module has a specific and usually unique purpose. They usually require different interfaces and data structures for each technical problem. The hard part is to define the specific interfaces and it is not clear that this can be done in a general way. It is difficult to see how a computer scientist will be able to anticipate what interfaces are needed so that a module that calculates the thrust from a rotor on a bacterium can be successfully integrated into a unified calculation of a swimming bacterium. Clearly new code development methodologies must be developed and tested on real problems. Identifying ways to develop these new methodologies and test them without unduly impeding application code development and greatly increasing application code development risk will continue to be a major challenge for the computational science community.

Another challenge will be to develop appropriate metrics for the development of technical software. Conventional function points are clearly inadequate. Technical software has additional complexity and challenges beyond those faced by the IT industry. Developing those metrics should be a key goal of any "lessons learned" activity. Gathering data on code projects will be essential. Without real data on the code development process and the codes themselves, it will be difficult to identify what is successful and what lessons can be applied to other projects.

Finally, code development in the future will almost certainly be done by "virtual teams," teams of non-collocated software developers at geographically separated sites. Such teams have the advantage of bringing varied skill sets to the project without the need to relocate and the potential for tapping the expertise of a number of institutions and generating the political as well as technical support of many institutions. Even collocated development teams face communication and coordination challenges. Those problems are more severe for virtual teams, and success will require addressing these challenges.

## 9. Conclusions and Path Forward

Computational science and engineering can play an exceedingly important role in society. The High Performance Computing community is meeting "The Performance Challenge" to provide us unprecedented power to tackle important problems. However, three additional challenges must be met before that potential can be realized. The first challenge is "The Programming Challenge." The development community must be able to efficiently develop programs for the ever more powerful and ever more complicated computer platforms. Secondly, the application models must become sufficiently accurate that they can be used for prediction with confidence— "The Prediction Challenge." Thirdly, the community must identify problems that can be addressed computationally and enlist the resources and commitment necessary to develop application codes to address those problems—"The Development Challenge."

To meet "The Programming Challenge," the High Performance Computer operations and development software community (industry, government and academia) must develop the tools and methods to facilitate the development and running of codes so that application codes can be developed quickly and reliably and can be run efficiently on the High Performance platforms. To meet "The Prediction Challenge," the computational science community (industry, government and academia) will need to become as mature as the theoretical and experimental scientific and engineering design communities. The computational science community must develop methods to ensure that the equations and models in the codes accurately reflect the real world, that the equations and models are solved correctly, that the applications are set up and run correctly by knowledgeable and careful users, and that the results are interpreted correctly.

The process must be consistent with the general "lessons learned" discussed in the foregoing. One of the most important "lessons learned" is that an intensive verification and validation program is an essential element of ensuring that computational results are accurate. Unfortunately, not only is the level of verification and validation usually insufficient, there is inadequate effort devoted to developing new methodologies and concepts for verification and validation. Much is needed and little is being done. The gap between the capabilities of scientific codes and code verification and validation processes is widening. Finally, those developing the code and those using the code must have a deep appreciation of the limits of the code and a deep-rooted appreciation that the results may not be correct.

As in other methodologies, retrospective case studies of past practices are an essential part of the path toward maturity. It is imperative that we as a discipline continuously examine and assess our mistakes and our successes. Without such a continuous re-assessment, we will continue to make the same mistakes. Our field will never be able to fulfill the tremendous promise that powerful computers give us.

Another way to look at it is as an issue of professional integrity. Unless the field of computational science and engineering has the same level of professional integrity as other methodologies (experiment, theory and engineering design), we will never be as credible as the other methodologies. We will continue to hear the refrain: "Who can believe that? It's just a code result and we know they can get anything they want if they play with the code enough." Scientists who conduct experiments irresponsibly find that their professional reputations are discredited quickly and thoroughly. The discoverers of "cold fusion" are no longer regarded as reputable by the scientific community [92]. It is rare that anyone in computational science gets even the slightest rebuke for a misleading or incorrect result. It is not enough for 95% of the work in computational science to be reliable, and 5% to be wrong. Unless the outside world can tell which 5% is bogus, none of the work will have the impact it deserves.

Finally, because it often takes 5 to 10 years and teams of 10 to 30 professionals to develop large, complex computer simulations, sponsors need to initiate and support code development projects well before the time they are needed. Indeed, if they don't do this, the codes will not be available when they are needed.

Looking to the future, the DARPA High Productivity Computing Systems (HPCS) project is focusing on reducing the time to solution for important problems by meeting the Performance, the Programming and the Prediction challenges. Improving productivity will help lower the barrier for developing new application codes. In its second phase, the DARPA HPCS program is working with three vendors, IBM, Cray and Sun to design and build Peta-FLOP/s scale platforms to be ready in 2010. Part of the HPCS project is the development of benchmarks for the platforms that are prototypical of real applications. Attention is being paid to the development of programming models and development tools for optimizing parallel performance. The HPCS project is sponsoring case studies of representative computational science projects in the DoD, DOE, NASA, NOAA, industry and academia to identify the lessons learned and document and publish them for the benefit of the computational science community. We have outlined a number of "lessons learned" that have already been developed from the comparative case study projects. As we assess a wider range of projects, we will refine those lessons and identify new ones. Adoption of these "lessons learned" by the computational science community will help the field to mature just as the development of "lessons learned" and their adoption has helped other fields to mature.

ACKNOWLEDGEMENTS

The authors are grateful for discussions with Vic Basili, Don Burton, Bill Carlson, John Cerutti, Linnea Cook, Larry Cox, Larry Davis, Tom DeMarco, Dale Henderson, Cray Henry, Fred Johnson, Leo Kadanoff, Jeremy Kepner, Joseph Kindel, William Krauser, Ken Koch, Dimitri Kusnesov, Steve Libby, Andrew Mark, Tom McAbee, Doug Miller, Pat Miller, Jim Rathkopf, Don Remer, Rob Thomsett, Tim Trucano, David Tubbs and Larry Votta and to the Department of Defense and Department of Energy for support.

REFERENCES

[1] Frank M.P., "The physical limits of computing", *Comput. Sci. Engrg.* **4** (2002) 16–26.
[2] Dongarra J., Foster I., Fox G., et al., *Sourcebook of Parallel Computing*, Morgan Kaufmann Publishers, Amsterdam, 2003.
[3] Post D.E., Kendall R.P., Whitney E.M., "Case study of the FALCON code project", in: *Proceedings of 2nd Workshop on HPC Applications, ACM/IEEE International Conference on Software Engineering, St. Louis, MO, 2005.*
[4] Joseph E., Snell A., Willard C.G., et al., "Study of ISVs serving the high performance computing market: The need for better application software", http://www.compete.org/hpc, 2005.
[5] Koniges A.E., *Industrial Strength Parallel Computing*, Morgan Kaufmann, San Francisco, 2000.

[6] Blondin J.M., Mezzacappa A., DeMarino C., *Astrophys. J.* **584** (2003) 971.

[7] Colgan J., Pindzola M.S., Robicheaux F.F., "Triple photoionization of the lithium atom", *Phys. Rev. Lett.* **93** (2004) 053201.

[8] Ethier C.R., "Bioengineering and biophysics", *Comput. Sci. Engrg.* **3** (2001) 382.

[9] Hase W.L., Scuseria G.E., "Computational chemistry", *Comput. Sci. Engrg.* **5** (2003) 12.

[10] Spotz W.F., Swarztrauber P.N., "Climate modeling", *Comput. Sci. Engrg.* **4** (2002) 24.

[11] Mesirov J.P., Slonim D.K., "Computational biology", *Comput. Sci. Engrg.* **1** (1999) 16.

[12] Chung T.J., *Computational Fluid Dynamics*, Cambridge Univ. Press, Cambridge, UK, 2002.

[13] Tohline J.E., Bryan G.L., "Cosmology and computation", *Comput. Sci. Engrg.* **1** (1999) 17.

[14] Schneier B., *Applied Cryptography*, second ed., John Wiley & Sons Inc., New York, 1996.

[15] Karypis G., "Data mining", *Comput. Sci. Engrg.* **4** (2002) 12.

[16] Asrar G.R., "A pathway to decisions on Earth's environment and natural resources", *Comput. Sci. Engrg.* **6** (2004) 13.

[17] Rundle J.B., "Computational Earth system science", *Comput. Sci. Engrg.* **2** (2000) 20.

[18] Saito T., Takayama K., "Applying shock-wave research to volcanology", *Comput. Sci. Engrg.* **7** (2005) 30.

[19] Hallquist J.O., "Current and future developments of LS-DYNA-1", in: *Proceedings of 4th European LS-DYNA Conference, ULM, Germany*, 2003.

[20] Northover K., Lo A.W., "Computational finance", *Comput. Sci. Engrg.* **1** (1999) 22.

[21] Vashishta P., Nakano A., "Dynamic fracture analysis", *Comput. Sci. Engrg.* **1** (1999) 20.

[22] Kumar S., Sastry S., "Biocomputation", *Comput. Sci. Engrg.* **4** (2002) 18.

[23] Winter C.L., Tartakovsky D.M., "Groundwater flow in heterogeneous composite aquifers", *Water Resources Res.* **38** (2004) 231.

[24] Lindl J., *Inertial Confinement Fusion*, AIP Press, Springer-Verlag, New York, 1998.

[25] Wesson J., *Tokamaks*, Oxford Univ. Press, Oxford, 2004.

[26] Kaxiras E., "Materials science", *Comput. Sci. Engrg.* **3** (2001) 14.

[27] Weinhous M.S., Rosen J.M., "Computing in medicine", *Comput. Sci. Engrg.* **2** (2000) 14.

[28] Ratner M.A., Chelikowski J.R., "Nanoscience, nanotechnology, and modeling", *Comput. Sci. Engrg.* **3** (2001) 40.

[29] Kupinski M.A., "Computing in optics", *Comput. Sci. Engrg.* **5** (2003) 13.

[30] Chonacky N., "Scientific databases", *Comput. Sci. Engrg.* **5** (2000) 14.

[31] McGlaun J.M., Thompson S.L., Kmetyk L.N., et al., "CTH: A three-dimensional shock wave physics code", *Internat. J. Impact Engrg.* **10** (1990) 351.

[32] Gombosi T.I., Powell K.G., DeZeeuw D.L., et al., "Solution-adaptive magnetohydro-dynamics for space plasmas: Sun-to-Earth simulations", *Comput. Sci. Engrg.* **6** (2004) 14–35.

[33] Lin S.J., Atlas R., Yeh K.S., "Global weather prediction and high-end computing at NASA", *Comput. Sci. Engrg.* **6** (2004) 29.

[34] Webb M.D., Balice R.G., "A real-time wildfire model for Los Alamos, New Mexico", *Internat. J. Technol. Transfer Commercialisation* **3** (2004) 226–242.

[35] Heath M.T., *Scientific Computing: An Introductory Survey*, McGraw–Hill, New York, 1997.

[36] Kalos M.H., Whitlock P.A., *Monte Carlo Methods*, John Wiley & Sons, New York, 1986.

[37] Thompson J.F., Soni B.K., Weatherill N.P., *Handbook of Grid Generation*, CRC Press, Boca Raton, 1998.

[38] Braginskii S.I., in: Leontovich M.A. (Ed.), *Reviews of Plasma Physics*, vol. 1, Consultants Bureau, New York, 1965, pp. 205–311.

[39] Roache P.J., *Fundamentals of Computational Fluid Dynamics*, Hermosa Publishers, Albuquerque, 1998.

[40] Post D.E., Kendall R.P., "Software project management and quality engineering practices for complex, coupled multiphysics, massively parallel computational simulations: Lessons learned from ASCI", *Internat. J. High Performance Comput. Appl.* **18** (2004) 399–416.

[41] Capers-Jones T., *Estimating Software Costs*, McGraw–Hill, New York, 1998.

[42] Post D.E., Kendall R.P., "Software project management and quality engineering practices for complex, coupled multiphysics, massively parallel computational simulations", *Internat. J. High Performance Comput. Appl.* **18** (2004) 399–416.

[43] Yin R.K., *Case Study Research, Design and Methods*, third ed., Sage Publications, Thousand Oaks, 2003.

[44] Paulk M., *The Capability Maturity Model*, Addison–Wesley, New York, 1994.

[45] Glass R.L., *Software Runaways: Monumental Software Disasters*, Prentice Hall PTR, New York, 1998.

[46] Ewusi-Mensah K., *Software Development Failures: Anatomy of Abandoned Projects*, MIT Press, Cambridge, MA, 2003.

[47] Phillips D., *The Software Project Manager's Handbook*, IEEE Computer Society, Los Alamitos, 1997.

[48] DeMarco T., *The Deadline*, Dorset House Publishing, New York, 1997.

[49] Thomsett R., *Radical Project Management*, Prentice Hall, Upper Saddle River, NJ, 2002.

[50] Moore G.E., "Cramming more components onto integrated circuits", *Electronics* **38** (1965).

[51] Frank M.P., "The physical limits of computing", *Comput. Sci. Engrg.* **4** (2002) 16–36.

[52] Dongarra J., van der Steen A., "Overview of recent supercomputers", http://www.top500.org/ORSC/2004/, 2003.

[53] Kuck D.J., *High Performance Computing: Challenges for Future Systems*, Oxford Univ. Press, Oxford, 1995.

[54] Gropp W., Lusk E., Skjellum A., *Using MPI*, MIT Press, Cambridge, MA, 1996.

[55] Graybill R., Kepner J., Lucas R., "DARPA high productivity computing systems program", http://www.highproductivity.org/, 2004.

[56] VanDeVanter M., Post D.E., Zosel M.E., "HPC needs a tool strategy", in: *Proceedings of 2nd Workshop on HPC Applications, ACM/IEEE International Conference on Software Engineering, St. Louis, MO*, 2005.

[57] Laughlin R., "The physical basis of computability", *Comput. Sci. Engrg.* **4** (2002) 27–30.

[58] Petroski H., *Design Paradigms: Case Histories of Error and Judgement in Engineering*, Cambridge Univ. Press, New York, 1994.

[59] Traweek S., *Beamtimes and Lifetimes: The World of High Energy Physicists*, Harvard Univ. Press, Cambridge, MA, 1988.

[60] Gehman H.W., Barry J.L., Deal D.W., et al., "Report of the Columbia Accident Investigation Board", National Aeronautics and Space Administration, Washington, DC, August 2003, 248 pp.

[61] Hallquist J.O., "Curent and future developments of LS-DYNA-1", in: *Proceedings of 4th European LS-DYNA Conference, ULM, Germany*, 2003.

[62] Taleyarkhan R.P., West C.D., Cho J.S., et al., "Evidence for nuclear emissions during acoustic cavitation", *Science* **295** (2002) 1868–1873.

[63] Shapira D., Saltmarsh M., "Nuclear fusion in collapsing bubbles—is it there? An attempt to repeat the observation of nuclear emissions from sonoluminescence", *Phys. Rev. Lett.* **89** (2002) 104302–104305.

[64] Glantz J., "Behind the official optimism, flawed projections", *Science* **274** (1996) 1600.

[65] Wakatani M., Mukhovatov V.S., Burrell K.H., et al., "ITER: Plasma confinement and transport", *Nuclear Fusion* **39** (1999) 2176–2249.

[66] Yushmanov P., Takizuka T., Riedel K., et al., "Scalings for tokamak energy confinement", *Nuclear Fusion* **30** (1990) 1999–2006.

[67] Glantz J., "Turbulence may sink titanic reactor", *Science* **274** (1996) 1600–1603.

[68] Glantz J., "Bright omens for giant reactor", *Science* **274** (1997) 1559–1560.

[69] Post D.E., Kendall R.P., "Software project management and quality engineering practices for complex, coupled multi-physics, massively parallel computational simulations", *Internat. J. High Performance Comput. Appl.* **18** (4) (2004) 399–416.

[70] Beck K., *Extreme Programming Explained*, Addison–Wesley, Boston, 2000;
van Vliet H., *Software Engineering, Principles and Practice*, John Wiley and Sons, Ltd., Chichester, 2000.

[71] Remer D., "Managing software projects", in: *Proceedings of UCLA Technical Management Institute, Los Angeles, CA* 2000.

[72] DeMarco T., Lister T., *Waltzing with Bears, Managing Risk on Software Projects*, Dorset House Publishing, New York, 2003.

[73] DeMarco T., Lister T., "Risk management for software", August, 2002, Arlington, MA, 2002.

[74] Capers-Jones T., *Estimating Software Costs*, McGraw–Hill, New York, 1998.

[75] Brooks F., *The Mythical Man-Month: Essays on Software Engineering*, Addison–Wesley Publishing Co., Menlo Park, 1995.

[76] Yourdon E., *Death March*, Prentice Hall PTR, Upper Saddle River, NJ, 1997.

[77] Verzuh E., *The Fast forward MBA in Project Management*, John Wiley, New York, 1999;
Ruskin A.M., Estes W.E., *What Every Engineer Should Know About Project Management*, Marcel Dekker, Inc., New York, 1995.

[78] Symons C.R., "Function point analysis: Difficulties and improvements", *IEEE Trans. Software Engrg.* **14** (1988) 2–11.

[79] Brooks F.P., "No silver bullet: Essence and accidents of software engineering", *Computer* **20** (1987) 10–19.

[80] Oberkampf W., Trucano T., "Verification and validation in computational fluid mechanics", *Prog. Aerospace Stud.* **38** (2002) 209–272.

[81] Roache P.J., *Verification and Validation in Computational Science and Engineering*, Hermosa Publishers, Albuquerque, 1998.

[82] Hatton L., Roberts A., "How accurate is scientific software?", *IEEE Trans. Software Engrg.* **20** (1994) 785–797.

[83] Roache P.J., "Code verification by the method of manufactured solutions", *Trans. ASME* **124** (2002) 4–10.

[84] Kamm J.R., Rider W.J., Brock J.S., "Combined space and time convergence analysis of a compressible flow algorithm", in: *Proceedings of AIAA Conference on Computational Fluid Dynamics, Orlando, FL*, 2003.

[85] Pautz S.D., "Verification of transport codes by the method of manufactured solutions: The ATTILA experience", in: *Proceedings of ANS International Meeting on Mathematical Methods for Nuclear Applications, Salt Lake City, UT*, 2001.

[86] Laughlin R.B., *A Different Universe: Reinventing Physics from the Bottom Down*, Basic Books Inc., 2005.

[87] Halberstam D., *The Reckoning*, William Morrow and Co., New York, 1986.

[88] DeMarco T., Boehm B., "The agile methods fray", *Computer* **35** (2002) 90–92;
Boehm B., "Get ready for agile methods, with care", *Computer* **35** (2002) 64–69;
Highsmith J., Cockburn A., "Agile software development: the business of innovation", *Computer* **34** (2001) 120–127.

[89] Herbsleb J., Zubrow D., Goldenson D., et al., "Software quality and the capability maturity model", *Comm. ACM* **40** (1997) 30–40.

[90] Humphrey W.S., *Winning with Software: An Executive Strategy*, Software Engineering Institute, Pittsburg, 2001.

[91] McConnell S.C., *Software Project Survival*, Microsoft Press, 1997.

[92] Huizenga J., Harris T.H. Jr., Happer W., et al., Report No. DOE/S-0073 DE90 005611, 1989.

# Author Index

Numbers in *italics* indicate the pages on which complete references are given.

# Subject Index

## A

Acceptability, 88–91
  components, 91
  effect of shortfalls on, 154, 156
  factors contributing, 90
  framework, 89, 127
  practical, 88
  tradeoff range for, 156, 157
Acceptability function, 91
Acceptance test, 115
Activity, definition, 178
Adaptive mesh refinement, 245
Adaptive networks, 231
Agile methods, 178, 180, 226–7
"Agile software" community, 293
Ambiguity, reduction, 121
Analysis, 116
  process, 117, 194
Analyze activities, 193–4
Appraisal costs, 17–18
Architecture definition interviews, 215–16
Artifact
  definition, 178
  states, 229
ASCI Q system, 261
Asset, definition, 178
Association rule mining, 50
Audit activities, 196
Authentication, 88, 110
Automobile industry, 291
Availability, 86–7, 93, 110

## B

B/CR, 6, 7
  examples for SPI methods, 18–19
Bagging, 49
Base classification techniques, 62

Base learners, 47
  categories, 48
Bayesian learning theory, 49
Behavioral requirements, 106–11, 117–18
Benchmarking, 285
Benefit/cost ratio *see* B/CR
Benefits (as ROI metric), 6, 7
BEP, 6, 7
  examples for SPI methods, 18–19
Best practices, 177, 178–9
Boltzmann equation, 244
Boolean rules, 50
Boosting, 49
Brainstorming workshops, 216–18
Branch Count metrics, 61
Break even point *see* BEP
Build-test-fix process, 82
Business-driven product planning case study, 204–6
  decision visualization, 223–4
  development effort ROI, 223
  evolution effort goals, 205
  evolution effort scope, 204–5
  evolution effort strategy, 205
  exercise-to-exercise influences, 206
  process evolution exercise, 205–6
  scaling to manage complexity, 233

## C

C, 263, 264
C++, 264
CAF, 262, 263
Capabilities, 98
Capability Maturity Model *see* CMM
Capability Maturity Model Integration *see* CMMI
Capacity requirements, 108–9
Capture activities, 192–3

311

# Contents of Volumes in This Series

323

Printed and bound by CPI Group (UK) Ltd, Croydon, CR0 4YY

03/10/2024

01040415-0006